PETE

GUIDE TO SOU

SAFARI LODGES

PRIVATE LODGES ■ REST CAMPS ■ BUSH CAMPS ■ COUNTRY HOTELS

STRUIK

Struik Publishers
(A member of The Struik Publishing Group (Pty) Ltd)
Cornelis Struik House, 80 McKenzie Street
Cape Town 8001

Reg. Nr. 54/00965/07

First published by Struik Publishers (Pty) Ltd 1993

Project co-ordinator Annlerie van Rooyen
Editor Tracey Hawthorne
Designer and DTP make-up Tamsyn Ivey
Picture researcher Nikki Newman
Cartographer Janine Blaauw
Indexer and proofreader Sandie Vahl

Reproduction by Unifoto (Pty) Ltd, Cape Town
Printed and bound by Singapore National Printers Ltd, Singapore

ISBN 1 86825 432 1

Every effort has been made to ensure factual accuracy in this book. Tourist facilities,
however, are in their nature subject to change, and some of the information will
inevitably become outdated during this edition's lifespan. Travellers are therefore
urged to consult travel agents, regional tourist bureaux, parks, publicity associations
and other sources for the latest details relating to their intended destinations.

ACKNOWLEDGEMENTS
The author and publishers wish to record their thanks to the following for their
invaluable help in compiling this book: David Steele and Patrick Wagner of *Getaway*
magazine; Sandra and Willie Olivier (Namibia); Peter Comley and Salome Meyer
(Botswana); Paul Tingay and Garth Thompson (Zimbabwe), and Marek Patzer (Zambia); and to the many safari operators, parks' authorities and management of private
lodges who willingly gave of their time and expertise.

FRONT COVER, CLOCKWISE FROM TOP LEFT: *Game viewing at Mabula Lodge; one of the
Mkuzi reserve's camps, Natal; canoe safari on the Zambezi River, Zimbabwe; Ngala
Lodge's dining area; elephants at Etosha's Okaukuejo camp, Namibia; Ruchomechi camp,
Zimbabwe.* TITLE PAGE: *The magical sundowner hour.* BACK COVER: *A bush camp at
Natal's Itala game reserve (left); bedroom interior at Ngala Lodge, eastern Transvaal (right).*

CONTENTS

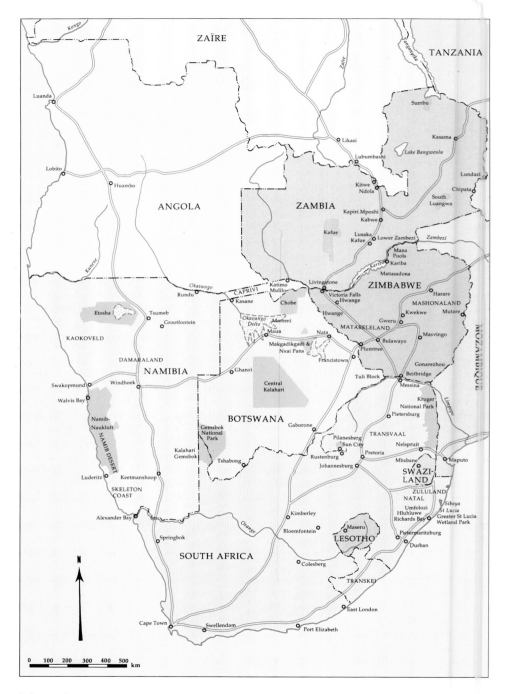

ZAÏRE

TANZANIA

Kongo

Luanda

Sumbu

Likasi

Kasama

Lake Bangweulu

Lobito

Huambo

ANGOLA

Lubumbashi

Zaïre

Kitwe
Ndola

ZAMBIA

Lundazi

Chipata

South
Luangwa

Kapiri Mposhi

Kabwe

Kunene

Kafue

Lusaka
Kafue

Lower Zambezi

Zambezi

Mana
Pools

Kariba

Matusadona

Etosha

Tsumeb

Grootfontein

Okavango

Rundu

CAPRIVI

Katimo
Mulilo

Kasane

Chobe

Livingstone

Victoria Falls
Hwange

ZIMBABWE

Harare

MASHONALAND

Kwekwe

Mutare

KAOKOVELD

Okavango
Delta

Moremi

Maun

Hwange

Gweru

Masvingo

MATABELELAND

DAMARALAND

Makgadikgadi &
Nxai Pans

Nata

Bulawayo

Plumtree

NAMIBIA

Ghanzi

Francistown

Gonarezhou

MOZAMBIQUE

Swakopmund

Windhoek

Central
Kalahari

Tuli Block

Beitbridge

Messina

Walvis Bay

Kruger
National Park

Limpopo

Namib-
Naukluft

Pietersburg

NAMIB DESERT

Gemsbok
National
Park

BOTSWANA

Gaborone

TRANSVAAL

Kalahari
Gemsbok

Pilanesberg
Sun City

Nelspruit

Luderitz

Keetmanshoop

Tshabong

Rustenburg

Pretoria

Mbabane

Maputo

Johannesburg

SWAZI-
LAND

SKELETON
COAST

ZULULAND
NATAL

Alexander Bay

Kimberley

Umfolozi
Hluhluwe
Richards Bay

Sibaya
St Lucia
Greater St Lucia
Wetland Park

Springbok

Orange

Bloemfontein

Maseru

LESOTHO

Pietermaritzburg

Durban

N

SOUTH AFRICA

Colesberg

TRANSKEI

East London

0 100 200 300 400 500 km

Cape Town

Swellendam

Port Elizabeth

THE SAFARI EXPERIENCE

Until quite recently – up to about the middle of last century – the broad grasslands of Southern Africa's central interior were perhaps the world's greatest treasure house of wildlife. Vast herds of springbok, buffalo, wildebeest and other plains game roamed the sunlit veld, free to follow ancient migratory paths, their numbers held in check only by seasonal drought, by sickness, by predators and by the modest needs of the scattered tribespeople.

Then came the white hunter with his guns and his lust for the killing sport, and the farmer to settle and fence the wild countryside. Between them they changed the nature of the land and took devastating toll of the herds. Especially destructive, and wantonly so, was the hunter: it is reckoned that by 1880 more than two million hides had been exported to Europe – a tragic enough figure, but one that belied the true extent of the slaughter. The Victorian 'sportsman' shot indiscriminately, for the highest possible tally, and only a very small fraction of the spoils served any useful purpose. The remaining carcasses, untold numbers of them, were left behind for the hyaena, the vulture and the bleaching African sun.

The first serious moves to create game sanctuaries north of the Vaal River were made in the 1890s by a Transvaal republican government acutely conscious of the region's dwindling natural resources. On President Paul Kruger's initiative, the Pongola segment of the Lowveld was declared a reserve, although the enterprise was later abandoned following an outbreak of stock disease. In 1897 the Natal Colony set aside the game-rich Umfolozi and Hluhluwe areas; a year later the Sabi reserve in the eastern Transvaal was proclaimed. Under the firm guidance of its first warden the Sabi flourished, expanded and, in 1926, was renamed after its principal founder to become South Africa's first and among the world's finest national parks.

The Kruger, however, is only one of several superlative Southern African wildernesses that beckon the visitor. Quite different in character but just as grand in their own way are Namibia's Etosha, Botswana's Chobe, Zimbabwe's Hwange, and the splendid Luangwa Valley in eastern Zambia. These, and the subcontinent's many other game areas, each with its distinctive plant and animal life, combine to form a wilderness complex that probably rivals that of Kenya in its magnificence, and certainly surpasses it in its variety and in what it can offer the visitor in the way of amenities.

Not that all is well with the Southern Africa's wild regions. On the contrary, they are under deadly threat – from poachers; from mining and industry; from domestic cattle and encroaching farmlands; from the voracious appetite of expanding rural communities for water, firewood, grazing, living room. These are the intractable problems of Africa – indeed of the entire Third World – and they are likely to remain with us for a long time to come.

There is, though, some light in the darkness. Society's priorities have lately undergone a dramatic change, and the voice of the conservationist is heard a lot more clearly today than it was even a decade ago. Man's assault on the environment must be halted if the earth as we know it is to survive. Moreover, those who make the decisions are coming to recognise that the wilderness is worth preserving for the *immediate* rewards it brings – in short, that eco-tourism is capable of generating vast amounts of money.

In this context two emerging trends are worth noting. First, there is now a general conviction that the wellbeing of the wildlife and the interests of tourism need not be in conflict with the needs of rural Africans, and recent years have seen the appearance of what is variously called the 'multi-use', the 'resource' and, in Zambia, the 'game management' area – integrated reserves in which the people of the countryside, instead of being relocated (as they have been, often controversially, in the past), stay where they are and help conserve the environment and, in return, share in its resources – and benefit from tourism development. It's a win-win rather than a win-lose situation, and it holds considerable promise for the future.

Secondly, the areas of responsibility are gradually being realigned. Up to now the various arms of government administered the great wildernesses and everything in them, but private ventures are becoming increasingly prominent in the running of the rest camps, lodges and other visitor facilities within the national and provincial parks. This makes sense: these ventures are, after all, specialists in the hospitality business. The operation of market forces – competition for the tourist trade – will, providing there isn't developmental overkill, benefit both the environment (by creating much-needed funding) and the people who come to explore and enjoy it.

ABOUT THIS BOOK
Guide to Safari Lodges covers Southern Africa's major game areas, which are concentrated within a broad arc stretching from the green and pleasant woodlands of northern Natal and Zululand in the southeast, through Swaziland, the eastern Transvaal Lowveld, the northwestern Transvaal bushveld, the sandy plains and great wetlands of Botswana to the Caprivi panhandle and the splendid Etosha National Park of Namibia. North of this arc is Hwange in Zimbabwe, home to one of the world's largest concentrations of game animals, and the Zambezi River, whose reaches take in the spectacular Victoria Falls and Lake Kariba. North again and we come to Zambia's Kafue River region, the Luangwa Valley and the limpid shores of Lake Tanganyika, the upper limit of our coverage.

This is a selective book, both geographically and in terms of the lodges and camps featured. There are other areas in which one can see Southern African wildlife, but they have been excluded partly for reasons of space (there simply isn't room to fit everything in) but chiefly because most of them are not in big-game country as the term is normally understood (or imagined). For example, far to the south, on the Cape coast, are the Transkei reserves, which have their animals but are visited principally for their scenic attractions. Not far away is the Addo National Park, world-renowned for its uniquely dense elephant population but otherwise somewhat lacking in diversity (though an environmental purist would dispute this). Other places have been omitted because they have few or no tourist amenities or because, like the great sandy wastes of Namibia, their appeal is quite different from that of the classic game region: here, admittedly, the desert-adapted animals and plants are among the earth's most fascinating, but they're very sparse on the ground.

The emphasis throughout the book is on the accommodation available in or close to the more prominent wildlife havens, the criteria for selection being comfort and attractive visitor facilities.

The regional chapters are broken down into their various component parts, which vary enormously in character from area to area. The main sub-sections – the individual entries – comprise:

■ Major national parks and wilderness areas, some of them – like Namibia's fascinating Caprivi and Zimbabwe's Kariba – grouped together for convenience (they form coherent wildlife regions), together with the public rest camps and private lodges enclosed within their boundaries.

■ Privately run lodges and camps – ranging from the luxurious safari establishment that offers five-star accommodation, cuisine and service to the more ruggedly informal bush venue – that lie outside the public parks (though they have ready access to them).

A few of these, notably the eastern Transvaal's more exclusive lodges, are the focal points of extensive private game reserves. The latter are formally proclaimed areas in which the cycle of predation and rebirth takes its natural course without interference, and where most of the species are able to migrate with the seasons. The environment is carefully (and expensively) nurtured, the human presence strictly controlled, and as a result tariffs tend to be on the high side.

■ Private game parks and farms, of which a select few are featured here. These are generally much smaller, invariably fenced areas that have been stocked with game to attract the tourist and, some of them, to serve as safe breeding grounds for endangered and other animals destined for sale or relocation (some of the farms also double as commercial hunting areas). Here there is little or no natural predation, mainly because restocking is so costly; predators, if any, have their own enclosures and are artificially fed; and, of course, the animals cannot migrate. Generally speaking, tariffs are lower than those of the private reserves.

■ Hotels that are located close to the major wildlife areas and which cater largely or even exclusively for the game-viewing public. Some of these, rather confusingly, call themselves 'lodges' – and in fact there isn't all that much difference, on the surface, between the more sophisticated safari lodge and the bush-oriented hotel. Both offer their guests game drives and walks, *en suite* accommodation, poolside relaxation, personalised service, full bar facilities and campfire barbecue meals in the boma, a (usually) reed-enclosed outdoor area marvellously suited to companionable evening get-togethers.

There are, of course, other ways of exploring Africa's wild spaces, notably through what is known as the mobile safari. This, as the name suggests, involves an extended trek through the wilderness – on foot or by land-rover, boat or other means of locomotion (including, in one instance, by elephant; see page 198) – as a member of a party led by professional guides. Mobile safaris do not feature in this book: there are just too many options and permutations.

Nor do we cover to any meaningful degree the hunting safari – not necessarily because there are moral inhibitions but because the subject appeals to an entirely different kind of reader. Indeed, most conservationists are in favour of controlled hunting: it's a valid alternative to the necessary but often wasteful and just as brutal practice of culling and, moreover, were it not for the income from hunting, most game ranches would be given over to environmentally destructive cattle.

USING THE BOOK

This is more of a compendium of ideas than a detailed practical manual: prospective visitors, having decided which areas and lodges hold the most appeal, will be able to find out a lot more about precisely what is on offer, how much it costs, and how to organise the trip from more specialised sources of information – from the parks and lodges themselves, travel agents, tour and safari operators. Nevertheless, there is much here of a functional nature.

Who to contact. At the end of the individual entries you'll find brief 'getting there' directions and, perhaps more useful, addresses for bookings and further information. The latter are the principal but in many instances not the only contacts: most of the lodges are associated with a number of agents and safari firms, and indeed any good travel consultant or touring company will be able to book you into the places of your choice and get you there and back.

Telephone numbers. Telephone and telefax numbers throughout the book are those applicable within the South African telecommunications system. In South Africa the prefix for international calls is 09, followed by the regional code, followed by the area code. The subscriber's numbers for locations within South Africa are preceded by the area code only. Callers from countries other than South

Africa should substitute the international code quoted with that relevant to their country, followed by the regional code, the area code and the subscriber's number.

Advisories. At the end of the book you'll find an Advisory of concise information about the different regions – climate, communications (road and air), suggested reading, useful addresses.

Tour and safari operators. A select but fairly lengthy list of these appears at the end of the book (pages 313-316). For those thinking of visiting the Southern African wilderness, the list will serve as an important reference.

Placing yourself in the capable hands of a professional safari outfit has a great deal of merit: in the first place, actually getting to some of the venues, especially in the farther-flung reaches, can be a complicated and frustrating business if you try to go it alone. Then again, a safari operator will have close associations with and may even own and run one or more of the lodges and camps. He will know the area intimately, will provide a comforting degree of personal service, and will make sure you extract the very most from your bush holiday. Moreover, he offers variety: his packages invariably take in more than one lodge, often more than one region; and the itineraries can be flexible, even customised. The options are set out in his catalogue, which he will send you free of charge.

The changing scene. The accommodation and other facilities described in *Guide to Safari Lodges* were a fair representation of what was available at the time of going to press in mid-1993. The eco-tourism world, though, is in its nature subject to rapid change, and while every effort has been made to ensure accuracy, some of the data will inevitably become outdated during this edition's lifespan. New lodges will appear on the scene, some existing ones will be upgraded, others may deteriorate, even close down altogether. Intending visitors are advised to seek the most up-to-date information – from sources quoted in the text, in the Advisories and in the list on pages 313-316 – before committing themselves to firm bookings.

ON SAFARI

Your venture into the African wilderness will be an exhilarating experience, one that will remain in your memory long after you return home. If this is your first visit, however, you will certainly be entering an alien and possibly confusing world, so a few preparatory pointers may be helpful.

Bush etiquette. Many visitors to the game regions explore them as clients of a safari company or guests of a private lodge, and they will be well looked after, conducted on drives, walks and other excursions by a ranger or trained guide. Follow his example, listen to his advice.

Independent travellers – game viewers embarking on self-guided drives – should bear in mind a few basic rules and a number of less formal conventions in the interests of safety, the convenience of others and for the protection of the environment.

■ Remember that parks and reserves have been proclaimed for the preservation of their wildlife, a generic term that encompasses all its living things – animals, birds, reptiles, amphibians, fish, insects, trees, shrubs and grasses. Here, in the wilderness, you are the intruder, your visit a privilege.

■ In some of the more remote wilderness areas you can explore on foot, but in most instances you're allowed to leave your vehicle only at designated areas – waterholes, viewing sites, picnic areas and so forth, all of which are (usually) clearly marked as such. Please observe the rules: you are in wild country, and although in some places the game is accustomed to and nonchalant about the human presence, appearances are dangerously deceptive: that lazy-looking lion basking at the roadside can spring to lethal life within a split second.

■ Similarly, light fires only at picnic sites and other appropriate places. Don't throw cigarettes from the car, especially during the dry winter months; after your camp site meal, kill the embers with a covering of earth. In the bush, fire is a very real hazard and the consequences of carelessness can be truly disastrous.

■ Don't pollute the countryside with litter. Keep a plastic bag in your vehicle for rubbish; use the camp's bins; leave your camp site absolutely spotless.

■ Do not feed the animals or disturb them unnecessarily. If a baboon gets used to easy pickings he will become a nuisance, possibly even a danger to other travellers: baboons learn to beg for food, the bolder ones raid cars and can turn nasty if thwarted – in which case they will have to be put down.

■ Stick to the roads; don't take short cuts over the open veld (an environmentally destructive practice, and potentially a hazardous one as well), or drive down firebreaks and closed routes. If you do stray from the beaten path and your car breaks down, you'll be stranded without any guarantee of early rescue. In most areas 'no entry' routes are clearly marked as such – not to hide anything from you but to safeguard the wilderness. These tracks are used by park staff only for essential management – as access to areas threatened by erosion, or which are being rehabilitated, or in which a culling programme is in progress.

■ Approach big game with caution; don't make any unnecessary movement or noise, and be prepared to drive on quickly if warning signs appear – if, for instance, an elephant turns head-on to you, raises its trunk, flaps its ears. Keep well clear of cow herds with calves. Be particularly careful on bush walks. Approach animals downwind if possible; don't try to get too close to them; remember that just about any species can pose a threat if startled, irritated or, most importantly, cornered. Don't under any circumstances cut off an animal's line of retreat; hippos can be especially dangerous if you block their escape route to water.

■ Approach and enter observation hides as silently as possible; remain quietly under cover for at least an hour – in your own interests (patience is the key to profitable game viewing) and in the interests of other watchers. The animals are keenly aware of movement to and from the hide and will take time to settle down.

Some game-viewing hints. Much of the time on safari is of course spent looking for and observing the animals and birds of the wilderness. Below follows a few suggestions to make the independent bush holiday as rewarding as possible:

■ Generally speaking, the most productive game-viewing period is the dry season – the winter (May-August) and the hot springtime months of September and October, when the vegetation has thinned out and the animals are concentrated near river, dam and waterhole. During the rains, on the other hand, water is plentiful, the animals widely dispersed, the ground cover thick and, in the less developed regions, the tracks very difficult to negotiate.

■ Get to know something of the habits and habitats of the wildlife before leaving on your trip; decide where your particular interests lie and what you would like to see. On arrival, arm yourself with a good map of the area and a guidebook containing game distribution lists, and then look for the animals in the places where they feed and find cover. Elephant, buffalo, lion, leopard, zebra and wildebeest; hippo and crocodile; fish eagle, vulture, hornbill – each has its favourite haunts. Grazers such as hartebeest will be found in grassland or lightly wooded countryside; browsers – bushbuck, for instance – in dense thickets; klipspringer among rocky outcrops, and so on. Where annual veld-burning programmes are customary, head for recently burned areas – grazers are attracted to the fresh growth.

■ The chances of spotting lion are better just after sunrise than at other times. Elephant, giraffe, rhino, eland and other large game are, in many regions, at their most visible in the hour before sunset.

■ Waterholes are usually more rewarding than the exploratory drive. As mentioned, one has to be patient, but there's always something to be seen – a mongoose, perhaps a brace of warthog, a kingfisher – and sooner or later the larger and rarer animals will appear on parade. In the warmer months most of the wildlife tends to lie up during the heat of the day (and so do the majority of visitors). Best times to set off on your drives are in the early mornings (first light up to about ten) and late afternoons. If you do emerge in the midday hours, scan the lower hillsides and shady clumps for signs of life.

■ If you have a choice of vehicle, bear in mind that a minibus is ideally suited to game viewing. Some of the wilderness areas, though, are too rugged for anything short of four-wheel drive.

■ Take along more than one pair of binoculars, if possible one for each member of the family or party. Having to share, particularly when something really special comes into view, can lead to irritation and argument.

Photography. Film tends to be in short supply and is sometimes unobtainable in several of the Southern African regions, among them Zimbabwe and Zambia. Take along a good supply. However, most international brands and sizes are available in South Africa, and processing is both quick and relatively cheap (enquire whether process charges are included in the price of the film). Ensure that your camera case is well padded and dust-proof. In the African bush, as elsewhere, light is at its best in the early mornings or early evenings; heat haze is a problem in midday hours.

What to pack. Informality and practicality are the keys, even in the most luxuriously upmarket of lodges.

Travel light: nobody dresses up, and most of the venues featured in this book provide laundry facilities, which means you can get away with maybe two changes of clothes. Shirts and shorts (for men) and shirts/blouses and skirts/shorts (for women) are the customary daytime wear; jeans and hard-wearing trousers valid alternatives. Avoid bright colours and white – they're difficult to keep clean and tend to look out of place in the bush. They are also said to attract the tsetse fly, a nasty little creature which has a bite that is both painful and capable of transmitting sleeping sickness (easily cured nowadays but, still, something to be avoided). Neutral hues – khaki, dull greens and browns – are best for game viewing and bird-watching. For walking, you'll need a good pair of hard-wearing, worn-in shoes, preferably of the ankle type for protection against scratches, stings and bites, though a pair of tough trousers will also do the job. Around camp one wears ordinary shoes, sandals, sneakers or 'slops'. Your sun-hat should shade the neck as well as the face.

Winter nights are chilly, even in the lowest lying of tropical valleys, and they can be bitterly cold in the plateau regions. Pack a warm sweater, tracksuit or anorak – and a light jersey for the sunrise and sunset hours.

Among other items in your luggage will be a swimming costume; personal toiletries that include lip salve and barrier cream; sunglasses (not a cheap pair – they do more harm than good); insect repellent; torch (fitted with new batteries).

Long-distance travel. Some of the game areas covered in this book – notably the Kalahari, much of Namibia and the outer reaches of Zambia – are vast, remote, their roads long, lonely and often rough, their signposts minimal or even nonexistent, facilities for travellers rudimentary and unreliable.

Check on route conditions before setting out: they can change dramatically with the weather. In the wet summer months stretches turn to quagmire; in winter the pits, potholes and sandy patches can be negotiated only by four-wheel drive. Leave word behind – with the police or local authority – of your destination and estimated time of arrival.

Self-sufficiency is the watchword. Stock up with plenty of provisions and water, extra fuel, motor spares. A basic checklist would comprise: route maps; a jack, wheelbrace and good set of tools; spare wheel and tyre in good condition, tyre lever, pump and tube; spare fanbelt; spare fuses; a container of brake fluid; jump leads; car instruction manual; fire extinguisher; first-aid kit and snakebite kit. Really careful drivers would also carry a set of contact-breaker points and condenser; radiator hose and clips; tyre valves; insulating tape; insulated electric wire; 'in line' fuel filter; and a selection of nuts, bolts, washers and split pins.

HEALTH HAZARDS

Malaria. Although malaria is more or less under control in the more developed parts of the subcontinent (Natal, the Transvaal), it is a serious health problem in the remoter, lower lying areas. In some parts the mosquitoes have become resistant to certain common drugs. Embark on a course of anti-malaria tablets before your departure. Prophylactics are available, without prescription, in pharmacies throughout Southern Africa. Tell the pharmacist which specific area or areas you intend visiting.

Bilharzia. Also known as schistosomiasis, this debilitating waterborne tropical disease is caused by a parasitical worm that inhabits the rivers and dams of the lower lying eastern and northern regions. The transmission cycle is complex: after developing its larval stage in a water snail, the bilharzia fluke may penetrate the skin of a person entering the water, later attacking the bladder, liver and kidneys. The eggs then leave the human body in the waste products, but will only hatch if discharged into fresh water, where the hatchlings will swim around until they find another snail host. When diagnosed (which can be difficult, as the symptoms are often vague), the disease readily responds to drugs. Precautions: be very circumspect about swimming in rivers and dams, unless there are clear assurances that they are bilharzia-free.

Aids. The virus is rampant in Zambia and increasingly widespread in the other countries. The risk of contracting Aids, though, is no greater in Southern Africa than it is elsewhere, provided of course that one takes the standard precautions.

CREEPIES AND CRAWLIES

Southern Africa has its fair share of venomous snakes, spiders, scorpions and sundry stinging insects, but surprisingly few safari travellers suffer serious attack or even discomfort. The confines of camps and lodges are usually free of risk, or nearly so, though obviously people on walking safaris should be rather more wary. Follow the group leader's advice.

Snakes. There are some 115 species of snake in Southern Africa, of which about a quarter are venomous enough to inflict a dangerous bite. The venom may be neurotoxic (affecting the nervous system), haemotoxic (affecting the blood vessels) or cytotoxic (destroying the body's cells).

But snakes are shy creatures, and will slither out of the way when they sense your presence (they should be allowed to do so), only striking if suddenly disturbed or provoked. Local back-fanged species include the boomslang and bird-snake, both highly poisonous but, because their fangs are too awkwardly positioned to allow them a good grip, they rarely cause serious injury. Among front-fanged species are the mambas, cobras, vipers and adders, coral snakes, garter-snakes and sea-snakes. Anti-snakebite serum is widely available in risk areas; snakebite kits may be bought at pharmacies.

Spiders. Around 5 000 species of arachnid (which includes the scorpions) are found in Southern Africa. Many will bite if provoked, and some of the bites may be very painful. Most dangerous (though rarely fatal to man) is the button spider (Latrodactus).

Scorpions. About 175 species are represented in Southern Africa, most of them occurring in the hot, dry areas of the subcontinent. All scorpion venom is toxic to the nervous system, though seldom dangerously so.

Ticks. The small, red, hard-backed tick most common in the bushveld areas (and not to be confused with the larger sheep or dog tick) can, if infected, transmit the typhus-type tick-bite fever. Symptoms are similar to those of malaria, with the addition of a severe neck ache and headache. The condition is treatable. If you see such a creature on your skin, don't brush or pull it off (the head will remain embedded) but rather suffocate it with an ointment or other covering.

Bees. African bees are notoriously aggressive, and some types of swarming colony can be dangerous to man and animal. Fortunately, attacks are rare and confined to certain brief spells during the year. In camp, take to cover; in the bush, remain motionless.

SOUTH AFRICA

South Africa covers less than one per cent of the earth's land surface, but contains more than ten per cent of its higher plants, eight per cent of its birds, and nearly five per cent of its mammals – a truly rich heritage, but a vulnerable one: over the decades the pressures imposed by human population growth and the encroachment of farmland have made savage inroads into the wildlife habitats. Of the bigger predators, only the leopard has managed to survive outside the reserves; the other carnivores, together with the elephant, buffalo, giraffe, zebra and many kinds of antelope, are now more or less confined to the larger protected areas, mainly in the northern savanna regions. Today, just one-twentieth of the country is given over to formal conservation – a long way short of the 20 per cent required by international convention.

Nevertheless, what has been set aside for the wildlife is of outstanding quality, and is likely to remain so for as long as tourism plays a part in the economic scheme.

At present there are a score of national parks and about 580 smaller (some not so small) reserves in South Africa, of which the most renowned is the Kruger, a vast chunk of game-rich bushveld occupying the north-eastern corner of the country. The Kruger,

OPPOSITE: Giraffe – one of the more common sights in the Kruger National Park.

for all the magnificence of raw Africa it encloses, is run very much with people in mind: thousands of visitors pour through its gates every day. Miraculously, though, the land remains relatively unspoilt, and the animals, birds and plants flourish – a testament to superb wilderness management. Along the western boundary are three of the largest private reserves and some of the most luxurious safari lodges in Africa, supremely comfortable places that provide five-star cuisine and service, and where personal rangers look after you from dawn to dusk.

The eastern Transvaal lowveld is generally considered South Africa's premier big-game destination, but it is only one of several, three of which are featured in these pages. To the south-east, just inland from the Indian Ocean coast, are the northern Natal and Maputaland reserves – the Umfolozi and Hluhluwe, established almost a century ago and today among the continent's finest conservation areas; Mkuzi, Ndumo, Tembe and Itala; and, fringing the shoreline, Kosi Bay, Lake Sibaya and Greater St Lucia. This last will, when its various elements have finally been drawn together, rank among the grandest of the world's wetlands. Far to the west is the most recently developed of the country's game regions, a broad swathe of northern bushveld that embraces, among other things, the Pilanesberg National Park.

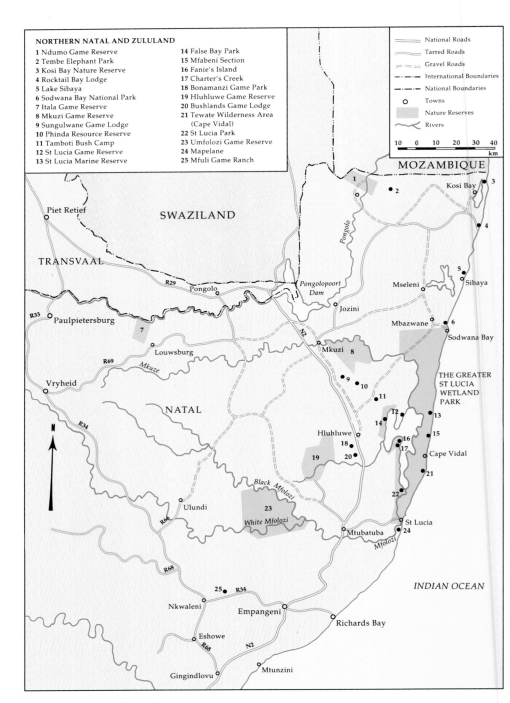

NORTHERN NATAL AND ZULULAND

1 Ndumo Game Reserve
2 Tembe Elephant Park
3 Kosi Bay Nature Reserve
4 Rocktail Bay Lodge
5 Lake Sibaya
6 Sodwana Bay National Park
7 Itala Game Reserve
8 Mkuzi Game Reserve
9 Sungulwane Game Lodge
10 Phinda Resource Reserve
11 Tamboti Bush Camp
12 St Lucia Game Reserve
13 St Lucia Marine Reserve
14 False Bay Park
15 Mfabeni Section
16 Fanie's Island
17 Charter's Creek
18 Bonamanzi Game Park
19 Hluhluwe Game Reserve
20 Bushlands Game Lodge
21 Tewate Wilderness Area
   (Cape Vidal)
22 St Lucia Park
23 Umfolozi Game Reserve
24 Mapelane
25 Mfuli Game Ranch

National Roads
Tarred Roads
Gravel Roads
International Boundaries
National Boundaries
○ Towns
Nature Reserves
Rivers

10 0 10 20 30 40
km

MOZAMBIQUE

Kosi Bay

SWAZILAND

Piet Retief

TRANSVAAL

Pongolo

R29 Pongola

Pongolopoort Dam

Jozini

Mseleni

Sibaya

R33

Paulpietersburg

7

Mbazwane

Sodwana Bay

Louwsburg

Mkuzi 8

R69 Mkuze

Vryheid

NATAL

9 10

11

12

THE GREATER
ST LUCIA
WETLAND
PARK

13

R34

14

15

Hluhluwe

18

16

17

Cape Vidal

19 20

21

Black Mfolozi

22

White Mfolozi

23

Ulundi

R66

St Lucia

Mtubatuba 24

Mfolozi

INDIAN OCEAN

R68

25 R34

Nkwaleni

Empangeni

Richards Bay

Eshowe

R68 N2

Gingindlovu Mtunzini

NORTHERN NATAL AND ZULULAND

Savanna, grass-covered hill, acacia thicket, evergreen woodland, river, lake, reedbed, swamp, blue lagoon and golden dune; rhino, elephant, giraffe, lion, hippo, crocodile; pelican, fish eagle, African jacana and forest bird – these are a few of the myriad elements that combine to create one of nature's great treasure houses.

The Natal and Zululand conservation areas are among the world's finest. The region's warm, humid climate and lush countryside, with its wonderful variety of grasses, shrubs and trees, provide ideal habitats for great numbers of animals and birds. Hluhluwe and Umfolozi together are, for example, one-twentieth the size of the Kruger National Park, yet they contain almost 70 per cent of the Kruger's animal and plant species. Umfolozi is famed for its white rhinos: it was here that the species was nurtured through the first five difficult decades of the century so that by the 1960s, Ian Player and his rangers were able to mount their highly successful capture and relocation campaign. Today both Umfolozi and Hluhluwe are keys to the future wellbeing, indeed survival, of the animal's grievously threatened black cousin. The splendid Mkuzi reserve is home to (among much else) a stunning number and variety of waterbirds. Itala, along the sluggish Pongola River, sustains Natal's largest concentration of klipspringer and a breeding colony of the rare bald ibis, and its new rest camp is setting standards of comfort and elegance that other parks, here and elsewhere on the Southern African subcontinent, are finding hard to match.

The far northern reaches of Natal and Zululand – the block bounded by Mozambique in the north, by Swaziland and the Lebombo mountains in the west and by the warm waters of the Indian Ocean in the east – is known as Maputaland, a region of great beauty and of stunning diversity. This is the transitional zone between the tropics and the

TOP: *Zulu women near the Umfolozi reserve; their headgear is traditional to the area.*
ABOVE: *Burchell's zebra is one of the Hluhluwe game reserve's 84 mammal species.*

subtropics, and within its bounds are half a dozen different ecosystems. Its visual variety is perhaps most evident, and most attractive, along the seaboard: fringing the coastline are three large lake systems, pre-eminent among them St Lucia, an extensive and environmentally unique wetland complex of shallow lagoon and estuary, lily-covered pan, game reserve, forest, high dune and sea.

Farther up the shoreline are two superbly pristine areas: Lake Sibaya, South Africa's largest natural expanse of fresh water, and Kosi Bay nature reserve, an 11 000-hectare wonderland of limpid bayou, dune and mangrove swamp, and of beaches that serve as the breeding ground of Southern Africa's giant and once endangered sea turtles – the leatherbacks and the loggerheads. Offshore are the world's most southerly and, for divers and snorkelling enthusiasts, some of its most rewarding coral reefs.

UMFOLOZI GAME RESERVE

This magnificent sanctuary, once the hunting ground of Zulu kings, sprawls over nearly 50 000 hectares of woodland savanna and lush floodplain between central Zululand's White and Black Mfolozi rivers and, together with its near-neighbour Hluhluwe (in fact the two are now administered as a single entity), is the mature product of one of Southern Africa's earliest conservation projects: both areas were proclaimed in April 1897, about a year before the establishment of the eastern Transvaal's Sabie, forerunner of the Kruger.

The countryside – sweetly grassed, warm and well-watered – supported huge numbers of game animals until the 1920s, when the authorities launched a massive, ill-conceived and near-disastrous campaign to eradicate the disease-bearing tsetse fly (more than 100 000 animals were slaughtered), but common sense eventually prevailed and, once chemical controls had replaced the hunter's rifle, the herds stabilised.

The reserve made a remarkable recovery, and is now home to healthy populations of elephant, buffalo, giraffe, zebra, lion, leopard, cheetah, blue wildebeest, spotted hyaena, wild dog, and a wide variety of antelope –

The lodge at Masinda, one of the Umfolozi game reserve's four attractive camps.

and to both white and black rhino, species that have been pulled back from the brink of extinction (see The Endangered Rhino, page 20). The lion population numbers something over 70, which in many respects is also quite remarkable: these predators, prime targets of 19th-century white hunters, had been regionally extinct for nearly six decades until a lone male made its erratic and elusive way from Mozambique to Umfolozi (a distance of about 400 km) in the late 1950s, to be joined later by a small group of females (brought in by the Natal Parks Board), and the resultant prides flourished. Around 400 different types of bird have been recorded in the area, among them black-bellied korhaan and Wahlberg's eagle.

UMFOLOZI'S CAMPS

The reserve has two attractive, hutted rest camps and two very comfortable bush camps. There is no restaurant; visitors bring their own food, which they either prepare themselves or have cooked for them by the resident staff, either *in situ* or in separate kitchens, depending on the type of accommodation. The nearest shop is at Mtubatuba, 50 km to the south, though petrol, cool-drinks, books and curios are on sale in the reserve. Bedding, linen, cutlery and crockery are provided.

MPILA CAMP offers three kinds of lodging: two fully equipped, self-contained and serviced, seven-bed thatched cottages that incorporate a bathroom, a lounge-dining room, and a kitchen presided over by a cook; six fully equipped, self-contained and serviced chalets, also incorporating a bathroom, a lounge-dining room and a kitchen but rather less luxurious, and less expensive, than the cottages (guests do their own cooking); and 12 three- or four-bed rest huts, equipped with fridges (meals are prepared by resident cooks in the central kitchen area), with access to separate (communal) bathroom facilities.

MASINDA CAMP has a seven-bed, self-contained lodge (much the same as but more comfortable than the standard cottage) and

BELOW: On the Umfolozi wilderness trail.
BOTTOM AND RIGHT: The Enselweni and Sontuli bush camps.

six four-bed rest huts with separate bathing and cooking facilities.

ENSELWENI and *SONTULI* bush camps, the latter on the banks of the Black Mfolozi River, have four fully equipped, two-bed huts each and may be hired on a block-booking basis.

Game viewing

The wildlife is more concentrated, and more visible, during the drier winter months; the reserve has 86 km of game-viewing roads and, unless you are a member of a tour party, you find your own way around. The route network encompasses designated picnic spots, viewing points, and a viewing hide. The 67-km self-guided Umfolozi Mosaic auto trail has been carefully contrived to provide an insight into the reserve's geography, history and management, and the interrelationships of its many life forms. A comprehensive trail guide booklet is available.

Some 24 000 hectares of the Umfolozi reserve have been set aside as a wilderness – an area that can be visited only by hikers on organised trails. Parties of eight are led by an experienced guide; pack donkeys carry hikers' personal effects from base camp to bush camp,

from which exploratory hikes in the company of a game guard are embarked upon.

The Wilderness Leadership School operates educational trails through the reserve, for scholars and adults. The organisers provide the camping requisites and transport from Durban.There are also what are known as 'primitive trails'. On these, you backpack from base camp and sleep in the open.

■ **Getting there:** The reserve is 270 km north of Durban. Take the main North Coast road (N2) to a point 3,4 km beyond the Mtubatuba turn-off; turn left onto the Nongama road and continue for 27 km, turning off again at the Umfolozi signpost.

■ **Reservations and information:** Natal Parks Board Reservations, PO Box 1750, Pietermaritzburg 3200, South Africa. Tel: (0331) 47-1981.

HLUHLUWE GAME RESERVE

Hluhluwe is not one of the region's larger reserves – it is just over 23 000 hectares in extent – but it ranks among those most highly regarded by the serious environmentalist and the casual tourist. And with good reason: the countryside is stunningly beautiful, a rich compound of misty forest, grass-covered hill, dense thicket and enchanting river (the Hluhluwe, which takes its name from the lianas, or monkey ropes, that festoon the riverine woodlands) that support a splendid diversity of plant and animal life.

An impressive 84 mammal species are represented in the reserve, including white rhino, black rhino (though, due to slight changes in the vegetation and other factors, the latter's population has declined somewhat in recent years), elephant, giraffe, buffalo, blue wildebeest, Burchell's zebra, waterbuck, nyala, kudu, bushbuck, baboon and, among the predators, lion, cheetah, leopard and wild dog (or Cape hunting dog).

For bird-watchers the Hluhluwe is a delight: no less than 425 species have been recorded in the area, including such notables as the whitebacked vulture and the bateleur.

Hluhluwe and nearby Umfolozi are two of Africa's oldest reserves – both were inaugurated in April 1897 – and until recently were separated by a narrow corridor over which the game moves freely. Consolidation of the areas makes ecological sense, and in fact the two are now managed as a single entity and are technically known as the Hluhluwe/Umfolozi Park.

OPPOSITE ABOVE: Crossing the White Umfolozi on one of South Africa's finest wilderness trails.
OPPOSITE LEFT: A ranger and his charges examine the Umfolozi's ground cover during their five-day wilderness trail.
OPPOSITE RIGHT: The spoor of lion – there are some 70 in the Umfolozi, all of them descendants of a lone male that wandered south from Mozambique in the 1950s.
BELOW: The view from a Hluhluwe camp site.

HLUHLUWE'S CAMPS

HILLTOP, the reserve's hutted camp, is set on the summit of a hill, from which there are splendid views of the surrounding countryside. It has been redeveloped to accommodate 710 people in chalets, simplexes and duplexes, all with *en suite* facilities. With the exception of the simplexes the units are fully equipped (stove, fridge, cooking utensils, linen, cutlery, crockery). Also available are rest huts, which are served by communal kitchens and ablution blocks. Among guest amenities are a restaurant and superette.

MTWAZI LODGE is more exclusive, comprising three bedrooms, a lounge, a dining room and a kitchen, together with a fourth bedroom and *en suite* bathroom in the annex. The lodge has its own pleasant garden; a cook is in attendance.

MUNTULU BUSH CAMP (accommodating eight guests) features an elevated lounge area looking onto the Hluhluwe River; the riverbank here plays host to a variety of thirsty animals, including elephant and rhino.

Game viewing

In summertime the ground cover is dense and, because there is plenty of water, the animals disperse throughout the reserve. In the drier

THE ENDANGERED RHINO

Between them, the Umfolozi and Hluhluwe game reserves are sanctuary to around 1 000 white rhino – a surprisingly healthy figure considering that at one time it seemed that nothing could save the species from extinction. But the southern subspecies, nurtured by far-sighted conservationists, survived and eventually flourished so that, in the 1960s, the Natal Parks Board was able to launch an ambitious translocation programme.

Led by the celebrated environmentalist Ian Player, the board's team of rangers and scientists pioneered and perfected drug-darting techniques to capture and move the animals, and the small breeding herds set down in distant places were nurtured until their survival and growth were assured. The white rhino still flourishes in the Umfolozi-Hluhluwe region.

Not so fortunate is its cousin, the black rhino, prime target of poachers and under threat everywhere in Africa. The two species, though related, differ in size, temperament, feeding habits and other characteristics. The 'white' rhino is in fact dark grey in colour; the term is thought to be a corruption of the Afrikaans word *wyd*, or wide, a reference to the square-lipped mouth of a grazing animal. By contrast the black rhino (again the name is misleading) is a browser, its pointed mouth well adapted to its diet of leaves and branches. It is also the smaller and more aggressive of the two species.

In 1970, the continent-wide population of black rhino numbered some 65 000; today, fewer than 3 500 remain, 400 of them in Natal. Rhino horn is much sought after, notably in the Far East as a fever suppressant, and in the Middle East for ornamentation; there are huge profits to be made from the illegal trade, and organised poaching is both rampant and ruthless throughout much of Southern Africa, though the Natal reserves have so far managed to contain the threat. The problem is especially serious in Namibia, and in Zimbabwe, where, in desperation, conservation authorities have resorted to de-horning the animals.

One of the Umfolozi/Hluhluwe area's white rhino – rescued from the brink of extinction.

ABOVE AND RIGHT: Hluhluwe's exclusive Mtwazi Lodge, one of the smaller venues in the reserve.

season (May to September), though, the herds and their predators tend to congregate on the riverbanks and at the pools and waterholes.

There are some 90 km of viewing roads; the route through the north of the reserve and those between Seme and the Gunjaneni gate are among the more rewarding. Two auto trails have been established (a descriptive booklet is available), together with a game-viewing hide, picnic spots, viewing points and a short (half-hour) walking trail into and through the lovely Mbhombe forest, on the fringe of the main rest camp. Rambles in the company of a game guard can be arranged; regular talks and film shows are held at the main camp.

■ **Getting there:** Hluhluwe is 280 km from Durban and 60 km north of Mtubatuba. By road from Durban, take the N2 to and through the village, continue for 50 km and turn left for the reserve's Memorial gate entrance. For the Gunjaneni gate, turn left onto the R618 just after Mtubatuba (signpost: 'Nongoma/Umfolozi game reserve') and then, after 17 km, right onto gravel.

■ **Reservations and information:** Bookings for Hilltop camp accommodation (simplexes, duplexes, chalets, rest huts) and Muntulu bush camp: Natal Parks Board Reservations, PO Box 1750, Pietermaritzburg 3200, South Africa. Tel: (0331) 47-1981. Bookings for Mtwazi lodge through Auxiliary Services, Natal Parks Board, PO Box 662, Pietermaritzburg 3200, South Africa. Tel: (0331) 47-1961.

BUSHLANDS GAME LODGE

This private lodge in central Zululand nestles in a pleasant setting of lushly green sand forest and indigenous shrubs close to the major northern conservation areas.

Bushlands is a small, imaginatively conceived, exclusive (16-guest) camp of seven luxurious 'tree houses' – chalets built on tall stilts and linked to each other by raised timber walkways (though in such a way that there is complete privacy). The rooms are attractively appointed: knotty pine floors and ceilings, half-timbered walls, mix-and-match soft furnishings in restful colours and a private bathroom. The recently completed honeymoon suite is especially appealing.

Moving spirits behind both lodge and safari company (see further on) are the Deane family: Norman Deane worked with the Natal Parks Board for 30 years before leaving to found the lodge; his son Rob, an experienced hunter and ranger, now runs the operation – and does so with a lot of flair.

Guests are outnumbered by staff, and are thoroughly spoilt from the moment they arrive. The main meals are taken in the

The stately blackbellied korhaan.

traditional boma; superbly prepared venison invariably features on the menu. Among other on-site drawcards are The Water Hole pub and the kidney-shaped swimming pool.

Game viewing
Bushlands' rangers conduct daily game drives to the major northern reserves – Umfolozi, Hluhluwe, Ndumo, St Lucia and Sodwana Bay and so on, which, taken together, cover some 120 000 hectares of splendidly wild country. Zululand Safaris, Bushlands' touring arm, offers fly-in safaris that take in the lodge and the reserves; there is a wide choice of itinerary. Also available are cultural tours across the border into Swaziland.

■ **Getting there:** Bushlands is located 10 km to the south of Hluhluwe village, and to the east of the St Lucia wetland complex. By road from Durban, take the N2 north past Empangeni and Mtubatuba to the Bushlands off-ramp about 39 km further on. The route is clearly signposted thereafter.

■ **Reservations and information:** Bushlands Game Lodge, PO Box 79, Hluhluwe 3960, South Africa. Tel and fax: 03562, ask for 144.

MFULI GAME RANCH
Tucked away in the deep-green lushness of central Zululand is Mfuli, a hospitable little retreat that offers a pleasant bush experience, considerable wildlife interest, and comfort in delightful surrounds.

This is not classic big-game country – that lies a day-trip's distance to the north – but the ranch does have its animals: zebra, wildebeest, impala, nyala and duiker, as well as other non-predatory species. There is also a marvellous array of birds, and an attractively diverse profusion of indigenous flora (some of the trees are truly lovely) can be observed and enjoyed in the area.

Accommodation comprises six rustic log cabins, raised above the ground, their verandahs looking out over the valley to the hills beyond. Each has two bedrooms, a lounge and a kitchenette. The décor is simple, with knotty pine much in evidence; air-conditioning holds the summer heat at bay. Mfuli staff keep the cabins clean and tidy.

Guests can either cook for themselves – the kitchenette is fully equipped, and each unit has its barbecue facilities – or take their meals in the licensed à la carte restaurant; in common with nearly all private game lodges, Mfuli's menu features delicious venison specialities. Other amenities include a bar, a swimming pool, a games room (with, among other things, a snooker table) and, deep in the bush, a secluded barbecue spot.

Among attractions farther afield are the sun-sea-and-sand enticements of the Natal North Coast, the battlefields and other historical sites of Zululand (this was the stamping ground of the great warrior-king Shaka), and Shakaland, a 'living museum' that started life as the location of a television epic and now introduces visitors to the ways of the traditional Zulu.

Mfuli is geared to host small conferences (maximum 30 delegates).

Game viewing
The Umfolozi, Hluhluwe and Mkuzi reserves and the splendid St Lucia wetlands are less than two hours' drive to the north. For the

rest, guests can view Mfuli's more modest game complement on walks through the densely thicketed and unspoilt terrain of the ranch. There are several trails, and they have a special appeal for the the botanist and lover of birds. Game drives are conducted in an open land rover, and there is also a snake park where the black mamba and African rock python, among others, reside. This park is primarily intended for educational purposes, but day visitors are welcome.

■ **Getting there:** By road from Durban, take the N2 to the R68 turn-off to Eshowe; drive through Eshowe to Nkwalini, turn right onto the R34 and follow the road for 12 km. Mfuli's entrance is on your left.

■ **Reservations and information:** Mfuli Game Ranch, PO Box 17, Nkwalini 3816, South Africa. Tel: (03546) 620; fax: (03546) 620, ask for fax, or toll-free 0-800-12-3000; fax: (011) 484-3160.

BONAMANZI GAME PARK

Tree houses are an unusual and charming feature of this private 4 000-hectare reserve, situated close to the village of Hluhluwe and within easy driving distance of the Umfolozi, Hluhluwe and Mkuzi game areas and of the lovely St Lucia wetlands. The tree houses are built high up among the foliage of forest giants, and they blend beautifully into their sylvan surrounds. Each is sited for maximum privacy, their double bedrooms (they have two apiece) leading out to a viewing verandah, the aspect of which is shared, as your hosts will tell you, 'only by the birds and the animals that pass by'. The chalets are self-contained, fully equipped and attractively appointed; beneath the high platform on which the living areas rest is a kitchenette, a barbecue site, and a toilet and shower (hot water on tap).

The cluster of chalets is one of Bonamanzi's four components, each of which has its own personality and amenities.

THE TREE LODGE consists of three luxurious bedrooms *en suite*, with private balconies and an open walkway leading to an airconditioned lounge and a verandah that looks out

The private Bonamanzi game park has four camps, including one with double-bedroomed tree houses.

towards the still waters of St Lucia. Here there is a fully equipped kitchen (a cook is available to help) and, close by, an attractive bush-barbecue area.

THE GAME LODGE is located in the centre of the reserve. This can accommodate six guests in its two double and two single bedrooms (the former have *en suite* showers; the latter share a bathroom). The lodge has a well-equipped kitchen, and an open-plan dining and lounge area.

LALAPANZI CAMP, at the northwestern corner of the reserve, is a pleasant complex of 10 thatched, family-type rest huts. They are set among lawns, shade trees and huge lala palms that host the rare lemonbreasted canary as well as colonies of palm swifts. Lalapanzi also has a secluded conference centre and a dining area raised (on tall stilts) above the lily-covered waters of a dam.

All four accommodation options are of the self-catering kind (guests shop at nearby Hluhluwe). Lalapanzi and the Game Lodge each has its own pool. There is a central pool for the tree houses and Tree Lodge.

Game viewing

The major northern Natal and Zululand parks, as mentioned, are virtually on your doostep. Bonamanzi itself – the name, incidentally, means 'good water' – is sanctuary for white rhino, giraffe, zebra, leopard, hippo, kudu, the shy suni and other buck, and for a host of smaller animals.

The reserve is divided into two sections: the 600-hectare park, and the more extensive conservation area, and between them they sustain more than 300 different kinds of bird, the species ranging from hoopoes, hornbills, sunbirds and the lovely Narina trogon to the pelicans, flamingoes and fish eagles of the lake shore. Plant life is diverse – habitats include grassland, thornbush, sand forest and palm stands – and there are some splendid trees to be seen, among them Natal mahogany and the wild silveroak.

Bonamanzi imposes few rules and regulations: guests are free to walk the wilderness paths (and to drive around the park). The Banded Mongoose trail is recommended: trees en route are identified. Conducted game drives and night excursions are also on offer, but their availability depends on the weather and, because Bonamanzi is a working ranch, on how busy the rangers are.

■ **Getting there:** From Durban and Johannesburg, take the N2 to the Hluhluwe off-ramp; drive 3 km to the village; turn right onto the Bushlands road and follow the road for 6 km. You will see the Bonamanzi turn-off on your left.

■ **Reservations and information:** Bonamanzi Game Park, PO Box 48, Hluhluwe 3960. Tel: 03562, ask for 181; fax: 03562, ask for 143.

THE GREATER ST LUCIA WETLAND PARK

One of the world's most remarkable wetland and marine wildernesses, the St Lucia complex lies along the Zululand coast, on the dividing line between the subtropical and tropical zones – an intricate and fascinating ecological compound of lake, lagoon, pan, marshland, papyrus swamp, sandy forest, palm veld and grassland stretching 90 km from Mtubatuba and Mapelane northwards to the soggy floodplain of the Mkuse River.

The wetlands are, in reality, an enormously extended estuarine system that runs parallel to the seashore, separated from it by the earth's highest vegetated dunes – they tower 120 m above the beaches and the necklace of coral reefs beyond. The food chain is intricate, the climate humid; annual rainfall ranges between 600 and 1 200 mm, depending on the area; hippo and crocodile, reptile and amphibian abound; and the diversity of plant, insect, bird and marine life is quite astonishing.

The central feature of the complex is the 'lake', a shallow, 36 000-hectare expanse formed some 25 000 years ago, when the ocean receded to leave a sandy flatland, parts of which were low-lying enough to retain both fresh and salt water.

The area's multiple elements – including the semi-arid savanna countryside to the west – were recently consolidated to create the 275 000-hectare Greater St Lucia Wetland Park. At present this magnificent complex has several distinct components.

St Lucia Game Reserve This comprises the lake (and its islands) which, as mentioned, is technically a system of lagoons extending northwards from the narrow sea outlet. It is at its widest – 30 km – in the northeast, at the junction of False Bay and the main lake. The lake's average depth is a modest one metre, the waters reed-mantled and especially marshy in the east, and it is home to a myriad fish, crustaceans, panaeid prawns (which are spawned in the ocean but come

LEFT: Yellowbilled storks feed from the shallow waters of St Lucia, one of Africa's finest wetlands. BELOW: Hippo at Mkuzi's Nsumo pan.

The St Lucia 'lake' – a series of lagoons extending north from their Indian Ocean estuary – is the centrepiece of a magnificent complex of elements: floodplain, pan and papyrus swamp; sandy flatland and dune forest; palm veld and savanna.
ABOVE LEFT: Viewing hippo from a safe distance.
ABOVE: Fishing in the nutrient-rich waters.
LEFT: The spiny frog, one of St Lucia's myriad aquatic creatures.
RIGHT: Exploring the lake by pontoon.

to maturity in St Lucia) and other nutritious creatures that sustain a huge number and variety of water-related birds – splendid fish eagles, thousands of white pelicans, 12 species of heron, great flocks of flamingoes, saddlebills, spoonbills, Caspian terns and many others. Hippo (about 700 of them) and crocodile are everywhere; the former tend to congregate in the south. Both must be treated with the utmost respect (no bathing or paddling permitted).

St Lucia Park covers the area around the estuary (or southern outlet) and a narrow belt of reed bed, woodland and grassland that runs around most of the lake's shore. The belt's average width is about a kilometre, its extent a little over 12 500 hectares, and it is sanctuary to a variety of antelope, bushpig, vervet monkey, a fantasia of frogs and toads, and a magnificent array of birds.

False Bay Park, the northernmost of the St Lucia reserves, is a 3 200-hectare conservation area on the western edge of False Bay. Most notable of its wildlife attractions are the 280 species of wetland, forest and bushveld bird to be seen. The park's sweet grasses nurture, among others, red and common duiker, nyala, suni, bushbuck, reedbuck, spotted hyaena and warthog.

The Mfabeni Section, which was formerly known as the Eastern Shores Nature Reserve, is a 15 200-hectare expanse of ecologically important dune forest and grassland country inhabited by leopard (reintroduced fairly recently), large numbers of water-loving reedbuck (more than 5 000 of them: the highest concentration of the species in Southern Africa), buffalo, kudu, waterbuck, jackal, red and grey duiker, and vervet and samango monkey.

Adjacent to and managed as part of the reserve is the Tewate wilderness area (formerly known as the Cape Vidal state forest), a 10 400-hectare area of tree-mantled sand dunes and marshy grassland to the northeast of Lake St Lucia. Again, a paradise for birdwatchers; game species include black rhino, buffalo and reedbuck, waterbuck, kudu and a variety of nocturnal animals.

St Lucia Marine Reserve This, together with the Maputaland coastline and offshore strip to the north, covers a full 84 000 hectares, which makes it Africa's largest marine reserve. The St Lucia segment extends from a point just south of Cape Vidal to one 11 km to the north of Sodwana Bay and out to sea for a distance of three nautical miles. Attractively prominent features are the coral reefs (the world's southernmost); a wealth of tropical fish; land-breeding turtles; and superb beaches on which can be found beautiful cowrie seashells. One can get to the shoreline by four-wheel-drive; no camping is allowed on the sands, and no bottom fishing, though spear, rod-and-line and skiboat are acceptable (with certain restrictions).

Sodwana Bay National Park The Sodwana Bay National Park, which lies within the marine reserve, is a small (413-hectare) coastal area that plays host to large numbers of summer vacationers; among the amenities provided are camp sites, log cabins, a supermarket, a community centre, fish-weighing points and fish freezers.

For all that, though, Sodwana has its beauty, its wildlife interest and its serenity. The beach-fringed bay is protected by reef and point; the dune forest, the swamps and lakelets of the immediate hinterland are home to reedbuck and suni, aardwolf, bushpig, the Tsonga red squirrel, trumpeter hornbill and a hundred other kinds of bird. The waters of the bay are crystal clear, the offshore coral reefs lovely, and both beckon the scuba diver and the snorkeller. Summer is the busy period. Winters are a lot quieter, though the fishermen still come in their scores – and with good reason: this is one of Southern Africa's finest game-fishing areas; remarkable catches of blue and black marlin, sailfish, tuna and other sporting species are recorded almost as a matter of course. During summer, too, the loggerhead and leatherback turtles come to nest (see pages 46 and 47); the Natal Parks Board conducts nighttime 'turtle tours' in January and February.

Other areas To the south of the St Lucia estuary are the Mhlatuze state forest and, a little farther west, the Dukuduku indigenous

Delightfully embowered huts at Charter's Creek.

woodlands, the latter an extensive (6 000-hectare) and precious stretch of coastal lowland forest. This is an environmentally fragile area that sustains several endangered bird species; the unique forest (it is one of the few coastal ones that is ecologically self-sufficient) is threatened by human encroachment. Attractions include the floral wealth, lovely butterflies, and a pleasant picnic spot. Beware of the rare gaboon adder.

Exploring the St Lucia region

This is not primarily game country: to see African wildlife at its classic best one visits the nearby inland reserves: Umfolozi, Hluhluwe and Mkuzi. But St Lucia's waters and their surrounds teem with hippo and crocodile; antelope of various kinds are plentiful, and the birds are a never-ending joy.

Those interested in the habits and habitat of *Crocodilus niloticus* should pay a visit to the St Lucia Crocodile Centre near the village of St Lucia Estuary – it is considered one of the finest of its kind in the world. The focus is of course on these giant reptiles, but there are also fascinating interpretive displays on the entire St Lucia system. The crocodiles are fed on Sunday afternoons. From the village, too, one can embark on launch trips across the waters of the lake – book well in advance. Also available for charter is the 80-seat *Santa Lucia*, on which there is a cocktail bar.

For those who prefer to explore on foot, there are some pleasant and most rewarding walks and hikes in the St Lucia area. The self-guided routes through St Lucia game park, Charter's Creek and Fanie's Island are designed to introduce you to, among other things, the area's splendid bird life. False Bay Park offers the Mpopomeni self-guided trail, which lasts three hours (or more, depending on how slowly you want to take things: there are lovely picnic spots en route), and the Dugandlovu trail.

The three-day Mziki (or Mount Tabor) trail covers the 22-km stretch of country between the estuary and Cape Vidal. There are also the five-day (Friday to Tuesday) St Lucia Wilderness tented trails, conducted from April to September; they start from Cape Vidal and wind their watery way among bird-rich pans.

ST LUCIA'S CAMPS

The area is served by five hutted rest camps and several camp sites – all run by the Natal Parks Board – and, in the lively little resort village of St Lucia Estuary, by a private hotel, timeshare units and holiday flats.

CHARTER'S CREEK, on the western lakeshore of St Lucia Park, is a pleasant little place of 15 rest huts (of various sizes), each equipped with a fridge, linen, bedding, cutlery and crockery. Bring your own food; meals are prepared by camp staff in the central kitchen area; bathroom facilities are communal.

There is also a seven-bed cottage incorporating a lounge-dining room, a kitchenette with a stove and a fridge. Here a camp cook prepares meals *in situ*.

Attractions include a pleasant swimming pool, self-guided walks, and facilities for fishing; petrol is available on site.

FANIE'S ISLAND, 11 km farther up the shoreline, offers much the same type of accommodation (a seven-bed cottage and twelve huts). Among the recreation options are swimming (in the pool), fishing (bait on sale), boating (boats for hire) and walking (self-guided trail).

MAPELANE, on the Mfolozi River south of St Lucia Estuary, has nine self-contained, two-bedroomed, five-person (three beds, one double bunk) log cabins, each with its own bathroom and kitchen (stove, fridge, cutlery, crockery). Linen is provided; the cabins are serviced on a daily basis; bring (and cook) your own food.

Attractions at this camp are the wonderful bird life (over 200 species have been identified); forest and beach walks; skiboating; rock and surf fishing; and musseling and cray fishing. The camp is rather remote, and the approach road sandy and in parts difficult to negotiate. There is no telephone; the nearest shop and petrol outlet is 40 km away, at KwaMbonambi.

FALSE BAY PARK The Dugandlovu rustic camp comprises four rather basic four-bed huts, each equipped with cutlery, crockery and utensils. Bring your own food and bedding; cook your meals on an open fire. Charcoal,

TOP: *A rustic log cabin at Cape Vidal.*
CENTRE: *Wilderness trailists crossing the dunes of Eastern Shores.*
ABOVE: *The end of a perfect St Lucia day.*

fishing bait, soft drinks and curios are on sale in the park, fuel and provisions at Hluhluwe village. Attractions include the walks and trails (see Exploring the St Lucia region, page 28), and canoeing (prior permission must be obtained) around the lakeshore. No swimming is, however, allowed (crocodiles are a hazard).

TEWATE WILDERNESS AREA (CAPE VIDAL), north of St Lucia Estuary, has 18 five-bed and 12 eight-bed log cabins, each with its own bathroom and kitchen, and five fishing cabins for larger groups. There is also an eight-bed bush camp available for hire (book three months in advance). Attractions are the dense dune forest; fishing (bait is on sale); and walking and hiking (see Exploring the area). Fuel and provisions can be obtained at St Lucia Estuary.

SODWANA BAY offers ten comfortable five-bed and ten eight-bed chalets, together with numerous camp sites; among visitor amenities are a well-stocked shop, fish freezers and fish weighing points.

CARAVAN/CAMPING There are attractive camp sites at Fanie's Island, Mapelane, the St Lucia Estuary resort, False Bay Park, Cape Vidal and Sodwana Bay.

TOP: *Bird's-eye view of Sodwana Bay, part of the Greater St Lucia area. The lovely offshore coral reefs are the world's southernmost.*
ABOVE: *The magical twilight hour.*

THE MAGIC OF MAPUTALAND

The region is known by a number of names – Tongaland, Northern Zululand, KwaZulu, and Makhatini Flats – but most people have now settled for Maputaland, after the river that flows through southern Mozambique. It lies between the Lebombo Mountains in the west and the Indian Ocean in the east, a 9 000-km^2 tropical wonderland of evergreen woodland, savanna, river, floodplain, lake and lagoon that has been compared in its character and extent to Florida's Everglades and the great Okavango wetlands of Botswana. A fragile land: low-lying, humid, lushly green, beautiful, pristine, it encompasses within its bounds a remarkable variety of floral and wildlife habitats. The wetter parts are home to great numbers of hippo and crocodile, and to a superb array of water-related and other birds.

Two major geophysical elements have combined to create Maputaland's stunning ecological diversity. A hundred million years ago the region lay beneath the sea, which, over the millennia, receded to leave a wide, sandy plain and a scatter of shallow depressions. These gathered fresh water from the Pongola and Mkuse rivers to form the lakes and lakelets that are now such a prominent feature of the area. Secondly, Maputaland is the meeting place of the tropical and subtropical zones, which accounts in part for its many and distinct ecosystems, and the kaleidoscopic nature of its soils, fauna and plant life.

Running eastwards from the Lebombo uplands is a 50-km-wide swathe of woodland that includes such splendid trees as giant sycamore fig, mahogany, riverine waterberry and wild date palm. Beyond, in the sandveld, are groves of ghostly fever trees, leadwood and winterthorn. Further towards the ocean one finds, successively, a belt of lala palms, then grassy coastal flats, coastal forest and a huge natural dyke of vegetated dunes, the highest in the world. Below the dunes, on their inland side, is a chain of estuarine systems and lakes; seaward are lovely beaches, rocky promontories and coral-encrusted offshore reefs.

In human terms Maputaland is still part of the old Africa. The people living here belong

to a number of groupings, largest of which is the Tembe; most of them still follow the traditional ways, fishing the estuaries and lakes, tilling the soil, gathering plants, and harvesting fruit in the manner of their forefathers. But despite its seclusion from the mainstream of development. Maputaland is under threat. Poverty, land hunger, the urge to modernise, forestry, organised agriculture and tourism are all bringing pressure to bear on the land.

The answer, according to environmental experts, is to consolidate the various ecosystems into one vast heritage site, provisionally named the Maputaland National Park. Vital to this ambitious scheme is the cooperation, the integration, and indeed the active involvement of the local communities. Understandably, distrust lingers at grassroots level – the forced removals of the recent past are not easily forgotten; promises of compensation and economic benefit are viewed with suspicion – but there has been some progress. It seems that the people on the ground are willing to accept an expanded conservation area provided the changes do not make inroads into their land and their access to traditional resources – fish, game meat, firewood, reeds for thatching, medicinal plants and water.

On these points they have been assured: the proposed park is to be a 'resource area' in which everyone shares and, moreover, the resultant growth in ecotourism will provide jobs and create opportunities for local entrepreneurs. According to a KwaZulu political leader, conservation and tourism are the most effective means of 'providing the economic stimulus that our people so desperately need'. The challenge is to gain broad popular support for the plan, and then to implement it with sensitivity.

From the Lebombo uplands eastwards to the sea: a land of stunning diversity.

PHINDA RESOURCE RESERVE

Phinda Izilwane, the original name of this impressive place, means 'return of the wildlife', and it refers to perhaps the biggest game-stocking exercise ever mounted on private land in Southern Africa.

Phinda started life when The Conservation Corporation, moving spirit behind the enterprise, bought up 15 000 hectares of land between the game-filled Mkuzi park and the St Lucia wetlands. The two blocks, which include the Zulu Nyala and Zinave, were already haven to white rhino, leopard, and the world's largest herd of the handsome, shaggy-coated nyala antelope; later (in 1991) more white rhino and cheetah were brought in and, later still, to complete the 'big five', a pride of lion made their appearance.

Resource reserves are a new breed of conservation area. The system is complex, though the fundamentals are simple enough: the scheme sets out to prove that Africa's priceless natural heritage can be used on a sustainable basis to the benefit of all – the game itself, the farmers, the owners of game lodges, tourists and, most important, the resident African communities. Londolozi (see page 80) helped lead the way; Phinda is the first such venture to be launched in Natal.

The exquisite, forest-fringed Mzinene River flows through the private Phinda reserve.

Neither money nor effort has been spared in creating one of the finest of ecotourism destinations. The Phinda reserve encompasses seven distinctively different ecosystems, among them open savanna, montane bushveld, palm belt and the rare and botanically fascinating sand forest (670 hectares of this are to be registered as a national heritage site). Flowing through these is the magical Mzinene River, its slow-moving waters fringed by fever tree and giant sycamore fig. The wetland areas of the river's reaches are rich in bird life; species include the African fish eagle, the rare finfoot, the pygmy goose and the pygmy kingfisher. Indeed, something over 350 kinds of bird make their home in Phinda's diverse habitats.

PHINDA NYALA LODGE is the first of two lodges planned for the reserve. Guest facilities are top of the range, and the buildings imaginatively designed. Phinda Nyala's consultant architect, Alan Louw, was asked to use natural and organic materials to create 'international sophistication', and he has carried out his brief with flair: the 46-bed lodge

RIGHT: Tranquillity and seclusion at Mkuzi. The reserve is home to, among much else, the handsome nyala (left) and the bushbuck (above).

Game viewing

This is excellent: the ranch sustains rhino, giraffe, zebra and many antelope species. If you're lucky you will also be able to spot the elusive leopard. A game scout will take you on bush walks; for the less energetic, conducted game drives (morning, afternoon and night) on an open vehicle can be arranged.

The game-filled Umfolozi, Hluhluwe and Mkuzi reserves are within easy reach; and the splendid deep-sea fishing grounds of the Sodwana Bay area beckon the sporting angler.

■ **Getting there:** By road from Durban, take the N2 highway to and through Hluhluwe; turn off onto the Sodwana Bay/Ngweni road 12 km beyond the village; turn left after the railway crossing and continue for 6,4 km to the Panata game ranch. The Tamboti camp is 5 km from the ranch entrance. By air: the nearest regional airport is at Richards Bay; Tamboti's transport will collect you (the service is not included in the daily rate).

■ **Reservations and information:** Tamboti Bush Camp, PO Box 2081, Petermaritzburg 3200, South Africa. Tel: (0331) 946-806; fax: (0331) 94-3942.

MKUZI GAME RESERVE

This medium-sized sanctuary is a splendid introduction to the Maputaland region and, for the wildlife enthusiast, one of the most rewarding of Southern Africa's conservation areas. It sprawls beneath the rugged Lebombo Mountains, a 35 000-hectare expanse of

TAMBOTI BUSH CAMP

A small lodge established within the 2 000-hectare Panata game ranch on the fringe of the game-filled Mkuzi reserve, Tamboti offers solitude, superb wildlife, and unpretentious comfort in its six two-bed rest huts. These are most attractive: they have thatched roofs, reed exterior walls, knotty interior pine walls and furniture, and an air of rustic charm about them. There is a central kitchen and lounge-dining room, but one usually takes lunch outside, beneath the spreading umthambothi trees, and dinner in cheerful company around a roaring fire in the reed-enclosed boma. Incidentally, umthambothi wood is much prized by the Zulu for its hardness, and by barbecue *aficionados* for its slow-burning properties. Tamboti's swimming pool is an inviting place to relax during the heat of the midday hours.

The tariff includes accommodation, all meals, game drives, and the services of a game scout. Guests should bring their own alcoholic beverages. Tamboti offers facilities for hunting and fishing.

dense thicket, open savanna, woodland, wetland and evergreen riverine forest. Ground cover is varied; scented thorns and the giant sycamore figs are among the more prominent floral species, wild wisteria and the scarlet flame-bush among the more attractive.

The reserve is bordered by the Mkuse River and its broad, shallow Nsumo pan, a place of dawn mists and phantom-like fever trees, crocodile and hippo, and a rich profusion of water-related birds – wild geese and duck, pinkbacked and white pelican, squacco heron, fish eagle, woolynecked stork and the hamerkop, a strange, solitary creature known to some rural folk as 'the bird of doom' (to disturb it, they say, will bring disaster). Among Mkuzi's 300 or so other avian species are sunbirds and African jacana, pinkthroated twinspot, the black cuckoo, the white-fronted bee-eater and the crested guineafowl.

The game is here, too – giraffe and black rhino, zebra, blue wildebeest, kudu, and the stately eland, largest of the country's antelope; klipspringer, mountain reedbuck, nyala, suni, bushbuck, waterbuck and warthog, and a host of smaller animals. Black-backed jackals are common; leopard and cheetah are present but elusive. One resident to beware of is the Mozambique spitting cobra, which lives, mainly, in the swampy grasslands and which can project its venom across more than two metres with deadly accuracy.

Sharing a common boundary – along the Mzunduze River – is a 4 200-hectare controlled hunting area (CHA) where, during the winter months, visiting sportsmen help remove animals that are surplus to the area's ecological carrying capacity. In summer their camp is available to non-hunting visitors. Animals move freely between Mkuzi and the CHA; the game viewing is excellent.

Game viewing

Mkuzi is renowned for its viewing hides, established at Kumahlala, Kwamalibala, Kubube and Nsumo pans. Here one can sit in secretive comfort to watch, and photograph, the parade of animals as they come to drink. The Malibali area, close to the entrance gate, is also the venue of a 'vulture restaurant', a place where these big, often threatened birds are fed their essential diet of bones broken down to digestible size.

The reserve encompasses an 80-km network of game-viewing roads; drives are generally very rewarding. Make sure you head for and

ABOVE AND LEFT: Mkuzi's Nhlonhlela bush camp has rustic huts set beside a bird-rich pan. The units are linked by raised boardwalks.

MKUZI'S CAMPS

MANTUMA, the reserve's hutted camp, is near the Mkuse River, in the northern part of the reserve, and offers a range of self-catering accommodation: two seven-bed cottages, four three-bed bungalows, five five-bed bungalows, and six three-bed rest huts (separate bathroom facilities). The bungalows are fully equipped with appliances, linen and bedding, utensils, cutlery and crockery. Bring your own food and drink. There are also four less sophisticated rustic huts, a caravan-camping site (maximum 60 persons) and a petrol-filling point at the entrance gate. The small camp shop sells cool drinks, books and curios; groceries and other provisions can be bought in Mkuze village.

NHLONHLELA BUSH CAMP, the pride of the reserve, is a cluster of four two-bed reed-and-thatch huts set beside the upper shores of the lovely three-kilometre-long Nhlonhlela pan. The units are linked togather by raised boardwalks that are lantern-lit at night. Each hut has a shower, toilet and wash basin; bedding

stop at Nsumo pan, where there are picnicking facilities and a bird-observation platform. Especially recommended is the 57-km self-guided auto trail (directions and informative notes are available at the camp office), which focuses on the ecology, history and trees of the Mkuzi area. Those who prefer to explore the reserve on foot have a choice of short, self-guided walks and longer (half- and full-day) conducted hikes. Book well in advance for the latter. Particularly worthwhile is the eight-kilometre Nhlonhlela trail, a three-hour stroll that leads you through splendid forest country and along the Mkuse River and the Nhlonhlela pan. The twice-monthly Mkuzi Bushveld trail is a three-day hike through largely flat, open, game-rich country.

and linen are provided; there is access to a fully equipped kitchen (fridge, freezer, gas stove) and, the *piéce de résistance*, to an open-sided dining enclosure and viewing platform. This last is a magical place in which to relax of an early evening: it overlooks the lily-covered waters of the pan and its backdrop of fever trees; in the distance are the Lebombo Mountains. The pan is a treasure house of bird life: it is at the junction of two ecosystems, and both savanna and water-related species are in evidence. The pan is also of more than passing interest to those interested in geology – at one time the area, indeed the whole of Maputaland, lay beneath the sea, and signs of enormously ancient marine life are to be seen here and there in outcrops containing fossilised mussels, crustaceans and so forth.

Surprisingly, there is no provision at Nhlonhlela bush camp for that most typical and enjoyable of bush pleasures – the beer-and-barbecue get-together. Apparently this is a deliberate omission, designed to conserve the area's precious wood.

In attendance at Nhlonhlela is a resident caretaker; a game guard will take you on bush walks.

TOP: *Mkuzi's bush camp. The reserve is haven to a wide variety of bird and mammal species.* ABOVE: *The strategically sited Nsumo hide.*

■ **Getting there:** From Durban, take the main North Coast road (the N2) to and through Hluhluwe, turning right onto gravel at the Mkuze signpost 35 km north of Hluhluwe village; continue for 15 km; turn off again, through the Lebombo uplands, and follow the signs. From the Transvaal, head for Mkuze village; follow the signposted road for 18 km to the reserve's entrance.

■ **Reservations and information:** Natal Parks Board Reservations, PO Box 1750, Pietermaritzburg 3200, South Africa. Tel: (0331) 47-1981. Camp site: Camp Superintendent, Mkuzi Game Reserve, PO Mkuze 3965, South Africa. Tel: 0020, ask for Mkuze 3.

LAKE SIBAYA

Sibaya is Southern Africa's largest natural lake, a clear, blue, limpid, 70-km^2 expanse of fresh water that was once, millennia ago, connected to the sea and still sustains 10 species of marine fish, although they have adapted over the centuries to their changed environment. Today, a narrow belt of immensely high (up to 165 m) forested dunes separates lake and ocean.

Sibaya and its surrounds are home to more than 100 hippo, some crocodile, a few reedbuck (they tend to be elusive), side-striped jackal, and a quite superb bird population. Here the African fish eagle is king, but there are scores of other species to be spotted, recorded and enjoyed – 280 in all, including cormorants (reed and whitebacked) and kingfishers (malachite, pied and giant).

SIBAYA'S CAMP

Baya, designated a 'wilderness camp', is situated about 150 m from the lakeshore, and its modestly appointed, boardwalk-linked wood, reed and thatch huts blend beautifully into the surroundings. Some of the units have four beds, others two, and each has a wash basin; bathroom facilities are communal. The huts have their own barbecue sites; visitors either cook their own food over the fire or have meals prepared for them, by the resident staff, in the central boma. Refrigeration and cooking are by means of gas, hot water by courtesy of the sun (it shines brightly most days of the year); the nearest shop and petrol outlet is at Mbazwana.

The camp is shaded by stately Umboni trees; huts, boardwalks, boma and pool are exceptionally well maintained. Languid relaxation beside the small swimming pool is a favoured pastime; pre-dinner drinks as the sun sets over Sibaya fill a magical hour.

Exploring the area

Sibaya is rather an isolated, quiet, tropically humid and very attractive area. Bird-watching is the principal drawcard – two hides have been established beside the pans, and there is an observation platform near the

The broad and beautiful waters of Sibaya.

camp. But one can also fish (in the lake or ocean surf), walk (there is a three-kilometre forest trail), picnic at Nine Mile Beach, and explore the waters of the lake. No private craft are allowed (powerboats and their coxswains can be hired), nor may one swim in or sail or water-ski on the lake: hippos, crocodiles and the bilharzia snail present too many risks.

■ **Getting there:** Sibaya is 20 km north of Sodwana bay. Take the N2 highway to the turn-off north of Hluhluwe village. The route is well signposted, but its condition varies: check beforehand with the AA or local authorities.

■ **Reservations and information:** KwaZulu Department of Natural Resources, 367 Loop Street, Pietermaritzburg 3201, South Africa. Tel: (0331) 94-6698; fax: (0331) 42-1948.

ROCKTAIL BAY LODGE

A rather lovely camp set close to the high dunes in the Maputaland Coastal Reserve, mid-way between Sodwana and Kosi Bay, Rocktail Bay Lodge is a cluster of just five attractive, steep-roofed timber chalets built on raised platforms. The rooms are spacious, furnished and decorated in pleasantly rustic style; high pole-and-reed ceilings keep the sleeping quarters cool on the notoriously steamy summer nights.

For those who prefer to cater for themselves, two of the chalets have kitchen and dining areas, but for the most part guests congregate either in the central lounge-dining room or outside, in the shade of the

THE WAYS OF THE HIPPO

The hippopotamus was once a prolifically prominent part of the African scene from the mouth of the Nile to the Cape Peninsula in the far south, but has disappeared from much of the continent, pushed out by human encroachment. In Southern Africa, this huge, semi-aquatic mammal is now found only in northeastern Natal, in the eastern Transvaal, in the riverine and wetland areas of Botswana and the Zambezi region, and in a select number of santuaries elsewhere.

Hippopotamus amphibius is usually seen in schools of between five and 20, resting in and alongside water during the day. At night the animals forage near river or pan, although when grazing is scarce they will travel up to 30 km on overnight forays in search of new pastures. Their appetites are enormous: a full feed for one adult is around 130 kg.

But water is their milieu – indeed, they cannot remain on dry land for very long: their thick skin is highly sensitive to the hot sun. They are excellent swimmers and divers, able to walk along the riverbed in deep water and to remain submerged for five minutes or longer. The single calf is born in the shallows, or in a secluded, trampled clearing in the reed beds, and can swim within a few minutes. For a time the mother will suckle her offspring while lying on the river bottom, the calf coming to the surface for air every half-minute or so. At this early stage, too, she will often carry the youngster through the depths on her back.

Hippos are generally placid, but when hurt or angered can be dangerous, attacking their tormentors with devastating effect. Fights between adult males, for dominance of herd or territory, are spectacularly ferocious affairs.

The hippo is amiable enough if unprovoked, but massive jaws make it a formidable enemy.

trees (and, at night, under the stars) for meals, and in the attractive thatched bar for relaxed sociability. The food is unpretentious, sustaining, and good.

It is hard to imagine a place less spoilt or more secluded: the lodge – a joint venture between the private Wilderness Safaris enterprise and the KwaZulu Department of Natural Resources – nestles beneath the high forest canopy behind the dunes and just a few metres from a golden beach and the blue and limpid waters of the Indian Ocean. The complex has been designed with the environment very much in mind: all the buildings blend into their sylvan surrounds; there are no overhead cables and no on-site generators: everything works on solar power and gas.

Part of the lodge's profits goes towards the protection and upkeep of the coastal reserve, and part to the regional authorities for rural upliftment projects. Like nearby Phinda, Rocktail Bay is a 'resource' venture in which all the parties – the local people, the entrepreneurs, the tourists – share, and from which the environment benefits.

Apart from the lodge, the only other accommodation in the reserve is down the coast at Mabibi, where there are 10 camp sites.

Exploring the area

Deserted beaches stretch to the far horizons; the crystal-clear reef waters are ideal for snorkelling; visitors who bring scuba equipment can embark on uncomplicated shore-centred dives. Marine life includes turtles (see pages 46 and 47), a variety of rays, clownfish, Moorish idols and a bright richness of other species. Underwater exploration is especially rewarding around Black Rock, a short drive northwards. Rocktail Bay itself is one of the region's premier line-fishing spots.

The turtle population in the area is monitored by a research centre at Bhanga Nek; in summer these creatures come ashore to lay their eggs in the beach sand. The area is also something of a bird-watcher's paradise; among the residents are wattle-eyed flycatchers, green coucal and Woodward's battis.

TOP: *The scorpion fish, deadly denizen of coral reefs.*
ABOVE: *Sunset over Kozi Bay.*

■ **Getting there:** The lodge is in the Maputaland Coastal Forest Reserve in Northern Zululand and reached via Jozini, which is the last refuelling point. The access route is complicated: Wilderness Safaris will let you have detailed directions prior to departure. Those who do not have 4x4 transport should park their cars at the Nature Conservation office at the Manzengmenya gate, where they will be met and driven the last 10 km to the lodge. By air: scheduled flights link Richards Bay, over three hours' drive away, with major centres.

■ **Reservations and information:** Wilderness Safaris, PO Box 651171, Benmore 2010, South Africa. Tel: (011) 884-1458/4633; fax: (011) 883-6255.

KOSI BAY NATURE RESERVE

The name is a bit misleading: the reserve encompasses a chain of four lakes running parallel to the most northerly segment of the Maputaland coastline and separated from the sea by a high rampart of forested sand dunes. The lakes – Amazimnyama (the southernmost), Nhlange (the largest), Mpungwini

and Makhawulani (which drains into a broad estuary that narrows to the Kosi mouth) – are filled with fresh water, though all but Amanzimnyama have a touch of salinity, which increases when storms blow in from the ocean. Summers are hot, and so are the waters of the lakes: 18 °C at their coldest, rising, in the shallows, to a high 30 °C.

The 11 000-hectare, 30-km-long reserve is a tropical paradise of limpid blue water and marshland, raffia, wild date and lala palm, mangrove swamp and sycamore fig forest that combine to provide a home for around 250 kinds of bird, among them fish eagle and palmnut vulture, whitebacked and night heron, and purple and reed kingfisher. Hippo and crocodile bask in and around the lakes; fish teem beneath their surfaces; and bushbuck, duiker and monkey inhabit the forested parts.

The stretch from Mpungwini to the estuary serves as a highly productive and, for the visitor, fascinating fishing ground: the local villagers erect 'kraals' – timber-boomed enclosures – into which the fish swim and are then guided though a series of basket

A fisherman of Kosi Bay. The pole and reed 'kraal' serves as a gigantic net.

'funnels' into smaller enclosures, where they are speared. At Bhanga Nek, just across the dunes from Lake Nhlange, is the Natal Parks Board's turtle survey station. The coastline here is unspoilt, and beautiful.

For recreation, there is good fishing in the lake and estuary (grunter, queenfish, the odd barracuda that comes in from the sea) and in the ocean; the small reef at the Kosi outlet is a favoured spot among snorkellers (you will need a four-wheel-drive to get there). No bathing is permitted in the lakes, for fear of crocodile, hippo and bilharzia. The sea here offers magnificent skindiving and spearfishing, but only if you are experienced: the currents between shore and reef can be strong, and there are such animate hazards as toxic firefish, scorpionfish and the deadly stonefish (the erect spines of which are filled with venom) – and sharks.

A number of walks have been laid out, the most demanding of them the four-day Kosi hiking trail, which takes in the swamp forests, mangroves and marshes of the lake-shore and the dunes and beaches of the shoreline. There is an appealing selection of undemanding day hikes, one of which leads you to the Kosi mouth.

KOSI BAY'S CAMPS

Permanent accommodation, established on Lake Nhlange's shore, comprises just three lodges or chalets (sleeping six, four and two respectively), and very attractive they are too. They have been constructed from local materials; the six-bedder has a tree-top verandah-platform; all are fully equipped, staffed, and very comfortable. Bring your own provisions; everything else is laid on; you're advised to book well in advance.

Scattered among the shade trees are 15 or so camping stands. There are also four trail camps; Sihadla, with its thatched huts built around a central barbecue area, is perhaps the most attractive. Mattresses and basic cooking equipment are provided.

The nearest shop and petrol outlet are at KwaNgwanase, 14 km away.

■ **Getting there:** Take the N2 to Mkuze village and then the R69 north; turn right towards Jozini and follow the generally well-maintained Sihangwe-KwaNgwanase road. The final 13-km stretch to odileKosi Bay is, however, unsurfaced.
■ **Reservations and information:** KwaZulu Department of Natural Resources, 367 Loop Street, Pietermaritzburg 3201, South Africa. Tel: (0331) 94-6698; fax: (0331) 42-1948.

NDUMO GAME RESERVE

Ndumo is a smallish conservation area – it covers just 10 000 hectares of the far-north-ern segment of Zululand – and there are no large herds of game. Many consider it, though, to be the most hauntingly beautiful of all the region's reserves – and, for the lover of birds (and of trees, too), it is certainly among the most rewarding.

Ndumo lies in the humid, low-altitude floodplain of the Pongola River, a lush, abundantly watered, ecologically fragile complex of lake and pan, marsh, reed bed, evergreen

TOP: *Ndumo's shady camp.*
ABOVE: *The reserve is known for its huge fig trees.*

forest and fig- and fever-tree woodland that is sanctuary to a fascinating array of mammals and reptiles, fish and fowl. Some of the 420-odd varieties of bird are tropical (East African) species at the southernmost limit of their range; aquatic birds in their thousands gather in and around the six-kilometre-long, water-lily-graced Banzi and the slightly smaller Nyamithi pans – pelicans and herons (among them the giant goliath), storks (yellowbilled, opensaddle and maribou), glossy ibis, plovers, avocets, flamingoes, Egyptian geese, whitefaced ducks, blackwinged stilts, egrets, Pel's fishing owl, the splendid fish eagle and a dense parade of small waders.

Beyond the pans is the drier sandveld country, a mix of reed bed, riverine forest and different types of woodland that provide habitats for a huge variety of other birds. Many of them can be observed, at leisure, from the verandah of your rest hut: flycatchers, weavers and shrikes, the Kurrichane thrush and the yellowspotted nicator, the

TOP: *The tropical luxuriance of Ndumo.*
ABOVE: *A dwarf chameleon of the Ndumo forest.*

greyrumped swallow, the floppet lark and sunbirds for Africa. Among Ndumo's raptors are the bateleur, the southern banded snake eagle, the gymnogene, the crowned and longcrested eagles, and, in the summer months, the eastern redfooted falcon.

Hippo (around 300 of them, which is the maximum the wetlands can sustain) and crocodile bask in and around all the larger stretches of water. Aerial surveys show that the reserve is home to about 400 crocs with a body length of more than a metre – which is a surprisingly healthy figure: at one time these giant reptiles had been reduced to the point of local extinction by the depredations of hunters, and by the proliferation of the barbel fish, which destroys the crocodile's food source. Ndumo's hatchery and breeding centre has been largely responsible for this remarkable recovery.

Many of the larger mammals are well represented in the Ndumo reserve: white and black rhino (which have been reintroduced), giraffe, buffalo, seldom-seen leopard, aardwolf, pangolin and bushpig, impala, duiker, reedbuck and the solitary suni.

The great 19th-century hunter Frederick Courteney Selous once came to the Ndumo area to collect nyala specimens for the London Zoo, and the reserve is still renowned for its population of these handsome, shaggy-coated antelope.

NDUMO'S CAMP

The main camp is an enchanting cluster of seven three-bed bungalows set atop Ndumo Hill. Cooking and bathroom facilities are communal; each bungalow is equipped with a fridge, linen, bedding, cutlery and crockery. It is a small camp, popular, and usually full to capacity (book well in advance).

There are also plans for two rustic bush camps (at the Shokwe and Banzi pans); for a bird hide; and for boardwalks leading over the reeds to raised viewing platforms. The new amenities may well be in place by the time this book is printed.

Game viewing

Bird life and scenic beauty are the main attractions, but there is plenty of game to be seen as well – though the cover is dense, and you really need to join one of the land rover tours (book in advance for these) or a scout-guided walk to get the best out of your stay. Most of the reserve is open to motorists; the road network is not all that extensive, but an unusually rewarding self-guided auto trail has been developed (an information brochure is available). Five game-viewing hides have also been established.

■ **Getting there:** By road from Durban, take the main North Coast road (the N2) to the Jozini exit, which is about 10 km north of Mkuze village; continue northwards for 66 km to the T-junction, and follow the signs to Ndumo village and, 14 km farther on, to the reserve's entrance gate.
■ **Reservations and information:** KwaZulu Department of Natural Resources, 367 Loop Street, Pietermaritzburg 3201, South Africa. Tel: (0331) 94-6698; fax: (0331) 42-1948.

NIGHT OF THE TURTLE

Each night between October and February scores of giant sea turtles crawl out of the sea to lay their eggs on Maputaland's beaches. Some have come from as far away as Kenya's Malindi area, 3 500 km to the north, others have covered the 2 000 km from Cape Agulhas, Africa's southernmost point. And their presence here in such numbers represents a signal victory for the conservationists.

The turtle is one of nature's gentlest creatures, slow-moving, vulnerable, its only defence a hard shell, but it has survived almost unchanged in form for almost 100 million years. Largest of the family (males reach a mass of 500 kg, and a body length of around two metres) are the leatherbacks; slightly smaller are the loggerheads. Other species seen along Southern Africa's shores are the green turtle and the hawksbill.

Leatherback and loggerhead turtles have been nesting along Maputaland's coast for

60 millennia, unerringly homing in, over huge distances, to the precise stretch of sand on which they were born, which, in the case of some individuals, could have been 50 or more years before. It is said that the male arrives first; mating takes place a little way offshore, and the female then finds her way through the reefs and the intertidal zone to the beach in search of a scent, a distinctive smell that surrounded her when she herself was a hatchling, and which was programmed into her impulse mechanism. When she finds a safe spot she digs a 60-cm-deep hole and drops her clutch of around 100 soft-shelled eggs, covers and carefully disguises the nest

BELOW: Scooping out the nest.
RIGHT: Around 100 eggs are laid.
OPPOSITE: Returning to the sea.

and then, exhausted, retreats back to the sea. A leatherback will lay up to 500 eggs in a season, in batches of approximately 100 and at intervals of around 10 days, and will return (perhaps the following year or perhaps not for another 15 years) to repeat the process. The hatchlings emerge, after a 70-day incubation period, at nighttime to brave the ghost crabs of the beach and plunge into an even more predator-infested ocean. Only one of every 500 that reach the water, it is thought, will survive to come back as an adult.

Despite the huge mortality rate, Maputaland's turtle populations flourished – until they began to fall victim to man's appetites and vanities. Valued for their meat, their eggs and the oil in their bodies, and as talismans and ornamentation, they were killed off in their thousands. In 1963, when the two species were well on their way to regional extinction, the Natal Parks Board (NPB) came to the rescue. Rangers mounted intensive shore patrols; the local village communities were asked for and willingly (and very effectively) gave their cooperation; large numbers of tagged hatchlings were collected and released. The outcome has been gratifying: in the years since, turtles have been returning to the beaches in increasing numbers.

Visitors to the area are able to see some of the results of this conservation effort on the organised night drives that are laid on by the NPB, from Sodwana Bay National Park, during December and January.

TEMBE ELEPHANT PARK

Tembe Elephant Park is a recently proclaimed conservation area, and a highly commend-able effort by the KwaZulu authorities to preserve the remnants of the once-great ele-phant herds of southern Mozambique's coastal plain.

Until the late 1970s South Africa's only free-roaming elephants were those that regu-larly migrated south across the border into the Sihangwane forest and Mosi swamp region of northern Maputaland, but the numbers were steadily being reduced as human settlement spread across the Maputo Elephant Reserve north of the border, and as a consequence of civil war.

By 1980 up to 10 000 villagers, it was reck-oned, had moved into the area. Those elephants that managed to survive the on-slaught – about 80 animals in all – are now protected by electrified fences within the 30 000-hectare park. The Mozambican authorities are keenly aware of the need to conserve their country's natural heritage, and in time, when peace returns to this troubled region, the fences will come down. Mean-while, the Tembe herd appears to be flourish-ing, its size increasing.

The park, comprising mainly dry-sand forest terrain with some shrub-veld and swamp areas, is also sanctuary to leopard, giraffe, white rhino, zebra, hyaena, suni, kudu, waterbuck and duiker. Bird life is prolific; the butterflies are gorgeous.

If hopes are fulfilled, Tembe and its near-neighbour Ndumo will be consolidated in the not-too-distant future: the corridor sepa-rating them is just six kilometres wide; Ndumo offers more nutritious vegetation, and the larger area would be able to accom-modate up to 250 elephant.

TEMBE'S CAMP

There is one luxury tented camp for overnight visitors (it sleeps eight), with a well-equipped kitchen tent, boma (barbecue area) and ablution facilities under thatch. Catering staff are on hand. A second camp is being planned.

Game viewing

The park is in its infancy; facilities are still being developed, and at the time of writing there were few facilities for visitors. Among these were three-day 4x4 expeditions, for groups of eight people. The best way to ob-serve the elephant will perhaps be from the hides that are planned – the animals, under-standably in view of the grievous persecution they have suffered in the past, tend to be temperamental.

■ **Getting there:** By road from Durban, take the main North Coast road (the N2) to the Jozini turn-off, which is 10 km north of Mkuze village, and continue northwards for 108 km (turning left at the T-junction at the 66-km mark) to Sihangwane and the park entrance.
■ **Reservations and information:** KwaZulu Department of Natural Resources, 367 Loop Street, Pietermaritzburg 3201, South Africa. Tel: (0331) 94-6698; fax: (0331) 42-1948.

ITALA GAME RESERVE

A little way off the beaten track and at one time something of the Cinderella of Natal's larger game reserves, Itala recently under-went a change of personality and now ranks as one of the region's most important – and for the visitor most rewarding – conservation areas. Ntshondwe, completed in 1991, is perhaps the finest of any public rest camp in Southern Africa.

The reserve, flanking the south bank of the Pongola River, covers 30 000 hectares of varied countryside. The land falls steeply, and spectacularly, from the highveld plateau in the east to the Nqubu basin in the west, a drop of almost 1 000 m; rugged cliffs and rocky, forest-clad slopes give way, suddenly and dramatically, to hilly grasslands, often bright with aloes, to bushveld, scented acacia thornveld and woodland savanna.

This is ideal country for viewing and photographing the wildlife, which includes among its 80 mammal species the white and black rhino, buffalo, elephant, giraffe, zebra, leopard, cheetah, brown hyaena, crocodile and waterbuck along the watercourses, and a

splendid array of antelope – eland, kudu, reedbuck, the rare roan, impala, nyala, tsessebe, blue wildebeest and, in the hillier areas, the country's largest population of klipspringer.

A number of rivers rise in or just outside the reserve, flowing down the valleys to join the Pongola. Along their winding courses are several pools, lovely waterfalls and the

Itala's new Ntshwondwe camp, pride of the Natal Parks Board, can host 200 guests in its comfortable cottages and chalets.
TOP: *The restaurant, set against the high escarpment and from whose windows there are superb views across the valley.*
CENTRE LEFT: *Ntshwondwe's pool deck.*
LEFT: *A corner of the lounge area.*
ABOVE: *Dinner for four, in splendid surrounds.*

ABOVE AND LEFT: *Mbizo bush camp offers seclusion and fine viewing from the verandah.*

deep-green magic of riverine forest. Breeding pairs of black eagle frequent the higher parts of Itala; among the reserve's rarer birds are the bald ibis, the goliath heron, the bat-hawk, the martial eagle, the brownnecked parrot and the Cape eagle-owl.

ITALA'S CAMPS

NTSHWONDWE REST CAMP is set, rather beautifully, against the high western escarpment, in a bush-mantled valley beneath the Ntshwondwe cliffs. Scenery and vistas are magnificent; there is a waterhole in front of the camp; walkways and hides make for trouble-free game viewing. The camp has been cleverly designed to complement, indeed blend into, its surroundings: thatched buildings nestle among the boulders and the giant euphorbias of the hillside; in winter the scarlet of erythrina blossom brings brilliant colour to the slopes.

Ntshwondwe can accommodate 200 people in its self-catering two- and three-bedroomed cottages and chalets. Each is equipped with appliances, kitchenware and tableware, although there is also a fully licensed à la carte restaurant, a take-away and a cocktail bar *in situ*. Other amenities include a curio shop, a pleasant swimming pool and a mini-supermarket. The camp's showpiece is its very luxurious three-bedroomed lodge, built high up on the escarpment. It has its own swimming pool, sundeck and barbecue area; each room has its private bathroom. A cook helps prepare meals (guests must supply their own provisions) and a maid keeps the place clean and tidy.

Itala also boasts a sophisticated conference centre, an impressive thatched building incorporating a main auditorium (90-seat capacity), two smaller halls (18 seats each), a foyer and a spacious, covered verandah. Delegates are lodged in the 28 adjacent two-bed chalets, each with study area, *en suite* shower and toilet; extra accommodation is available at nearby Ntshondwe camp.

Bush camps Itala has three of these delightful retreats, sited away from the main tourist routes, each different in character, each with its boma, and each designed with the environment very much in mind. They are self-catering: bring your own food, drink, torches and towels; a caretaker keeps things in order; a game guard will take you on bush walks.

THALU, beside a large pool on a bend of the Thalu River, comprises a single timber-and-thatch unit with kitchen and separate bathroom facilities; and two bedrooms, on either side of the open lounge/dining area.

MBIZO, overlooking the rapids and pools of the Mbizo River, has two four-bed reed, thatch and timber buildings, each with a separate bathroom; and a communal barbecue and campfire area.

MHLANGENI, in a tranquil setting on a rocky knoll above the Nsense stream along the upper reaches of the Pongola River, consists of five two-bed units; a central lounge, dining room and kitchen; a lovely sundeck and a barbecue area.

Each of the bush camps in the Itala game reserve has its distinctive character.
RIGHT: Shower time.
BELOW: Last light.

Game viewing

Well maintained gravel roads lead through the best game areas to viewpoints and picnic sites. The network was recently extended and is still under development; a visitor's self-drive guide booklet is available.

For those who prefer to be shown the way, the Natal Parks Board has established five-day guided wilderness trails: they are conducted during winter (March to October, beginning on a Friday and ending the following Tuesday), and are limited to parties of eight. Trailists spend all four nights at the base camp (tents, but with flush toilets), making daily excursions into the veld. All camping gear, including sleeping bags, is provided, but bring your own food and drink. The provisions are invariably pooled.

■ **Getting there:** Itala is close to Louwsburg in northern Natal. By road from Durban, take the tarred route via Hlobane. From the Transvaal, go via Piet Retief and Paulpietersburg to Vryheid and then north. From the Natal North Coast, take the main road to Pongola, left to Magudu and right onto the Vryheid/Louwsburg road. By air: the reserve has its own 1 200-m tarred airstrip, which can take most types of private aircraft. Private pilots must make prior arrangements with the camp office, Tel: (0388) 7-5105; fax: (0388) 7-5190.
■ **Reservations and information:** Natal Parks Board Reservations, PO Box 1750, Pietermaritzburg 3200, South Africa. Tel: (0331) 47-1981. Last-minute reservations: Tel: (0388) 7-5190.

HOTELS AND RESORTS

In contrast to South Africa's other major game regions – notably the eastern Transvaal Lowveld – northern Natal and Zululand have not been extensively developed by the hotel industry. There is plenty of comfortable and even luxurious accommodation, however, available at Richards Bay (the three-star Karos Bayshore Inn, for instance, and the two-star Karos Richards Hotel), a busy coastal port that is fairly conveniently situated for visits to the wildlife areas. The following are closer to the reserves.

Mhlangeni bush camp: a peaceful place over-looking the upper reaches of the Pongolo River.

ZULULAND SUN LODGE

A sophisticated mix of three-star country hotel and luxury game lodge, Zululand Sun Lodge is located within the Ubizane reserve, a 1 500-hectare, privately run conservation area near the village of Hluhluwe. The reserve is sanctuary to around 2 500 head of game, among them white rhino, Burchell's zebra, blue wildebeest, nyala, kudu, waterbuck and other antelope, ostrich and crocodile. The bird life here is also quite magnificent.

The hotel is an attractive scatter of quite beautifully thatched buildings: rondavel-type suites clustered around a main complex. Each of the rooms has its private bathroom, radio and telephone; laundry and valet services are among the guest amenities.

Food and drink: Excellent carvery/buffet fare is served in the Kudu Grill restaurant, casual meals on a terrace which overlooks the waterhole, and snacks on the pool deck. Guests intent on early-morning game view-ing are treated to an especially sustaining start-of-the-day breakfast.

Amenities: The swimming pool and waterhole are set in lovely grounds. Also on offer are conducted safaris in open vehicles and on foot, night drives, and guided game-spotting trips farther afield – to the Umfolozi, Hluhluwe and St Lucia reserves. Other excursions introduce guests to some of the Zulu people's splendid cultural heritage.

The Zululand Sun Lodge is part of the prestigious Southern Sun group; a major development programme is under way.

■ **Getting there:** 50 km north of the village of Mtubatuba. Turn left at the Hluhluwe game reserve sign; the Ubizane entrance is 6 km farther on; follow the signs to Zululand Sun Lodge.
■ **Reservations and information:** PO Box 116, Hluhluwe 3960, South Africa. Tel: (035) 562-0241/2; fax: (035) 562-0193. Central reservations: Johannesburg (011) 783-5333, or toll-free within South Africa 0-800-11-7711.

HLUHLUWE PROTEA HOTEL

This attractive and good-value two-star establishment is situated close to the Hluhluwe and Umfolozi reserves; Lake St Lucia is just a few kilometres to the east. Accommodation is in 65 well-appointed double rooms, each with its private bathroom, air-

conditioning, television (with video channel) and telephone.

Food and drink: Guests have a choice of à la carte, set menu, buffet and carvery fare in the restaurant, and barbecue meals outside. The hotel has a cocktail bar and a pool bar.

Amenities: These include a lovely swimming pool and tennis court set in pleasantly tropical grounds.

■ **Getting there:** Hluhluwe Village is just off the N2 highway, between the Hluhluwe game reserve and St Lucia.
■ **Reservations and information:** PO Box 92, Hluhluwe 3960, South Africa. Tel and fax: (035) 562-0251 (ask for fax).

RIGHT: White rhino graze Zululand Sun's lawns.
BELOW: Hluhluwe Protea's pleasant pool area.

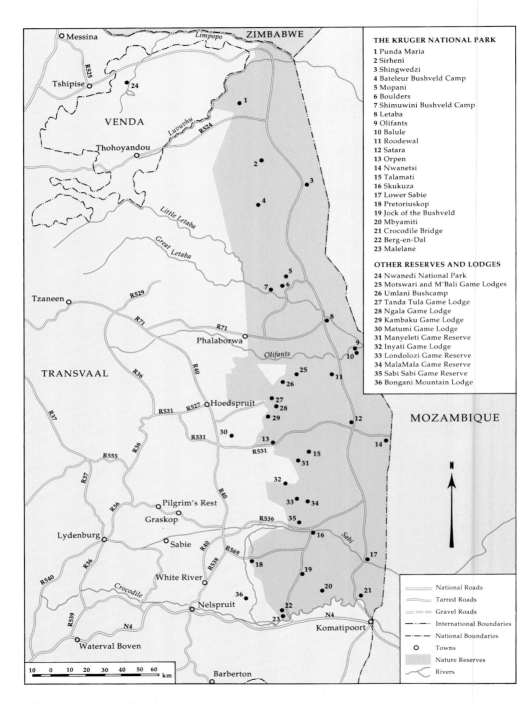

THE KRUGER NATIONAL PARK
1 Punda Maria
2 Sirheni
3 Shingwedzi
4 Bateleur Bushveld Camp
5 Mopani
6 Boulders
7 Shimuwini Bushveld Camp
8 Letaba
9 Olifants
10 Balule
11 Roodewal
12 Satara
13 Orpen
14 Nwanetsi
15 Talamati
16 Skukuza
17 Lower Sabie
18 Pretoriuskop
19 Jock of the Bushveld
20 Mbyamiti
21 Crocodile Bridge
22 Berg-en-Dal
23 Malelane

OTHER RESERVES AND LODGES
24 Nwanedi National Park
25 Motswari and M'Bali Game Lodges
26 Umlani Bushcamp
27 Tanda Tula Game Lodge
28 Ngala Game Lodge
29 Kambaku Game Lodge
30 Matumi Game Lodge
31 Manyeleti Game Reserve
32 Inyati Game Lodge
33 Londolozi Game Reserve
34 MalaMala Game Reserve
35 Sabi Sabi Game Reserve
36 Bongani Mountain Lodge

National Roads
Tarred Roads
Gravel Roads
International Boundaries
National Boundaries
○ Towns
Nature Reserves
Rivers

THE EASTERN TRANSVAAL LOWVELD

Stretching northwestwards from the White River area for some 300 km, to the town of Tzaneen and the magically lovely Magoebaskloof upland forests, is a splendidly imposing ridge, part of South Africa's Great Escarpment and here known as the Transvaal Drakensberg. The mountains are, on average, 1 000 m above sea level, and they present a stunning visual composite of peak, buttress and deep ravine, densely wooded slope, verdant valley, crystal stream and charming waterfall that, for sheer scenic beauty, is rivalled by few other segments of the southern subcontinent. The eastern faces are steep, precipitous in parts, plunging dramatically down to the coastal plain that rolls away through Mozambique to the Indian Ocean.

The plain is known as the Lowveld: a harsh land, sun-blistered and heat-hazed during the long summer months, dry and dun-coloured for the greater part of the year, but with its own distinctive character, its beauty, and its bounty. The soil is fertile, the grasses are sweet, and the area supports a magnificent variety and density of game, much of it concentrated in the world-famed Kruger National Park, some of it in the flanking regional and private reserves.

The Kruger dominates the entire Lowveld, and is perhaps South Africa's greatest single tourist attraction. Sprawling over nearly 2 000 000 hectares (about the size of Wales; larger than the state of Israel), this park plays host to around 5 000 people daily and, for the inexpensive game-viewing holiday, is probably unsurpassed anywhere: its 20 or so rest camps are pleasant, tree-shaded oases in a splendidly pristine wilderness that is home to the 'big five' and well over 100 other mammal species, and to an impressive 500 different kinds of bird.

Beautifully maintained game-viewing roads (some 2 600 km of them) lead visitors to splendid viewing sites and to waterholes that often teem with wildlife.

ABOVE: The sturdy buffalo. Hunters regard the species as among the most cunning and dangerous of game animals.
PREVIOUS PAGES: A lone cheetah at dusk.

Along the Kruger's western boundary – which was fenced until recently, but the barriers are now coming down and the animals are able to move freely – are three of the world's largest private reserves: Klaserie, Timbavati and Sabi Sand.

Each of these comprises a number of farms and independent game properties, some of whose owners have – at least in the latter two cases – clubbed together to create and operate commercial lodges: exclusive and mostly luxurious camps that offer, at a price, a bush experience that will linger in the memory. Here, at MalaMala and Londolozi, Ngala, Motswari and M'Bali, Tanda Tula, Sabi Sabi and a score of other venues, guests enjoy five-star accommodation, cuisine and service in the heart of the rugged African bushveld, and they are introduced to the ways of the wild by some of the most knowledgeable, and personable, of hosts.

THE KRUGER NATIONAL PARK

The Kruger is South Africa's premier game sanctuary, huge in extent, fascinating in its many moods, majestic in its wealth of wildlife. It sprawls across nearly 20 000 km² of low country between the Crocodile River in the south and Kipling's great and grey Limpopo in the north, a vast expanse of savanna and woodland that is home to more kinds of animal and bird life than any other sanctuary in Africa.

The park sustains 147 species of mammal, 112 species of reptile (including 50 of snake), 34 of amphibian, 49 of fish (among them the 'living-fossil' lungfish, and an ocean-living shark that has been found in one of the rivers) and nearly 230 species of butterfly. For the bird-watcher, the Kruger has special appeal: more than 510 avian species have been recorded, including ostrich, African fish eagle, vulture, bateleur, secretary bird, lourie and lilac-breasted roller, oxpecker and woodpecker, owl, francolin, hawk, babbler, hornbill and korhaan.

It's a fascinating region, too, for the botanist and especially for the lover of trees: there are some 336 varieties of the latter, many with

A herd of Kruger elephant. The park is home to about 8 000 of these gentle giants.

evocative names – velvet bushwillow, mountain syringa, live-long, mahogany and fever tree, ironwood, leadwood and yellow-wood, ancient baobab, peeling plane, bride's bush, sumach bean – and a vast array of shrubs, grasses, worts, aloes and bulbous plants. All these life forms, together with the uncountable insect species and micro-organisms, combine to create a coherent habitat, a complex system of gene pools in infinitely delicate balance, in which the cycle of life, fragile and miraculous, is maintained through collective dependence.

In broad terms, the Kruger can be quartered according to plant type. South of the Olifants River, which runs from west to east through more or less the centre of the park, the western section is distinguished by its acacia, combretum, marula and red bushwillow cover, while to the east there are broad grazing lands of buffalo and red grasses shaded by knobthorn. The lands to the northwest of the Olifants are dominated by fairly tall, butterfly-leafed mopane and the ubiquitous bushwillows, and those to the northeast by stunted mopane. Distinct from all these are the strips of dense riverine vegetation in which Natal mahogany and giant sycamore fig feature prominently.

Plant life and climate change as you reach the Kruger's far northern parts. This is a unique and, in geophysical terms, quite remarkable region, the meeting place of nine of Africa's major ecosystems. Here there is bushveld and wetland, sandveld, grassy plain and deep-green forest, woodland and broad lava flat, granite hill and dramatic ravine: a land of stunning contrasts, the kaleidoscopic elements complemented by a startling variety of reptiles and insects, trees and bushes. Many species are found in few other areas; some occur nowhere else in the world. Special are the splendid ebonies and the phantom-like fever trees standing pale in the silent reaches of the Luvuvhu River, the weird baobabs of the Mashikiri, the massive Lebombo ironwoods, and the teeming game of the Hlamalala plain.

The Kruger's climate is generally subtropical, though the northern region has tropical characteristics. Summer temperatures often reach a high 40 °C and more (though the daytime average is around 30 °C, cooling down to a comfortable 20 °C or less at night). Summer is also the wet season: on a typical day during the months from November through to February the storm clouds – great, dark, billowing banks of cumulonimbus – start building up from about lunchtime, to unleash their full fury in the late afternoon. The summer rains – in good years – are torrential. Winters, on the other hand, are bone-dry, the days sunny and pleasantly warm, the early mornings cool, the nights often downright cold (temperatures sometimes fall below zero).

All of which should be taken into account in deciding when to visit the Kruger, though each season has its attractions. In wintertime the streams – there are six perrenial rivers

The imperious martial eagle: found in the Kruger even though mountains are its preferred habitat.

and many sporadically flowing watercourses in the park – are reduced to a trickle, the wildlife tends to congregate around what water there is, and the ground cover is generally thin, so it is a lot easier to see the animals, and see them in greater numbers, during the cooler months. But in winter the park looks at its worst: the earth is parched and dusty, the colours drab, the game in poor condition. In startling and refreshing contrast is the green abundance of summer, when the rivers flow again, the pools fill, and the bushveld takes on a rich luxuriance, nurturing the animals back to health and vitality, enticing the migrating flocks of birds.

Among the Kruger's game species are the 'big five' – lion, leopard, elephant, buffalo and rhino. Of these, the first is the average game viewer's quarry, and most people manage to spot at least one of the prides during their stay. There are around 1 500 lion scattered throughout the park, though they are most commonly found in the grasslands of the central region and in the Crocodile Bridge and Lower Sabie areas of the south – terrain in which wildebeest and zebra, favourite prey of the big cats, are concentrated.

ABOVE: *Lion in the Kruger's southern region.*
OPPOSITE: *The baobab – 'upside-down tree' of African lore.*

A lot more elusive is the leopard, a shy, solitary and beautiful animal that hunts at nighttime and hides away during the daylight hours among the rocks of granite outcrops or in dense bush, or in the branches of a tree. Occasionally it will venture into open ground, but is still difficult to discern: its lithe, tawny-yellow body is spotted with black rosettes, creating a colour pattern that enables it to blend perfectly into its surrounds. There are around 900 leopards in the Kruger park.

In somewhat greater evidence are the park's 200 cheetah, fastest of all land animals, capable of reaching speeds of 75 km/h and more in short, explosive bursts of sinuous movement. Their numbers are few because they have to compete for food with larger predators and, moreover, the Kruger does not have too many patches of clear grassland, the type of country that this plains-loving cat needs in order to run down its prey.

Elephant, the third of the big five, are everywhere in the park, usually found in groups of 30 or so individuals (though herds of 100 and more have been seen, most often in the northern region) and 'tame' enough for humans to approach within a few metres. Do so, however, with caution: do not make any unnecessary movement or noise, and be prepared to drive away quickly if warning signs appear – if the animal turns to face you, raises its trunk and flaps its ears.

Even more numerous are the Kruger's buffalo: about 25 000 of them are distributed throughout the region, many of them congregated in herds of up to 200. This large relative of the antelope should also be treated with respect: it may appear to be docile, but hunters regard it as one of the most cunning and dangerous of Africa's game species, especially when wounded or cornered. Solitary males, exiled from the herd after losing a mating battle and often seen close to streams or waterholes, can be particularly aggressive and unpredictable. Ordinary visitors to the Kruger, though, are not at risk providing they apply common sense and follow the rules.

Rhino are relative newcomers to the Kruger – or rather, they became regionally extinct some decades ago, and have only recently been reintroduced. The first few of the 'white' variety (see page 20) were brought in from Zimbabwe and Zululand in the early 1960s, thrived, and were later joined by 300 more. Today white rhino number about 1 500, and black rhino approximately 300.

Perhaps the most visible of the larger mammals are the impala. There are some 120 000 in the Kruger, and one sees them everywhere. But, though very familiar, they're worth more than a passing glance: they are graceful animals, and remarkable ones too, when in flight – the entire herd moves in synchronised fashion, leaping prodigiously and in concert over the ground with the choreographed precision of a hundred-strong ballet troupe.

Other game figures – approximate ones, since censuses are periodically taken and the numbers change each time (recent droughts have had their tragic effect) – are: 30 000 zebra, 5 000 giraffe, 13 500 wildebeest, 6 000 kudu, 3 000 waterbuck, 3 000 hippo, 3 000 warthog, 1 500 sable, 800 reedbuck, 700 tsessebe, 500 eland and 350 wild dog. Crocodile and hippo are a common sight in the riverine parts.

THE KRUGER'S CAMPS

The park, as mentioned, plays host to around 5 000 people at any given time (though many of these are day visitors), and it has few

pretensions to exclusivity: it takes an un-ashamedly popular approach to introducing people to South Africa's natural heritage. Comfort and easy access to wildlife are the keynotes, and there is little of the classic African safari about one's stay there. There are 22 rest camps, five of which are smallish, private clusters of huts and chalets available on a block-booking basis and one of which is reserved for caravaners and campers. Also on offer are five attractive, rather isolated bush camps. Accommodation facilities are also available at the Crocodile Bridge and Orpen entrance gates.

The camps are pleasantly restful places, fenced against the animals, neatly laid out, most of them graced by lovely indigenous trees, flowering plants and expanses of lawn. Many of the units are surprisingly comfort-able and spacious: a typical family cottage will have two two-bed rooms, a bathroom, a toilet, a small kitchen (gas stove, fridge, uten-sils, cutlery and crockery provided), a gauzed-in verandah, airconditioning and, just out-side, a barbecue site. Lower down the scale are one-room, two- and three-bed units each

with a shower and toilet, and even more basic two- to five-bed huts (with a cold-water handbasin only) close to communal ablution facilities. Each rest camp (except Mopani and Olifants) has a caravan-camping area.

Top of the range are the guest cottages, built by private organisations or individuals for their own occupancy but available for hire when not in use. They differ in size and style – some can accommodate up to nine people – and, usually, they are most attrac-tively fitted out. There are guest cottages at Skukuza, Berg-en-Dal, Letaba, Lower Sabie, Olifants, Pretoriuskop, Satara, Shingwedzi and Mopani; bookings should be made at last three months in advance.

Camp routine is casual and undemanding, the emphasis on low-cost outdoor living. Vis-itors usually cook their own meals, indoors if the bungalow has its own kitchen, or at the barbecue site just outside. There are also communal field kitchens, and barbecue facili-ties at the park's many designated picnic spots. One either stocks up with provisions before one arrives or at the camp's shop, which sells fresh meat, groceries, dry goods,

alcoholic beverages, photographic film, reading matter, curios and oddments. A pleasant alternative to self-catering is the licensed restaurant (which all the major camps have), an informal place that serves adequate food in a friendly atmosphere. Many of the Kruger's restaurants are strategically sited to overlook a waterhole, river or deep valley.

The public camps The Kruger's public rest camps, from south to north, are:

CROCODILE BRIDGE Located on the bank of the Crocodile River next to one of the park's southern gates. It's a smallish, pleasant place – just 20 or so three-bed huts (bathroom, fridge, no kitchen) and a petrol-filling station.

There is no restaurant; basic provisions are on sale at the shop. This is acacia country, the grasses sustaining large herds of buffalo, wildebeest, zebra, kudu and impala. Lion and cheetah are also present. About eight kilometres along the road to Malelane is a pool that serves as home to a herd of hippo, and as a waterhole for elephant and other animals.

BERG-EN-DAL A more modern camp than most of the others, sited in the woodland country northwest of the Malelane gate. The Afrikaans name means 'mountain and valley', which more or less describes the landscape. The general layout and building style are attractive: the architects have made clever use of natural materials; the accommodation

is well spaced out; the camp, which overlooks the Matjulu stream and a dam, is graced by beautiful shade trees and walkways. On offer are six-bed family bungalows, two- and three-bed chalets (bathroom, kitchen), some of them specially designed for the physically disadvantaged, and two very nicely appointed guest cottages. Among the amenities are a licensed restaurant, a snack bar, a lounge, an information centre (audio-visual displays), a shop that sells fresh produce and much else, an imaginatively designed swimming pool, laundry facilities, a petrol-filling station, and provision for conferences (the conference hall is quite superb). Berg-en-Dal can cater for nearly 300 guests in its permanent units; 70 stands are available to caravaners. The surrounding countryside is notable for its marulas, acacias, red bushwillows, tree-fuchsias and stately jackalberry trees; among animals commonly seen in the area are giraffe, rhino, zebra, kudu and other bovids; also visible but less so are lion.

LOWER SABIE A lovely, medium-sized camp on the Sabie River bank, it is set in an especially game-rich area: the animals are drawn

OPPOSITE: An aerial view of Letaba rest camp.
TOP LEFT: Lower Sabie, on the banks of the Sabie River.
ABOVE LEFT: Punda Maria, northernmost of the Kruger's camps.
ABOVE: Cheetah are the swiftest and among the most graceful of all land mammals.

to it by the good grasses and foliage, the river and the abundance of waterholes (the Mlondosi and Mhlanganzwane dams are also nearby). Lawns and shade trees lend charm to the setting. Accommodation is in five-bed family cottages (bathroom, kitchen); two- and three-bed chalets (bathroom, fridge), and in three self-contained and well-appointed guest cottages. One three-bed unit is designed for the physically disadvantaged. There is a licensed restaurant, a shop and a petrol-filling station. The flat plains of the region teem with buffalo, and with various antelope species, which attract lion and other predators. There are hippo, crocodile and an array of water-related birds on and around the dams.

PRETORIUSKOP This is the Kruger's oldest camp, an attractive collection of huts, family

ABOVE LEFT: *Heavy traffic; the Kruger has a splendid network of game-viewing roads.*
ABOVE: *Hippo in their element.*
LEFT: *Satara, on the central grasslands.*
OPPOSITE: *Olifants, set high above the river.*

cottages, two- and three-bedroomed chalets and two comfortable guest cottages, the whole set in an area of tall grasses, sicklebush and marula just to the east of the Numbi gate. It has a shop, a licensed restaurant, a petrol-filling station, a natural-rock swimming pool, and shady, lawn-covered open spaces. The vegetation is dense, but with luck you will spot rhino and wild dog.

SKUKUZA 'Capital' of and by far the largest camp in the Kruger, Skukuza is named in honour of the park's first warden, James Stevenson-Hamilton (the word means 'he who sweeps clean', a reference to his ruthless war against poachers). In fact, Skukuza is more of a busy little village than a bush camp, its centrepiece the spacious restaurant and reception complex (thought to be the world's largest thatched building). Among the visitor amenities are a supermarket, à la carte restaurant, a 'train' restaurant (a converted dining car and lounge) and a snack bar; a post office, a bank, a police station, a doctor's surgery; a petrol-filling station, a workshop and AA service; an airport, and Comair and Avis offices. The information centre is very well organised, and houses a good library and

exhibition hall. Nearby is a nursery – worth visiting for the baobabs, palms, cycads and other indigenous plants on sale. On offer is the full range of accommodation, from fairly basic units to splendid guest cottages.

ORPEN A small, peaceful, pleasant camp in the west-central plains country, close to Orpen gate, notable for its grounds graced by tall acacia and marula trees, red bushwillows, aloes and rock gardens. It has a shop (which doubles as the reception area) but no restaurant; accommodation comprises modest two- and three-bedroomed huts; kitchen and bathroom facilities are communal. Nearby is the Maroela caravan-camping ground. Most common of the area's larger game species are zebra and wildebeest (in the direction of Satara), giraffe and elephant; lion, leopard and cheetah along the Timbavati River; and, to the south, splendid sable antelope.

SATARA Second largest of the Kruger's camps, Satara is located on the flat grassland country-side of the east-central region and although, in contrast to most of the others, it does not enjoy any special views, it is one of the more attractive: majestic Natal mahogany and marula shade the lawned grounds, and the bird life is prolific – buffalo weavers, horn-bills, cheeky sparrows and what seems like a million starlings enliven the area around the terrace and pleasant self-service restaurant.

The latter is sited close to a waterhole. This is good grazing country, ideal for wildebeest, zebra, buffalo, kudu, impala and other buck, which in turn attract prides of lion. Elephant can also be seen around Satara.

Accommodation consists of six-bed family cottages, two- and three-bed chalets (bathroom and fridge; two are designed specially for the disabled), and three comfortable, self-contained guest cottages. Amenities include a restaurant, snack bar, lounge area, shop, an information centre, an AA workshop, and a petrol outlet.

BALULE A satellite of the much larger Olifants camp just to the north (see below), Balule is a modest cluster of six three-bed rondavels, a caravan camp and bathroom block on the central region's Olifants River. Among the few amenities are a communal freezer and barbecue sites (firewood available in camp). The camp does not have electricity.

OLIFANTS A modern, pleasantly designed camp magnificently set on cliffs that rise 100 m above the river, Olifants offers spectacular views down to the lushly evergreen, game-rich valley below and to the distant hills beyond – the vistas are lovely at all times, but especially so at sunrise and sunset. Thatched chalets (some with a kitchen, some with a fridge only, but all with a bathroom or shower and toilet) and the family and guest cottages are built along rising, aloe-decorated terraces, all of which enjoy the view. There is a licensed restaurant, a shop, a museum and an information centre, an amphitheatre in which wildlife films are screened, and a petrol-filling station. Olifants is well placed between the grazing lands of the central region and the mopane country of the north. Recommended is the river drive.

LETABA One of the park's most handsome camps, it's quite beautifully sited above a sweeping bend of the Great Letaba River; the terraces are ideal for riverine game viewing, the grounds attractive with lawn, aloe, flowering shrubs, shady mahogany and lala palm. Letaba is also well positioned – at the junction of three major routes – for game drives to the south, west and north. Choice of accommodation includes two- and three-bed huts (bathroom; fridge), six-bed family cottages, and two guest cottages sleeping eight and nine respectively. The camp has a shop which sells, among other things, fresh produce; and

an above-average licensed restaurant, a laundromat, a petrol-filling station and an AA repair workshop.

Opening during 1993 is the Environmental Education Centre, which houses the tusks and history of the 'Magnificent Seven' – legendary elephants with exceptional tusks. Known as the Elephant Hall, the history, morphology and physiology of the African elephant are to be displayed.

MOPANI A newish camp, cleverly designed to blend in with the natural surrounds, Mopani is located in the northern region about half way between Letaba and Shingwedzi. It is set into a rocky incline, and the view down towards Pioneer dam is quite splendid. The bungalows are of stone and thatch, and they're built to allow guests a fair degree of privacy. The area is less well endowed with game than the park's more southerly parts, but one can see plenty of elephant, buffalo, zebra, wildebeest and buck species; and some sable, eland and roan. Recommended drives include those along the Letaba River to Letaba camp, and between Letaba and the Engelhardt dam. Accommodation consists of six-bed family cottages and three-bed huts.

The somewhat old-fashioned charm of Shingwedzi. The trees here are especially lovely.

There is a licensed restaurant, a swimming pool, a shop and a petrol-filling station.

SHINGWEDZI An atmospheric, rather old-fashioned camp, large, rambling, and notable for its spacious grounds, handsome trees (mainly mopane but also palms) and bright pink-and-white impala lilies. Some of the older bungalows have colonial-style charm, though they are quite modern inside.

There are many possible game-viewing drives in this rewarding area; those to the southeast (towards Letaba) and the secondary route to Satara (the well-patronised Kanniedood dam is along this road) are especially recommended. Accommodation comprises two-, three- and four-bed huts (some with bathroom) and a self-contained, seven-bed guest cottage. Shingwedzi has a licensed restaurant, a cafeteria, a shop, an information centre and a petrol-filling station.

PUNDA MARIA Located in the tropical far northwestern part of park and named after the wife of an early ranger, Punda Maria is a smallish, unassuming, quite charming camp, popular for its sociable atmosphere and its setting among groves of evergreen trees and rocky hills. In contrast to the some of the southern camps, it has an evocative wilderness feel about it. Recommended is the short Mahogany loop drive on the evening you arrive: it's a superb introduction to this most attractive of areas. Next day, be sure to make your way to the jungle-like banks of the Luvuvhu River. Accommodation comprises of four-bed family cottages, and two- and three-bed huts (the latter with kitchen) set along hillside terraces.

Amenities include a licensed restaurant, a shop and a petrol-filling station.

The private camps Much smaller and more exclusive are the five private camps – secluded, peaceful places that limit access to their resident guests. They're ideal for groups (they must be reserved *en bloc*), and for people who have specialist interests. Bungalows have either overhead fans or airconditioning, and are cleaned and serviced each day; bed linen, towels, cooking and eating equipment and barbecue facilities are provided.

MALELANE is an 18-guest camp of five well-appointed, even luxurious, cottages in tree-shaded surrounds, with a communal kitchen complex (fridge, freezer, stove). Check in at Berg-en-Dal.

JOCK OF THE BUSHVELD An atmospheric little 12-person camp, its character recalling the early days of the gold-diggers and transport riders. The neat, rustic, white-painted, jackalberry tree-shaded buildings are set at the confluence of the Mtomenispruit and Mbyamiti River. There are three self-contained, four-bed cottages; solar panels provide the electricity. Check in at Berg-en-Dal.

NWANETSI Set on the lily-mantled Nwanetsi riverbank close to the Mozambique border, with the Lebombo mountains forming its backdrop, this is an especially attractive and tranquil camp (its name in Shangaan means 'river with clear water' or 'reflections'). It can accommodate 16 guests in its four three-bed huts and two two-bed bungalows (shower and toilet). There is a communal kitchen area

TOP: *The 19-guest Roodewal private camp.*
CENTRE: *The redbilled oxpecker.*
ABOVE: *Giraffe – tallest of land mammals.*

and a summerhouse for quiet relaxation. Check in at Satara.

ROODEWAL The tree-shaded A-frame buildings of this 19-guest camp are set on the Timbavati River between Satara and Olifants: a truly superb game-viewing area. There are three five-bed huts (shower and toilet), a fully equipped four-bed family cottage and a communal kitchen fitted with a stove and fridge. Check in at Satara.

BOULDERS Just four two-bed bungalows (bath, shower, toilet) and a four-bed family cottage. The camp is unfenced, quite beautifully designed and set among massive boulder formations; the thatched buildings are raised up on stilts, and each has its pleasant verandah. Solar power provides the electricity. There's a sociable kitchen-cum-relaxation area; domestic help is available. Guests should check in at Mopani.

The bushveld camps The five bushveld camps offer standard accommodation but are smaller, more secluded and generally less sophisicated, and offer fewer amenities than the larger rest camps.

MBYAMITI Set on the Mbyamiti River bank, five kilometres from its confluence with the Crocodile River in the extreme southern part of the Kruger, this camp has 10 five-bed and five four-bed family cottages.

SHIMUWINI On the Shimuwini dam (filled with the waters of the Letaba River), west of the tarred road between Phalaborwa and Mooiplaas picnic site. The riverbank is lined with some lovely trees (among them giant sycamore figs), and the river is favoured by the fish eagle. The area's bird life is splendid. The camp offers one six-bed and five four-bed family cottages, all with kitchenettes.

BATELEUR Located 43 km southwest of Shingwedzi, beside the mostly dry Mashokwe stream. A splendid timber viewing platform overlooks a pool which fills during the rains, and to which the animals come to drink. The area is rather off the beaten tourist track, and the camp is more a part of the 'real Africa' than most. Nearby are the Silverfish and Rooibosrand dams, which Bateleur's guests regard as their own. Bird life is prolific and fascinating. Bateleur has four four-bed and three six-bed family cottages, all with kitchenettes equipped with fridges. Solar panels provide the electricity.

TALAMATI On the Nwaswitsontso River bank (the river is dry for most of the year) near the park's western boundary (Orpen gate), Talamati offers ten six-bed and five four-bed

family cottages, each with kitchenette. The game viewing and bird-watching is excellent.

Sirheni On the Sirheni dam near Talamati (see above), Sirheni also has ten six-bed and five four-bed family cottages. A superb scenic, game-viewing and bird-watching area.

Game viewing

The Kruger's eight gates and 20 or so rest camps are linked by a 2 600-km network of main (tarred) and secondary (graded gravel) roads. Within leisurely driving distance of every camp are waterholes, viewing sites, pic-nic spots and a wealth of scenic and wildlife splendour. Most people – those who are not members of tour groups – explore the Kruger on self-drive excursions. The park is open throughout the year, though some of the lower-lying areas may be closed off during the heavy summer rains. There are petrol-filling stations at all the larger rest camps, and at the Crocodile Bridge and Orpen entrance gates.

Despite the massive tourist presence, the Kruger remains unspoilt. Everything intro-duced by man – the rest camps, the 'designa-ted areas', the routes and the 'visual bands' that run along either side of them – takes up less than four percent of the total area. The remaining 96 percent belongs to nature. The camps and roads, as one writer has put it, are 'merely windows looking out into the wilder-ness'. Some hints:

❏ This is low-lying country and can be uncomfortably warm during the summer months, and much of the game tends to rest up during the heat of the day (as do the majority of visitors), so the best times to set off on your drives are the early mornings (from first light to around 10h00) and late afternoons (15h30 to dusk). Travel is restrict-ed to daylight hours.

❏ Stick to the speed limits (between 40 and 50 km/h, depending on the route, which is sensible enough since you won't see much if you travel faster), and don't leave your vehicle unless you're in a designated spot.

The Kruger, as we've noted, is huge, and one has to plan one's viewing. Before starting out, decide where your special interests lie

OPPOSITE: Malelane camp comprises five attractive cottages.

TOP: Game-viewing at the Talamati bushveld camp, near the Kruger's western boundary.

ABOVE: The bateleur, distinguished by its short tail and long wings, is among the most hand-some of the park's birds of prey.

and what you would like to see. Elephant, lion, croc and hippo, buffalo, giraffe, birds of prey – each species has its favourite haunts. Arm yourself with a good map and a guide-book containing a game distribution list – both will be available from the rest-camp shop, together with a useful selection of spe-cialist publications describing the Kruger's wildlife in detail. Also available is a checklist of the park's 300 or so tree species. Many of the more prominent specimens you will see during your drives have been numbered to correspond with the listed items.

❏ Generally speaking, waterholes are more rewarding than the exploratory drive. One has to be patient, but there is always some-thing to be seen – a mongoose, a hornbill, perhaps a brace of warthog – and sooner or

ABOVE: *The huts of the Wolhuter trail camp.*
ABOVE LEFT: *Hikers on the Bushman trail survey the terrain ahead. The area is graced by a variety of Bushman rock paintings.*
LEFT: *Lion in repose. These big cats hunt mainly at night, their prey ranging from massive giraffe down to the smaller mammals. Full-grown males weigh in at around 200 kg and stand a full metre at the shoulder.*
OPPOSITE: *The shady Nyalaland trail camp.*

later the larger and rarer creatures will make their appearance. There are plenty of water-holes to choose from; two of the more pleasant are those at the Orpen dam, near Tshokwane, and the Mlondozi dam, near Lower Sabie, each of which has a shady viewing point with chairs *in situ*.

For those with more energy, more time, and a wish to get closer to the Kruger's wildlife, there are a number of wilderness trails on offer, foot safaris led by rangers who know the lore of the wilderness and are able and willing to share their expertise. The walks are neither competitive nor challenging: they are designed simply to stimulate the mind and the eye, and to provide enjoyment, relaxation and good companionship in the most pristine of surrounds. They tend to be meandering, go-where-you-will affairs, leading wherever the mood and interest of the group dictate, stopping now and then to examine a particular tree perhaps, a flower, an insect, a herd of antelope, or the nest of a bird. The ranger will talk with knowledge and enthusiasm about each. Accommodation is fairly basic (simple, thatched, A-frame huts are a

feature of several base camps), but bedding, food and utensils are provided. The campfire evenings, spent in conversation and anecdote with the sounds of the nighttime veld all around, are memorable indeed.

The seven established trails are the Bushman, the Sweni and the Wolhuter in the southern region (the last-mentioned is named after Harry Wolhuter, a local ranger who, in 1903, killed a full-grown, marauding lion with his sheath-knife); the Olifants and the Metsi-Metsi in the central region, and the Naphi and the Nyalaland in the north. The Nyalaland's base camp is sited among kudu-berry trees near the Luvuvhu River, in an area of superb game, bird and plant life.

■ **Getting there:** By road from Johannesburg: take either the N4 to Nelspruit – the distance is 358 km – or the N1 north, turning off to the east on the R71 (for Tzaneen and Phalaborwa) or the R524 at Louis Trichardt (for the northern Kruger), for the gate nearest to your camp. The eight public entrances are, reading clockwise from the park's southeastern corner, Crocodile Bridge, Malelane, Numbi, Paul Kruger, Orpen, Phalaborwa, Punda Maria and

Pafuri. The Kruger gate is the busiest. Visitors should arrive well before nightfall; the gates have opening and closing times, which vary slightly with the seasons. Coach travel: a luxury coach operates between Johannesburg and Nelspruit; consult your travel agent on this and other coach services. Air travel: Comair, Link Airways, Metavia and Letaba Airways operate scheduled services connecting Johannesburg and Durban with Skukuza, Phalaborwa and Nelspruit (see Visitor's Advisory, page 303), and, of course, aircraft may be chartered. A new airport at Malelane, on the Kruger's southern boundary, came into operation in 1990. Car and minibus hire: there are Avis offices at Skukuza and

Phalaborwa; make reservations through Avis, Comair or your travel agent. Contact numbers are: Avis (01311) 6-5651 (Skukuza) and (01524) 5169 (Phalaborwa), and Comair (01311) 6-5644.

■ **Reservations and information:** Bookings for both the camps and the wilderness trails should be made through The Chief Director, National Parks Board, Reservations, PO Box 787, Pretoria 0001, South Africa. Tel: (012) 343-1991. A regional National Parks Board office may be contacted at Cape Town: PO Box 7400, Roggebaai 8012. Tel: (021) 419-5365. Alternatively, call in at the Parks Board's head office in Leyds Street, Muckleneuk, Pretoria.

BONGANI MOUNTAIN LODGE

Bongani, an attractive blend of game lodge and upmarket country hotel, is situated in the 8 000-hectare Mthethomusha reserve on the uplands bordering the southwestern segment of the Kruger National Park. The place has a superb setting: it's built atop a granite plateau that looks over the Lowveld plains to the lofty Transvaal Drakensberg beyond. In the early morning, before the air is hazed by the heat, you can see the animals – herds of antelope and zebra, sometimes giraffe, occasionally elephant – moving through the grasslands far below.

The lodge, which can comfortably accommodate up to 60 people, is a handsome complex, designed and decorated in ethnic Swazi style; timber, thatch and strikingly coloured fabrics are the visual keynotes. You reach the reception area through a narrow rock passage – local legend holds that renewed fertility is conferred on those who pass through this natural corridor. The luxurious double chalets incorporate twin bathrooms; some of the larger units have a lounge area that can also be used as an extra bedroom; and all have wooden verandahs that afford both privacy and splendid views. There is also an especially large and luxurious two-bed-roomed main suite. The attractive central area encompasses a lounge, a safari bar, a timber game-viewing deck, and a cosy dining room. Close by is the swimming pool and the traditional boma, where tribal dancing, good food and good company are enjoyed on warm, firelit evenings.

Among the sights to see in the general area are Bushman rock paintings and places of archaeological interest. The lodge and reserve are within the KaNgwane region, inhabited by people of Swazi stock, and, although the old ways are fast disappearing, the ancient rituals and celebrations, the music, dance and regalia still bring colour and vitality to special occasions. Of these, the Incwala, held during the first new-moon phase of the year, and the Umhlanga, a sustained reed-dance performed in either July or August, are the most notable.

The 60-guest Bongani lodge: luxury living on the edge of the Kruger wilderness.

Game viewing

Mthethomusha was once used for cattle grazing, but it has now been restored to its original wilderness splendour and restocked with a profusion of game, including white rhino, Burchell's zebra, giraffe, buffalo, nyala and other antelope. Leopard, lion and elephant are also present – and, of course, the great spaces of the Kruger National Park are just beyond the horizon.

The reserve has some lovely trees – kiaat, marula and the scarlet-blooming *Erythrina*; among the wide variety of bird species are crowned eagle and bateleur.

To preserve the integrity of the wilderness, private vehicles are not permitted beyond the picnic and parking areas; professional guides conduct guests on game drives aboard 4x4 vehicles.

■ **Getting there:** By road from Johannesburg: take the N4 to and through Nelspruit, leaving your car in the foothills 35 km east of the town (the parking area is well signposted, and secure). There will be an open land rover there to meet you and take you up the mountain road to Bongani. By air: there are scheduled flights to Nelspruit, from where a helicopter will collect guests and ferry them the 12 km to Bongani. You fly low, following the course of the Crocodile River: a fine introduction to the wilderness.

■ **Reservations and information:** Bongani Mountain Lodge, PO Box 1990, Nelspruit 1200, South Africa. Tel: (01311) 5-3931; fax: (01311) 2-3153.

THE AFRICAN LION

The Kruger is home to around 1 500 lion, largest of Africa's land predators and hunter supreme. The prides range throughout the park and its neighbouring reserves, but tend to be more numerous in areas that support large numbers of herbivores – on the plains of the central region and in the south, around Crocodile Bridge and Lower Sabie.

Lion are a territorial species, usually living in prides of six or so (though larger groups, of a dozen and more individuals, are sometimes found), hunting and killing by a subtly complex process – one in which the female plays the more prominent role. Most kills take place near waterholes, especially during periods of drought. The male, in his lordly fashion, tends towards indolence, though his physical strength is quite remarkable: he can break the neck of a full-grown wildebeest with one pass of his massive paw. He is also able to show a phenomenal turn of speed, covering 100 m in just four to six seconds. And his appetite is prodigious: when really hungry he can consume a full quarter, or even a third, of his own body mass in meat at one sitting.

Both males and females are usually tawny-brown in colour, enabling them to merge into the brown-yellow grasses of their savanna and bushveld habitat. The male's mane often darkens with age, from a dull yellow to black; cubs, born at any time of the year in litters of two to five, have darker patches which disappear as they grow older.

Lion have no natural enemies, but mortality is surprisingly high among the prides, the heaviest toll taken by starvation among the cubs in the lean seasons, and by parasite-borne diseases that attack the young when they are in poor condition. Adults are also prone to injury during the hunt – from the horns of a buffalo, for instance, or the lethal kick of a giraffe. Death often results, too, from overly familiar contact with the porcupine – the needle-sharp quills pierce the flesh to set up an infection that spreads, slowly weakening the lion until it can no longer hunt for food.

Once widely dispersed over the Southern African veld, the lion is today found mainly in parks, reserves and other protected areas. Some of the largest populations occur in the Kruger and the Kalahari Gemsbok National Parks, the Hwange in Zimbabwe and in Zambia's Luangwa Valley.

The regal male of the species: lazy, but capable of swift and lethal action.

Sabi Sabi Game Reserve

Sabi Sabi, part of the Sabi Sand reserve bordering the Kruger National Park, has two lodges: River Lodge (20 chalets), a private camp on the banks of the perennial Sabie River, and Bush Lodge (25 chalets), set deep in the veld 10 km to the north. The habitat is diverse, ranging from dense riverine forest along the Sabie River to acacia thornveld, and is home to a splendid array of wildlife.

Both lodges nestle among stately indigenous shade trees; each has its filtered pool, its fully licensed and amiably sociable pub, and its pleasant terrace where one sips long drinks in the heat of the Lowveld day. Décor is rather special: one of the country's leading architects was recently engaged 'to bring the bush into the buildings', and the results are splendid. Each lodge has its plant-filled courtyard; the dining, lounge, bar and reception areas are open plan under thatch; and scattered around are eye-catching wooden carvings by celebrated sculptor Geoffrey Armstrong, each piece created from bushveld materials. The boma is linked to a viewing deck, which overlooks the waterhole. Your chalet doesn't have many frills: no telephone, television or radio (here, in this pristine environment, one does not need these distractions), but it is comfortable, spacious and restfully cool. Each chalet has its *en suite* bathroom, a shower and a private verandah; there is fruit on the table, iced water at the bedside, and a personal note of welcome from the housekeeper.

Pride of Sabi Sabi are its four new luxury suites, one at Bush Lodge and three at River Lodge. The Mandleve unit is arguably the most inviting: it has beautifully appointed living, dining and kitchen areas, and two bedrooms and two bathrooms, all located under a dramatically high, open, thatched ceiling; an 'alfresco' shower (open to the stars); a large deck, built out into the trees to overlook the river; a private swimming pool; and its guests have their own land rover and ranger-tracker team.

On arrival, you are introduced to your ranger, who will look after you throughout your stay. Mealtimes, announced by the sounds of kudu horn and drum, are companionable affairs. Breakfast and a sumptuous buffet lunch are taken on the dining terrace or in the Safari Lounge; the menu features a range of salads (try the shrimp), four meat dishes (including venison, of course), assorted desserts, cheeses and home-made bread.

When the weather is good – which it nearly always is – it is the reed-enclosed boma that provides the focus of conviviality. Sabi Sabi is known for the warmth of its hospitality; the barbecue dinners are special – for the glowing fire, the food, the animated conversation and the ambience. The rangers are young and, for all their expertise and serious commitment to their work, full of ingenuous fun. During the evening Shangaan women perform their traditional dances, singing with superb gusto and rattling their 'castanets' (made from bottle tops) as they go through the prescribed movements of an ancient choreography. When the dancing is over they resume, rather incongruously, their main role and serve you your food. The service is informal and cheerful, and the evenings invariably turn into a roaring party.

Game viewing

The Sabi Sabi reserve is exceptionally well endowed with game, and the day and night drives are almost always highly rewarding: the trackers display impressive skill, and the search is exacting and exciting. Present are lion, leopard, elephant, buffalo, rhino (though very few of the black variety), cheetah, jackal, hyaena, wild dog and a profusion of antelope. There's perhaps more game than the area originally supported or was meant to support, but the reserve has an excellent habitat-management programme. Sabi Sabi's lodges, like all the others in the area, are commercial enterprises, but there is much more at work here than the simple profit motive. Behind the sophistication of a successful tourist venture lies a deeply felt commitment to the land and its abundant wildlife, to conservation.

Sabi Sabi has launched an imaginative 'ranger-training course', designed largely but

OPPOSITE, LEFT: Sabi Sabi's inviting pool area.
OPPOSITE, ABOVE: The dining terrace offers excellent cuisine in pleasant surrounds. On fine nights dinner, a convivial barbecue occasion enlived by traditional music and dance, is enjoyed in the reed-enclosed boma.
OPPOSITE, BELOW: Embarking on a game drive.
ABOVE: Buffalo in the Sabi Sand reserve. Many of the Lowveld's herds number 200 and more; the Kruger alone is home to around 25 000 of these powerful relatives of the antelope.

not exclusively for business executives, to provide a deeper insight into the ways of the wild than one can get from a few days' game viewing. Groups of up to seven spend five days and four nights in a bush camp; subjects covered by the ranger and tracker tutors include wildlife and spoor identification, tracking, the edible and medicinal plants of the veld, 'orienteering', bush survival, snakes, snake bite and first aid, habitat management, the astronomy of the southern skies, and the handling of a four-wheel drive vehicle.

■ **Getting there:** By road from Johannesburg: take the N4 to Nelspruit, the R40 north to Hazyview and the R536 towards the Kruger park's Paul Kruger gate and Skukuza camp; turn left after 38 km – at the collection of signposts, one of which is Sabi Sabi's. You drive the last eight-kilometre stretch on gravel. By air: there are daily Comair flights to Skukuza, from which a Sabi Sabi ranger will collect you.
■ **Reservations and information:** Sabi Sabi Private Game Reserve, PO Box 52665, Saxonwold 2132, Johannesburg, South Africa. Tel: (011) 483-3939; fax: (011) 483-3799.

MALAMALA GAME RESERVE

This part of the Sabi Sand area has five different and highly distinctive components, each with its own attractions, and its own pleasant character.

MALAMALA itself, the largest of the camps, is generally rated as one of the most exclusive and best-run camps in the world. It provides the ultimate in safari luxury: an airconditioned and beautifully appointed complex that offers supreme comfort, fine cuisine and five-star service in a wilderness area that boasts the greatest concentration of big game on the African continent.

The camps's clientele is cosmopolitan; many of the guests jet in from Europe and the States for a brief taste of the real Africa, and they are superbly looked after from the moment they set foot in MalaMala. MalaMala has room for a maximum of 50 people, and there are 10 rangers in attendance, which amounts to very personalised service indeed. The rangers are courteous, helpful, well versed in the ways of the wild, and they look after you from dawn to dusk.

The camp is a neat cluster of exquisitely thatched buildings of an ochre colour nestling among shade trees. Most of them are

sited to overlook the game-rich Sand River. Each of the units has two bathrooms (a 'his' and 'hers'), direct-dial telephone, airconditioning and comfortable three-quarter beds.

Public areas include a swimming pool, a cocktail bar, a pleasantly shaded verandah and a spaciously cool, Out-of-Africa lounge where original bronzes, carvings and trophies are displayed. Décor generally has been cleverly devised to create a bush atmosphere, though there are none of the discomforts of the bush. MalaMala has an impressive boma shaded by an enormous, 800-year-old jackalberry tree; dinners are splendid occasions.

Special mention should be made of the Sable Suite, an ultra luxurious, self-contained little complex on the southern edge of the

OPPOSITE, ABOVE: *The focus of MalaMala's Kirkman's Kamp is a 1920s' homestead, restored to its original charming condition.*
OPPOSITE, BELOW: *One of the main camp's bedroom suites.*
ABOVE: *MalaMala's cottages are beautifully thatched, luxuriously appointed.*

camp. Designed for a maximum of 16, it has a lounge, viewing deck and boma which overlooks an illuminated waterhole, and is ideal for business getaways and family parties.

HARRY'S, smaller than MalaMala but friendly and most comfortable, is also on the Sand riverbank and comprises seven twin rooms (each with its *en suite* bathroom) decorated on the outside with geometrical, Ndebele-style wall patterns. The emphasis here is on outdoor living: home-style meals are served under the trees, overlooking the river, on the verandah, or in the intimate boma area – unless the weather is especially bad, in which event you retire to the lounge. The food is simple, and very good. There is also a bar, a lounge and a swimming pool. The general setting is entrancing; antelope and warthog sometimes wander into the grounds.

KIRKMAN'S KAMP, the third component, comprises 10 twin cottages next to an old homestead which Colonel Stevenson-Hamilton, architect of the early Kruger park, used to visit regularly for Sunday tennis and luncheon. Mike and Norma Rattray bought it a few years ago and restored it to its original 1920s style. The lounge-dining room is especially evocative of a more romantic, bush era; the pub and the spacious verandah are places for relaxed sociability. The semi-detached guest cottages are decorated with sepia photographs of the old days and have bathrooms fitted with ball-and-claw tubs. The tennis court was laid half a century ago (though since upgraded, of course) and players still sit on the old and bent marula tree trunk to take a breather between sets. A swimming pool and boma complete Kirkman's Kamp's complement of amenities; its elevated position commands fine views of the river and surrounding wilderness.

KIRKMAN'S COTTAGE, a recent addition to the MalaMala reserve, is situated close to the Kamp and modelled along similar lines. The Cottage accommodates a maximum of eight guests in four twin rooms, each with its *en suite* bathrooms. It is a completely independent camp with its own swimming pool, lounge, bar and boma.

TREKKER TRAILS, the fifth camp, is for guests who want to get really close to the wild. Here there are three comfortable twin tents with reed-enclosed, *en suite* bathrooms where one can enjoy a hot shower under the stars. The emphasis at Trekker Trails is on ranger-guided walking safaris designed to introduce guests to the lore of the bush. Evening spotlight game drives are also laid on.

Game viewing

Outstanding opportunities. MalaMala covers 18 500 hectares of pristine Lowveld bush country, and is renowned for the relative ease with which you can spot the 'big five' – lion, leopard, elephant, rhino and buffalo. But there's a great deal more to be seen and enjoyed, of course, including some rare and lovely birds. Day drives, night excursions and walks are on offer; the rangers are knowledgeable (many are degreed) and informative, the trackers superb.

■ **Getting there:** By car from Johannesburg: take the N4 east to Nelspruit; turn north on the R40, continuing to Hazyview via White River. At Hazyview, turn right, onto the R536 (signpost: Paul Kruger Gate - Skukuza Camp) and follow the road for 36 km, turning left at the MalaMala sign. A fee is payable on entry into the conservation area. By

THE WILD DOG: A HUNTER IN JEOPARDY

During a game drive in the Sabi Sand reserve, MalaMala guests spotted a wild dog caught in a poacher's snare. Their ranger radioed for help, and one of the Kruger park's veterinarians arrived on the scene to immobilise, release and treat the injured animal. It made a full recovery: a week later it was seen again, at an impala kill and, later still, mating with the pack's alpha female (which indicated it was the group's dominant male).

The rescue had more than sentimental significance. The wild dog, or Cape hunting dog (*Lycaon pictus*), is Africa's most endangered carnivore. For decades settlers regarded the species as vermin, a ruthless killer to be hunted down and exterminated. In South Africa today, just 350 remain in the wild, and each individual is important, a bearer of the precious seed that keeps the gene pool viable.

Although a member of the dog family Canidae, the wild dog is not closely related to the domestic animal. It has large, rounded ears, a bushy white-tipped tail and 'tortoise-

shell' (black, yellow and white) colouring. It is the only member of the family to have four toes on each forefoot rather than five. The wild dog hunts in packs in the more open savanna country, running its victims to exhaustion. In the Kruger, its favourite prey are impala and kudu.

The wild dog is one of the most fascinating of the region's larger species. Of all the predators, it has perhaps the most intricate social order: each individual's seniority within the pack, its place in the hunt and its rights to the spoils are subtly and precisely defined. The order changes over the seasons as cubs are born, adults grow old and dominance is challenged. Group survival is the overriding impetus; all is sacrificed to the wellbeing of the pack as a whole.

Allen Reich, a scientist who observed the wild dogs of the southern Kruger, noted that the animal that led the hunt invariably stood back at the carcass. 'All were eating peacefully,' Reich wrote of one incident, 'save for the subordinate male. He had made the kill; he had trotted back to the others; he had let them taste the blood on his mouth, and he had led them back to the kill. Now he waited for what, to our human minds, was rightfully his. He eventually managed a few scraps ... What a remarkable creature!'

TOP: A dog pack unmoved by tourist traffic.
LEFT: Portrait of defiance.

air: MalaMala's own tarred runway accommodates charter aircraft. In addition, Rattray Reserve Air Charters operates fully pressurised King Air C200 turbo-prob aircraft from any destination in South Africa directly into MalaMala. Guests flying to or from Botswana are processed for immigration purposes at the MalaMala airfield. There are daily scheduled flights on Comair from Jan Smuts Airport to Skukuza Airport, where you will be met by a MalaMala representative.

■ **Reservations and information:** MalaMala Game Reserve, PO Box 2575, Randburg 2125, South Africa. Tel: (011) 789-2677; fax: (011) 886-4382. United Kingdom: 185-187 Brompton Road, London SW3 1NE. Tel: (071) 584-0004; fax: (071) 581-8122.

INYATI GAME LODGE

A splendid wilderness venue on the banks of the perennial Sand River in the heart of the Lowveld. Inyati is the African name for 'buffalo', and the area is indeed sanctuary for numbers of these giant bovids, but for much else as well – for the other four members of the 'big five', for giraffe and wildebeest, hippo and crocodile, zebra, several varieties of antelope and for the occasional cheetah.

The lodge itself is a collection of lovely, thatched, luxuriously appointed buildings set among shade trees and broad sweeps of lawn. You'll find little of the classically rugged bush camp here: there are nine spacious chalets; each has wall-to-wall carpeting, a tiled *en suite* bathroom, a walk-in dressing room, custom-built furniture, and attractively coherent décor (bedding, curtains and lamp-shades in matching colours). The main lodge comprises an elegantly appointed lounge and dining area (five-star cuisine; excellent wine list), a cocktail bar (the Warthog Wallow), a filtered pool, gymnasium, and a river patio overlooking the Sand – and, of course, the traditional boma, where guests enjoy good food and good company on warm summer evenings.

Game viewing

Morning and afternoon safaris are conducted in open land cruisers; the rangers and their Shangaan trackers are knowledgeable and

The bushbuck: a shy and mostly nocturnal animal.

highly skilled. Inyati Tree Tops is a large (two-decked) and quite magnificent timber-and-thatch viewing complex, set beside the Sand River, to which guests have daily access. For day visitors staying nearby, there are morning and evening game drives, with breakfast provided during the former and dinner during the latter.

■ **Getting there:** By road from Johannesburg: take the N4 to Nelspruit; turn north to Hazyview, and then east along the R536 to the Kruger park's Paul Kruger gate and Skukuza camp. Turn left after 35 km and follow the signs for Sabi Sand Wildtuin and Inyati. By air: Inyati has its own 900-m airstrip; a high proportion of the guests arrive by charter aircraft (the flight from Johannesburg takes an hour). Alternatively, take one of the scheduled flights to Skukuza or Phalaborwa (see Visitor's Advisory, page 303). On arrival you will be met by Inyati's courtesy bus and driven to camp.

■ **Reservations and information:** Inyati Game Lodge, PO Box 38838, Booysens 2016, South Africa. Tel: (011) 493-0755; fax: (011) 493-0837.

LONDOLOZI GAME RESERVE

The Zulu name means 'protector of living things', and it is apt: Londolozi is one of the most exclusive of the Lowveld's private lodges, and its owners among the most enterprising of conservationists. Among other things, they are the moving spirits behind the Conservation Corporation (see page 34).

The Varty family have lived in the Sabi Sand area since 1929; brothers John and Dave took over the lodge in the early 1970s, when it was a modest little huddle of rudimentary rondavels set in a desecrated wasteland. With the steady encroachment of man over the decades, with drought, soil erosion, the decline of the water table, and with the fencing of the Kruger park's western boundary in 1961 (as a measure to prevent the spread of foot-and-mouth disease), the once-teeming wildlife of the area had become depleted to the point, in some cases, of local

extinction. Instead of game-sustaining grasslands and the scattered canopies of indigenous woodland, there was the dense, choking mantle of alien bush. The celebrated Kruger ranger, Harry Kirkman, recalled a few years ago that at one time 'we used to see thousands of wildebeest trekking from the Park to the Sabie River here. You could see the dust of the trek from the Drakensberg'. No more. Gone were the roan and sable, the tsessebe, the reedbuck and many of the other animals.

The Varty brothers, impelled by youthful energy and by something akin to crusading zeal, set about restoring the area – and to showing that good land management can be combined with tourism. They began clearing away the exotic vegetation (at a crippling financial cost), restoring the seep lines, and returning the veld to its original character. And the game came back. Now, too, the fences that blocked the free movement of

animals between the Kruger and its neighbours are coming down, giving added impetus to Londolozi's progress.

Partly to defray expenses and partly to prove a fundamental and very significant point, the Vartys launched what they call the 'multi-use' or 'resource' system, which simply means making maximum use of the land. For instance, bush clearance produces firewood (a commodity only less precious to rural Africans than food), which is sold through a network of distributors, thus meeting a need for many, providing a living for some, and helping pay for the bush recovery programme. Similarly, game management means culling, and the surplus meat is sold off. Some of the game is culled by hunters, who pay well for the privilege. The hunters, and the tourists, need rangers, trackers and camp staff, and this creates jobs – and so on: everyone benefits. Much the same principle underlies the two other lodge ventures the Vartys are associated with (and which are also featured in this book): Ngala, in the Timbavati area just to the north, and the Phinda Resource Reserve in northern Natal. In tourist terms, especially, Londolozi has proved a huge success: its reputation (and most of its clientele) is international.

The lodge has three components, each different in character from the others.

TOP: *Londolozi's eight-guest Tree Camp – comfort and privacy in lush riverine surrounds.*
ABOVE: *The interior of one of Bush Camp's eight 'rock' chalets. Each has its private verandah.*
LEFT: *One of Londolozi's famed leopards.*

MAIN CAMP, which accommodates 24 people, is a scatter of luxurious double chalets with elevated private balconies and *en suite* bathrooms, a superb open dining verandah (English breakfasts; sumptuous buffet lunches), a swimming pool and the traditional boma, all overlooking the richness of the Sand River banks. Dinner is served in the boma, which has a bar set beneath an explosive growth of purple bougainvillea, and the evenings are hugely enjoyable. The Vartys are often there to play host; Dave is the raconteur, his enthusiasm infectious; John plays the guitar (sometimes). He also makes wildlife films, applying skill and endless patience to his craft. One of his outstanding productions is *The Silent Hunter*, which tells the story of the famed leopards of Londolozi. Most of the camp's rangers have been there a long time and have the confidence, the easy charm, that comes from familiarity with and enjoyment of a worthwhile job.

BUSH CAMP is separately run, and has its own hostesses, rangers and staff. Its eight 'rock' chalets, with their raised verandahs, are luxurious (each has its *en suite* bathroom and outdoor shower). The swimming pool is elevated, attractive, set into the Sand River bank and shaded by stately ebony trees.

ABOVE: Manyeleti's Khoka Moya plays host to elephant.
OPPOSITE: Viewing warthog from a game hide.

TREE CAMP Some distance away is the unusual, eight-person Tree Camp, pride of Londolozi. The chalets are supremely comfortable, even luxurious, but without ostentation, designed both for privacy and to complement the lush riverine surrounds. Here, too, each has its bathroom, outdoor shower and balcony. The central area is built into an ancient leadwood tree; guests take their meals on a balcony suspended on branches 25 m above the ground – the vista is magnificent. Tree Camp also has its swimming pool (natural rock surrounds and a waterfall), its own hostess, rangers and trackers, and it has been described as 'the most beautiful camp in Africa'. Tree Camp, like Bush Camp, has its own boma.

Game viewing

Very rewarding. There are the 'big five', of course, and more leopard than you are likely to see elsewhere – thanks largely to the Vartys' work with these large and graceful cats. Those which have featured in John's films have become accustomed to the land rover, so one can approach fairly closely – a real

bonus if you're a photographer. A pride of lions has made its home in the area; wild dog are regularly sighted.

And, as a consequence of the bush-clearing programme, a lot of plains game, including wildebeest and zebra, have returned to Londolozi's 14 000 hectares. Clearing the bush has also brought back several species of sweet and sour grasses which, in turn, have enticed animals such as white rhino, waterbuck and warthog to the area.

More than 200 resident bird species have been identified, and if you have a sharp eye you will be able to spot as many as 150 of them on a two-day sojourn. Many of the larger raptors, such as the giant eagle owl and, in winter, the fish eagle, are common sightings; less so are the black-headed heron, the kori bustard and the cuckoo hawk.

■ **Getting there:** By road from Johannesburg: take the N4 to Nelspruit, travel north on the R40 to Hazyview, then east on the R536 towards the Kruger park's Paul Kruger gate and Skukuza camp for 36 km (1 km past the Lisbon store) before turning left onto a gravel road. The final 28 km-stretch to Londolozi is well signposted. By air: there are scheduled Comair flights from Johannesburg to Skukuza, from where Londolozi's private aircraft will fly you to the reserve. Air charters can be arranged; private aircraft may land at Londolozi's 1 200-m airstrip.

■ **Reservations and information:** Londolozi Game Reserve, PO Box 1211, Sunninghill Park 2157, Johannesburg, South Africa. Tel: (011) 803-8421 or 803-8616; fax: (011) 803-1810.

MANYELETI GAME RESERVE

The 23 000-hectare Manyeleti shares boundaries with the Kruger National Park, and its game population is varied and prolific: the reserve is sanctuary to, among much else, rhino, buffalo, lion, leopard, cheetah, wild dog, breeding herds of elephant and many antelope species.

Public accommodation (the reserve is run by the regional Gazankulu parks authority) comprises self-catering and ordinary rondavels, dormitories (for school groups), a restaurant, bar, shop, post office and a swimming pool: a large and busy venue, though attractive enough and good value for money. There is also an educational bush camp for groups of up to 45.

Far more exclusive are the two privately owned camps that cater mainly, though not entirely, for trailists and, unlike many others with the same purpose, do so in style.

KHOKA MOYA The name, in translation from the Shangaan language, means 'capture the spirit', an oblique reference to the open grassland spaces and ambience of the reserve. The amenities are rustic; accommodation (for up to eight people) consists of comfortably informal, kerosene lamp-lit 'bandas' – timber and thatch bungalows opening out onto spacious verandahs. Each banda has its *en suite* shower (hot water on tap), washbasin and toilet. There is a fully stocked bar *in situ*; guests eat alfresco – a sustaining 'hunter's brunch' after the morning trail; a companionable dinner around the cheerful open fire in the evening. A splash pool helps keep you cool during the heat of the day.

HONEYGUIDE Manyeleti's second private venue is, according to the literature, the 'only traditional luxury safari-style tented camp' in South Africa. The six East African-style tents certainly aren't typical of trail accommodation: they are in effect comfortable canvas bedrooms, each with twin beds (inner-sprung mattresses), a fitted carpet, a wardrobe, an *en suite* bathroom (again, hot water on tap), a flush toilet and solar-powered electric lighting. Honeyguide also has its splash pool and separate bar area, plus a walkway through the riverine forest around the camp. Meals are invariably taken outdoors, in the boma. Close by is a waterhole and its attendant viewing hide. The camp is set among huge indigenous trees.

Game viewing

Khoka Moya has resident rangers and trackers who accompany guests on daily walking trails, and optional spotlit night drives. Owners Bruce and Judy Meeser recently extended the game-viewing horizons with the launch of their Khoka Moya 'Wildlife Encounters': four- and five-day forays designed to bring you as close to the wilderness, its fauna and flora as it is possible to get. Itineraries include a 'night watch'; the identification, location and tracking of one of the 'big five'; an insight into the behaviour patterns and 'languages' of animals and birds, and into the intricate interrelationships that sustain the ecosystem. Guests use Honeyguide as their base, but spend most of the time in the wild, sleeping out, on some nights, at a bush hide overlooking a waterhole.

■ **Getting there:** By road from Johannesburg: take the N4 to Nelspruit, the R40 north to the R531 turn-off towards the Kruger park's Orpen gate; continue for 36 km; turn right at the Manyeleti sign.
■ **Reservations and information:** Public camps: The Manager, Manyeleti Game Reserve, PO Manyeleti 1362, South Africa. Tel: 0020, ask for Manyeleti 3. Khoka Moya and Wildlife Encounters: Safariplan, PO Box 4245, Randburg 2125, South Africa. Tel: (011) 886-1810/1/2/3/4; fax: (011) 886-1815.

MATUMI GAME LODGE

This is a medium-sized, pleasantly informal lodge located some 45 km to the west of the Kruger National Park's Orpen gate, and an ideal bush getaway for the whole family. Your hosts are Theo and Elsie Rosslee, and they make you feel very welcome.

The camp comprises a cluster of twelve four-bed and two eight-bed thatched-roofed chalets, airconditioned, comfortably appointed (each has its private bathroom) and set among the tall trees that grace the Klaserie

River banks – a lovely spot, lushly green in the wet summer months and with a different kind of attractiveness, starker perhaps but no less appealing, in the dry season. The reeds and dense thorn thickets of the river are home to a fine array of birds; in its waters, and at the nearby Jan Wassenaar dam, there is excellent angling for bream and yellowfish.

The lodge, like nearly all the Lowveld camps, has its reed-walled boma where guests gather in the evenings to sip a relaxing sundowner and then to make their enjoyable way through Elsie's renowned traditional game dishes. There is also a more orthodox, indoor restaurant, a cosy pub (both feature a lot of timber and thatch in their décor), a swimming pool and a small recreation hall (table tennis, darts and so on).

Game viewing

Self-guided day drives to the Kruger are an option, of course, but Matumi does lay on its own conducted trips in an open land rover: the general area is rich in wildlife. For the more intrepid, the lodge will organise a night spent in the bush lapa (enclosure): one cooks and eats in the company of a game guard; sleeps under the stars; listens to the sounds of the African night. Walking enthusiasts can explore on foot, following a bush trail and stopping, perhaps, for a rewarding hour or two at one of the established game-viewing hides. There is opportunity to hunt the 'big five' as well as other trophy game. A professional hunter will take you out; contact Matumi Big Game Hunting Safaris (see address below).

■ **Getting there:** By road from Johannesburg: take the N4 to the R539 turn-off to Belfast and then the R36 north through Lydenburg. Turn right onto the R531 (Klaserie road) 30 km beyond the JG Strijdom tunnel, continue for 34 km, turn left onto the Orpen road and left again, after 3 km, onto the Guernsey road. Matumi is 6 km along this route.
■ **Reservations and information:** Matumi Game Lodge, PO Box 57, Klaserie 1381, South Africa. Tel: (01528) 3-2452. Matumi Big Game Hunting Safaris: same address and telephone number.

STEAM TREK TO GAME COUNTRY

The first group of tourists to visit the Kruger park – in 1923, three years before it was formally proclaimed a national asset, and before there were any proper roads in the area – were brought in by train as members of what was known as the 'round in nine' package. The trip took in the scenic uplands of the eastern Transvaal, the Lowveld wilderness and some of Portuguese East Africa (now Mozambique; the itinerary included an exotic evening in the coastal town of Lourenço Marques), and it lasted nine days. In the Kruger, the passengers detrained at Skukuza for a short walk in the bush, and then got together for a festive evening around the campfire. Grand old days indeed, but long gone.

Something of that less restrictive, more romantic era, has reappeared with the recent introduction of the Rovos Rail steam train excursions. These take the 46 passengers on a

four-day trip from Pretoria to and through the spectacular mountains and dense pine plantations of the Transvaal Drakensberg and then down to the plains below. Here tour members spend at least a night at one of the more luxurious private lodges, and see some of the world's finest big-game country. The itinerary is quite flexible, and other digressions can be fitted in as well.

On board, passengers are treated to cordon bleu cuisine and five-star service in the most elegant of settings. The dining car dates from 1924 (though its carved-timber arches and roof supports evoke an earlier period); one of the coaches from 1919, and its best suite has richly panelled walls, twin beds, a private bathroom and a plush little sitting room; the observation car is glassed in at one end and has a fully stocked bar at the other. The locomotives, venerable old workhorses that may be changed at various stages of the journey, include an 1893 Class Six ('Tiffany') and three 1938 Class 19Ds.

Reservations and information: Rovos Rail, PO Box 2837, Pretoria 0001, South Africa. Tel: (012) 323-6052; fax: (012) 323-0843.

BELOW: *En route to the game-rich Lowveld.*
LEFT: Dining car – legacy of a bygone era. The cuisine is cordon bleu.

Tanda Tula Game Lodge

The oldest and one of the most exclusive of the eastern Transvaal's private lodges, and for the wildlife enthusiast one of the most challenging and rewarding.

The camp comprises eight twin-bedded bungalows (all with *en suite* bathrooms and showers, airconditioning and overhead punkah-fans) huddled in the shade of mature acacia trees. Among the thatched buildings is a kitchen and dining area, and a kind of open-on-one-side bar and informal lounge which looks out onto the swimming pool and, beyond that, the waterhole with its game-viewing hide. Nearby is the reed-enclosed boma, where you sit under the stars facing the fire, eat barbecued food and listen to the night sounds, and to people who really know their wilderness lore. Tanda Tula is an unusually companionable, often highly sociable and always enjoyable place. Your host is the renowned Pat Donaldson, a man with a 'big' personality, and a real feeling for the African veld. For all that, though, it is also a place of peace. Aptly enough Tanda Tula, in translation, means 'to love the quiet'.

Game viewing

The lodge is in the heart of the Timbavati private nature reserve, which is home (though they wander) to those rare and beautiful animals, the white lions. They really are snow-white – not albinos, because they have deep colour in their eyes, but rather the product of a recessive gene. In the early 1990s the pride had two females, one of them white, but she disappeared towards the end of 1992. These animals range freely between Timbavati and Tshokuane, and you will be lucky indeed if you see them.

For the rest, the area supports lion, leopard and cheetah, wild dog, buffalo, white rhino, and plenty of antelope but no roan or sable. The Timbavati has the highest density of giraffe in the world; the Tanda Tula area is home to a breeding herd of elephant – some 65 of them – and they tend to be a bit aggressive, but you are always with a ranger and there's no risk. Over 300 species of bird have

One of Tanda Tula's bungalows. The lodge is among one of the Lowveld's smaller, more intimate venues.

been recorded in the vicinity, among them many species of raptors.

The bush here tends to be dense, comprising mainly acacia and combretum, which is of the bushwillow family. The 'rivers' (they are dust-dry most of the time) sustain handsome jackalberry, raintree, date-palm and weeping boerboom, and it is a joy to walk along them.

The lodge has access to more than 7 000 hectares of varied game country; game drives are conducted in custom-built safari vehicles; the 'bush breakfast' on the early-morning one fills a memorable hour. There are two waterhole hides.

■ **Getting there:** The lodge is about five hours' drive from Johannesburg. Take the main highway east past Witbank and Middelburg to Belfast; turn onto the R540 to Lydenburg and then follow the R36 through the JG Strijdom tunnel; turn east, following the R531 and the R527 to Hoedspruit. Turn right onto the R40 towards Klaserie and then, after 7 km, left onto the Argyle road. Continue for about 36 km; the Tanda Tula entrance is on your right. By air: Comair runs scheduled flights from Johannesburg to Phalaborwa, and will transfer passengers to Tanda Tula by road. Charter flights are available: the lodge has its own (tarred) 1 000-m private airstrip.

■ **Reservations and information:** Country Lodge Marketing, PO Box 32, Constantia 7848, South Africa. Tel: (021) 794-6500; fax: (021) 794-7605.

UMLANI BUSH CAMP

Umlani, on the banks of the Shlaralumi River bed, has been aptly described as 'a place where one can walk the line between comfort and a true bush experience': it is a charmingly informal thatched and reeded camp set among a profusion of handsome Lowveld trees – jackalberry and knobthorn, leadwood, tamboti and weeping boer-bean – in the heart of the Timbavati game reserve.

There are just six rest huts, unpretentiously rustic. The routine is fairly standard: a trail guide and tracker take you out on an early-morning bush walk; the hot middle hours are spent relaxing around camp or bird-watching from the treehouse overlooking a nearby waterhole; come late afternoon there is a game drive followed by sundowners, a night drive, and then back home for a companionable campfire dinner.

Game viewing

Umlani has access to 10 000 acres of the Timbavati's central section, an area cut through by three dry but life-giving riverbeds. Among the larger animals you may see are elephant, lion, white rhino, blue wildebeest, buffalo, giraffe, zebra, kudu, nyala and other buck; present but more secretive are leopard and cheetah, spotted hyaena, serval and caracal. Around 200 bird species have been identified locally, among them the Egyptian vulture.

■ **Getting there:** By road from Johannesburg: take the main highway east past Witbank and Middelburg to Belfast; turn onto the R540 to Lydenburg and then follow the R36 through the JG Strijdom tunnel. Turn east, following the R531 and the R527 to Hoedspruit. Turn right onto the R40 towards Klaserie and then, after 6 km, left onto the Argyle road. Continue for 19 km on tar and a further 12 km on gravel. The Umlani gate is on your right. By air: there are three Metavia flights a week to Hoedspruit; transport from the airfield can be arranged. Comair operates a regular service to nearby Phalaborwa, where Avis car hire is available.

■ **Reservations and information:** Umlani Central Reservations, PO Box 26350, Arcadia 0007, Pretoria. Tel: (012) 329-3765; fax: (012) 329-6441.

MOTSWARI AND M'BALI GAME LODGES

These sister lodges, situated on 70 000 hectares of the Timbavati game reserve bordering the Kruger park, are among the best known and most imaginatively conceived of the region's private venues: both are exclusive, intimate, luxurious, exceptionally attractive, and they each offer a memorable bush experience.

Motswari, which in rough translation means 'to keep and conserve', can accommodate up to 26 guests in its thatched, charmingly appointed *en suite* rondavels (11 twin, four single). Focal point of the camp is a large and shady verandah that looks down on the waterhole (buffalo are regular visitors) and which serves as both viewing site and companionable place in which to linger at the sundowner hour.

Somewhat smaller (16 guests) and even more distinctive is M'Bali, nine kilometres distant – an enchanting collection of seven 'habitents' (luxury rooms under canvas) that hint of a more romantic era (Kenya, perhaps, in the colonial days). Each tent is perched on its platform high above the ground to look over the dam, the Shlaralumi River and the bushveld plains beyond. Each has its private bathroom; there is fine game viewing from the timber balcony outside your bedroom; bush sounds fill the night air.

Among the amenities at each camp is a fully stocked bar and – so welcome in the middle hours of a Lowveld summer day – a sparkling swimming pool. Both are renowned for the excellence of their cuisine. Dinners – cheerfully informal and hugely enjoyable affairs – are usually served in the firelit boma. A 10-minute air transfer to Phalaborwa will enable you to play golf on the highly regarded Hans Merensky course.

Game viewing

There is plenty to see, including the 'big five', without even moving from camp (and, at M'Bali, from your private sleeping quarters). Motswari is known for its lion sightings (most guests manage to see the big cats at

least once during their stay), its nocturnal animals and its intriguing bird life; M'Bali for its elephant and buffalo – the Timbavati reserve sustains large breeding herds of both species. Giraffe and many kinds of antelope are also in residence. The area is known for the presence of the renowned white lions (see also page 86).

Game drives in open vehicles are conducted twice a day by professional rangers.

Guided walks are also on the programme – indeed, they are something of a speciality at Motswari-M'Bali. Wildlife author Michael Smith recalls 'the thrill of walking with a tracker on recent lion spoor, and the adrenalin-producing close encounter with an elephant ...', while Ross Nugent, the head game ranger, assures you that the 'threatening charge and waving ears are only for show ...'.

■ **Getting there:** The camps are about 530 km (five to six hours' drive) from Johannesburg. Take the N4 to Belfast; turn onto the R540 and continue to Lydenburg; take the R36 over the Abel Erasmus pass to Hoedspruit; turn right onto the R40, continue for 7 km; turn left onto the Argyle road and follow this for 58 km (39 km on gravel). The Motswari sign is on your right. By air: there are daily scheduled Comair flights to Phalaborwa, from where Motswari aircraft will collect you for a 10-minute air transfer along the Olifants River. For charter flights, Motswari has its own landing strip.

■ **Reservations and information:** Motswari Game Lodges, PO Box 67865, Bryanston 2021, South Africa. Tel: (011) 463-1990/1; fax: (011) 463-1992.

NGALA GAME LODGE

Ngala, which is the Shangaan word for 'lion', fits into the upper range of Lowveld lodges: its chalets cluster around a beautiful thatched complex in the mopane woodlands of the Kruger National Park's western region, the whole recently remodelled to 'international five-star standards'.

The lodge is also something of a pioneer in the field of ecotourism: its owners have signed an accord with the National Parks Board Trust, the first such between private enterprise and the public sector, which allows its management to concentrate on what it knows best – the hospitality business – while the Kruger park's experts look after the land and its wildlife. It's an eminently sensible division of responsibility that

promises to set the pattern of future developments countrywide. The moving spirit behind the venture is Dave Varty's Conservation Corporation, which also administers Londolozi in the Sabi Sand reserve just to the south, and the pathfinding Phinda Resource Reserve in northern Natal. The corporation offers 'eco-adventure' tourist packages taking in all three venues.

Ngala has 20 airconditioned, twin-bedded chalets in all, each with its *en suite* bathroom, as well as one luxurious Safari Suite with its own private swimming pool and sole use of a land rover. The central complex comprises a lounge, dining room, cocktail bar, swimming pool, and a lovely Out-of-Africa verandah overlooking a waterhole to which elephant and many other animals come to drink.

TOP: *Guests relax on Ngala's spacious verandah.*
OPPOSITE, LEFT: *The elegant Safari Suite.*
ABOVE: *Ngala's entrancing outdoor eating area.*

When the weather is good, one dines beneath the stars. Cuisine, service, and visitor amenities generally are geared to a sophisticated, cosmopolitan clientele.

Game viewing

The Ngala area has one of the densest populations of lion in Southern Africa; each one of the 'big five' can be spotted on the ranger-conducted game drives; nocturnal species are located and observed on the organised night excursions. Walking safaris, led by superbly skilled Shangaan trackers, introduce you to many of the smaller but no less intriguing denizens of the Kruger wilderness. For those who want a more intimate and sustained acquaintanceship with the wildlife, there is a 'sleep-out' boma or hide.

■ **Getting there:** By road from Johannesburg/ Pretoria: Take the N4 to Belfast; turn onto the R540 and continue to Lydenburg; take the R36 over the Abel Erasmus pass to Hoedspruit; turn right onto the R40 and continue for 7 km. Turn left onto the Argyle road and continue for 31 km and turn right at the Ngala sign. The lodge is 9 km further on.
■ **Special packages:** Several permutations on offer: self-drive, fly-and-hire and other 'eco-adventure' itineraries covering the Ngala/Londolozi/Phinda triumvirate. Bookings only through the central package office (see Reservations below).
■ **Reservations and information:** The Conservation Corporation, PO Box 1211, Sunninghill Park 2157, South Africa. Tel: (011) 803-8421; fax: (011) 803-1810.

KAMBAKU GAME LODGE

Kambaku is a small safari lodge tucked away in the bushveld countryside of the Timbavati reserve. The eight thatched chalets, each with its private bathroom, are set among the knobthorn and weeping boer-bean trees beside a waterhole: a real get-away-from-it-all place, informal, friendly – and relatively affordable. A swimming pool provides welcome relief from the heat of a Lowveld day; in the evening, guests relax around an open-air bar and then savour a companionable venison barbecue around the campfire.

Game viewing

Pleasantly rewarding hours can be spent in the hide; farther afield, one can expect to see all the animals associated with the western section of the Kruger park, including the 'big five' (elephant often make their way into the lodge's immediate vicinity). On offer are the standard day and night drives on specially equipped land rovers, together with guided bush walks.

■ **Getting there:** By road from Johannesburg: take the main highway east past Witbank and Middelburg to Belfast; turn north on the R540 and continue through Lydenburg, following the R36 through the JG Strijdom tunnel, and then take the R531 and R527 to Hoedspruit. Turn south onto the R40 and, after 7 km, left onto the Argyle road, continuing for 31,5 km to the Timbavati boundary. Turn right, following the road for 6 km before turning left into the reserve. Turn left again after 1,8 km.
■ **Reservations and information:** Bushveld Breakaways, PO Box 926, White River 1240, South Africa. Tel: (01311) 5-1998; fax: (01311) 5-0383.

NWANEDI NATIONAL PARK

The 11 170-hectare Nwanedi, in the far north-eastern corner of Venda, extends over the foothills of the scenically lovely Soutpansberg range. Centrepieces of the park are its twin man-made lakes, created when the Nwanedi and Luphephe rivers, which join a little farther on to flow into the Limpopo, were dammed in 1960. The dams, a short distance above the main camps, are a focal point for those who enjoy fishing, or watching the game and bird life from a launch or canoe.

The resort is set among beautiful indigenous riverine shade trees; accommodation comprises 15 fully-equipped four-bed rondavels, each with a kitchenette and *en suite* bathroom; 10 split-level four-bed luxury rooms (these are not self-catering); and 10 ordinary two-bed rooms (again, no kitchen). There is also a fully licensed à la carte restaurant *in situ*, together with a cocktail bar and a well appointed conference centre. Fishing permits are available. There are canoes for hire, and launch trips can be arranged.

Nwanedi: embowered by lovely shade trees.

The Nwanedi park's game population is fairly modest – the main attractions are the splendid scenery and the fish-filled waters of the lakes – but visitors can see white rhino, giraffe, zebra, blue wildebeest, eland, hartebeest, nyala and other antelope. The riverine woodlands provide habitats for a number of bird species, among them the fish eagle.

Game viewing

Several self-guided game drives have been established, and conducted tours to other areas (to scenic attractions, Bushmen paintings and ancient ruins) can be arranged.

Walking in the park is not permitted, though one can make one's way on foot to the dams and the Tshihovhohovho waterfall on the Luphephe River. There is safe bathing in the rock pools below the falls; the dams are much favoured by keen anglers.

■ **Getting there:** The park's entrance is 75 km north of Thohoyandou. Usual access route from Johannesburg, however, is via the N1 north to the R525 turn-off, 50 km beyond the town of Louis Trichardt. Follow the R525 eastwards past Tshipise, 24 km beyond which is the Nwanedi turn-off.

■ **Reservations and information:** Central Reservations, Venda Tourism, PO Box 9, Sibasa, Venda. Tel: (0159) 4-1577; fax: (0159) 4-1048.

HOTELS AND RESORTS

Within easy reach of one or more of the Kruger park's entrances are a number of delightful hotels and country hideaways that are ideal for those who fancy combining their bush experience with a more general eastern-Transvaal holiday. They provide easy access both to the Lowveld's game areas and to the splendours of the Escarpment, or Transvaal Drakensberg, a high mountain range of magical beauty. Most spectacular of the range's natural features is the Blyde River Canyon, a majestically massive red sandstone gorge, the sheer faces of which plunge almost a kilometre to the waters below. Among other major attractions are the 'living museum' town of Pilgrim's Rest, once a thriving little centre of the gold-mining industry and now given over to timber and tourism, and the Sudwala Caves, a remarkable complex of chambers that are thought to extend for 30 km and more (though only 600 m are open to the public).

Several of the hotels offer organised excursions to the Kruger; others have special arrangements with one or other of the private game lodges.

CYBELE FOREST LODGE

Cybele, near White River, is the very best kind of small, exclusive, home-from-home country lodge – indeed, Britain's *Tatler* magazine placed it, in 1992, among the 50 best hotels in the world, describing it as 'the smartest hideaway in South Africa', and British Airways ranked it as one of its 37 favourite hostelries worldwide. It received local recognition when it was voted South Africa's top country hotel for 1992.

The lodge has accommodation for 28 guests, and its snug scatter of cottages and suites has a very distinctive appeal: English-farmhouse in atmosphere, colonial and Cape Dutch in appointment, each room individually and charmingly furnished and decorated. The general setting is deep-green pine woodland, dark and cool. Around the lodge itself, though, there is plenty of colour and grand shade trees, including giant turpentine,

tibouchina, African flame and a spreading jacaranda under which guests sit to take breakfast and luncheon. The gardens and pool area are pleasantly informal, rambling, and full of secluded corners.

Food and drink: Cybele is a member of the enormously prestigious, Paris-based *Relais et Chateaux* chain, which says everything: the cuisine is exquisite; the menus are simple and thoughfully chosen; presentation is immaculate, with wines to complement. The lodge is part of a 120-hectare farm, and the food is as fresh as you could wish; on offer are home-grown Arabica coffee, home-baked bread, special fruit jams and preserves. The dining room is candle-lit and intimate, the bar fully licensed.

Amenities: Six suites have their own swimming pools, and a main swimming pool is tucked away down the slope; also set well apart are the stables (there are enchanting bridle-paths through the forest). Cybele has its own stretch of rainbow trout-stocked stream. For the rest, there is walking beside the riverbank and through woodland, and bird-spotting: the area is rich in bird life.

OPPOSITE, ABOVE: Cybele Forest Lodge's welcoming lobby area.
OPPOSITE, BELOW: Farmhouse Country Lodge.
TOP: A corner of Jatinga's drawing room.
ABOVE: Pink Tibouchina – light and airy.

Cybele is well positioned as a base for exploring virtually the whole of the eastern Transvaal. Available are Dragonfly helicopter trips (the itinerary takes in a mountain-top champagne lunch) and safaris by luxury minibus. The lodge has a reciprocal arrangement with Londolozi; on offer are five-day, four-night Cybele/Londolozi packages that can be combined with the Rovos Rail steam train excursion (page 85).

Location: Near White River, and half-an-hour's drive to the Kruger's Numbi gate.

Reservations and information: PO Box 346, White River 1240, South Africa. Tel: (01311) 5-0511; fax: (01311) 3-2839.

FARMHOUSE COUNTRY LODGE

The very best kind of country hotel: small, elegant, created by people with exquisite taste, run by perfectionists. The lodge is a restored and extended, gabled, thatched and whitewashed 80-year-old farmstead set on 160 hectares of subtropical countryside to the west of the Kruger National Park; accommodation comprises 14 cottage suites and studios, each with its full bathroom (showers as well as baths; bathrobes provided), king-size bed, wool carpeting, cosy fireplace (there's also under-floor heating), colour co-ordinated furnishings and its lovely terrace view. Fruit, chocolates, a bowl of fresh flowers and a decanter of good sherry are among the thoughtful little touches that lift the rooms far above the ordinary.

The main guest lounge opens out onto the palm-graced pool area and landscaped gardens. All is quietly luxurious; the lodge deserves its four stars and more.

Food and drink: The table d'hôte fare, prepared by three lady-chefs and served in the intimate dining room, is of cordon-bleu quality. The cuisine is country-style with French undertones; a typical meal will start with a lightly curried pear soup (unusual, but delicious), followed by julienned smoked salmon with black and red caviar; roast quail stuffed with guinea-fowl pâté and, to finish, perhaps a chocolate velvet gateau with Jersey cream from the farm's prize dairy herd. Light meals and drinks are enjoyed on the pool patio.

Amenities: Pool and, for strolling, the beautiful grounds (there are strategically placed benches for bird-lovers). The surrounding farmlands sustain cattle, avocados and emerald banana plantations. Among activities laid on for guests are afternoon game drives through parts of the Sabi Sand reserve, with a break for sundowners and a boma barbecue thrown in, followed by a night drive. Also hiking trails and walks, horse-riding, river-rafting, micro-liting, hot-air ballooning (a splendid way to see the countryside) and helicopter trips to and champagne breakfasts among the high hills of the escarpment.

Location: The lodge is situated between White River and Hazyview on the R40.

Reservations and information: PO Box 40, Kiepersol 1241, South Africa. Tel: (01317) 6-8780/1/2; fax: (01317) 6-8783.

FRANGIPANI LODGE

This charming lodge is set on 22 hectares of fertile countryside between Nelspruit and White River – a half-hour's drive from the Kruger National Park. The gardens are tropically lush, cared for, and embowered by lovely indigenous trees; antiques and elegant furnishings grace the interiors. Each of the five guest rooms is individually decorated, and has its private bathroom. Guests are beautifully looked after by owners Jan and his actress wife Louise Mollett-Prinsloo.

Food and drink: Louise provide delicious fare; the dining room is candle-lit and graced with fresh flowers from the garden.

Amenities: Frangipani offers tranquillity, and friendly and attentive hospitality in the most gracious of surrounds. It also serves as a congenial base from which to explore both the game areas and the scenic delights of the Transvaal Drakensberg.

Location: Take the R40 north from Nelspruit; turn left at the Heidelberg sign; continue for 7,5 km and turn left.

Reservations and information: PO Box 1236, White River 1240, South Africa. Tel: (01311) 3-3224; fax: (01311) 3-3233.

JATINGA COUNTRY LODGE

A farm lodge, and one which offers the ultimate in comfort, cuisine and thoughtful hospitality, Jatinga is run by a two-man team: Mike Hobson is front-of-house manager, and Ken Sanders looks after the kitchen, décor and the grounds, and both do a superb job.

Jatinga is in fact the Lowveld's oldest country lodge. It was born in 1928 on ground that was part of a tea estate started in the early 1900s by Indian Army expatriates, and the place still has something of the Raj in microcosm about it. It comprises seven hectares of attractively landscaped and mature gardens girded by a small stream (the White River) and about eight hectares of untouched bush. The entrance driveway is a long avenue of Christ-thorn and stately pine; the grounds are cared for, shaded by graceful trees counterpointed by a riot of bougainvillea, and there are some lovely birds to be seen.

The main building (the old homestead) houses a Regency-style lounge, a cane-and-cushion-furnished sunroom, and a dining room; clustered around are the 10 deep-thatched, pleasantly appointed guest cottages, each with its bathroom, brass beds (double or twin; state your preference when booking), rosewood mirrors, the occasional antique, fresh fruit, and freshly cut flowers.

Food and drink: This is faultless: exquisite cuisine in the heart of the bush. People come from all parts of the region to eat at Jatinga. Breakfasts are solid and sustaining, dinners cosy and candle-lit. The vegetables are grown on the estate. Guests setting out on day excursions are provided with a delectable food hamper.

Amenities: In the grounds is a swimming pool and its attendant pool bar, a bowling green and a crocquet lawn; nearby there is golf, tennis, water sport and horse riding.

Jatinga is well-placed as a base from which to explore the game areas of the Lowveld and the splendours of the uplands. Mike can arrange sightseeing trips by helicopter (this concludes with a mountain-top picnic lunch or a hot-air balloon flight). A delightful alternative to driving or flying to Jatinga is the journey by Rovos Rail, one of the world's premier steam-train trips (see page 85): the train departs from Pretoria and takes 24 hours to get to Hazyview, from which pre-arranged transport will collect you.

Location: The lodge is 8 km east of White River, and about an hour's drive from the Kruger park.

Reservations and information: PO Box 77, Plaston 1244, South Africa. Tel: (01311) 3-1963; fax: (01311) 3-2364. For information on Rovos Rail, see page 85.

HIGHGROVE HOUSE

A broad avenue of jacarandas, gloriously lilac-flowered in springtime, leads down the hillside through avocado orchards to an elegant, colonial-style farmhouse girded by lawn, gardens and stately trees. This is Highgrove House, a converted farmstead and centrepiece of an enchanting lodge complex.

Malelane Lodge: strategically situated close to the Kruger National Park.

There are just eight guest chalets, each with its lounge and open fireplace, *en suite* bathroom, and balcony; two of the suites have a private swimming pool and sauna; one of them – the honeymoon – is graced by a quite magnificent four-poster bed. Inside the main house are two drawing rooms, a dining room, a pub, and a cane-furnished verandah.

Food and drink: The table d'hôte consists of classical cuisine, superbly prepared, presented and served. Breakfast is served in the Victorian gazebo in the garden on fine mornings. Dinner is a four-course affair to be lingered over in the silver-filled dining room. The wine list is excellent.

Amenities: There is a fern-fringed swimming pool in the grounds; pleasant walks through the forest and among the avocado orchards; bass and other fish in the private dam; and excellent bird-watching.

Location: Highgrove House is just off the R40 between White River and Hazyview, and a half-hour's drive from the Kruger park.

Reservations and information: PO Box 46, Kiepersol 1241, South Africa. Tel: (01311) 5-0242; fax: (01311) 5-0244.

MALELANE LODGE

David Steele, editor of *Getaway*, South Africa's newish and now leading travel magazine, recalled that he could not fault this lodge in any way: 'Its situation, ambience, friendly staff, excellent food and attention to detail,' he wrote, 'make it the best resort hotel in which I have stayed.'

Malelane Lodge, a four-star member of the Southern Sun group, is set in a 400-hectare private nature reserve fronting the Crocodile River, the southern boundary of the Kruger park. It's a visually pleasing complex in which natural materials feature; the gardens are lush and attractively landscaped; the public rooms spacious, airy, and decorated to give a vaguely ethnic impression; and indoors and outdoors are integrated coherently and most pleasantly. Accommodation comprises 100 airconditioned, semi-detached chalet-rooms, some with twin beds, others with doubles, all with a private bathroom, television, radio, and a telephone. In addition, there are two 'presidential' suites, each with two bathrooms (one with spa bath), marble fittings, a private garden and a pool.

Food and drink: À la carte plus buffet in the Kingfisher restaurant; game dishes are a speciality (try the crocodile stirfry).

The Mount Sheba complex viewed from the Sheba Lookout. The surrounding tree-mantled slopes have been set aside as a private nature reserve; the rainforest is in climax condition.

Amenities: There's a splendid swimming pool in the grounds, and the hotel, together with the next-door country club, provides facilities for, among other things, tennis, squash, bowls and golf (nine-hole course).

Leopard, lion and elephant sometimes wander across from the Kruger; a viewing platform has been erected to overlook the Crocodile River and the southern strip of the park. Safari Services offers excursions from Malelane Lodge to the Kruger, together with night drives on a private reserve close by. Also available are helicopter trips, notably to the wondrous Blyde River Canyon.

Location: The hotel is close to the southern Kruger's Malelane gate.

Reservations and information: PO Box 392, Malelane 1320, South Africa. Tel: (01313) 3-0331; fax: (01313) 3-0145, or central reservations Johannesburg (011) 783-5333; Durban (031) 32-3419; Port Elizabeth, East London and Bloemfontein toll-free 0100-173.

MOUNT SHEBA HOTEL

One of the finest of Southern Africa's country hotels, and one of the most beautifully positioned: it lies in the valley far beneath the crest of Mount Sheba massif in the Transvaal Drakensberg, surrounded on all sides by steep slopes carpeted by evergreen trees – dense, lush and lovely.

The green-mantled hillsides are in fact part of the hotel's own nature reserve, a 400-hectare sanctuary in which more than 1 000 different plant species have already been identified (many more await the inquisitive botanist). Some of the yellowwoods are more than 1 000 years old, and there is a wealth of Cape chestnut, massive cusonias, red pears, and towering, incredibly hard ironwoods. The rainforest is in what is termed 'climax condition' – the trees are left to mature and die of old age without interference, though they are protected against such alien threats as pine and wattle. It is a stable floral community which, together with its indigenous fauna – birds, and the smaller animals – forms a complete ecosystem.

The hotel and its attendant timeshare units comprise a neat cluster of stately buildings;

first impressions are of whitewashed walls, generous expanses of thatch and elegant symmetry, the whole surrounded by trim lawns and, beyond and around, the great green mantle of woodland rising tier upon tier – a stunning setting.

There are not many public areas – just two small, elegantly furnished drawing rooms, the restful dining room, and a modest bar. Accommodation is in 25 spacious, tastefully decorated suites, 10 of which are of the duplex kind, 14 standard and one an especially luxurious and exclusive Executive suite. The timeshare section comprises 20 self-contained and well-designed cottages, available for casual bookings when not in use: they sleep four to six people, and are fully equipped.

Food and drink: Table d'hôte is served in the handsome Chandelier dining room; the menu is extensive enough, and the food good enough, to invite you to linger – which you are encouraged to do. Part-owner and manager Graham Ledger says he likes guests 'to spend at least an hour and a half over dinner, from hors d'oeuvres right through to their Cognac'.

Amenities: The hotel has a pleasant swimming pool, together with the Prospector pool-deck bar (open all day; tables set out for breakfast and lunch), a sauna and solarium, tennis and squash courts, and a snooker table. Trout fishing and golf are available in the area. There are no newspapers, no radio and no television – but here, you don't really need them.

The Kruger National Park is a little over an hour's drive away; the historic mining town of Pilgrim's Rest, an evocative 'living museum' with lovingly restored buildings reflecting the period 1880 to 1915, just up the hill and down the road. Guided tours around the village is available.

Then there's the Mount Sheba forest reserve all around you – it's a joy to walk the paths. They are well signposted; many of the trees have been numbered for identification; recommended walks range from the gentle Golagola to the five-kilometre stroll to

Marco's Mantle, which is a rather lovely waterfall. Most strenuous is the hike to the trout and aloe pools: this involves steep slopes and wonderful views of gorge and water. The hotel also lays on game-viewing and nature drives in a specially converted land rover.

Location: In a deep valley to the southwest of Pilgrim's Rest. Take the Lydenburg road (the R533) from the town and turn left at the 11-km mark; the last stretch is very steep.

Reservations and information: PO Box 100, Pilgrim's Rest 1290, South Africa. Tel and fax: (01315) 8-1241.

PINK TIBOUCHINA LODGE

The lodge has been named after, and is as charming as, the subtropical shrub whose dense foliage is garlanded in springtime and summer by lovely pink flowers. It's a small lodge, a renovated and cosily furnished farmstead set in the foothills west of the forestry village of Graskop, close to the Timbavati and Klaserie private game reserves and conveniently placed for day trips to the Kruger. All is light and airy, the rooms decorated in pinks and pastels brightened by imported floral fabrics; each of the 11 suites has its private bathroom and patio, from which there are fine views across the valley.

Food and drink: The set menu offers home cooking with a continental flavour. The lodge has a wine and malt licence, and the wine list is thoughtfully contrived.

Amenities: Include a guest lounge (with library and television), a swimming pool, and pleasant gardens. There are rewarding walks through the forest. A saligna gum plantation fringes the banks of the farm dam, where anglers can fish for black bass. The lodge's minibus takes guests on day visits to the Kruger park.

Location: North of Hazyview; take the R40 to the R533 (Graskop) turn-off and follow the road for 7 km.

Reservations and information: PO Box 53279, Saxonwold 2132, South Africa. Tel: (011) 447-3263; fax: (011) 442-6525, or at the lodge: (01315) 7-1157.

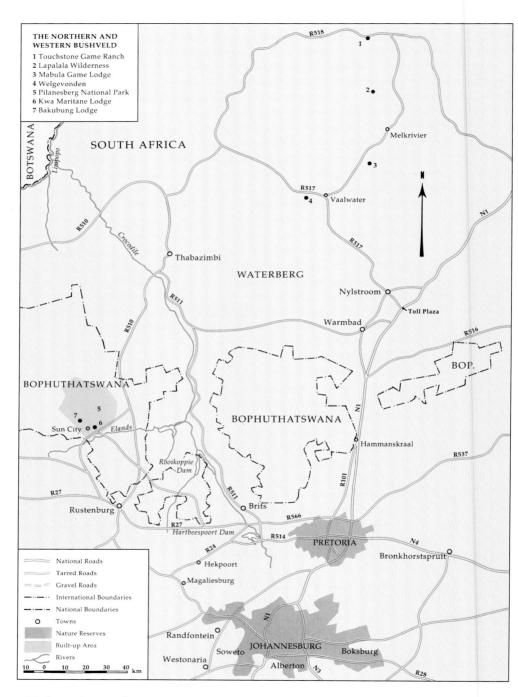

THE NORTHERN AND
WESTERN BUSHVELD

1 Touchstone Game Ranch
2 Lapalala Wilderness
3 Mabula Game Lodge
4 Welgevonden
5 Pilanesberg National Park
6 Kwa Maritane Lodge
7 Bakubung Lodge

SOUTH AFRICA

BOTSWANA

Limpopo

R518

1

2

Melkrivier

3

R517

Vaalwater

4

R510

Crocodile

Thabazimbi

WATERBERG

Nylstroom

Toll Plaza

Warmbad

R511

R510

BOPHUTHATSWANA

5

7

6

Sun City

Elands

BOPHUTHATSWANA

BOP.

R516

Hammanskraal

R537

Rooikoppie
Dam

R27

Rustenburg

R511

Brits

R566

Hartbeespoort Dam

R27

R24

R514

PRETORIA

N4

Bronkhorstspruit

Hekpoort

Magaliesburg

R101

National Roads
Tarred Roads
Gravel Roads
International Boundaries
National Boundaries
Towns
Nature Reserves
Built-up Area
Rivers

10 0   10   20   30   40
km

Randfontein

Soweto

JOHANNESBURG

Boksburg

Westonaria

Alberton

R28

N1

N1

N3

R517

N1

THE NORTHERN
AND WESTERN BUSHVELD

The Magaliesberg ridge, which runs from a point just east of Pretoria to the area around Rustenburg in the western Transvaal, rises barely 300 m above the surrounding, flattish countryside, but the hills have a distinctive beauty of their own and, in the more rugged parts, even grandeur. They are well wooded, rainfall is relatively generous, and the upper slopes are the source of crystal streams that feed into the northward-flowing tributaries of the Limpopo River.

In bygone years the water, the warmth and the lushness that these two elements create combined to attract a profusion of wild game to the region and to the great grasslands that stretch northwards to and beyond the Pilanesberg, a volcanic mountain that takes its name from the impala that roamed the sunlit spaces. But the game species, and the elephant in particular, were a magnet to the early white hunters, who came with their guns for the killing sport and slaughtered the

ABOVE RIGHT: The distinctive saddlebilled stork.
BELOW: The infinite serenity of the bushveld at last light.

animals in their tens of thousands. The hunters were followed by pastoralists and farmers – and the countryside was finally tamed, the wilderness turned over to cattle and crops, its wildlife gone, seemingly for ever. Then, in the late 1970s, the Bophuthatswana

authorities decided to restore a large part of their bailiwick, 55 000 hectares in all, to its original condition, and in the event accomplished something of an environmental miracle. Resident farmers agreed to move to new land, farmsteads were demolished, telephone lines rerouted, power lines replaced by solar panels, alien trees felled, dongas filled, and animals – a great many of them – were brought in from all parts of the subcontinent. Within a remarkably short time the Pilanesberg National Park, one of the finest of Africa's conservation areas, had opened its gates to its first visitors.

The need to conserve – or rather, rediscover – the region's natural heritage was, however, only part of the impetus. There was also tourism, and the much-needed money that tourists would bring into this relatively poor part of the subcontinent. To supplement the area's attractions, a vast hotel and casino complex made its appearance on the southern perimeter of the park. Today, Sun City ranks among the world's largest and most lavish resorts.

Cutting through the northwestern Transvaal bushveld is another range of hills. Named the Waterberg for its many perennial streams, it runs from the Thabazimbi area close to the Pilanesberg's eastern boundary across to Pietersburg on the main Johannesburg-Zimbabwe road. Between the hills and the Limpopo River to the north is the Waterberg district, a 16 000-km^2 slice of rugged bush terrain, and in the past it too supported great numbers of wild animals, until the farmers and ranchers moved in. Here some of the larger properties have been retained as private game areas, though they are perhaps less pristine in character than those of the eastern Transvaal, where there are coherent habitats in which predator-prey relationships determine the natural balance. Nevertheless, these properties, and their lodges and bush camps, rank among the country's more rewarding game-viewing destinations.

ABOVE RIGHT: One of Mabula's two pool areas.
RIGHT: Returning from the afternoon game drive.

MABULA GAME LODGE

Mabula falls somewhere between a classic safari lodge and a country resort, a busy, cheerful and popular place that owes much of its success to its fair proximity to the densely populated Pretoria-Witwatersrand-Vaal Triangle (PWV) conurbation; to its relatively cheap rates (although higher than those of the public parks, they are considerably lower than those of the average private luxury lodge); to its unusually sociable staff; and to a wildlife complement that is both abundant and highly visible.

Mabula's game populations inhabit around 8 000 hectares of the northern Transvaal's Springbok Flats, along the foothills of the Waterberg range, and include the 'big five' – or rather, the 'big six', as the management prefers it, adding hippo to the orthodox list of elephant, rhino, lion, leopard and buffalo. Keeping these company is a host of other animals, among them giraffe, zebra, warthog, baboon, civet, lynx, crocodile (in and around the reserve's nine earth dams) and numerous buck (nyala, tsessebe and springbok are among the 23 different species). The elephant were translocated from the Kruger; the white

rhino population is the largest of any private sanctuary anywhere; cheetah and lion are bred in special (separate) reserves on the property. The flora is rich and well protected, sustaining 250 different species of bird, among them the endangered Cape vulture.

The lodge itself is a rambling, high-ceilinged building housing a reception, a spacious and companionable bar area and a dining room; attached is a patio and a cascade pool. Other amenities include a second swimming pool and tennis and squash courts; facilities for volleyball and snooker; a gymnasium, a sauna, a games room, and a shop that sells bush gear, curios and a range of essentials. The lodge has three fully equipped conference rooms. Accommodation comprises deep-thatched, refurbished chalets with *en suite* bathrooms and private verandahs. Other units are available from the timeshare pool.

There are several happy options when it comes to wining and dining. Mabula has six venues: the restaurant at the main lodge (carvery); the open-air boma nearby (barbecues with all the trimmings, plus African music and dancing); the Hippo Pool (finger lunches, cocktail parties for groups); the Fig Tree Plain, two kilometres away (champagne breakfasts and brunches); the Bush Boma (an intimate evening-barbecue site) and other bush-barbecue spots.

One of Mabula's graceful springbok, for long South Africa's sporting emblem. Among other animals to be seen are the 'big five' – lion, hippo, leopard, rhino and buffalo.

Game viewing

A fairly recent addition to Mabula is the hippo-pool-cum-waterhole, complete with game-viewing hide, which is linked to the lodge by a stoutly fenced passage. There are also the standard game drives in open vehicles, two in the morning (at six and nine) and one in the afternoon. The rangers are cheerfully talkative and very knowledgeable, and the trips are extremely rewarding. Game walks may appeal to the more serious naturalist, and unique horse trails (through the bush) to the adventurous. Some of the excursions are enlivened by champagne breakfasts and bush barbecues.

■ **Getting there:** By road from Johannesburg/Pretoria: take the N1 north to Warmbaths, turn left onto the R516 and drive 34 km to the gravelled turn-off to your right. Follow the signs. The lodge is 159 km from Johannesburg and 103 km from Pretoria. By air: Mabula has its own 1 300-m landing strip.

■ **Reservations and information:** Mabula Game Lodge, Private Bag X22, Bryanston 2021, South Africa. Tel: (011) 463-4217; fax: (011) 463-4299.

LEFT: *One of Lapalala's six bush camps; remote and tranquil, they have been conceived for the real lover of the African veld.*
ABOVE: *Rather more sophisticated is Kolobe Lodge.*

LAPALALA WILDERNESS

The Lapalala conservation area covers some 24 000 hectares of plateau terrain among the hills of the Waterberg range between Potgietersrus and the Botswana border. This is relatively well-watered, largely unspoilt countryside, which the celebrated conservationist and author Clive Walker and his partner Dale Parker are developing in four segments – though the word 'developing' perhaps gives the wrong impression, since one of the blocks of land, the rugged northwestern wilderness, will remain entirely untouched, and another impressive 7 500-hectare expanse has been set aside and kept in its pristine condition for environmental education.

The other two divisions are of rather more interest to game viewers, but of the kind, as one visitor aptly put it, 'who have graduated beyond looking just for the big five'. Lapalala offers a total wilderness experience rather then a simple wildlife adventure.

Six bush camps have been established on 7 000 hectares along the Palala (or Lephalala, which is the Sotho word for 'barrier', a reference to its once-formidable flow) and Blockland rivers, each camp named after a local tree species. They are remote, unstaffed and unpretentious; four of them consist of just a single thatched cabin or hut. Some have separate living and eating areas, and all have hot-water showers and flush toilets and are equipped with the essentials (gas-fired hotplates, paraffin, a fridge, bedding, utensils, tableware and so forth). These camps are for the person who likes to find his own way around the veld, on foot, without the help of an expert guide.

Then there's Kolobe Lodge, a cluster of four comfortable, two-roomed, four-bedded rondavels with *en suite* bathrooms, a tennis court, a filtered swimming pool and a pleasantly cosy pub. Meals are served in the open-air boma, beneath the spreading branches of a giant wonderboom fig. Dinners around the campfire are companionable, the conversation full of interest, and the roasts (of both domestic and game meat) delicious. Breakfast is often taken out in the bush, during the early-morning game-viewing excursion.

Game viewing
Lapalala was the first area of private land to receive a breeding group of the endangered black rhino. There are also white rhino, giraffe, zebra, hippo, buffalo, leopard, wildebeest, red hartebeest, kudu, impala, sable, the rare roan antelope and eland. (The last of the lion disappeared from the region in the 1950s, shot out by hunters.) Some of the numerous nocturnal animals, such as brown hyaena, antbear, caracal and civet, may be spotted on returning from a late afternoon or evening game drive.

Although there are an impressive number and variety of game species, in Lapalala the animals are not all that visible. One really has to search for them, which adds a challenge, a special quality, to your open-vehicle game drives and guided walks, which are conducted by experienced rangers.

Bird life is surprisingly prolific – more than 275 species have been identified. Lapalala also sustains a splendid variety of trees: 150 different types in all, which is apparently more than you'll find in any other single area in Southern Africa, with perhaps the sole exception of the northern Kruger park's Luvuvhu River valley.

Kolobe offers one of the more rewarding, less expensive kinds of bush holiday, and it is very good value for money.

■ **Getting there:** By road from Johannesburg/ Pretoria: take the N1 highway to the Kranskop toll road (117 km from Pretoria); turn off to Nylstroom and continue on to Vaalwater; turn right to Melkrivier (40 km) and then left onto gravel. Kolobe is 21 km along this road. By air: Kolobe has its own 1 000-m gravel airstrip.
■ **Reservations and information:** Lapalala Wilderness, PO Box 645, Bedfordview 2008, South Africa. Tel: (011) 453-7645; fax: (011) 453-7649.

The beautiful reaches of the Palala River, which runs along Touchstone's western boundary.

TOUCHSTONE GAME RANCH
This ranch extends across 17 500 hectares of the Waterberg region of the northern Transvaal, and neighbouring properties cover another 40 000 hectares, which makes the combined area the biggest privately owned conservancy in the country. The terrain is wild and lovely, the sweeping, koppie-studded grasslands plunging down to the Palala River which, on Touchstone's western perimeter, has carved a 22-km canyon out of the highveld landscape. The great spaces support a splendid richness of fauna – Touchstone is home to around 90 game species.

Accommodation is varied, designed to suit different preferences and budgets. On offer at one end of the scale are hiking and horse-trail camps and self-catering units. At the other end are two more exclusive lodges.

Welgevonden's terrain ranges from well-watered valleys to the peaks and cliffs of the uplands.

MILLSTONE is a thatched-roofed, slate-floored, refurbished farmhouse set among shady marula and red bushwillow trees. The lodge sleeps eight guests in its boldly decorated double rooms, each with an *en suite* bathroom. Home-style meals are enjoyed in the dining room, venison barbecues around the boma fire, and picnics in the bush. Millstone also has bar facilities.

FLAGSTONE can accommodate 10 people in its thatched and rather unpretentiously but comfortably furnished rondavels. This lodge has an especially pleasant boma area (venison is, again, the speciality) and an attractive swimming pool.

Game viewing

Guests are conducted on bush walks and on open-vehicle day- and night-drives by an experienced ranger. Among the animals to be seen are elephant, white rhino, giraffe, buffalo, wildebeest, hippo, crocodile, the rare roan antelope, black impala, kudu, sable and tsessebe. Leopard and cheetah are also present. More than 300 species of bird have been recorded on the ranch. Especially notable are the raptors: black, martial and Wahlberg's eagles, the lanner falcon, the gymnogene and the secretary bird. Bow-hunting safaris can be arranged.

■ **Getting there:** By road from Johannesburg: take the N1 north to Potgietersrus and the 518 north-west to the Moerdyk turn-off. Alternatively, turn

onto the R517, through Nylstroom, Vaalwater and Melkriver, to its junction with the R518; turn left and left again at the Moerdyk signpost. By air: Touchstone has its own landing strip.

■ **Reservations and information:** Touchstone Game Ranch, PO Box 57, Marken 0005, South Africa. Tel: (01536) 5-0230; fax: (01536) 5-0108.

WELGEVONDEN

This private 13 500-hectare ranch, located in the wilds of the northern Transvaal's Waterberg region, shares one of its boundaries (at this stage still fenced) with the Kransberg National Park (projected for proclamation at the time of writing). The countryside is ruggedly attractive, beautiful in parts, the open grasslands sweeping up to the splendid peaks, cliffs and gorges of the highlands. Game comprises animals indigenous to the region and includes white rhino, giraffe, plains zebra, kudu, oryx, waterbuck, sable, nyala and other antelope, leopard in the less accessible places, black-backed jackal, baboon and vervet monkey.

Welgevonden offers luxury (two-person) as well as standard (family) 'leisure and photo' game safaris. Trophy and biltong (dried meat) hunting facilities are also available. The ranch is geared towards the self-sufficient guest: its camps are staffed – domestic helpers will make fires, clean and tidy the chalets each day, make sure there is plenty of ice, set the table, lay out the drinks and so forth – but one brings and cooks one's own food.

ABOVE LEFT: Welgevonden's attractive Bobbejane se Biertuin hideaway.
ABOVE: One of the Mini Ha-Ha camp's bedrooms.

Full catering facilities are, however, available at some of the camps. A tent camp for hikers is also on the property.

STERKSTROOM is self-catering and consists of two thatched-roofed, two-bedroomed chalets, each with a bathroom and fully equipped kitchen, set near a waterhole and bush hide, amid lawns and a swimming pool.

BOBBEJANE SE BIERTUIN (literally 'baboons' beergarden') was originally a family picnic spot set high on cliffs overlooking the Suikerbos River, its dam and lovely valley, home to swarming troops of baboons. Now it is a bush hideaway for just two people – very private, very exclusive. The intimate complex has a bedroom and bathroom, a separate shower and toilet, two kitchens (the interior one is small, the exterior fully equipped), a cosy bar area, a boma for campfire meals, and a swimming pool. Catering facilities are available.

MINI HA-HA REST CAMP, once the name of the owners' family farm near the Maluti Mountains of Lesotho, is the oldest of Welgevonden's camps. A sprawling bush house of brick, iron, stone and thatch, it sleeps a maximum of 12 people in five bedrooms. Everything is informal, and is ideal for the gregarious family; the boma and its open fire are the focus of sociability. Catering facilities are available.

The pleasant communal area at Mankwe camp, on the shores of Pilanesberg's lake.

The *EDDIE YOUNG HUNTING CAMP* accommodates eight guests in its two large chalet bedrooms. Features include a fully equipped kitchen, a boma with an outside bar, a pleasant swimming pool, and a verandah overlooking a waterhole. In summer the camp is used by families, in winter by biltong hunters who have the use of a separate 650-hectare segment of the ranch administered by a hunting manager.

■ **Getting there:** By road from Johannesburg: take the N1 to the toll gate (180 km), bear left to Nylstroom (10 km) and drive on to Vaalwater (60 km) and for 15 km beyond on the Ellisras road. The Welgevonden sign on your left is for Bobbejane se Biertuin and Mini Ha-Ha camps only; carry on for a further 10 km to the second Welgevonden sign for the other two. By air: there is a landing strip 15 km from Welgevonden, and a helicopter pad at Mini Ha-Ha rest camp.

■ **Reservations and information:** Welgevonden, PO Box 72298, Parkview, Johannesburg 2122, South Africa. Tel: (011) 883-7980; fax: (011) 883-8427.

PILANESBERG NATIONAL PARK

In the Bophuthatswana region, some two hours' drive northwest of Johannesburg, one of the strangest of Southern Africa's geological features rises skywards from the flat Highveld plain. This is the Pilanesberg massif, a 1 200-million-year-old relic of volcanic convulsion made up of a series of four concentric mountain rings. They average around 3 000 m in height; the loftiest of the peaks is the Pilanesberg itself, towering 600 m above Mankwe Lake, which is at the dead centre of the ancient volcano's bowl, a circular area 27 km in diameter and the site of the 60 000-hectare Pilanesberg park.

The Pilanesberg, today one of the subcontinent's premier tourist attractions, is the product of Operation Genesis, launched in 1979 and rated among the most imaginative of the world's game-stocking enterprises. Eland were brought in from Namibia, zebra and waterbuck from the Transvaal, white and the precious black rhino from Natal (there are now 38 individuals in the Pilanesberg, and because the habitat is ideal the number is likely to increase), and elephant and buffalo from the Cape's Addo National Park. Currently some 10 000 head of game graze, browse, hunt and scavenge on the rolling grasslands and in the dense bush and wooded riverine valleys. They include, in addition to the species mentioned, giraffe, hippo, kudu, eland, sable, gemsbok, red hartebeest, tsessebe, waterbuck, warthog, cheetah, leopard, and the rare brown hyaena. Indeed, the Pilanesberg is one of the few Southern African parks that contain a near-complete assembly of the area's original fauna.

The area is a transitional zone between two major vegetation groups – the sour moist bushveld and the dry Kalahari thornveld – and this has created a wonderful diversity of habitats. The vegetation is varied; it includes, among much else, the extremely rare Transvaal red balloon tree, *Erythrophysa transvaalensis*, of which there are about 100 here and fewer than 10 recorded elsewhere.

More than 300 bird species have been identified, among them 30 types of raptor, prominent among which are the martial, fish and black eagles, the bateleur and the endangered Cape vulture. This last lives among the high, ledged cliffs of the Transvaal Magaliesberg range to the south, but its traditional habitat has been under severe threat: during the breeding season the survival of the species depends on a diet of bones from carcasses crunched to digestible size by the strong-jawed hyaena; the hyaena has all but disappeared from the western Transvaal, pushed out by the encroaching farmlands, so the vultures have come north to feed. To save this shy and stately bird from regional extinction environmentalists have created a number of 'vulture restaurants', one of which is in the Pilanesberg, located at the scavenger hide near the Manyane gate. For the benefit of visitors, an ingenious hide has been established: the viewing point is slightly below ground level, its tinted-glass front angled away from the rays of the sun. Clear-glass portholes are incorporated for the convenience of naturalists and photographers.

Observing leopard on a Pilanesberg game drive. The park is home to around 10 000 animals.

Game viewing

The park has something over 100 km of well-surfaced roads, much patronised by visitors from the next-door Sun City resort complex and its satellite hotels. Picnic sites, viewing hides and self-guided wilderness trails are among the established facilities. The viewing is probably at its most rewarding along the valleys; game is at its most concentrated and visible during the dry winter months.

More hides and another 40 km of roads are being developed in response to the growing tourist demand, along with additional picnic and viewing sites. The game populations are also being increased – among other things, lion may be introduced. According to Bophuthatswana Parks Board director Roger Collinson, the authorities 'have been very conservative in determining the wildlife populations the park could carry, but having monitored the game carefully over the past 10 years we are now confident it can carry double the number of animals'.

Of special interest to bird lovers is the huge walk-in aviary at the Manyane gate: it has been cleverly landscaped to simulate natural habitats, and is fully accessible to visitors: one strolls through while, all around, the inmates carry on with their daily lives.

THE PILANESBERG'S CAMPS

The park is served by one hutted rest camp, three bush camps, a superb caravan complex which also incorporates permanent accommodation, and a 'dormitory' camp for larger groups. In the middle of the park is the Pilanesberg Centre, a lovely old building that once served as the local magistrate's court.

Exploring the Pilanesberg by hot-air balloon.

MANKWE CAMP lies on the shore of the lake and offers 10 two-bedded safari tents; guests supply their own utensils, food and drink; and bathroom facilities are communal.

KOLOLO CAMP is especially secluded, has four tents, and meals are provided on request.

MANYANE CAMP ranks among Southern Africa's top 10 caravan parks. The five-star, thatched-roofed central complex has a fully licensed restaurant, swimming pools and well-appointed ablution facilities. The restaurant, described by a visitor as 'one of the finest to be encountered in any national park', specialises in venison dishes. Hutted accommodation is also available at Manyane.

Here there are informative displays, a shop, and an excellent little restaurant (the menu is small but carefully contrived, the beer ice-cold). There are also two sophisticated private lodges, Kwa Maritane and Bakubung, which are situated within the Pilanesberg. Close by is the giant Sun City complex and the Sundown Ranch Hotel.

TSHUKUDU, a luxury rest camp set on the crest of a ridge in the park's southwestern segment, was under development and closed to the public at the time of writing, but was scheduled to reopen its gates in the not-too-distant future. In 1992 Tshukudu comprised four self-contained, two-bed thatched chalets, each incorporating a kitchen, a lounge-dining area and a bathroom.

METSWEDI SAFARI CAMP, deep in the wilderness, overlooks a waterhole, has six tents, a lounge-dining area with a cosy log fireplace, laid-on meals, and two sets of ablution facilities (bathrooms, showers and flush toilets).

Pilanesberg Safaris

A splendidly unusual way of exploring the park and its wildlife is by balloon. Pilanesberg Safaris, which has a permanent presence both at the Manyane gate and at the Sun City complex, run early-morning, Kenya-type, four-hour aerial excursions over the game-rich grasslands; passengers sip champagne as the sun rises over the plains. Also on offer are morning game drives (with bush breakfasts) and drives at night (with bush barbecues); ranger-led hiking trails; horseback trails; and conducted tours of the magnificent Manyane indigenous bird aviary and the Kwena crocodile farm.

Reservations and information PO Box 79, Sun City 0316, Bophuthatswana. Tel: (014651) 2-1561; fax: (0142) 2-3002.

Hunting

The Pilanesberg offers controlled and closely monitored facilities. Much of the concession area comprises rugged terrain that is not accessible to vehicles, and hunters should be prepared to do a fair amount of walking. There are excellent habitats for such species as bushbuck in the densely covered valleys and klipspringer in the higher, more rocky parts. Reservations and information: Kgama Safaris, PO Box 2799, Rustenburg 0300. Tel: (01466) 5-5587/8 or (0142) 2-1736.

By road from Johannesburg and Pretoria: drive west to Rustenburg and then north on the R510 towards Thabazimbi for 56 km before turning left for the Pilanesberg's Manyane (eastern) gate. Alternatively, take the R565 from Rustenberg towards Sun City for the signposted Bakgatla, Bakubung and Kwa Maritane gates. Coach travel: there are daily coach services between Johannesburg and Sun City. By air: Bop Air operates scheduled flights between Jan Smuts international airport and Sun City airport.

■ **Reservations and information:** Reservations Officer (information: Public Relations Officer), Pilanesberg National Park, PO Box 1201, Mogwase 0302, Bophuthatswana. Tel: (01465) 2-2405 or 2-2409.

KWA MARITANE LODGE

This is not the usual kind of game lodge, but rather a luxury hotel and timeshare resort complex (and a very attractive one, too) set within the bounds of the game-rich Pilanesberg National Park – nature, as it were, brought to a very sophisticated doorstep.

Your introduction to Kwa Maritane – the name means 'place of the rock' – is a quite charming pool area, a kind of tropical, palm-festooned oasis (the cliché is very apt in this instance) enclosed by a circle of thatched buildings housing a lounge, a two-level à la carte restaurant and other pleasantly appointed and decorated public rooms. Indeed, from a décor point of view, the lounge is rather special: high-roofed and beautifully furnished in solid woods, it looks out to the Rock (a massive granite outcrop) through picture windows.

Accommodation is in self-contained chalets and duplex cabanas sleeping up to five people, and luxury chalets sleeping eight. All the units are furnished in solid oak and appointed in rustic style; each is airconditioned (though the high, thatched roofing keeps the

LEFT: *Inside one of Kwa Maritane's chalets.*
BELOW: *The Kwa Maritane complex, within the Pilanesberg park.*

rooms cool enough, even in the blistering heat of summer) and provided with television, radio and a telephone. Chalets have their own private patios, and the luxury units an upstairs loft bedroom and a plunge pool.

The restaurant offers à la carte and table d'hôte fare, and excellent it is too. Less formal poolside meals are a pleasant alternative on hot days. The Kwa Mazout pub, which leads off the pool's courtyard, is a cool place of thatch, stone and wood; the Kwa Baneng bar and a fast-food counter lead onto a second pool area.

Kwa Maritane is very well placed to serve two major purposes: on the one hand there's the cornucopia of pleasures that is Sun City, a couple of minutes' drive down the road, and on the other it's a supremely comfortable base from which guests can enjoy a taste of the wide-open bushveld spaces. The lodge has floodlit tennis courts and volleyball facilities; and outdoor amenities at Sun City (there's a courtesy bus service between the two resorts) include golf, squash, watersports, bowls, tenpin bowling and horse riding.

Business conferences are well catered for: there are four fully equipped rooms, the largest – the Rhino – seating 100 people in cinema format.

Game viewing

Guests have immediate access to the wildlife splendours of the Pilanesberg National Park; experienced rangers conduct you on sunrise, late-afternoon and, for the more self-indulgent, champagne drives – one stops for a refreshing glass or three of Buck's Fizz at the tail end of the morning expedition – by open land cruiser (seats are raised high for better observation). The afternoon drive ends with a barbecue in Kwa Maritane's bush boma. Night excursions are also on offer.

There are also informative, and fascinating, walking trails. The emphasis on the shorter (two-hour) walk is on bird identification; your guide on the longer (three-hour) trail will concentrate on spoor, bird life, vegetation and game identification, and will explain the approach to game management

ABOVE: *The busy scene in Bakubung's public area. The terrace overlooks a hippo pool.*
OPPOSITE: *Bakubung guests encounter rhino.*

within the Pilanesberg. More unusually, there is a 180-m underground tunnel that takes you from the lodge to a well-appointed game-viewing hide (carpeted flooring; pedestal stools) the windows of which overlook a small waterhole. Best times to see the animals are early morning and late afternoon, but the nocturnal hours come a close second: the waterhole is illuminated.

■ **Getting there:** By road from Pretoria and Johannesburg: take the route west to Rustenburg and then north towards Sun City, on the R565. The lodge is 8 km beyond Sun City; turn left into the Pilanesberg National Park before the airport, and follow the signs. An alternative route from Rustenburg is via the R510 towards Thabazimbi, turning left towards and into the Pilanesberg park after 56 km. Coach travel: there are daily services between Johannesburg and Sun City. By air: Bop Air operates frequent flights between Jan Smuts international airport and Sun City; a bus service links Sun City airport with Kwa Maritane.

■ **Reservations and information:** Kwa Maritane, PO Box 39, Sun City 0316, Bophuthatswana. Tel: (01465) 2-1820/2/3/4; fax: (01465) 2-1147.

BAKUBUNG LODGE

This lodge is similar in many ways to Kwa Maritane – both are hotels and timeshare resorts located within the splendid Pilanesberg National Park – but it is rather more affordable and its setting is quite distinctive: the 22 studio rooms and 50 chalets, all handsomely thatched, are arranged in a sweeping horseshoe configuration around a specially created hippo pool. Bakubung means 'people of the hippo', and in 1991 two of these giants were brought in from Bloemfontein to make their home at the lodge.

The complex is sited near the southern Pilanesberg's busy Bakubung gate, though you're not aware of its proximity: the wilderness all around remains undisturbed except

for bird-song and the occasional movement of antelope and other game on the wide, grassy plain to the north. The lodge's buildings blend beautifully with their surrounds.

The rooms are comfortably, even luxuriously appointed, and have been decorated, in vaguely ethnic style, by someone with excellent taste. Each has two double beds, a bath and shower, a lounge facing out onto the veld, an overhead fan, a television and a direct-dial telephone. The timeshare chalets, naturally, are more spacious, consisting of two *en suite* bedrooms, a small kitchen fitted with a hob, microwave and fridge and with plenty of cupboard space, a lounge-dining area, and two patios, one of them equipped (with gas barbecue-grill) for alfresco eating.

Bakubung's hotel building – which you enter through a porte-cochere and along a rather lovely breezeway leading to the terrace and hippo pool – houses a pleasant reception area, a lounge, the Motswedi cocktail bar, the excellent buffet and à la carte restaurants, and two fully equipped conference rooms. Recreational amenities include a swimming pool, two floodlit tennis courts and a volleyball court; a courtesy bus service links the lodge to the pleasure-palace of Sun City.

Game viewing

Facilities are much the same as those at Kwa Maritane, and include conducted drives through the Pilanesberg in high-seated land cruisers. There are two excursions, the sunrise and the champagne ones (guests sip a refreshing glass of bubbly and orange at the end of the trip) in the morning, and a choice of five in the afternoon and evening, one of them a 'sundowner' expedition (drinks en route; game viewing by spotlight on the return leg), and two others enlivened by a bush barbecue.

Foot trails are conducted in the mornings. One of them is designed to introduce guests to the Pilanesberg's impressive bird life (more than 300 species have been recorded); another takes in the animals, their spoor, game identification, vegetation and the principles of game management.

■ **Getting there:** By road from Johannesburg/Pretoria: drive west to Rustenburg and then north on the R565 towards Sun City; continue west past the Sun City entrance gates for about 4 km and through the Pilanesberg's Bakubung gate. The turn-off to the lodge is just inside the gate. Bakubung can also be reached from Sun City itself (take the road past the Cascades and Palace hotels). An alternative route from Rustenburg is via the R510 towards Thabazimbi, turning left towards and into the Pilanesberg park after 56 km. Coach travel: there are daily services between Johannesburg and Sun City. By air: Bop Air operates frequent flights airport with Bakubung.

■ **Reservations and information:** Bakubung Hotel and Timeshare Lodge, PO Box 6021, Rustenburg 0300, Bophuthatswana. Tel: (01465) 2-1861; fax: (01465) 2-1621.

THE GIRAFFE: AN EVOLUTIONARY WONDER

Reaching nearly six metres in height, the adult giraffe is the tallest creature on earth and ranks among the four heaviest land mammals (it can weigh up to an incredible 1,5 tons). But, for all that, the animal is able to make itself surprisingly inconspicuous in its natural habitat: it is a master of camouflage, its dappled hide and ability to stand perfectly still enabling it to blend into and become an almost indistinguishable part of its woodland surrounds.

The species is gregarious, forming small herds of up to 20 individuals to feed on the tender young leaves of trees – a diet that, over countless generations of natural selection, led to the evolution of its freakishly long neck. This in turn triggered the development of other, not so apparent but equally extraordinary, physical features. To compensate for the enormous distance between heart and head, for instance, nature has devised a rather special adaptation of the arteries to pump blood 2,5 m up to the brain, together with a unique arrangement of valves in the larger veins to prevent the blood from running back. Without these ingenious mechanisms, the brain would be either starved of blood when the animal stands erect, or flooded when it bends down to drink.

The giraffe's principal natural enemy is the lion, to which it is especially vulnerable when drinking at riverbanks or waterholes – with its legs awkwardly splayed, it is virtually immobilised. Away from water, though, the giraffe more than holds its own: it is fleet of foot, and it can deliver a lethal kick with both its forefeet and its hind legs.

Once widespread, giraffe are now found only in the subcontinent's northern parts.

HOTELS AND RESORTS

Casual visitiors to the Pilanesberg have a pleasant choice of accommodation outside the boundaries of the national park. Close to the southern entrance are the Sundown Ranch Hotel and the pleasure palaces of the huge Sun City complex.

Farther south, among the green hills and valleys of the lovely Magaliesberg area, there are other splendid venues – holiday destinations in their own right but also strategically sited for forays into the game-rich north-western grasslands.

HUNTER'S REST HOTEL

There is more than a hint of the colonial country club about Hunter's Rest, an impression conveyed by the riding paddock and golf course, the spacious, trimly kept grounds, the shady terraces, and the comfortably solid buildings with their cool reception areas. A stately and most attractive three-star hotel, it is set in the fertile plain below the Magaliesberg range and an hour's drive from the Pilanesberg park. It is large for a country hotel: there are 90 or so well-appointed and pleasantly decorated single, double and family rooms, each with a private bathroom, sitting area and patio.

Food and drink: Table d'hôte, offering ample, wholesome and delicious fare. The dining room has large windows and a fine view. There's a lively barbecue lunch laid on on Saturdays, a dinner-dance on Saturday evenings, and a smorgasbord lunch on Sundays. The hotel has a full liquor licence and an impressive wine-list; there is a Tudor-style cocktail bar leading off the lounge.

Amenities: A superb swimming pool is set in the charming surrounds; sauna; horse riding, bowls, croquet, tennis, squash, volleyball, mini-golf, and a nine-hole par-three golf course. For joggers, there is a recommended eight-kilometre run to Olifantsnek dam and back. The hotel offers full conference facilities for a maximum 250 delegates.

Location: Astride the R24 road, 12 km south of Rustenburg; 90 km from Pretoria and 100 km from Johannesburg.

TOP: Hunter's Rest – set below the Magaliesberg.
ABOVE: The hilltop charm of Mount Grace.

Reservations and information: PO Box 775, Rustenburg 0300, South Africa. Tel: (0142) 9-2140; fax: (0142) 9-2661.

MOUNT GRACE COUNTRY HOUSE

The name is apt: this is a charming venue, both visually and in the courteous, attentive way in which the staff looks after the guests – English country-house luxury in a family atmosphere probably sums it up. The double rooms and suites are spacious, elegantly appointed, and expensively and tastefully decorated, and they are clustered in three sections: Thatchstone Village, Grace Village and Mountain Village. Each has its own character, and the whole is set beneath mature shade trees, among beautifully landscaped gardens, on a high hill overlooking the Rietpoort valley and the uplands beyond.

Food and drink: Quality fare, tending towards the simple and wholesome, with the emphasis on country-style cooking. Breakfast and lunch are served in The Copperfield restaurant, from the large-paned windows of which

ABOVE: Sun City, on the edge of the Pilanesberg park, offers four hotels and a kaleidoscope of recreational and entertainment attractions. The surrounds are enchanting.
OPPOSITE, ABOVE: One of the Sun City pool areas.
OPPOSITE, BELOW: Shops are among the myriad visitor amenities.

there are fine views; dinner and Sunday lunch are taken in the dark-oak Thatchstone, where there is delicious table d'hôte fare; English afternoon teas, complete with scones and cream, are enjoyed in the lounge, and drinks in the Hartley's cocktail bar.

Amenities: A large central pool area, bowling green, tennis court, and croquet, squash and billiards. Strolling in the extensive grounds is a delight: there is a network of pathways, with rustic seats en route, and a small dam garlanded by lush vegetation through which a quite enchanting walk meanders.

Location: Just off the R24 road to Rustenburg, on the hill above Magaliesburg village.

Reservations and information: PO Box 2536, Parklands 2121, South Africa. Tel: (011) 880-1675; fax: (011) 880-3582.

SUNDOWN RANCH HOTEL

This is a large, three-star hotel set in 1 600 hectares of African bushveld some 10 km from Pilanesberg and Sun City. The pleasantly furnished bedrooms (101 in total) have private bathrooms, and balconies that look down onto a central complex graced by gardens, a stylish pool area, and a red-tiled bar and bistro. Also sited on the grounds are 300 chalets, each sleeping up to six people.

Food and drink: Excellent à la carte and buffet can be enjoyed in the plush Pilanesberg restaurant; light meals are served in the Maroela Coffee Shop.

Amenities: Sun City is just down the road, but for those who want to relax nearer home there is tennis, swimming and snooker *in situ* and walking, jogging and horse-riding trails in the immediate vicinity. Of interest on the extensive property are the ruins of two African villages dating to the 17th century.

Location: On the R565, 10 km from Sun City.

Reservations and information: PO Box 139, Boshoek 0301, South Africa. Tel: (0142) 2-8320; fax: (0142) 97-1038; or through Central Reservations (011) 339-5979.

SUN CITY

This vast complex, close to the southern perimeter of the Pilanesberg National Park, is the flagship of Sun International's fleet of hotel-casino resorts: an enormous, opulent extravaganza of luxurious hotels, glittering entertainment centres, restaurants, gaming rooms, shops, discos and hugely extensive, beautifully landscaped grounds, the whole set, rather incongruously, in one of the bleaker regions of the subcontinent.

Sun City is nearly 20 km in circumference, and what it sets out to do – entertain, divert, amuse and spoil the holidaymaker – it does on a grand scale, and in style. Visitors have a choice of four hotels, each designed for different pockets and preferences.

THE CABANAS These are the least expensive of the various types of accommodation; they are for families, the rooms opening out onto pleasantly lush gardens that lead down to the lake and Waterworld, the focus of fun in the sun. There are 284 rooms in all, divided into the standard units (twin beds, shower, toilet) and the deluxe (twin beds, fold-out queen-size bed and private bathroom); all are airconditioned, carpeted and equipped with a radio and television. The Cabanas have their own and very attractive pool area and poolside bar; the Palm Terrace restaurant (self-service for breakfast) and the Morula Steakhouse (contemporary décor); light snacks and drinks from the Boathouse bar; and, for the children, Adventureland.

SUN CITY HOTEL Middle-of-the-range, and very comfortable. Its 340 units are divided into double, family and luxury suites, and two presidential suites, all with the standard appointments (private bathrooms, television, telephone and so forth), all facing the pool. Restaurants include the Calabash (à la carte and carvery), Raffles (sophisticated supper, and dancing in the adjacent disco), the Silver Forest (French cuisine), and the Sun Terrace (breakfast and lunch buffet); among the bars are the Aquarius (dancing), Lobby, Pool, and Raffles Cocktail. The hotel is close to the Entertainment Centre (see next page) and the Extravaganza Theatre, where nightly shows are staged, and the famed Casino. Guests can also relax around a swimming pool that has an island at its centre; the island sustains transplanted palms, including *Cocos plumosa* (indigenous to the Pacific), and phoenix dates from the oases of the Sahara.

CASCADES HOTEL A superb, five-star establishment that can accommodate 486 people in its twin, standard corner and spa-fitted luxury rooms, six suites and three presidential suites. Excellent international fare is served in the Peninsula restaurant; cocktails and snacks in the Grotto. There are two cocktail bars, two jacuzzis and three observation lifts servicing the hotel's 15 floors. The grounds are extensive and lovely: more than 50 000 m² of the surrounding countryside have been sculpted to produce a kaleidoscope of lawn, pools, grottos, waterfalls, tropical plants and exotic bird life. The flowerbeds alone cover nearly 6 000 m².

THE PALACE is the centrepiece of The Lost City, a new development at Sun City which makes the combined complex one of the world's biggest and most opulent resorts. The Palace, an elaborate affair of domes and minarets, columns and curlicues, has 350 luxurious rooms and suites, an entrance hall rising three storeys, and two restaurants, one set on an island surrounded by cascades of water, the other embowered by jungle foliage. The Valley of Waves, which links The Palace with the Entertainment Centre, has its own 'instant' jungle of 3 500 trees, plus a 100 m x 60 m swimming pool with 1,8-m-high artificially created surfing waves. Among other features are water chutes for the courageous, and a Lazy River Ride for the very young.

Indoor amenities: The Entertainment Centre is a vibrant concentration of restaurants, bars, discos, shops, conference rooms, cinemas, slots and a 200-seat computerised bingo hall. Its core is the Superbowl, used for conventions, banquets (seating for 3 500), lavish promotions, big-name shows (Sinatra, Minelli and Queen have performed here) and international sporting events, including world title fights. In the main Sun City Hotel, the Casino offers the standard gaming range plus the ubiquitous slots, a *salon privé* (punto banco and chemmy) for devotees, and the 620-seat Extravaganza Theatre.

Outdoor amenities: On offer are horse riding, tennis, squash, bowls, swimming, tenpin bowling; an animal farm for the children; and game-viewing in the Pilanesberg (conducted drives) and in the next-door Letsatsing reserve. The Gary Player Country Club boasts a magnificent 18-hole golf course that has

hosted most of the world's greats and the annual Million Dollar Golf Challenge. A second Arizona desert-style course recently opened as part of The Lost City development. The Valley of Waves incorporates 22 different regions of vegetation, from a rocky outcrop of ancient baobabs to lush tropical jungle. Strollers are also enticed to the Waterscape, a huge arrangement of interlinked pools, a kilometre of low weirs and two kilometres of walkways that lead through gardens and over, and under, rock formations. Among the Waterscape's permanent residents are swans, herons, and the rare South African black duck. The Waterscape is illuminated at night.

Much activity revolves around Waterworld below the Cabanas – a 750-m-long manmade lake, designed both for the idler and the sporting enthusiast (water-skiing, windsurfing, parasailing, jet skiing and so on).

ABOVE: The opulent Palace of The Lost City.
OPPOSITE: One of the Palace's quiet sitting areas.
RIGHT: Chefs display barbecue fare.

Well worth a visit (it is at the entrance gate) is Kwena Garden, a reptile park and ranch distinguished by its dramatic architecture, its lushly tropical surrounds, and by the giant Nile crocodiles it contains.

Location: Sun City is on the southern boundary of Pilanesberg, 167 km from Johannesburg and 152 km from Pretoria; many of its guests fly in from Jan Smuts airport; others come by coach (daily scheduled services).

Reservations and information: Sun International Central Reservations, PO Box 784487, Sandton 2146, South Africa. Tel: (011) 780-7800; fax: (011) 780-7449. Regional telephone numbers: Cape Town (021) 418-1465; Durban (031) 304-9237.

SWAZILAND

The country is small: it covers less ground than the Kruger National Park, which is fairly close by, and is small enough to take in almost all its 17 000-odd km², at a glance, from the viewpoint atop a humped mountain called Mlembe, which is part of the Khalamba range that runs along the northwestern border. The range is the northern extension of the towering Natal Drakensberg, and if you enter Swaziland by the Nelspruit-Havelock-Pigg's Peak route you will see some truly spectacular scenery. The area is well watered, blessed with good rains; the countryside is rich, its hills and wide valleys mantled by grassland and the deep green of endless pine forest.

Coming down towards Mbabane, Swaziland's modest but attractive capital, the landscape changes: here there is the undulating, fertile savanna of the middleveld, at its loveliest perhaps in the Great Usutu, or Ezulwini, rivervalley. Ezulwini means 'place of heaven' – an apt name, for this is indeed an exquisite corner of Africa, lush, densely populated, prosperous looking, the skyline dominated by twin peaks known as Lugogo, more informally as 'Sheba's Breasts' and said to have inspired the setting for Rider Haggard's *King Solomon's Mines*. Ezulwini is Swaziland's most developed and busiest holiday area,

OPPOSITE: The lush terrain of the Mlilwane wildlife sanctuary, part of the Ezulwini valley.

its major attractions the renowned Mlilwane wildlife sanctuary and the hotels, their golf courses and casinos.

Eastwards again, and the terrain assumes a classic bushveld character, hot and humid, the lowland plains rarely rising more than 300 m above sea level. The vegetation is generally dense, almost impenetrable in some places but often yielding to open savanna and to the emerald green of sugar plantations. Finally, there is the Lubombo plateau that rises sharply up to the Lebombo mountains that form the country's eastern border with Mozambique.

A varied and beautiful country, peaceful, unhurried in its lifestyle, amiable in its welcome to travellers – and full of interest for the visitor. Swaziland is a kingdom, its people steeped in the traditions of their forebears and addicted to ritual and ceremony, which is conducted most dramatically in huge gatherings where the vividness of dress, regalia, music and movement combine to create occasions of unforgettable vibrancy.

Among Swaziland's other drawcards are its conservation areas. They cannot compare in size or content with those of the subcontinent's larger countries: there are just five major reserves, none of them extensive by African standards. But each has its distinctive character and its special wildlife complement, and each offers a memorable wilderness experience.

MLILWANE WILDLIFE SANCTUARY

In the 1970s, like so many other African countries where good farming land is at an ever-increasing premium, Swaziland was fast losing its wildlife heritage – a situation brought sharply into focus when a party of King Sobhuza II's hunters returned from one four-day foray bearing just two impala! Up to then Mlilwane had been a family farm and private reserve – the oldest in the region – but owners Mickey Reilly and his wife, sharing the general concern and determined to do something about the depredation of game, decided to donate their land to the nation. It was a magnificent gesture. King Sobhuza became the new sanctuary's patron, Ted Reilly (Mickey's son) its first warden.

Today Mlilwane represents one of the most impressive success stories in the annals of Southern African conservation. Under Ted's guidance the reserve has been transformed from a virtually empty wilderness into a superbly managed, flourishing, 4 500-hectare haven for a remarkable variety of animals and birds – and into a prime tourist attraction.

Mlilwane straddles the escarpment between Highveld and Lowveld, an area that was once the terminal point of both easterly and westerly game migrations. The scenery is magnificent; most of the sanctuary lies within the Usutu River valley, otherwise known as Ezulwini ('place of heaven'), a stunningly beautiful sweep of countryside dominated by the twin peaks of Lugogo. The Ezulwini valley is Swaziland's pride; nearby are some fine hotels as well as the Royal Village (Lobamba) and the parliament buildings.

MLILWANE'S CAMP

Visitors have a fairly wide choice of accommodation; none of it is in the luxury class; all of it is simple, comfortable, and very well maintained. On offer are thatched huts (with communal ablution facilities), log cabins (two double bunks, lounge, kitchen, dining room, separate bathroom facilities), a self-contained two-bedroomed cottage (lounge, verandah, bathroom, kitchenette) and a

TOP: *A corner of Mbabane's busy market place.*
ABOVE: *Swazi women in traditional garb.*

cluster of seven rather basic 'beehive' huts. Centrepiece of the camp is the hippo pool, and some of the animals in and around it are endearingly tame. There's also a largish caravan/camping ground.

Mlilwane is essentially for the do-it-yourself guest (bring your own food, crockery and utensils; meals are cooked over the campfire), though the Hippo Haunt restaurant, which is licensed, offers venison barbecues and stews (especially popular is warthog cooked in a ploughshare with onions and tomatoes). Beer and wine are on sale in the camp shop. Among visitor amenities is a swimming pool.

Game viewing

The wildlife is varied and plentiful: Mlilwane sustains rather more than 50 kinds of large and small animal, including leopard, giraffe, buffalo, blue wildebeest, zebra, eland, kudu, mountain reedbuck, blesbok, sable, nyala, klipspringer, oribi, hippo, crocodile, and a

ABOVE: Hikers pause to enjoy breathtaking scenery in Mlilwane.
LEFT: On the Mlilwane guided horse trail.

■ **Getting there:** From Mbabane, follow the road south towards Manzini; turn right at the Mlilwane signpost and continue for a further 2 km.
■ **Reservations and information:** Central Reservations, Mlilwane Wildlife Sanctuary, PO Box 234, Mbabane, Swaziland. Tel: (09268) 4-5006, ext. 245; fax: (09268) 4-4246.

kaleidscopic bird life – around 240 species have been identified, among them crane, stork, the martial and black eagle, waterfowl and sunbirds for Africa. Some of these creatures are charmingly visible: the birds around Mlilwane's camp are fed at three in the afternoon, and the animals – hippo and warthog among them – habitually move in to purloin a morsel or two.

Game drives are either self-guided or (for a fee) conducted by a Mlilwane ranger in open land rovers by day or night. The more active visitor is enticed by the Macobane trail, an undemanding self-guided walk that brings into view the granite splendour of Nyonyane peak. Shorter walks and bridle paths have been laid out; guided horse trails are popular.

MALOLOTJA NATURE RESERVE

The Malolotja is a magnificent wilderness of mountain, gorge, river, waterfall and dense riverine forest, covering 18 000 hectares in northwestern Swaziland. The area is dominated by the Ngwenya, Silotfwane and Mgwayiza mountain ranges. The Malolotja River, rising in the east, tumbles down in a series of spectacular cascades and waterfalls – including Swaziland's highest, the Malolotja Falls (90 m) – to join the Nkomati River 900 m below. The varied landscape and its different habitats sustain many lovely and rare plants, among them proteas and ericas, aloes, orchids and amaryllids. Species of the ancient cycad also occur here. Worth visiting is the reserve's small herbarium.

ABOVE: *Sundowner hour in Mlilwane's rest camp.*
RIGHT: *The Hippo Haunt restaurant – venison is a speciality, barbecued warthog a popular dish.*

The birds, too, are rather special: more than 250 species have been recorded, including the nesting blue swallow, the blue crane and a flourishing colony of bald ibis (on the cliffs above the Malolotja Falls). The rich nectar of the proteas that dot the higher slopes sustain sunbirds and Gurney's sugarbirds; among other notables are Stanley's bustard, striped flufftail, blackrumped buttonquail and Knysna loerie. A bird checklist is available.

Among Malolotja's other claims of interest to the visitor is the site of the world's oldest known mine: 41 000 years ago men dug down into the earth here for the red and black iron that gave them the materials and the colours for their mystical and now long-forgotten rituals.

MALOLOTJA'S CAMP
The reserve caters mainly for backpackers, who have the use of a number of camp sites consisting of clearings in the bush next to water. For less adventurous overnight visitors there are five furnished, self-catering, six-bed log cabins, each provided with a fridge, a

stove, crockery, cutlery and linen. The main camp site has communal bathroom facilities (hot water on tap), a central barbecue area and 15 individual sites, some suited to caravans.

Exploring the area
Malolotja's wildlife complement is modest enough, but it has its interest. It is home to blesbok, mountain reedbuck, blue and black wildebeest and zebra. Klipspringer, oribi, grey rhebok and two duiker species are also found in the reserve. Predators include jackal, caracal and aardwolf. Visitors can undertake self-guided game-viewing drives – most of the roads are gravelled and there are three kilometres of all-weather roads (these traverse the eastern section). But the reserve is really

ABOVE: Malolotja's enchanting Upper Potholes.
ABOVE RIGHT: A self-catering cabin at Malolotja.
OPPOSITE: Hutted accommodation in Hlane.

for the hiker: there are superb two- to seven-day wilderness trails to the remote corners of the reserve, the Majolomba, Maphandakazi and Malolotja falls, and to the Mahulung-wane gorge. Here and elsewhere one can take a dip in the clear waters, but be careful of the strong currents in the rainy season.

■ **Getting there:** The reserve flanks a section of Swaziland's northwestern (Transvaal) border. From the Oshoek border post, take the route towards Mbabane and turn left, after 7 km, in the direction of Pigg's Peak. You'll reach the Malolotja entrance (on your left) after another 18 km.

■ **Reservations and information:** The Senior Warden, Malolotja Nature Reserve, PO Box 1797, Mbabane, Swaziland. Tel: (09268) 4-3060 (information). Malolotja Bookings, PO Box 100, Lobamba, Swaziland. Tel: (09268) 6-1516 or 6-1178/9; fax: (09268) 6-1875.

HLANE NATIONAL PARK

A royal hunting preserve until the mid-1960s, when it was proclaimed a national sanctuary – principally because the hunters and, more destructively, the poachers had virtually denuded the area of its animals. Today Hlane is Swaziland's largest repository of game, home to, among others, elephant and giraffe, white rhino (these have been dehorned, to render them commercially valueless), zebra and wildebeest, hyaena, jackal, impressive numbers of buck species – and, currently being reintroduced, lion, emblem of the Swazi monarch.

Hlane extends over 30 000 hectares of open parkland savanna, scrubland and dense low-lying bushveld and hardwood forest in the northeast of the country. Flowing across the northwestern and western parts of the area is the Black Mbuluzi River, a magnet for the animals during the bone-dry winter months. In summer, when the rains come, the game disperses to the south. Bird life is prolific and some of it unusual: Hlane has the densest population of raptors to be found in Swazi-land, and is home to Africa's most southerly colony of marabou stork.

HLANE'S CAMPS

There are two of these, each different in setting and character, each offering fairly modest self-catering accommodation.

NDLOVU CAMP is a pleasant, tree-shaded little complex of just two furnished huts (one three-bedded, the other a larger affair that sleeps eight, four of them in the loft) and a

camping ground. Close by is a waterhole; the birds are a joy. There is a central bathroom block; one brings one's own food and cooks it in the open, over the campfire. The huts have gas fridges; kitchen- and tableware are supplied; lighting is by paraffin lamps and candles.

Elephants and other animals roam freely in the area, but there is a low (and unobtrusive) electrified fence around Ndlovu camp to keep out the larger species, allowing the smaller ones to enter and wander at will. In spring, a marvellous array of hole-nesting birds – glossy starling, crested barbet and woodland kingfisher – delight visitors with their calls and colours.

BHUBESI CAMP has a lovely position overlooking the gently flowing Mbuluzwana River and its sandbanks and hardwood trees. Here there are three fully furnished, self-contained cottages (two bedrooms, bathroom, lounge, kitchenette), each sited for maximum privacy, electrified, fitted with a stove, a fridge and a Jetmaster fireplace. Each, too, has its own verandah and a view across and footpath leading down to the water. Very pleasant.

Game viewing

Hlane offers self-guided drives only. One of the routes running through the park has, regrettably, been upgraded to a public trunk road, which takes something away from the wilderness and one's enjoyment of it, but makes it easily accessible. Game walks in the company of a ranger can be arranged.

■ **Getting there:** From Mbabane, drive to and through Manzini, to Simunye, from where Hlane is signposted. The park is 67 km from Manzini.
■ **Reservations and information:** Central Reservations Office, Hlane National Park, PO Box 234, Mbabane, Swaziland. Tel: (09268) 4-5006, ext 245; fax: (09268) 4-4246.

MLAWULA NATURE RESERVE

The 16 000-hectare Mlawula sanctuary, which incorporates the Ndzindza Nature Reserve, straddles the Lebombo mountains of the eastern (Mozambique) border, its western parts sweeping down into the Swaziland lowveld – a visually quite splendid area of peak and upland plateau, seasonal pan, river valley and grassland that is popular more for its scenery and floral fascination, and for the magnificent bird life of the region, than for its larger animals.

The game is there, though, and it has its interest – Mlawula is home to white rhino, zebra, kudu, oribi, mountain reedbuck and other bovids, spotted hyaena, prolific crocodile along the Mbuluzi and Mlawula rivers, and many smaller, more secretive and (some of them) rare creatures. Altogether, 64 different kinds of mammal, 30 of amphibian, 25 lizards, 27 snakes and 31 varieties of fish have been identified within the reserve. But it is the birds that distinguish the wildlife complement – notable among the 350 species are African broadbill, finfoot, yellowspotted nicator, the lovely narina trogon, and a fine array of raptors. A 'vulture restaurant' provides visitors with a rare opportunity for close-up observation.

Intriguing features of the area are its 'busholumps' – huge, vegetated termite ('white ant') mounds rising from the flat grasslands of the plateau. Notable too is the rich plant life, most especially that found in the depths of the mountain gorges. Here there are rare stands of Lebombo ironwood and, growing in their shade, a species of primeval cycad, *Encephalartos umbeluziensis*, that is found nowhere else in the world. More than 1 000 different plants have been recorded in the Mbuluzi valley.

ABOVE: The roan antelope, one of several rare animals to be seen in the game-rich Mkhaya nature reserve.
OPPOSITE: The conducted walks in Mkaya bring guests into close contact with the wildlife.

MLAWULA'S CAMP
Accommodation, at Sara camp, is modest: it comprises just three two-bed tents (bedding, kitchen- and tableware provided). Visitors must bring their food and drink. At Siphiso there's a campsite with ablution block (caravans welcome).

Exploring the area
The game can probably be seen at its best in the Siphiso valley, a dryish area of knobthorn savanna and, on the rocky ridges, bushwillow. The Mbuluzi gorge is also rewarding. Mlawula is excellent walking country; backpacking trails and gentler rambles are being developed. Drives and walks are either self-guided (an informative booklet is available) or, on request, accompanied. There are also facilities for camping and canoeing.

■ **Getting there:** From Mbabane, drive to and through Manzini; bear left 6 km beyond the town, drive past Hlane and look for the Mlawula signposts after Simunye.

■ **Reservations and information:** Bookings: Swaziland National Trust Commission, PO Box 100, Lobamba, Swaziland. Tel: (09268) 6-1151 or 6-1178/9; fax: (09268) 6-1875. Information: Senior Warden, Mlawula Nature Reserve, PO Box 312, Simunye, Swaziland. Tel: (09268) 3-8885.

MKHAYA NATURE RESERVE
This smallish (6 200-hectare) private reserve, situated in Swaziland's acacia-dominated lowveld region to the southeast of Manzini, is the newest and perhaps, for the game spotter, the most rewarding of the country's conservation areas: it sets out to provide a genuine 'into-Africa' experience and the chance to see the larger animals at unusually close quarters, and succeeds admirably in both endeavours.

The reserve, together with Mlilwane, is run by the renowned conservationist Ted Reilly who, some years ago and with the backing of the Swazi royal family, began reintroducing the indigenous game species, many of them threatened or endangered, that had long gone from the area, among them elephant and buffalo, hippopotamus, roan and tsessebe, and the white rhino and its highly vulnerable black cousin. The last-named animal is probably more visible in the Mkhaya nature reserve than in any other Southern African sanctuary.

Also on view are giraffe, zebra, blue wildebeest, kudu, eland and other buck, crocodile, ostrich and a host of small animals. Of the big cats only the leopard is present; other carnivores are the African lynx, the side-striped and black-backed jackal and the occasional spotted hyaena.

The reserve is haven to an impressive number and variety of birds (over an average weekend a keen birder can expect to see more than 120 species), among them some fine raptors: vultures (four species are now nesting in the area, which is heartening – the birds were ruthlessly poisoned during the colonial days), booted, crowned and Wahlberg's eagles, hawk and, also reappearing recently after an absence of two decades, the extravagantly coloured, oddly shaped and remarkably aerobatic bateleur. Other notables include the purplecrested lourie, Swaziland's national bird (its feathers, by tradition, adorn the costumes and regalia of the royal family), the beautiful narina trogon, the brownheaded parrot and the pinkthroated twinspot.

MKHAYA'S CAMP

Safari-type accommodation is provided in the reserve's remarkably attractive Stone Camp, a complex comprising tents, a stone-and-thatch open cottage, and a thatched summerhouse and kitchen built from and among the dolorite boulders.

The 10 tents (some four-bedded, others three-bedded) are comfortably, even luxuriously, fitted out and discreetly sited under the hardwood forest canopy. The stone cottage, named Nkonjane ('swallow's nest'), has two double beds, two single beds and a bathroom. Camp staff prepare meat dishes (game sausage, venison and so on) over the open fire; the bread is homemade; vegetables and fruit are fresh; meals are washed down with soft drink, beer or good South African wine. Lighting is by paraffin lamp; and the night air is filled with the evocative sounds of the bush – the sudden laughter of a hyaena, the bark of a kudu, the call of a nocturnal bird, the cacophany of frogs and crickets. Into Africa indeed.

Game viewing

Mkhaya offers splendid opportunities for observing and photographing animals – and unique ones, possibly, when it comes to black rhino. One cannot, however, set out on self-guided excursions: the terrain is rugged, and some of the roads, bush tracks and river crossings are simply too challenging for private vehicles.

Day and night drives are conducted in open land rovers by expert and very informative rangers whose speciality is the close wildlife encounter. Day tours run between 10 in the morning and four in the afternoon, and lunch is provided. Entry into the park is by prior arrangement; both day and overnight guests are met at the pick-up point just outside the reserve, escorted to the ranger base and transferred to 4x4s. Guided walks bring visitors into even more intimate contact with the wilderness and its residents.

Also on offer (between December and May) are exhilarating one-day trips by raft through the sometimes white, though more often

ABOVE: White-water rafting on the Great Usutu River is for the more intrepid of Mkhaya's guests.
RIGHT: Mkhaya's charming cottage.
OPPOSITE TOP: The Royal Swazi Sun complex.
OPPOSITE BELOW: Ezulwini Sun's leisure area.

gently placid and (generally) crocodile-infested, waters of the Great Usutu River and its Bulungu gorge. Propulsion and navigation are either by oar (which your guide wields: you simply hang on) or by paddle (here everyone pitches in: good teamwork is the key), depending on personal preference and on the mood of the river.

■ **Getting there:** From Mbabane, follow the tarred road to the Big Bend turn-off 6 km beyond Manzini and continue, for 44 km, to Phuzamoyo, which is the pick-up point. Pick-up times are 10h00 and 16h00. Note that *all* visits are by prior appointment. By air: Mkhaya is an hour's drive from Matsapha airport.

■ **Reservations and information:** Central Reservations, Mkhaya Nature Reserve, PO Box 234, Mbabane, Swaziland. Tel: (09268) 4-5006, ext 245; fax: (09268) 4-4246.

HOTELS AND RESORTS

The country boasts a well-developed tourism infrastructure; visitors are well served by hotels ranging from the small and informal to pleasure palaces of five-star quality, complete with gaming rooms and the full range of sporting amenities. Swaziland is, as we have noted, a small country and, wherever you stay, you'll be within easy driving distance of the major game and nature reserves.

ROYAL SWAZI SUN AND CASINO

The resort and its two satellites, the Lugogo Sun and the Ezulwini Sun (see below), are situated in the lovely Ezulwini valley and, together, these elements form Swaziland's premier playground.

The Royal Swazi received its prefix from King Sobhuza II, both in recognition of the huge contribution it makes to the coffers of a relatively poor country and as a tribute to its regal, or at least stately, character. The hotel is set in lushly tropical and superbly land-scaped grounds of sweeping lawn, bright bed-ding, palm, flatbush and crimson flame tree, fountain and sparkling pool. The buildings are grand – enormous public areas, marble floors, chandeliers, mirrors everywhere, and throngs of people.

The hotel has 147 rooms and suites, all of them spacious, some with balconies, and all with views (of golf course or mountain). The nine luxury suites are truly luxurious; two of them are, literally, fit for a king.

Food and drink: The Royal Swazi Sun is part of the Sun International group and, as one might expect, the cuisine is varied and excellent. Most people eat in the Terrace restaurant (buffets with international themes, among much else). Gigi's offers à la carte fare as well as dancing and cabaret. There is a poolside barbecue area.

Amenities: These include the casino, a cine-ma, an expansive swimming pool, and one of the largest open-air aerated spas in the world. There are tennis, squash, bowls and golf at the adjacent country club – the 18-hole course is renowned – and mineral springs (just down the hill) that really do seem to be therapeutic, a gymnasium, a solarium, a sauna and a beauty treatment centre.

Location: A few kilometres to the south of Mbabane and close to the Mlilwane wildlife sanctuary.

Reservations and information: Private Bag, Ezulwini, Swaziland. Tel: (09268) 6-1001, or through Sun International Central Reservations, PO Box 784487, Sandton 2146, South Africa. Tel: (011) 780-7800; fax: (011) 780-7449.

EZULWINI SUN

This is the Royal Swazi Sun's smaller and rather more modest cousin, a rambling place with delightful views of the Ezulwini valley and the mountains. The hotel has 120 air-conditioned and very comfortable two-double-bed rooms, and a splendid outdoor leisure area.

Food and drink: The Forrester's restaurant serves excellent à la carte fare; the poolside terrace is also a popular venue for meals (Italian dishes plus a display by the Sibhaca traditional dancers on Saturdays; Indonesian cuisine on Sundays). Ezulwini Sun also has a popular cocktail bar.

Amenities: The pool, of course; also tennis, horse riding, and the gambling and other enticements at nearby Royal Swazi.

Location: In the Ezulwini valley, just south of Mbabane.

Reservations and information: PO Box 123, Ezulwini, Swaziland. Tel: (09268) 6-1201, or through Sun International Central Reservations, PO Box 784487, Sandton 2146, South Africa. Tel: (011) 780-7800; fax: (011) 780-7449.

LUGOGO SUN

Much the same is on offer here as at the Ezulwini Sun, though this hotel tends to specialise in group hospitality. Accommodation comprises 202 two-double-bed rooms, recently upgraded and pleasant.

Food and drink: The Lugogo's buffets, stir-fries and waffles, enjoyed in the Ilanga restaurant, are famous. There's also a pool terrace and barbecue area; a 'Swazi braai' and a display by the Sibhaca dancers on Saturdays; and a Caribbean buffet on Sundays.

Location: In the Ezulwini valley, just to the south of Mbabane.

Reservations and information: Private Bag, Ezulwini, Swaziland. Tel: (09268) 6-1201, or book through Sun International Central Reservations, PO Box 784487, Sandton 2146, South Africa. Tel: (011) 780-7800; fax: (011) 780-7449.

FORESTERS ARMS

The hotel, an attractive mix of English country inn and pine-scented German forest lodge, with an overlay of pure Africa, is set in the misty, deep-green magic of the Usutu woodlands.

It's a charming place, rather rambling – the buildings seem to have happened by happy accident rather than architectural design. Pine-log fires in the beam-ceilinged public rooms are a pleasant wintertime feature; the clientele tends to be cosmopolitan and very sociable; the 24 bedrooms (the poolside ones are recommended) have delightful views of forest and valley.

Food and drink: À la carte and a set menu; the country-style food is served in an informal atmosphere. The hotel's Sunday buffet-lunches are famous. Meals are preceded by drinks in the wonderfully convivial pub.

Amenities: The grounds are extensive and parklike; there's a swimming pool, sauna and croquet lawn *in situ*. Horse riding and trout fishing (in the six well-stocked dams) are popular pastimes. The forest is crisscrossed by foot and bridle paths. Close by is the Usutu golf club.

Location: The hotel is some 30 km southwest of Mbabane.

Reservations and information: PO Box 14, Mhlambanyatsi, Swaziland. Tel: (09268) 7-4177, 7-4377 or 4-5707; fax: (09268) 7-4051.

MEIKLES MOUNT COUNTRY ESTATE

This guest farm comprises fully equipped cottages set in 300 magnificent hectares of woodland. Seven perennial streams have their sources on the Mount; the hills are mantled by over 100 000 eucalyptus trees (the property produces timber on a commercial basis); the air is clear and sweet, the quietness infinite. Accommodation is in seven thatched, self-contained cottages; each has its bathroom; the largest has three bedrooms. The views are splendid.

Food and drink: One brings one's own; there's a shop on the estate that sells meat, basic provisions and some vegetables. A domestic help keeps your cottage clean and tidy, and will also cook for you.

Amenities: These include a swimming pool, riding stables, tennisette, badminton, croquet, and walking on the forested slopes. Features of the area are enchanting waterfalls, picnic spots and, for climbers, two challenging rock faces. For anglers: yellowfish and bream in the river that borders Meikles Mount – but with its rapids and sandy little beaches, the river is worth exploring even if you're not a fisherman.

Location: 22 km from Mbabane off the Mhlambanyatsi road.

Reservations and information: PO Box 13, Mhlambanyatsi. Tel: (09268) 7-4110.

PHOPHONYANE LODGE

A scatter of self-catering cottages surrounded by a nature reserve in the lovely mountains around Pigg's Peak in northern Swaziland. Waterfalls, rock pools, riverine forest and an entrancing bird life are features of the area.

The 'lodge' in fact comprises three separate little camps; one has the choice of double-storeyed cottages, comfortably appointed and decorated in ethnic style; the luxurious 'Top Cottage' (A-frame; bathrooms *en suite*); and the tented safari camp (the tents have hand-woven cotton carpets, double beds and easy chairs). The main complex's grounds are lush, dense with indigenous flora, and criss-crossed by walkways of timber, stone and gravel. All very attractive.

Food and drink: Guests cater for themselves, though there's also The Dining Hut, a licensed à la carte restaurant at the main camp.

Amenities: Among these are a swimming pool, nature walks, hikes, and bird-watching excursions. Phophonyane is strategically placed for trips to Swaziland's Malolotja reserve and to the Kruger National Park, across the border in the eastern Transvaal. Conducted drives by 4x4 can be arranged.

Location: In northern Swaziland, 3 km off the main road; 70 km from the Kruger park.

Reservations and information: PO Box 199, Pigg's Peak, Swaziland. Tel: (09268) 7-1319.

NHLANGANO SUN AND CASINO HOTEL

The name in Siswati means 'meeting place of the kings', and commemorates the 1947 encounter between England's George VI and Sobhuza II of Swaziland. From the public rooms, two wings of A-frame bedrooms (48 in all) extend like the horns of a Swazi regiment in battle formation; the horns embrace a vast lawn and a swimming pool; beyond is the Makhosini valley.

Food and drink: There is excellent à la carte cuisine, dancing and entertainment in the Makhosini restaurant.

Amenities: These include a small but lively casino, disco and cinema, none of which interferes with the hotel's principal function as a country inn.

OPPOSITE: *The Lugogo Sun in its lovely setting.*
TOP: *Enjoying the view from Phophonyane's 'Top Cottage', one of the lodge's three venues.*
ABOVE: *Guest suite at Phophonyane's main camp.*

Location: Nhlangano is in the southwestern part of the country; the nearest entry point is the Mahamba border post.

Reservations and information: Private Bag, Nhlangano, Swaziland. Tel: (09268) 7-8211; fax: (09268) 7-8402; or through Sun International Central Reservations, PO Box 784487, Sandton 2146, South Africa. Tel: (011) 780-7800; fax: (011) 780-7449.

NAMIBIA & THE KALAHARI

Namibia, a fledgling republic that gained its full independence only in 1990, extends over more than 800 000 km² of the western subcontinent between the Orange River in the south and the Kunene and Okavango rivers in the north – a vast and mostly desolate land of arid deserts and rugged uplands, harsh in its climate and terrain, hauntingly beautiful in its stark emptiness. Major towns are few and far between; the biggest is Windhoek, the nation's capital, which is located at the geographical centre of the country. For visiting motorists, getting about can be a wearisome business: distances are immense, the terrain often monotonous, the heat and dust constant discomforts – but, still, there is something magical about the great Namibian spaces that seduces the senses, and lives in the memory long after the journey is done.

In very broad geophysical terms Namibia can be divided into three regions. A high central plateau runs up, like a spine, from the southern to the northern borders, sloping away on either side to desert. Running parallel to the plateau and fringing the Atlantic Ocean to the west is the Namib, the southern section of which is characterised by gigantic, shifting sand dunes sliced through by ancient underground rivers, their bone-dry beds surprisingly rich in plant life. Farther to the north the dunes give way to a harder plain from which the occasional granite mountain rises. Here the shoreline has been named the Skeleton Coast, a bleak and savagely inhospitable seaboard from which the terrain rises inland to the rugged hills and sparse grasslands of the Kaokoveld. To the east of the central highlands is the Kalahari, commonly termed a desert because its sandy soils cannot retain surface water, but in reality a life-sustaining wilderness that is home to huge numbers of game animals. Most of what Namibia has to offer in terms of wildlife interest, however, is to be found in the plateau's better watered, more fertile northern region which, for the most part, comprises a great alluvial plain created by the Okavango and by the other rivers that flow southwards from Angola to feed the wetlands of northern Botswana and the huge depression known as Etosha Pan.

The famed Etosha National Park is the finest of Namibia's game sanctuaries – but for the natural history enthusiast there are other enticing options. The desert areas, rather surprisingly, support an intriguing diversity of life forms (though they are not featured prominently in these pages). Better endowed are the conservation areas of the north-central grasslands and, especially, the new and still developing Caprivi parks in the moist lushness of the far northeast.

OPPOSITE: Quiver trees, or kokerbooms, stand like silent sentinels in the Namibian twilight.

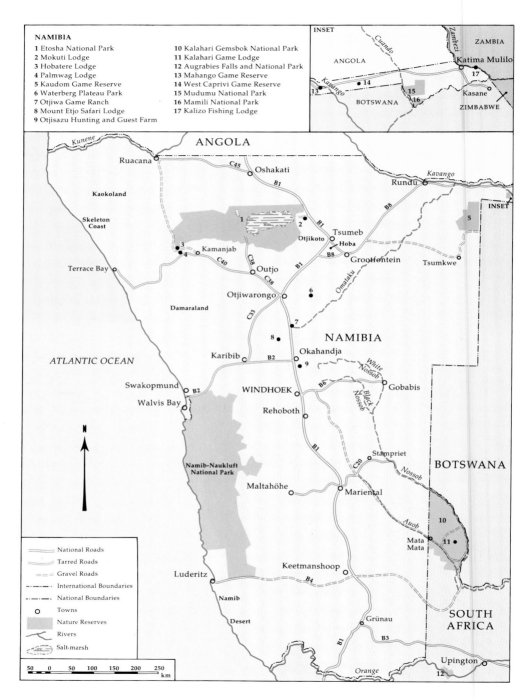

NAMIBIA

1 Etosha National Park
2 Mokuti Lodge
3 Hobatere Lodge
4 Palmwag Lodge
5 Kaudom Game Reserve
6 Waterberg Plateau Park
7 Otjiwa Game Ranch
8 Mount Etjo Safari Lodge
9 Otjisazu Hunting and Guest Farm

10 Kalahari Gemsbok National Park
11 Kalahari Game Lodge
12 Augrabies Falls and National Park
13 Mahango Game Reserve
14 West Caprivi Game Reserve
15 Mudumu National Park
16 Mamili National Park
17 Kalizo Fishing Lodge

INSET

ZAMBIA
ANGOLA
Katima Mulilo
17
Cuando
Zambezi
Kavango
● 14
15
Kasane
16
BOTSWANA
ZIMBABWE

National Roads
Tarred Roads
Gravel Roads
International Boundaries
National Boundaries
○ Towns
Nature Reserves
Rivers
Salt-marsh

50 0 50 100 150 200 250
km

ANGOLA

Kunene
Ruacana
Oshakati
C45
B1
Rundu
Kavango
Kaokoland
B8
INSET
Skeleton
Coast
1
2
B1
5
Tsumeb
Otjikoto
Hoba
3
Kamanjab
C40
B8
Grootfontein
Tsumkwe
4
C38
Terrace Bay
Outjo
B1
C38
Damaraland
C33
6
Otjiwarongo
Omataku
7
ATLANTIC OCEAN
8 ●
NAMIBIA
Karibib
B2
Okahandja
White Nossob
9
Swakopmund
B2
WINDHOEK
B6
Gobabis
Walvis Bay
Black Nossob
Rehoboth
Namib-Naukluft
National Park
B1
Stampriet
C20
BOTSWANA
Maltahöhe
Nossob
Mariental
Auob
10
Mata Mata
11
Luderitz
Keetmanshoop
B4
Namib
Grünau
SOUTH
AFRICA
Desert
B1
B3
Upington
Orange
12

THE NORTH-CENTRAL REGION

The pride of Namibia's parks is located in the great spaces to the north of Windhoek. The name Etosha, it is said, translates as 'place of the mirages' and, although experts differ on the precise meaning of the word, that imagery captures the essence of the pan, or shallow depression that extends across 6 000 km² of the harsh, semi-arid north-central countryside. The pan is the focal part of the famed Etosha National Park.

The region, though, has more to offer the safari traveller. Just over 200 km from the capital is the Waterberg Plateau, a surprisingly well-watered area well worth visiting for both its wildlife and its striking landscapes; elsewhere there are private reserves and game ranches that offer a more personalised, more informative introduction to the Namibian wilderness.

WATERBERG PLATEAU PARK

The plateau, a place of grandly rugged red-sandstone formations and wooded hillsides, emerges abruptly and rather surprisingly from the north-central plains, an island of vivid greenery in an otherwise monochromatic countryside. Steep cliffs on three sides rise to a flattish summit, forming a natural boundary for the 42 000-hectare park and its splendid wildlife. Only where the high ground slopes gently away to the north is there a need for man-made barriers.

The Waterberg gets its name – a refreshing one in this country of deserts and drought – from the life-giving, free-flowing springs of the southern foothills. These sustain thick acacia and wild fig and a profusion of emerald Waterberg ferns, but it is in the higher parts – on the broad grasslands and around the rocky outcrops of the plateau itself – that the flora is at its richest and most varied. Here there are luminescent silver terminalia and the laural fig, bushwillow, wild syringa, flame acacia and wild plum, apple leaf and coffee mimosa and the golden springtime

TOP: *Ovahimba girls of the Kaokoveld region. The forebears of their people, a highly distinctive group that clings tenaciously to the old ways, were Herero herders dispossessed and driven from their eastern lands by the warlike Nama.*
ABOVE: *An all-purpose 'cuca' store (named after an Angolan beer) in Ovamboland.*

glory of weeping wattle, lavendar bush and billowing white bauhinia.

The water and the vegetation, and the natural food sources these create, nurture some 200 different species of bird, among them three kinds of hornbill, coqui francolin, starlings, lovebirds, and a fine array of raptors – Ovambo sparrowhawk, barrel owl, booted and black eagle, rock kestrel, peregrine and lanner falcon, and the country's only breeding colony of the threatened Cape vulture. These last make their home on the cliffs of the Okarukuwisa mountain. In the 1950s there were about 500 of the birds in the park, but changes to the vegetation and the poison put down by the region's stock farmers (to eliminate predators) drastically reduced their numbers. By 1980 there were only 20 or so left. Now the colony is flourishing once more, thanks to controlled bush-burning, the cooperation of surrounding landowners, and the establishment of a 'vulture restaurant'.

The plateau had long been a haven for eland, largest of the Southern African antelope (an adult male weighs in at a full 700 kg), for other buck, and for such carnivores as leopard, cheetah and hyaena. Then, in the late 1960s the authorities, prompted by the closure of the militarily strategic West Caprivi park in the far northeast, decided to turn the Waterberg into a major wildlife sanctuary, the special function of which would be the preservation of rare and endangered animals (including those of the Caprivi: the vegetation types in the two areas are similar), and a large-scale relocation programme was launched. More eland were brought in – there are now over 1 000 in the park – to be followed by giraffe (from the north), blue wildebeest, white rhino (from the northern Natal reserves), buffalo (from the Cape's Addo park), duiker, impala and tsessebe, sable and the rare roan and, in 1989, black rhino from the poacher-plagued Etosha.

All these species are indigenous to the Waterberg, so their translocation was more of a homecoming than an introduction. Nevertheless each is quarantined on arrival, to make sure no diseases are brought in, and then consigned for several weeks to a 1 000-hectare acclimatisation area, where the animal gets the feel of its new home – becomes accustomed to its climate, to the terrain, plant life and predators – before graduating to the wider wilderness.

WATERBERG PLATEAU'S CAMP

An impressive new camp, sited among the southern foothills and named the Bernabé de la Bat after one of Namibia's leading conservators, opened its hospitable gates in mid-1989. A great deal of care went into its design and construction: the red-brick and stone buildings complement the sandstone formations of the area and, all in all, the place blends beautifully into its natural surrounds. The contractors left much of the indigenous vegetation undisturbed; the grounds are graced by gardens and rockeries and by some lovely shrubs and shade trees.

Accommodation is in comfortable, self-contained, five-bed chalets, ordinary three-bed bungalows and what are called 'bus quarters', or 'tourisettes'. There is also an extensive caravan/camping ground.

Visitor amenities include a shop that sells the basics, an information centre, a museum (being developed at the time of writing) and, in the historic and now renovated Rasthaus – which started life in 1908 as a police post, later serving as a guest house – an à la carte restaurant, beer garden and cocktail bar. The renovators wisely retained the building's charming period character; there are splendid views from its windows.

Game viewing

The plateau is not really an 'open' tourist venue. The terrain is rough and most of the roads are rudimentary – deliberately so – so movement around the area is restricted to preserve its untamed character and rare species. Nevertheless the park's directorate provides a specially equipped 4x4; there are also other open vehicles for hire, and an enclosed bus takes visitors on tours. Observation points and carefully sited hides have been established.

Probably the best way to explore the plateau, though, is on foot. Ranger-guided three-day, three-night hikes start on the second, third and fourth Thursday of each month from April through to November; groups leave from Onjoka and stay overnight at a small camp in the wilderness atop the plateau. No fixed routes have been laid out – again a deliberate omission to lessen the environmental impact. Hikers follow game paths, gullies and dry river beds. Shorter walking trails have also been charted.

■ **Getting there:** By road from Windhoek, take the B1 north; after some 200 km turn right onto the C101 and follow the road for 42 km before turning left for the Waterberg. The last 26-km stretch is gravelled.
■ **Reservations and information:** The Ministry of Wildlife, Conservation and Tourism, Private Bag 13267, Windhoek 9000, Namibia. Tel: (061) 3-6975/6/7/8 (reservations) and (061) 3-3875 (information); fax: (061) 22-4900. Telephone bookings can be difficult: the lines tend to be busy.

OTJISAZU HUNTING AND GUEST FARM

Otjisazu in the Herero language means 'land of the red cattle', and this is indeed a working ranch, but it is also a three-star guest establishment – the highest possible rating in Namibia. It is situated in the wide, sunlit, bush-covered plains of the central region, 100 km north of Windhoek, its homestead an attractive and historic complex (it was built in 1872 as a mission station) of main house and nine pleasantly appointed *en suite* double rooms. Your amiable hosts are Hagen and Allison Detering.

The homestead's grounds are refreshingly green, graced by tall shade trees, traversed by walkways; and the pleasant pool beckons during the hot midday hours. Activities include horse and pony rides, and health courses (specially contrived health menus, plus supervised exercise).

Otjisazu's restaurant (there is also an outdoor eating area) recently won an award for its service and ambience, and for Allison's cuisine. The culinary routine provides for a full breakfast (English, American or German), a three-course lunch and a light meal in the evening. The barbecue fare – venison cooked over camelthorn coals – is delicious. The guest farm is fully licensed.

Game viewing

Otjisazu caters, and does so very well, for the safari photographer, the trophy hunter, and the lover of the great wilderness spaces. The wildlife complement is not nearly as varied and spectacular as that of, say, Etosha farther to the north, but there is plenty to see; game animals include mountain and plains zebra, springbok, blesbok, impala and the magnificent eland. Bird life is surprisingly prolific and interesting. On offer are game drives, pony treks and walking trails.

The hunting season runs from the beginning of February to the end of November; trophy hunters have access to an impressive 89 000 hectares of Otjisazu and other properties in the northeastern and eastern parts of the country. Otjisazu's 10-day package takes in six days' hunting and bird-shooting, a two-day excursion to Swakopmund on the coast, and two days spent among the splendours of the Etosha National Park.

■ **Getting there:** By road from Windhoek, follow the main road north to Okahandja (70 km); turn right on to the D2102 and continue for 27 km, to the Otjisazu signpost. If you are arriving at Windhoek by air, Hagen will meet you at the airport and drive you to Otjisazu.

■ **Reservations and information:** Hagen and Allison Detering, Otjisazu, PO Box 149, Okahandja 9000, Namibia. Tel: 06228 (Okahandja), ask for farmline 8-1640. Windhoek telephone and fax number: (061) 3-7483.

OTJIWA GAME RANCH

A two-star guest farm located in the north-central thornveld country some 220 km from Windhoek, Otjiwa is an all-purpose, relatively inexpensive venue that caters as much for the family holidaymaker as for the serious game viewer.

Otjiwa is a member of the Namib-Sun hotel group. Accommodation is in three camps. The main one comprises a cluster of 12 'park homes' (singles, doubles and four-bed family units, all with private bathrooms) and a central complex of restaurant and campfire barbecue area (Namibian venison is quite superb), lounge, cocktail bar, swimming pool and, close by, a children's playground and a conference venue.

The other two camps, Hilltop and The Nest, are much smaller and exclusive: they provide self-contained accommodation for eight people; Hilltop is eight kilometres from the main complex, The Nest is four kilometres, and their guests have full use of Otjiwa's dining and recreational amenities (courtesy transport is laid on).

Game viewing

The ranch is home to various kinds of game animal, including white rhino, eland, kudu, gemsbok and waterbuck. On offer are guided drives and hikes through the bush. Packed lunches are provided.

■ **Getting there:** The guest farm is on the B1 route north, between Okahandja and Otjwarongo.

■ **Reservations and information:** Namib-Sun Hotels, PO Box 2862, Windhoek 9000, Namibia. Tel: (061) 3-3145; fax: (061) 3-4512. Local address: Otijwa Game Ranch, PO Box 1231, Otjiwarongo 9000, Namibia. Tel and fax: (0658) 1-1002.

MOUNT ETJO SAFARI LODGE

Situated in the north-central part of Namibia some 250 km from Windhoek, Mount Etjo is one of Southern Africa's better endowed and more luxuriously attractive private game lodges (though technically it is classed as a guest farm), the broad savanna and woodland spaces of its reserve blessed with a generous number of waterholes and dams and a fine profusion of wildlife. Much of the latter has been reintroduced to the area, including elephant, giraffe and white rhino, mountain and plains zebra, blue wildebeest, kudu, eland, red hartebeest, roan antelope, blesbok, gemsbok, nyala and impala. Predators are represented by lion, leopard and cheetah; the waterholes attract a great many birds.

In the late 1980s the lodge hosted leading politicians, diplomats and officials involved in the painfully protracted but ultimately successful Namibian peace process leading to the country's full independence in 1990. This says a lot about Mount Etjo's character: accommodation and amenities are at the top of the range. Guests have a choice of hotel-type rooms, each with its private bathroom. The lodge has sophisticated conference, bar and restaurant facilities (dinner is usually served in the spacious boma) and a swimming pool.

Game viewing

This is outstanding: hides have been established at several of the watering places; at one, buck carcasses are left out for the lions, which creates fine opportunities for close-up observation and photography. The lodge lays on ranger-guided game drives in open safari vehicles, and conducted bush walks. Of passing interest are the fossil footprints to be seen on the nearby farm Otjihaenomaparero.

TOP: *The green and pleasant grounds of the Mount Etjo lodge. Accommodation is luxurious.* ABOVE: *Mount Etjo guests on a game drive.*

There are several tracks, the most prominent that of a 150-million-year-old kangaroo-like dinosaur. Also in the vicinity are caves once inhabited by Bushmen.

■ **Getting there:** By road from Windhoek, follow the main route north for about 135 km, turning left on to the 2483 (dirt road) towards Kalkfeld. You will see the Mount Etjo sign on your right. By air: the lodge has its own airstrip.

■ **Reservations and information:** Mount Etjo Safari Lodge, PO Box 81, Kalkfeld 9205, Namibia. Tel: 06532, ask for 1602; fax: 06532, ask for 44.

ETOSHA NATIONAL PARK

For most of the year, from about March to November, Etosha Pan presents a strange, infinitely austere winterscape of hard, dazzlingly white flatland where the air shimmers in the heat and mirages deceive the eye. The physical origins of this remarkable feature – it is 130 km at its longest, 50 km at its widest – are also something of a mystery. The legend of the Heiqum (who are sometimes, but incorrectly, referred to as Bushmen) has it that a group of strangers once wandered into the region and were set upon by hunters, who killed all the men and the children, and the tears of the women made a great sea. The waters were then drawn up by the sun, leaving only salt. Science has a more prosaic explanation: millennia ago the depression was a vast lake fed by the waters of the Kunene before that river, at some point in the distant past and for reasons that can only be guessed at, changed its course. The lake dried out, bequeathing a briny, mineral-rich, dead-flat plain – a 'salt desert' of hard, deeply cracked clay incapable of sustaining life. (Elsewhere, though, the terrain is more hospitable, much of it covered by sparse but sweet grasses, deciduous trees, acacia and mopane woodlands.)

But the saline and mineral residues of the pan, and the moisture from the summer rains and the overflowing rivers – which combine to fill the cracks, to lie in pools and, sometimes, in exceptional years, to re-create

the ancient lake itself – attract an immense number and variety of game animals, and birds too. The waters sustain, briefly, a rich profusion of micro-organic life, which in turn entices thousands of flamingoes. The birds migrate to the pan to breed, and to do so they must race against time, for when the water evaporates at the end of summer the predators move in.

The pan is the centrepiece of the Etosha National Park, pride of Namibia and one of Africa's finest wildlife sanctuaries. A few decades ago the proclaimed area covered nearly 100 000 km^2, which made it the world's largest natural reserve, but in the mid-1960s political considerations intervened – parts of it were hived off to make room for ethnic 'homelands' – and its area is now a more modest, though still very impressive, 23 000 km^2.

Etosha park is haven for about 2 500 elephant; for rhino and giraffe; lion, leopard and cheetah; spotted and brown hyaena; for 7 000 zebra, 2 600 blue wildebeest; for eland, kudu, red hartebeest, springbok, gemsbok, roan antelope; for the rare black-faced impala and the tiny Damara dik-dik (see page 146) and many other buck: altogether, 93 different types of mammal have been listed (the avifauna is equally varied: well over 300 species, ranging from miniscule prinias to the giant ostrich, are found in the park).

The rhino population includes some 300 of the highly endangered black variety,

LEFT: *Some of the Etosha park's 2 500 elephant. These animals are voracious, and their growing numbers pose a serious threat to the environment.* TOP: *Zebra slake their thirst at a waterhole. The animals are gregarious, inquisitive, and endowed with exceptionally keen eyesight and hearing.* ABOVE: *Giraffe are preyed upon only by lion.*

descendants of 43 animals captured in Kaokoland and Damaraland in the 1960s and translocated to flourish (at least initially) in Etosha – in striking contrast to the situation in Africa as a whole, where the species, prime target of the poacher, has suffered a 95 per cent numerical decline during the past 20 years. It would perhaps be too much to hope that the poachers will prove kinder to Etosha and indeed, now that it is probably the most tempting of the few remaining sanctuaries, they are establishing an ominous presence in the park. On the other hand various counter-measures are in force, others being considered, and perhaps one of them – dehorning the animals, for instance – will make the difference between survival and extinction.

At one time the animals of Etosha were wholly free, able to roam at will over the wider northern region, going where the seasons dictated. But then, with the consolidation of the area, the fences went up and this, together with veld-fire control, and other well-intentioned moves that altered the ecosystem's emphasis from savanna to woodland, had its effect on migration patterns and the intricate balance between the wildlife species. It was by no means a traumatic effect (the park is big enough to remain ecologically coherent, and to continue to accommodate all its original fauna) but there were changes in the relative numbers of game. The blue wildebeest and Burchell's zebra declined, for instance, as did a cheetah population faced with increased competition from other predators (notably lion), while giraffe, elephant and lion thrived.

The rapid growth of the elephant herds has been especially dramatic. In 1955 the park held between 50 and 100 individuals; now there are about 2 500, which poses a particularly serious environmental problem. These animals are voracious and destructive feeders. If the herd is allowed to become too large for the available space the consequences for the habitat can be devastating. The usual (and obvious) answer is kill off the surplus, though up to now Etosha's conservationists have been lukewarm in their support for this

ABOVE: Okaukuejo's water tower, from which there are fine views of the game-rich plains. OPPOSITE TOP: The waterhole at Okaukuejo – floodlit at night, and a magnet for the animals. OPPOSITE BELOW: The pool at Okaukuejo camp.

approach. A much happier solution to the proliferation of lion is being explored. Here, time-release contraceptive capsules have been implanted into some of the females, which will hopefully lower the birth rate without reducing the gene pool.

ETOSHA'S CAMPS

There are three of these, strung out on the long road running east-west past the southern shores of the pan. All offer comfort, without too much in the way of luxurious trimmings, in self-catering bungalows and rooms. There are caravan/camping grounds at all three. Each rest camp has a swimming pool, picnic spots, a licensed restaurant, and a shop that sells dry goods, frozen meat, barbecue firewood, alcoholic beverages, maps and information booklets. Petrol is on sale at all of them; a qualified mechanic at Okaukuejo undertakes minor repairs. Book well in advance: demand is heavy, especially during the South African school holidays.

There are two park public entrance gates: the Von Lindequist, 11 km from Namutoni, and the Anderssen, 17,5 km from Okaukuejo. The camps are open from sunrise to sunset; leave yourself plenty of daylight time to get to them after passing through the gates.

The private Mokuti Lodge is just outside the Von Lindequist gate. Otjovasandu camp in

lights don't appear to bother the animals at all) attracts all manner of wildlife, including lion and elephant, black rhino, and spotted and brown hyaena. The night watch is a magical experience. Rising high above the camp is its water tower, from the top of which there are fine views of the plains and the hills beyond (these are known, rather improbably, as the Ondundozonananandana Mountains). The camp has an information centre; on view are displays illustrating the nature of and life within Etosha.

Clustered around the waterhole are the accommodation units, which comprise:
❑ Luxury two-bedroomed rondavels, each with a kitchen, a shower and a toilet
❑ Ordinary one-roomed bungalows with two beds, a washbasin, a shower, a toilet and a kitchenette
❑ One-bedroomed, two-bed 'bus quarters' or 'tourisettes' (bath, toilet) accommodate visitors who arrive by coach
❑ Tents sleeping four people, with communal facilities
❑ An extensive caravan/camping ground with communal facilities.

the far west (reached via the Galton gate) did not, at the time of writing, offer tourist accommodation: it serves primarily as a base for the conservators who look after rare and endangered wildlife.

OKAUKUEJO, Etosha's administrative centre, is the most westerly of the public rest camps and, for instant game-viewing, the most rewarding: its superb waterhole, which as mentioned is illuminated at night (the bright

HALALI Midway between Okaukuejo and Namutoni and fairly recently upgraded, Halali is a pleasant, tree-shaded camp – attractive enough to boast an established walk within its bounds. A waterhole with floodlights has also been created. Here there are two-bedroomed luxury bungalows (kitchen, shower, toilet), ordinary one-bedroomed bungalows with two beds (communal facilities), 'bus quarters' or 'tourisettes' (bath and toilet), and a caravan/camping ground.

NAMUTONI This is an unusual and, in the game-park context, unique place: its focus is a romantic, palm-girded, Beau Geste-type fort built by the German military colonists in the first years of the century. In the early days its commander, First Lieutenant Adolf Fischer (who became a renowned conservationist) and its garrison acted as warden and rangers respectively of the three large nature reserves, among them one around Etosha Pan, that were proclaimed in 1907. The fort was occupied by South African forces after their defeat of the Germans in 1915, declared a national monument in 1950 and, after extensive renovation, welcomed its first tourists in

1957. Today's visitors are still lodged in the building. The two- (with toilet and bath) and three-bed (with communal facilities) rooms are ordinary enough (the 'bus quarters' are outside the walls), but the setting is splendid. Shades of the military past are all around: the whitewashed battlements served a very real purpose not so very long ago; bugles call and flags are raised and lowered at each end of the day; and there is a little museum in the lookout tower. An adjacent complex houses a restaurant and fully stocked shop, and the good German-style beer goes down a treat after a long spell on the dusty plains.

Game viewing

This is excellent throughout the year: the countryside is generally open; the wildlife remarkably prolific and relatively 'tame' – the animals seem accustomed to and unafraid of human presence (though visitors should treat a breeding herd of elephant with great circumspection). Tour parties are of course conducted; self-guided drives are the norm. Large parts of the park are off limits, but there is an extensive network of roads connecting the three camps with waterholes and viewing spots. The routes are well maintained (road gangs are on permanent duty), but they can become rough in wet weather and so dusty during the winter months that one's vision is obscured. At these times the waterholes – there are about 30 of them in the central and eastern regions – are a lot more rewarding. And rather than make a tour of them, as you would in most parks, select just one, settle down to wait, and be patient: you'll have a clear view, and the animals will sooner or later make their appearance – simply because there is precious little water for them elsewhere. The game is especially concentrated towards the end of winter (October and November); in the rainy reason it tends to disperse to the west.

Tourist officers at the camps will advise you on the best viewing spots at any given time, though if you're staying at Okaukuejo you don't really have to leave the grounds: the waterhole here is very well patronised, and you can observe the parade in comfort, from behind a low wall, both during the day and, by floodlight, at night. Among other venues and their special attractions are:

❏ Klein Namutoni waterhole near the Namutoni rest camp (probably the best place to see black-faced impala)
❏ The extensive Fischer's Pan, also near Namutoni (springbok, wildebeest, and good bird-watching)
❏ The road between Okaukuejo and Namutoni (views of Etosha Pan, and digressions leading down to waterholes)
❏ The Bloubokdraai road (for Damara dik-dik)
❏ Chudob waterhole, 7 km from Namutoni (a reed-fringed artesian spring which attracts many game species, known especially for its eland and giraffe)
❏ Batia, between Namutoni and Halali (elephant, blue wildebeest and springbok)
❏ Andoni (the northernmost waterhole, a swampy place rich in bird life)
❏ Salvadora, Sueda and Charitsaub (a cluster of waterholes between Okaukuejo and Halali, teeming with plains game, and cheetah)

OPPOSITE: Lion are among the 93 mammal species to be found within Etosha.
ABOVE: The historic fort at Etosha's Namutoni.

❏ The far west of Etosha (for summertime game viewing, and to see some of the rarer species, for which an extensive predator-free zone has been created; the public has limited access to the area).

■ **Getting there:** By road from Windhoek to Okaukuejo, follow the road north via Otjiwarongo and Outjo (distance to the Anderssen gate: 447 km). From Windhoek to Namutoni, go via Otjiwarongo and Tsumeb (distance to the Von Lindequist gate: 553 km); the road is tarred all the way. By air: there are scheduled flights from Windhoek's Eros airport via Mokuti to Tsumeb, where Avis car hire is represented (see Visitor's Advisory, page 306-7). Each of the camps also has its own airstrip; private pilots must arrange landings in advance with the relevant camp authority. Transport from airstrip to camp is undertaken by a private concern operating within the park. Aerofuel is not available at Etosha.
■ **Reservations and information:** The Ministry of Wildlife, Conservation and Tourism, Private Bag 13267, Windhoek 9000, Namibia. Tel: (061) 3-6975/6/7/8 (reservations) and (061) 3-3875 (information); fax (061) 224900. Telephone bookings can be difficult: the lines tend to be busy.

ETOSHA'S UNUSUAL ANTELOPE

The Damara dik-dik (*Madoqua kirkii*) is the smallest and perhaps the most endearing of Etosha's bovids: an adult weighs in at a mere five kilograms and stands no higher than 400 mm at the shoulder (which are the approximate dimensions of a scrub hare). The animal, whose rather odd name is thought to derive from the sharp, squeaky grunt it emits when disturbed, is distinguished by its long, mobile, trunk-like snout, by the tuft of hair on its brow, and by its tiny false hoof. Only the males have horns, which are spiky, ringed and about 10 cm long.

Dik-diks are not especially gregarious: one usually sees them alone or in pairs, or in family groups of three (and occasionally, in the dry winter months, in parties of up to six). They are shy creatures, elusive to the eye: 'Even when running,' wrote one zoologist (GC Shortridge, in the 1930s), 'the shadows cast are more conspicuous than the animals themselves as they vanish like wisps of smoke.' Generally speaking, they keep to the sheltering woodland and scrub on the fringes of rocky outcrops and hills, and to riverine thickets that act as avenues to the semi-desert country that is their natural habitat. Their diet comprises high-nutrient plants – seed pods, leaves, fruits and so on – which they search for, and test, by extending their proboscis-like snouts this way and that. Much of their day is spent in rumination.

These antelope occur in two quite separate regions of the continent – northern Namibia extending to southern Angola, and East Africa. The groups are divided by a distance of some 2 000 km, and there is no intermediate distribution.

The second of Etosha's more noteworthy bovids is the black-faced impala, a comparatively rare animal: there are only about 1 000 of them in existence, all in northern Namibia. At one time the animal and its more common cousin were thought to be separate species but they are now considered too closely related. Still, there are very clear differences between the two: the black-faced variety is heavier (63 kg compared to 50 kg) and darker in colouring, and its face and ears have black markings. Its tail is also bushier and its coat duller, lacking the rich reddish-brown of the ordinary impala.

LEFT: *The graceful black-faced impala.*
BELOW: *The Damara dik-dik.*

Mokuti Lodge

The word 'lodge' tends to be a little misleading: this is not your classically rugged safari establishment, but rather a most attractive three-star hotel that offers two major inducements: a touch of easeful elegance in an otherwise uncompromisingly harsh environment, and close proximity to one of Africa's most outstanding game sanctuaries.

Mokuti is sited just 500 m from Etosha park's eastern (Von Lindequist) gate and 12 km from its historic Namutoni camp, and it has all the comforts: a pool set in the green lushness of lawn and shade tree; restaurants, cocktail bars, spaciously cool public rooms and agreeable private ones. Accommodation is in thatched, airconditioned luxury chalets (double bed, bathroom *en suite*, cane-furnished lounge with TV, mini-bar); two-bedroomed (five-bed) family chalets, and two-bed double 'tourist rooms' – 96 units in all.

The lodge has two restaurants, each named after an indigenous tree: à la carte fare is served in the Tambuti (the menu is smallish but thoughtfully contrived; try the venison) and a lavish buffet/carvery in the Onduli. The décor of both is very African. There are, though, other culinary options: lunch is usually taken in casual style next to the pool or on the thatched verandah; barbecues are enjoyed in the firelit boma. Drinks are offered in either the Marula or the pool bar.

Among on-site facilities are a tour operator, curio shop, petrol outlet and an Avis agency.

Game viewing

Namib Wilderness Safaris, based at Mokuti Lodge, lays on day tours to and through Etosha park; the guides are experienced and they know where to go for the best game viewing. One can also of course embark on self-guided drives; packed lunches are provided. Closer to home, the lodge's grounds are also worth exploring, especially by bird lovers: Mokuti has its own 100 hectares of natural bush, through which there runs a nature trail. On the property, too, is the Klein Begin game reserve, a recently launched project (animals are still being introduced).

Mokuti Lodge, next door to Etosha, is an oasis of comfort in a harsh land.

■ **Getting there:** Either drive from Windhoek (the road is tarred all the way), or take one of the scheduled flights from Windhoek's Eros airport to Tsumeb (Avis car hire is represented in the town; alternatively, Mokuti will organise transport to the lodge); or take the twice-weekly flight from Eros directly to the lodge. The 19-seater Beechcraft turbo-prop flights leave Windhoek on Tuesdays and Thursdays.

■ **Reservations and information:** Mokuti Lodge, PO Box 403, Tsumeb 9000, Namibia. Tel: (0671) 3084; fax: (0671) 3084. Namib-Sun Central Reservations, PO Box 2862, Windhoek 9000, Namibia. Tel: (061) 3-3145; fax: (061) 3-4512.

Hobatere Lodge

Hobatere is billed as the 'Gateway to Damaraland', the wonderfully unspoilt northwestern region that is home to the famed desert elephants – and to a surprising number of other game species. The three-star lodge, surrounded by its own 35 000-hectare reserve (one of five concession areas in Damaraland), is close to the undeveloped western section of Etosha National Park and some 200 km from Etosha's Okaukuejo camp. This is an exclusive place, relaxed, friendly, run by dedicated conservationists and geared to the more discerning game enthusiast and photographer.

A maximum of 22 guests can be accommodated in the 11 comfortable, two-bedroomed *en suite* units. Among the lodge's central amenities are a lounge, a dining room, a

PALMWAG LODGE

Even more remote than Hobatere, Palmwag and its surrounding concession area are the base from which Desert Adventure Safaris (DAS) operates. Here too you will find the desert elephant, and much else. Palmwag, set among fan palms beside a perennial spring (in the otherwise dry Uniab River), has a rest camp of reed huts, which boast all the amenities except a kitchen (cooking poses a fire hazard). There are outdoor barbecue areas, however, and à la carte meals are served in the restaurant. There is also a companionable pub, and two swimming pools.

boma and barbecue area and, that most welcome antidote to the fierce heat of a Damaraland day, a swimming pool. A rustic bush camp, situated four kilometres from the lodge, can accommodate a further 16 people.

Game viewing

Apart from the desert-adapted elephant, this desolate, beautiful area is home to, among others, lion, leopard, various kinds of buck and to an intriguing bird life: Hobatere's specially devised ornithological excursions introduce visitors to such typical Namibian species as the Damara rockjumper and the barecheeked babbler. There are game drives in open vehicles, both by day and by night, and guided nature walks. Also on offer are day visits to the western Etosha National Park (which has only recently been opened, on a restricted basis, to tourists). One can explore this pristine region's broad plains, granite outcrops and ranges of dolomite hills in the company of a Hobatere guide.

■ **Getting there:** By road from Windhoek, take the main route north to Otjiwarongo and Outjo and then to and through Kamanjab, following the route to Ruacana. The Hobatere signpost is about 65 km beyond Kamanjab; from there, the lodge is another 15 km away. By air: Hobatere has its own airstrip.
■ **Reservations and information:** Hobatere Lodge, PO Box 110, Kamanjab 9000, Namibia. Tel: 0020, ask for Kamanjab 2022.

ABOVE: One of Hobatere's neat rondavels.
RIGHT: Palmwag panorama.

Game viewing

Among the game species to be found are elephant and black rhino, the habits of the latter – like those of the elephant – uniquely adapted to the harshness of their bone-dry environment (and threatened here, as everywhere else, by poachers). There are also giraffe, mountain zebra, kudu, gemsbok and steenbok. Visitors with 4x4s can follow the many and rather rugged tracks that traverse the area – Palmwag's staff will give practical advice on routes – but it would probably be wiser to put yourself entirely in DAS's capable hands and book a guided safari.

■ **Getting there:** Desert Adventure Safaris will handle their clients' travel arrangements. Independent guests are advised to take the route from Windhoek north through Otjiwarongo, Outjo and Kamanjab and then along the D3706 (the signpost is Sesfontein). The turn-off to the lodge is 6 km along the D3706. An alternative route is eastwards from Torra Bay on the coast. Guests can be flown in from Swakopmund or Windhoek on request.

■ **Reservations and information:** Desert Adventure Safaris, PO Box 1428, Swakopmund 9000, Namibia. Tel: (0641) 4072 or 4459 (after hours: 4054); fax: (0641) 4664.

KAUDOM GAME RESERVE

The 385 000-hectare Kaudom, flanking the Botswana border in the northeast of the country – the region known as Bushmanland – is one of Namibia's newest conservation areas: a rugged, rather featureless expanse of dry Kalahari sandveld, much of it covered by acacia and leadwood, Rhodesian teak, false mopane and manketi.

To get there one drives via Tsumkwe; the last sandy stretch of road is negotiable only by four-wheel-drive. There are also tracks leading in from the north. Visitors must by regulation travel in convoys of at least two 4x4s, and self-sufficiency is the order: stock up beforehand with plenty of petrol, spares, food and water. The tracks are rough; sand makes the going heavy; the most rewarding routes are those that follow the courses of the dry and ancient rivers of the region, along which there are occasional watering places, some fed by springs.

This is a remote land indeed – but well worth exploring if you're an adventurous spirit, and if you want to see Africa and its wildlife at their most pristine. A less troublesome and probably less expensive option is to book with a safari operator, of which two offered trips to the park at the time of writing: Charly's Desert Tours, PO Box 1400, Swakopmund 9000, Namibia; Tel: (0641) 4341; and Namib Wilderness Safaris, PO Box 6850, Windhoek 9000, Namibia; Tel: (061) 22-5178. The latter's Johannesburg address is: PO Box 651171, Benmore 2010, South Africa; Tel: (011) 884-1458.

KAUDOM'S CAMPS

There are two of these, both very small: Sikereti in the south and Kaudom in the north. Both offer four-bed huts, a camp site, a barbecue area and communal bathroom facilities (water is heated by a donkey boiler; the toilets flush). The huts, built of kiaat wood, are rustic, evocative of the 'real' Africa, and each is simply furnished with a table, chairs, and four beds and mattresses (visitors must bring their own bedding). Note that the camps are not fenced.

ABOVE: *A kudu senses danger.*
OPPOSITE: *The north-eastern plains, dry for most of the year but covered by sweet grasses that are enriched by the brief rains of summer.*

Game viewing

The Kaudom is well endowed with game and especially so when the rains enrich the grasslands. The viewing, though, is at its best in the dry winter months, when the animals – elephant and lion, giraffe, wildebeest, spotted hyaena, wild dog, eland, roan and gemsbok among others – stay near the waterholes.

■ **Getting there:** Four-wheel-drives are mandatory. From the south, go via Grootfontein, Tsumkwe and Klein Dobe (the final 60-km stretch is very sandy). From the north, travel via Rundu and along the southern bank of the Okavango, turning south at Katere (the final 44-km stretch is very sandy). Check the condition of the route beforehand.
■ **Reservations and information:** The Ministry of Wildlife, Conservation and Tourism, Private Bag 13267, Windhoek 9000, Namibia. Tel: (061) 3-6975/6/7/8 (reservations) and (061) 3-3875 (information).

THE CAPRIVI REGION

The Caprivi 'strip' is a long (482 km) and narrow (35-80 km) panhandle probing eastwards from the Mahango game reserve and the Okavango to and along the Zambezi River, its extremity the meeting point of Namibia, Zambia, Zimbabwe and Botswana.

This is a land of rivers, some of them many-named. The Okavango flows for some 1 600 km southeast from Angola (where it is known as the Kubango), forming part of Namibia's northern border before slicing through West Caprivi and into the Kalahari regions of Botswana, where it empties into the immensity of the Okavango wetlands. For the local Kavango and Caprivi peoples the river and its inundations are life itself, nurturing the land, sustaining the herders and their cattle, and serving as a broad thoroughfare for the mokoros – the traditional dugout canoes – of the fishermen. The Zambezi, largest of the waterways, rolls eastward to plunge over the Victoria Falls 80 km from Kazungula. Fringing much of Caprivi's southern boundary is the Linyanti River (also known as the Chobe for part of its course); to the west, bisecting the strip, is the Kwando.

All very complicated – not only in geographical terms but in historical ones too. Caprivi is an oddity, one of the more eccentric legacies of that extraordinary flurry of 19th-century European expansionism known as the Scramble for Africa which, here, prompted an attempt by the German imperialists to link their western and eastern possessions in Africa by means of a 1 500-km cross-continental corridor. The region was militarily strategic during the low-intensity but hugely destructive bush war of the 1970s and 1980s, and remains largely undeveloped. It does, however, boast four superb conservation areas, some of them shot out during the war but now recovering. Each of them is enriched by one or more of the rivers.

LEFT: *The Zambezi River at Katima Mulilo, principal centre of the Caprivi panhandle.*

MAHANGO GAME RESERVE

Like the Kaudom (see page 150), the Mahango is a new area, but is much smaller (it is just 25 000 hectares in extent) than its sandy southern neighbour and quite different in character. This is an ecologically diverse, magical expanse of grassland and broadleafed woodland, floodplain, lush riverine forest, and reed and papyrus bed, all of these elements combining to sustain a wonderful variety of animals, birds and plants.

Much of the reserve is enriched by the Okavango River; hippo and crocodile abound; giant baobabs, wild date palms and a profusion of other tropical flora flourish in the fertile alluvial soil; among the 60 mammals present are four of the 'big five' – elephant, buffalo, lion and leopard – together with cheetah, wild dog, spotted and brown hyaena, blue wildebeest, reedbuck, bushbuck, kudu, oribi and other buck, and a splendid array of smaller species. The bird life is fascinating: there isn't a complete list yet, but among what is believed to be more than 300 species are such notables as the hamerkop (the 'bird of doom' in African lore), lappet-faced and whitebacked vultures, western and banded snake eagles, Pel's fishing owl and African fish eagle.

There are no overnight facilities within the Mahango game reserve, but the Popa Falls rest camp lies 15 km north of the entrance and the privately run Suclabo Lodge, situated between Mahango and Popa Falls, offers basic accommodation.

POPA FALLS REST CAMP This attractive cluster of chalets is set on the Okavango River, near the four-metre-high waterfall that is best seen in the dry season – during the rains the higher flow obscures its modest drop. The chalets are built of hard wild teak and thatch; visitors have the use of a field kitchen and communal bathroom facilities. There is excellent tiger-fishing in the river; and pleasant walks on *terra firma* and, when the Okavango's level is low enough, over boulders to some of the islands (which are rich in bird life). Footbridges lead from river bank to one or two of the larger islands.

Reservations and information: Ministry of Wildlife, Conservation and Tourism, Private Bag 13267, Windhoek 9000, Namibia. Tel: (061) 3-6975/ 6/7/8 (reservations) and (061) 3-3875 (information); fax: (061) 22-4900.

BELOW: Chalets at the Popa Falls rest camp.
OPPOSITE LEFT: Canoeing on the Kwando River.
OPPOSITE RIGHT: Sunset over the West Caprivi.

Suclabo Lodge Again, there are not many refinements on offer here, but there's plenty of atmosphere, and plenty of things to see and do. Suclabo is very Out of Africa, German-run, the clientele interesting, the food sustaining, and the beer cool and good. Accommodation is in basic huts and a camp site. There is a swimming pool, but it is the river that entices: the lodge lays on tiger-fishing, rafting, and mokoro dug-out excursions, boat trips to the Popa waterfall and to the islands, as well as visits to the nearby Mahango game reserve.

Reservations and information: Suclabo Lodge, PO Box 894, Rundu 9000. Tel: (067372) 6222.

Game viewing

Two roads lead through the reserve, one of which is part of the main route from Namibia to Shakawe in Botswana, the other suitable only for four-wheel-drive vehicles. Petrol is usually available at the turn-off to the reserve. From the picnic site on the river bank one can view the Okavango and its myriad life forms. Here, a dip in the cooling waters may appear inviting, but beware the crocodiles.

WEST CAPRIVI GAME RESERVE

The reserve covers an enormous part of the western segment of the 'strip' between the Okavango and Kwando rivers and, until the peace agreement of 1989, was out of bounds to casual visitors. The area is destined to become one of Namibia's most splendid eco-tourism destinations.

Environmentally the West Caprivi is very similar to the Mahango reserve – savanna, woodland, lush floodplain and riverine forest. The fauna is more or less the same, too: here you can expect (or rather, hope) to spot elephant, buffalo, lion, reedbuck, water-buck and, of course, the ubiquitous hippo and croc. The water-related bird life is magnificent, seen at its best perhaps on a boat ride past the islands and sandbanks.

A good gravel road runs from west to east through the West Caprivi (there are modern bridges over the rivers at either end). Kalizo Fishing and Photographic Safaris (see page 158) operate fully equipped photographic excursions into the reserve.

MUDUMU NATIONAL PARK

This 85 000-hectare conservation area flanks the Kwando River close to its dissipation into the Linyanti swamp (see Mamili, page 157), a splendid wetland in which crocodile and hippo and tropically colourful birds flourish. Larger animals to be found around the swamp and in the adjacent savanna and woodland country include elephant, buffalo, zebra, giraffe, sable, roan antelope, kudu, the water-adapted sitatunga and the lechwe.

Carnivores are represented by cheetah, lion, leopard, spotted hyaena and wild dog. Bird life: 450 species have been identified, among which are Pel's fishing owl, fish eagle, narina trogon, painted snipe and rock pratincole.

LIANSHULU LODGE is a complex of eight attractive reed-and-thatch chalets and an expansive lounge and leisure area, all overlooking the waters of the Kwando. The units are comfortably fitted out; each has *en suite* facilities (hot water on tap), and guests have the welcome use of a plunge-pool. Mealtimes are sociable affairs: the lodge is known for its excellent cuisine; dinner is preceded by

ABOVE: Game-viewing from Lianshulu's pontoon.

sundowners and accompanied by most palatable wines. Among the activities on offer are fishing; sunset cruises on the Lianshulu pontoon; small rivercraft for game viewing and bird spotting; and a resident naturalist to take guests on walks.

Reservations and information: Wilderness Safaris/ Afro Ventures, PO Box 651171, Benmore, Johannesburg 2010, South Africa. Tel: (011) 884-1458/4633; fax: (011) 883-6255. Desert & Delta Safaris, PO Box 2339, Randburg 2125, South Africa. Tel: (011) 789-1078; fax: (011) 886-2349.

MVUBU LODGE Also on the Kwando River but situated beside a quite lovely oxbow lake in the backwaters – a spot habitually used by elephant and other game as a watering place – the camp, which the owners describe as 'semi-civilised' but is in fact very comfortable, comprises permanent, two-person luxury tents and a central complex of restaurant, bar and a pleasant outdoor eating area. Bathroom facilities are communal (hot water, flush toilets).

On offer are conducted game-viewing and bird-spotting walks and drives, fishing and photographic expeditions, small-boat and mokoro excursions, and overnight visits to the Linyanti swamp and Mamili park, where guests stay in a 'fly camp'. Kalizo Fishing and Photographic Safaris are among the independent safari ventures who make use of Mvubu's facilities.

Reservations and information: Kalizo Fishing and Photographic Safaris, PO Box 195, Wilgeheuwel 1736, South Africa. Tel and fax: (011) 764-4606. PO Box 501, Ngwezi, Katima Mulilo 9000, Namibia. Tel: 067532, ask for 346.

MAMILI NATIONAL PARK

The Mamili was proclaimed in the early 1990s to protect some 40 000 hectares of floodplain and Linyanti swampland, a wetland created when, for complicated geophysical reasons related to a fault line of the Great Rift Valley system, the Kwando River changed its course to the northeast.

This magnificently unspoilt, almost inaccessible area serves as a sanctuary for elephant, buffalo, lion, leopard, and for buck species that include the sitatunga and lechwe. The former, which tends to be elusive elsewhere, can be fairly easily spotted among the papyrus reeds. In times of drought, game migrates from northern Botswana to enhance Mamili's wildlife attractions. The marshes and inundated grasslands enclose two prominent islands, Nkasa and Lupala, which are worth exploring for their bird and plant life.

Kalizo Fishing and Photographic Safaris operate a tented fly camp within the Mamili National Park.

KALIZO FISHING LODGE

A fisherman's and birder's paradise, this lodge is set on the Zambezi River bank some 40 km downstream from Katima Mulilo. The river rises rapidly with the main rains, which begin in late January, and the water pushes into its floodplain to surround the lodge (guests are boated to camp during these months).

The lodge's two types of chalet – reed-and-thatch and wood-and-thatch – are comfortably appointed. All 12 units have beautiful views of the river; nearby are the shared bathroom facilities (his and hers; with hot water and flush toilets). Guests enjoy three meals a day in the restaurant and sociable drinks in the Tugger's Nook pub, which also looks out to the Zambezi. Sundowner hour, with the day closing in around you in a glorious explosion of colours, is a time to be savoured.

Fishing is excellent throughout the year: tiger-fish are the principal game species, but there's a lot more: about 20 different kinds of 'bream' (the term is loosely applied; nemwe and three-spot reach four kilograms in weight), barbel (30 kg) and eel can be caught. Kalizo operates 12 fully equipped St Lucia and Firefly Viking fibreglass boats powered by 60- and 40-horsepower outboards. The Kalizo international tiger-fishing tournament takes place at the lodge in August each year: around 120 anglers are invited to compete in teams of three and four.

The bird life along this stretch of the river is superb, but the game is rather sparse at the moment (as mentioned, much of it was shot out during the bush war). However, there is wildlife aplenty in the Mudumu and Mamili parks around the Kwando/ Linyanti wetlands to the southeast, where Kalizo operates two tented camps. The venture also runs photographic safaris to the two areas.

■ **Reservations and information:** Kalizo Fishing and Photographic Safaris, PO Box 195, Wilgeheuwel 1736, South Africa. Tel and fax: (011) 764-4606. PO Box 501, Ngwezi, Katimo Mulilo 9000, Namibia. Tel: 067532, ask for 346.

ABOVE: A young East Caprivi fisherman displays his day's catch of bream and catfish.
OPPOSITE : The handsome Zambezi Queen *takes visitors on week-long river safaris.*
OPPOSITE BELOW: The Caprivi reaches of the Zambezi: a paradise for the fisherman and bird-watcher.

KATIMA MULILO

This small Zambezi riverside settlement is the administrative capital of the Caprivi region: a remote place that has slept soundly in the sun for most of the century, it hosted army personnel during the 1970s and 1980s, then received a commercial shot-in-the-arm in 1989 with the arrival, in Namibia, of the Untag peacekeeping forces, and is now becoming an increasingly popular tourist destination. All the basics needed for your bush holiday are available in town: it has a supermarket, butchery, bank, and an Avis agency; worth visiting are the open-air market and the Caprivi Art Centre (wood and soapstone carvings on sale). Scheduled flights connect the local airport with Johannesburg and Windhoek (see Advisory, page 200).

ZAMBEZI LODGE The hotel, two kilometres from Katima Mulilo, comprises attractive double and single chalets with private facilities, all set in tropically lush riverside surrounds. One of its less conventional attractions is a floating bar; other more standard amenities include a licensed restaurant, an outdoor eating area, a swimming pool, a gymnasium, a sauna, and a nine-hole golf course (where hippo occasionally pose a golfing hazard). The Katima Mulilo yacht club is nearby.

Boats – powered ones and the more romantic mokoros – can be hired for fishing, photographic and birding excursions. Among the less common birds to be found along the river reaches here are honey-buzzard, broad-tailed paradise whydah and blackcheeked lovebird, and of course there are hundreds of other, more widely distributed species.

The Caprivi game areas are easily accessible from the hotel, as is the Chobe park just across the border in Botswana (see page 200) and, a little farther away, the Victoria Falls.
Reservations and information: Ms Alta Visagie, PO Box 98, Katima Mulilo 9000, Namibia. Tel: 067352, ask for 203.

Zambezi Queen

This elegant, 45-m, three-deck riverboat offers luxurious seven-day cruises along the Zambezi and neighbouring watercourses; passengers are accommodated in 13 airconditioned double cabins, and have the use of an entertainment deck, cocktail bar, dining room and two lounges. A typical voyage on the *Queen* takes you from the mooring at the Zambezi Lodge (see above) to the village of Mwandi Khutu (barbecue and traditional African dancing); Mpalila Island (meeting point of four countries), where you board the game-viewing barge *Eagle*, which takes you up the Kasai channel and Chobe River to the famed Chobe park (in Botswana) and then to Kasane, where there is a coach transfer to Victoria Falls.
Reservations and information: Ms Alta Visagie, PO Box 98, Katima Mulilo 9000, Namibia. Tel: 067352, ask for 203.

■ **Getting to the Caprivi**: By road from Namibia, travel via Grootfontein and Rundu; the route is gravelled for the last 150-km stretch and is being tarred to Popa Falls. A gravel road then runs west-east through Caprivi to the Kwando River and from there a tarred road to Katima Mulilo. The shortest route from South Africa, however, is through Botswana via Gaberone, Francistown, Nata and Kasane; customs and immigration formalities are processed at Ngama Bridge, about 60 km from Kasane along a fairly good dirt road. The route runs through Chobe. By air: there are scheduled Air Namibia, South African Airways and Air Zimbabwe flights (the latter two via Victoria Falls) to Katima Mulilo's Mpatcha airport. Safari operators will of course make all the travel arrangements on behalf of their clients. Lianshulu Lodge has its own airstrip.

■ **Reservations and information:** For private accommodation and Popa Falls, see individual entries. At the time of writing, no public accommodation had been established within any of the four pro-claimed areas. For general information, contact the Ministry of Wildlife, Conservation and Tourism, Private Bag 13267, Windhoek 9000. Tel: (061) 3-6975 or 3-3875; fax: (061) 22-4900.

THE NAMIB: MOST ANCIENT OF DESERTS

The Namib is a long, narrow desert: it stretches almost 2 000 km from the Orange River northwards to and beyond the Kunene, and for an average 150 km inland, the terrain gradually sweeping up to the central plateau that runs parallel to the coast. An inhospitable area, searingly hot by day, often bitterly cold at night, bone-dry for the most part, it is a region of emptiness, an immensity of solitude and infinite silence.

In the south is a sea of sand, where rank upon serried rank of massive shifting dunes, some of them fully 30 km long and 250 m high, march to distant horizons. Here and there you will find the occasional salt and mud flat – relics of sporadic streams that tried, and failed, to make their way to the sea – and underground rivers, the dry beds of which are refreshingly mantled in greenery. Farther north the land levels out to a hard plain from which isolated granite hills rise, and the bedrock of which is slashed by deep ravines. Part of this stretch is known as the Skeleton Coast, the treacherous, rocky shoreline the graveyard of a thousand ships and named for the many mariners who survived the wrecks only to die in the waterless wastes.

None of this can be regarded as classic African safari country – indeed for the most part the region appears utterly barren. Yet it does have its life forms, a rich diversity ranging from conventional big game to a fascinating array of small, specialised animals, reptiles, insects and plants. Some of the wildlife – sand-digging and sand-diving lizards, for example – is unique: this is the world's oldest desert and the long millennia have given free rein to the evolutionary process. One of the most remarkable of desert flora is the welwitschia, a primitive conifer described by the great Charles Darwin as 'the platypus of the Plant Kingdom'. It lives for more than 1 000 years, but in all that time

TOP: *A view from the Kuiseb canyon.*
ABOVE: *The shovel-snouted lizard.*
OPPOSITE: *The Namib's dunes are ever shifting.*

manages to produce just two leaves. These grow continuously, splitting into strips, the outer parts withering before the onslaught of burning sun and driven sand.

Much of this life is nurtured not by rain and ground cover (there are very little of these) but by the mists that roll in from the sea, and by breezes from the interior that bring in grass segments and other nutritious bits and pieces. Larger game is sustained by the odd pan and spring. Mountain zebra and gemsbok roam widely in the 50 000-km^2 Namib-Naukluft park of the central region; on the sandy flats of the Skeleton Coast park to the north are springbok, gemsbok and lion; and

elephant and black rhino have been observed just 10 km from the desolate shoreline.

Still in the north, but inland, are Damaraland and Kaokoland (jointly known as the Kaokoveld), scenically spectacular regions, but still untamed and almost entirely undeveloped for commercial tourism. The grassy plains of the eastern parts and the sandy wastes of the west support small but wide-ranging populations of elephant and rhino, giraffe and other animals, most of which have adapted their lifestyles to survive the harshness of the desert. The elephants, for example, will travel up to 70 km a day in search of food and water and, unusually, do not destroy trees in their quest for forage. The herds suffered grievously from the guns of poachers and illegal hunters until the early 1980s, when estimates put their number at just 70. The remnant is now carefully protected.

The Namib and the Kaokoveld have few visitor amenities; roads are non-existent over much of the land and rudimentary in the rest; what little permanent accommodation is available tends to be basic, though there are one or two well-founded lodges in Damaraland. Most travellers to these regions – and there is an increasing number – book their excursions through one or other of the several safari and tour operators (see page 314).

THE KALAHARI

The Kalahari extends over the eastern parts of Namibia, most of Botswana, western and southwestern Zimbabwe, some of Angola, and a small segment of South Africa north of the Orange River – an immense, parched-looking region that, although termed a desert, is in fact a wilderness: its great plains are covered by sparse but sweet grasses that sustain an enormous number and variety of game. It is also the last refuge of the traditional Bushman people, nomadic hunter-gatherers who subsisted largely on game, honey, and the roots and fruits of plants such as the wild cucumber and tsamma melon. The few Bushmen who remain untouched by Western culture live in total harmony with nature, posing no threat to the environment, their routines prescribed by the seasons, the availability of water and the movement of animals. Only the South African portion of the Kalahari has been developed in any significant way for tourism.

In Botswana the desert areas are conserved within a national park, but access to this is restricted, and the fringing Mabuasehube game reserve has no permanent accommodation. No part of the Namibian Kalahari has been proclaimed a conservation area, though people do visit the region for its wildlife, and there are some privately run tourist facilities.

ABOVE: A solitary lion drinks its fill in the vastness of the Kalahari Gemsbok park.
LEFT: Gemsbok on the Kalahari plains.

KALAHARI GEMSBOK
NATIONAL PARK

This reserve covers the South African portion of the desert: a 9 600-km^2 expanse of northern Cape red-sand territory wedged between Namibia and Botswana. When combined with Botswana's Gemsbok National Park, the area extends across some 80 000 km^2.

There are no fences to mark the common border, and the animals are free to migrate, which they do in their tens of thousands, the dust from their massed ranks darkening the sun – an unforgettable sight. Much of the countryside between the bone-dry river beds of the Auob and the Nossob (the latter flows once in every hundred years or so) is red duneland, scantily clad by grass and scatters of bush and trees. The plant life, richer near and along the river courses, includes camelthorn, blackthorn and other acacia species.

The park began life in the early 1930s as a sanctuary for gemsbok and springbok, antelope that had up to then been indiscriminately slaughtered by trophy and biltong

hunters. Today it contains these and much more: giraffe, blue wildebeest, eland, steenbok, red hartebeest, duiker and many smaller animals. The predators include lion, leopard and cheetah, wild dog, and spotted and brown hyaena; among the more than 200 bird species are tawny, martial and two types of snake eagle, and the noble bateleur.

Wind-powered boreholes have been sunk to tap the underground water, and the dams and waterholes attract great concentrations of game. Many of the Kalahari's animals, however, obtain their moisture as well as their food from the hardy and uniquely adapted desert succulents.

KALAHARI GEMSBOK'S CAMPS

There are three of these: Twee Rivieren, near the confluence of the two rivers; Mata Mata, on the Auob to the west; and Nossob, on the Botswana border. Twee Rivieren has airconditioned, fully equipped chalets with either three or four single beds or two single beds and a double sleeper. Nossob and Mata Mata have six-bed, fully equipped cottages and three-bed huts with communal kitchen and ablution facilities. Nossob also offers three-bed huts, each with a fully equipped kitchen, a shower and a toilet. Each has a shop selling groceries, though only Twee Rivieren stocks fresh meat, bread, margarine and eggs. Alcoholic beverages, barbecue firewood and petrol are also on sale; fresh vegetables and film are not available. Twee Rivieren boasts a swimming pool and a restaurant.

Game viewing

The main public roads follow the courses of the Auob and Nossob (which forms part of South Africa's border with Botwana) – plus a track over the dunes linking two riverside picnic spots. Do not stray from the established routes – your vehicle could come to grief in the soft sands. Before setting out, inform the camp office of your route and destination for the day. Petrol is on sale at all the camps. There is an information centre at Nossob camp, and the rangers and park officials at the others will know where to go for the best game viewing.

BOTSWANA

In the old colonial days this vast, landlocked, dry country was known as Bechuanaland, one of the three British High Commission territories in Southern Africa. Its modern name, conferred at independence in 1966, is derived from the Tswana people, or Batswana, largest of the eight major groupings who, in sparse and uneven fashion, inhabit the region.

Botswana extends across well over half a million square kilometres of the great African plateau; its people number a little over a million. Most of the groups are historically and culturally interrelated, though each occupies its own areas, has its own traditional chiefs and enjoys proprietary rights over its own lands. The population is at its densest in the southeast, along the common border with South Africa's Transvaal province; Gaborone, the capital, is barely three hours' drive from the giant Johannesburg-Pretoria conurbation. Botswana also shares frontiers with Zimbabwe in the east and northeast, and with Namibia's desert wastelands in the west. To the north, in sharp geophysical contrast, is Namibia's Caprivi 'strip', a long, narrow, lushly vegetated panhandle noted for its rivers and marshlands.

For the most part Botswana is a flat, dun-coloured, dry, hot country of sandy soils, scantily covered grasslands and rugged woodland savanna. Its people – the majority of whom are rural, self-employed and dependent on their livestock for survival – are accustomed to droughts that often last for years. The rains, most of which fall between November and March, are sporadic, at their heaviest in the north and at their least generous on the great red-dune Kalahari spaces of the southwest.

Huge tracts of the country have no surface water. The only permanent sources are the rivers of the north and east: the Okavango, the Linyanti/Chobe system and to a much lesser degree the Shashe and the Limpopo. These watercourses, however, and especially the first two, combine to make Botswana one of Africa's finest tourist destinations.

The Okavango flows down from the uplands of Angola to form an immense and wondrous inland delta of lagoon and labyrinthine channel, palm-graced island and papyrus bed, riverine forest and fertile flood plain. Scores of safari camps have been established in and around this watery wilderness, and in the game-rich Moremi and Chobe parks a little farther to the north. Between them, they offer the best of several worlds, appealing variously to the sporting fisherman and the bird-watcher, the game viewer, the explorer of hidden places and the lover of Africa at its most fascinating and least spoilt.

OPPOSITE: A typical safari venue in the Okavango, a magical region of reed-fringed flood plain.

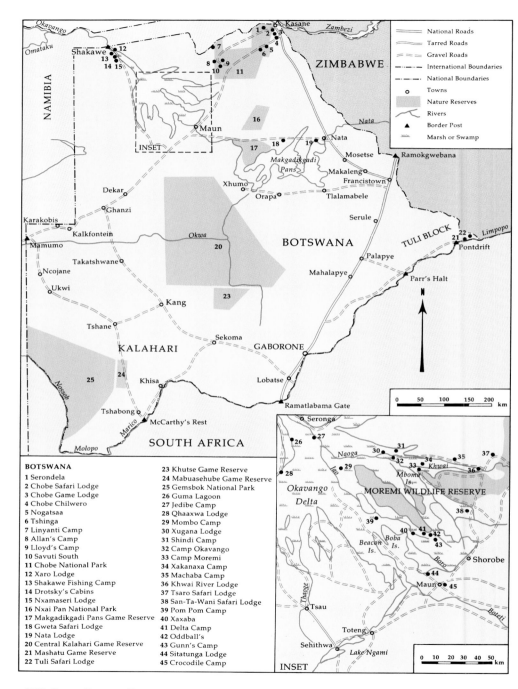

National Roads
Tarred Roads
Gravel Roads
International Boundaries
National Boundaries
○ **Towns**
Nature Reserves
Rivers
▲ **Border Post**
Marsh or Swamp

ZIMBABWE

Kasane · Zambezi

NAMIBIA

Okavango

Omataku

Shakawe

Maun

INSET

BOTSWANA

Nata

Mosetse

Ramokgwebana

Makgadikgadi Pans

Makaleng
Francistown

Xhumo

Orapa · Tlalamabele

Dekar

Ghanzi

Karakobis

Kalkfontein

Okwa

Serule

TULI BLOCK

Pontdrift

Limpopo

Mamumo

Takatshwane

Ncojane

Ukwi

Palapye

Mahalapye

Parr's Halt

Kang

KALAHARI

Tshane

Sekoma

GABORONE

Lobatse

Khisa

Tshabong

McCarthy's Rest

Molopo

SOUTH AFRICA

Ramatlabama Gate

0 50 100 150 200 km

BOTSWANA	23 Khutse Game Reserve
1 Serondela	24 Mabuasehube Game Reserve
2 Chobe Safari Lodge	25 Gemsbok National Park
3 Chobe Game Lodge	26 Guma Lagoon
4 Chobe Chilwero	27 Jedibe Camp
5 Nogatsaa	28 Qhaaxwa Lodge
6 Tshinga	29 Mombo Camp
7 Linyanti Camp	30 Xugana Lodge
8 Allan's Camp	31 Shindi Camp
9 Lloyd's Camp	32 Camp Okavango
10 Savuti South	33 Camp Moremi
11 Chobe National Park	34 Xakanaxa Camp
12 Xaro Lodge	35 Machaba Camp
13 Shakawe Fishing Camp	36 Khwai River Lodge
14 Drotsky's Cabins	37 Tsaro Safari Lodge
15 Nxamaseri Lodge	38 San-Ta-Wani Safari Lodge
16 Nxai Pan National Park	39 Pom Pom Camp
17 Makgadikgadi Pans Game Reserve	40 Xaxaba
18 Gweta Safari Lodge	41 Delta Camp
19 Nata Lodge	42 Oddball's
20 Central Kalahari Game Reserve	43 Gunn's Camp
21 Mashatu Game Reserve	44 Sitatunga Lodge
22 Tuli Safari Lodge	45 Crocodile Camp

Seronga

Ngoga

Khwai

Mboma Is.

MOREMI WILDLIFE RESERVE

Okavango Delta

Boba Is.

Beacon Is.

Boro

Shorobe

Maun

Tsau

Toteng

Sehithwa

Lake Ngami

Boteti

INSET

0 10 20 30 40 50 km

Less well endowed are the vast, sandy wastelands of central and southern Botswana, once inhabited by Iron Age peoples known as the Kgalagadi. The name, in corrupted form, is now applied to the desert spaces that occupy much of the country, and to the complex of huge salt pans in the east-central region. In all, about 17 per cent, or 90 000 km², of Botswana's land surface has been set aside for conservation as national parks and game reserves – an impressive allocation by any standards, and one that is being supplemented by an increasing number of what are called wildlife management areas, broad expanses of terrain in which the game takes precedence over man and his cattle.

All of which paints an inviting picture for the visitor bent on a big-game safari. However, a few mildly cautionary words.

Do not expect as easy game viewing as you would enjoy, say, in South Africa's Kruger National Park or on the plains of Kenya's Serengeti. The animals are there, but they tend to be highly mobile and in many places the wildlife is not all that prolific or varied. Come to Botswana, rather, for the *total* wilderness experience, one in which the game is a significant but by no means the only element.

Secondly, movement around the country can be difficult and frustrating for the independent traveller intent on exploring the wilder spaces: distances are huge; facilities are few; to get to a particular destination often involves two and sometimes even three modes of transport (car or 4x4, light aircraft, boat). Finding your own way through the Okavango swamplands and, to a lesser degree, parts of the Chobe area is especially problematic; journeys to and through the central and southern Kalahari regions can be downright hazardous. Some visitors are happy to settle for the more developed fringes of the wilderness, and an ordinary saloon car and a good map will safely see them there. But for the rest – unless you're one of those intrepid sorts who appreciates a challenge – you are advised to use the services of a reputable safari operator.

Horseback safaris are among the more adventurous ways to explore the Okavango Delta.

OKAVANGO AND MOREMI

The Okavango River, known as the Kubango in its upper reaches, rises in Angola's well-watered Benguela plateau to flow 1 600 km southeastwards until it divides into a number of lesser watercourses. These make their way into Botswana's Kalahari desert to form a vast, fan-shaped, astonishingly luxuriant wilderness of flood plain and forest, stream and pool, lagoon, lakelet, the occasional large expanse of open water and a myriad labyrinthine channels. In times of peak flood the wetlands extend over almost 15 000 km², and embrace about a thousand islands, some of them several kilometres in diameter and thickly wooded, most of them small, and the water that flows around and past them moves so languidly that there's no sediment to blur its clarity, though the channels are often difficult to discern through the dense profusion of reed, papyrus, hippo grass and water lily.

This magical region – one of the world's few major inland deltas – is the product of a movement, or a series of movements, in the earth's crust that diverted the Okavango from its original course to send it rolling down to die in the thirsty desert wastelands. The annual floods begin between January and March, a gentle rather than a spectacular process: the waters that seep over the river banks to inundate the slightly lower-lying plains take several months to reach their southern extremity. From a visitor's point of view, therefore, the region is at its best from about April through to September, though the main channels remain fairly full throughout the year.

The northeastern segment of the Delta has been set aside as the Moremi wildlife reserve, an 1 800-km² expanse of pristine wilderness that bears testament to the foresight of conservationists Robert and June Kaye, and to the resolve of the local Tswana people. The latter, a predominantly hunting community, witnessed the savage depletion of their precious game resources during the 1950s and early 1960s and, in a ground-breaking move, decided to convert part of their tribal territory into a formal sanctuary – even though this meant, for many, an unsettling move away from their traditional land. Later on the 100-km by 15-km Chief's Island was added to the reserve and, together, the two tracts comprise the only protected area within the Delta.

Most of the Okavango's western and northern swamplands have modest game populations – in terms of the number and variety of their larger animals these areas cannot compare, for instance, with the splendid Chobe National Park to the northeast. Nevertheless

there are plenty of buffalo to be seen, together with the water-adapted lechwe and sitatunga antelope, hippo and crocodile, and a host of smaller species.

The animals, though, are just one of many elements that combine to make the Delta a treasure-house for the naturalist, the photographer, the fisherman, for the lover of solitude and of beauty. The brooding quietness of the waterways, the plaintiff cry of the African fish eagle, the flash of a kingfisher

ABOVE: *Most camps offer trips by mokoro, the dugout canoe guided by an expert poler.*
LEFT: *Scented lilies grace the Delta's waters.*

among the reeds, the scent of the water lilies, the moist heat of the day, the caressing coolness of the evening and its glorious sunset – the images are sharp, and kaleidoscopic, and they remain in the memory long after one has departed this enchanted land. Unforgettable, especially, are the birds of the Okavango: more than 400 different species have been identified, among them 16 kinds of heron, spurwinged goose and saddlebill stork, sacred ibis, wattled crane, egret, cormorant, bittern, darter, hoopoe, roller, copperytailed coucal and chirping cisticola.

Like so many of Africa's wilderness areas, the swamps are under threat from human need. There is a shortage of good grazing in the adjacent lands, and such green luxuriance in an otherwise parched country is a standing temptation to the stock farmers, especially in times of drought. In a so-far successful effort to keep the cattle out and the animals in, a veterinary cordon has been erected along the Delta's western and southern edges; less effective are the fences to the north, half-completed at the time of writing, the work delayed pending the results of a proper environmental impact study. Whatever the outcome of the latter, though, and however laudable the intent, the man-made barriers will, inevitably, continue to go up, which worries some conservationists: they believe that the wetlands cannot support their present wildlife populations if the animals are hemmed in; many species, they say, need to migrate to water and to more nutritious pastures in the dry season.

More serious, perhaps, are the demands of Botswana's diamond-mining industry and the expanding town of Maun, both of which are apparently thirsty for water, though major (and highly controversial) proposals to siphon off some of the Delta's abundance have, for the time being, been shelved.

And then there is tourism, described by one senior parks official as 'the greatest threat of all' to the swamps. This issue, however, is by no means clear: the Delta is certainly becoming an increasingly popular destination, and in 1993 plans were being finalised to treble the number of concessionary areas (blocks of land reserved for individual safari firms), which will add substantially to the human presence, especially around the Moremi reserve, the boundaries of which are to be extended to cover the northwestern papyrus swamps. But on balance the scheme could prove highly beneficial: the new 15-year lease arrangement will encourage private operators, long plagued by having to renew their leases each year, to become more active in conservation. And, of course, tourism generates the income so desperately needed to preserve this, the greatest and perhaps most fragile of Africa's remaining wetlands.

Exploring the Delta

It is possible to embark on an independent tour of the Okavango Delta but, for the ordinary visitor, generally it is inadvisable to do so (though some sections, including the Moremi, are fairly comfortably accessible to 4x4 vehicles). The region is remote, distances are huge, public facilities few and far apart, and to get there and get around invariably involves water as well as land and, in many instances, air transport. Moreover, although the swamps have been charted, the web of channels is so intricate and so obscured by vegetation that only those with years-long familiarity with its complexities can hope to find their way over the watery terrain.

Far better to put yourself in the hands of a professional safari outfit, of which there are many. They have an intimate knowledge of their particular areas of operation, and they

will handle all the arrangements and provide all the services – the package includes, among other things, travel to and accommodation in Maun; transport to the lodge (by light-aircraft and/or road and/or boat); a comfortable bed, food, drink and good company in camp; game-viewing, fishing and photographic expeditions; professional guides (a very important element), boat hire – and trips by mokoro, a traditional dug-out canoe expertly negotiated through the watery maze by an African poler. Swift, silent, unintrusive, the mokoro skims lightly over the placid surface, providing probably the best and certainly the most restful means of seeing this entrancing world.

Accommodation There are around 40 lodges and camps in the Delta region – some comprising tents, others reed-and-pole structures, still others brick under thatch – and dozens more are likely to be established as new concession areas are opened up. Conventional hotel accommodation is currently confined to the Maun area in the south.

OPPOSITE: The Delta is a bird-watcher's paradise; over 400 different species have been recorded.
TOP: Overland access can be difficult; most visitors arrive by charter aircraft.
ABOVE: The enchanting malachite kingfisher.

IN AND AROUND MAUN

The town of Maun, capital of Ngamiland and the administrative centre of northern Botswana, lies on the southeastern rim of the Okavango, and serves as a convenient staging post for journeys into the swamplands.

Once a rather sleepy, dusty, goat- and donkey-infested little settlement, the town has been expanding rapidly over the past few years: the goats and donkeys still wander where they will, but now the streets are alive with Mercs and brand-new 4x4s and the press of busily outward-bound humanity (nearly everyone seems to be on his way somewhere). Many of the safari firms are either based or represented in Maun; here one can organise a lodge or mobile safari, a game-viewing, birding, fishing, photographic or hunting expedition, hire a vehicle or powerboat, charter an aircraft. In town are banks, service stations, outlets that sell curios, liquor and fresh produce and pretty well everything you could possibly need for your Delta holiday from a bush jacket to an aluminium boat.

Maun's social scene is lively and informal, its focus The Duck Inn, a place where you'll meet characters that seem to have stepped straight from the set of the *African Queen*. Adding to the local colour is a largish community of traditionally garbed Herero people, descendants of refugees that fled the German colonists of neighbouring Namibia during the war of 1904-1905.

RILEY'S HOTEL

A well-known and well-loved hostelry which the Cresta group took over and renovated fairly recently. Something of the old colonial days comes across in the cool, deep verandah. The 52 double rooms are very comfortably appointed (telephone, radio, television, hair dryer, tea/coffee-maker), pleasantly decorated, and airconditioned; each has its private bathroom. Larger and more luxurious suites are also available. Guests enjoy à la carte fare in Riley's Grill; drinks are served at the Pool Bar (which overlooks the river), in Harry's Bar, or at the Motswiri Pool Bar. The hotel has a lovely swimming pool; there is also a curio shop, a hairdressing salon and a tour operator's desk on the premises. There are conference facilities for 75 delegates.

■ **Location:** Riley's Hotel is in Maun.
■ **Reservations and information:** PO Box 1, Maun, Botswana. Tel: (09267) 66-0204/66-0320; fax: (09267) 66-0580. Or central reservations: Gaborone (09267) 31-2431; fax: (09267) 37-5376; Harare , tel: (092634) 70-3131; Johannesburg , tel: (011) 453-7630.

CROCODILE CAMP

An old-established and charming camp set among shade trees on the Thamalakane River north of Maun. Accommodation is in reed-and-thatch bungalows, some fitted with showers and flush toilets, most with access to communal facilities; central amenities include a swimming pool, a fully licensed

TOP LEFT: Maun is the Delta's main centre and staging post for those bound for the remoter parts.
LEFT AND OPPOSITE: The attractive Crocodile Camp, close to Maun.

restaurant – the place is famous for its cuisine – and a most sociable pub. There is also a caravan/camping ground whose reed-enclosed sites offer an unusual degree of privacy.

The camp is jointly owned and operated with cheerful efficiency by Karl-Heinz Gimpel and Jane Elliot; on offer are boating (including canoes), fishing, game-viewing and photographic excursions, and a variety of ranger-conducted mobile safaris.

■ **Getting there:** Crocodile Camp is 13 km north of Maun on the road to Moremi. From Maun, take the Moremi road and turn left at the traffic circle.

■ **Reservations and information:** Crocodile Camp Safaris, PO Box 46, Maun, Botswana. Tel: (09267) 66-0796; fax: (09267) 66-0793.

SITATUNGA LODGE

Essentially for the do-it-yourself visitor, Sitatunga offers a pleasantly shady camping ground within a 60-hectare, game-fenced property 14 km south of Maun. The camp incorporates a modern ablution block (plenty of hot water on tap); each camp site has its own barbecue grill; among other amenities are a small shop (bread, butter, cheese, bacon, meat – including crocodile fillets and barbecue packs – tinned foods and toiletries) and a liquor outlet There is no restaurant or bar facilities on site. Also available are a number of furnished, equipped and serviced chalets (double bed, single bed, gas cooker) and a few tents (linen provided).

Sitatunga shares the property with Botswana's largest crocodile farm, which visitors may tour. Well worth exploring is the riverine forest, haven to a splendid variety of water-related and other birds, including fish eagle, marabou stork, vulture and five different types of owl. Among the more organised attractions on offer are mokoro excursions through the Delta region and mobile safaris into the Moremi reserve.

■ **Getting there:** Coming into Maun, cross the bridge and turn left at the traffic circle towards Ngami/Shakawe; follow the tarred road for 12 km; turn left at the Sitatunga sign.

■ **Reservations and information:** Sitatunga Camping Safaris, Private Bag 47, Maun, Botswana. Tel and fax: (09267) 66-0570.

THE NILE CROCODILE: KING OF THE INLAND WATERS

Together with their cousins the alligators and caimans, crocodiles are the largest and heaviest of present-day reptiles and the closest living relatives of the long-gone dinosaurs. *Crocodilus niloticus*, the Nile crocodile – the only species found in the rivers and swamps of Southern Africa – can reach a length of six metres, or over 20 feet, though a specimen of this size would be an especially long-lived one (well over a hundred years old, it is reckoned).

The crocodile is a predator, at its most active at night, its diet made up of fish, waterfowl, small animals and, rather less frequently, medium-sized mammals that come to the water's edge to drink. It catches the latter by remaining motionless, or floating passively to resemble a log, and then, with lightning speed, seizing its sizeable victim in massive, many-toothed jaws and dragging it down to drown beneath the surface. There, the croc will rotate its body rapidly in order to twist manageable chunks of meat from the carcass.

The crocodile's eyes, ears and nostrils are so positioned, at the top of the head, that it can remain for long periods almost fully submerged, barely noticeable to unsuspecting birds and animals – and to people: in Africa, it accounts for more human deaths than elephants, lions, leopards and snakes put together. During the day, though, it likes to sun itself on river bank or island (it does this to gain heat), often in company of others of its species. For the rest, it lives alone within its established territory, which it defines for the benefit of its neighbours by emitting a short, loud, resounding roar.

The female lays between 25 and 30 hard-shelled eggs in shallow holes in the sand or in the sandy soil above the water line. She then guards the nest during the three-month incubation period, and when she hears the squeaks of her 250-mm-long hatchlings, she helps them emerge and carries them to water in her mouth. Once there, they remain together in a 'crèche' for several months, defended by their parents during this, the most critical phase of their life. Nonetheless, mortality among the young remains high.

Of all reptilian brains, the crocodile's is the most advanced: the creature is capable of showing curiosity, and of adapting to a strange environment. If caught when young enough, for instance, individuals may learn to recognise their keepers, show neither anxiety nor hostility, and allow themselves to be handled.

A familiar sight in the Delta.

THE PANHANDLE AND NORTHWESTERN DELTA

This is a region of permanent water, of papyrus and reed and water lily, deep channel, broad lagoon and island – terrain that can best and sometimes only be explored by boat. Along the western rim of the Delta there are remote villages whose residents are superbly skilled in the art of basket weaving. If you're travelling up by road, it is worth making a 50-km detour to the four Tsodilo Hills: they rise 400 m above the vegetated dunes of the Kalahari, and some 2 500 examples of Bushman rock art are to be found among their rocks, overhangs and caverns. In the far northwest is the so-called Panhandle,

BELOW: *Two carmine bee-eaters hitch a ride on a ground-living kori bustard.*
BOTTOM: *The water-adapted red lechwe.*

the comparatively narrow, 100-km-long main channel and flood plain of the Okavango before it divides into its offspring watercourses to fan out over the Delta proper. Here the river, fresh from the Angolan highlands and still rich in nutrients, sustains a wonderful number and variety of fish, which in turn support a wide diversity of water-related birds. Several inviting camps have been established in this magical land, the majority of which specialise – though not to the exclusion of any other delights – in fishing safaris.

Many of the camps can be reached via the newly tarred road that runs from Maun along the Delta's western perimeter, but the journey is long and tiring, the Okavango is not really suited to independent travel, and most visitors book through and are flown in by professional safari operators.

DROTSKY'S CABINS

Named after owners Jan and Eileen Drotsky, the lodge is set high on the Okavango River bank about five kilometres from the far northwestern village of Shakawe. There's a choice of accommodation (A-frame chalets, reed huts and camp sites), all of it unpretentious, comfortable and surprisingly inexpensive. The camp is shaded by beautiful indigenous trees; the broad waters here are a paradise for fishermen.

Guests can hire powerboats, Leisure Liner houseboats or self-contained pontoons on a daily or hourly basis. The craft are a capacious five metres long, so it's possible to load up and take off southwards into the watery wilderness on one's own for a couple of secluded days. Also on offer are nighttime boat trips (an exhilarating experience) and conducted excursions to the Tsodilo Hills (see above).

■ **Getting there:** Drotsky's is one of the farthest lodges from Maun. One can drive the 350-odd kilometres, but most guests book through Merlin Services and are flown in.
■ **Reservations and information:** Merlin Services, Private Bag 13, Maun, Botswana. Tel: (09267) 66-0351; fax: (09267) 66-0571.

SHAKAWE FISHING CAMP

One of the older, larger, better-known and best-run of the Panhandle's angling venues. The owners are Barrye and Elaine Price, expert fisherman and dedicated ornithologist respectively – and opportunities in both disciplines are outstanding: the river's bream and tigerfish offer splendid sport; the area's diversity of habitats (riverine vegetation, grassland and sandveld) are haven to a marvellous variety of birds.

Accommodation is also varied, comprising comfortable, *en suite* brick-under-thatch chalets, a tented camp (each Meru tent has its own flush toilet), and a camp site with communal facilities. Among guest amenities is a most refreshing swimming pool. On offer are river cruises, and trips to the Tsodilo Hills and to the beautiful Nxamaseri Valley.

■ **Getting there:** It is possible to drive in from Maun but, again, most visitors entering from South Africa make the journey by air: charter services link Shakawe airfield (where one goes through customs and immigration formalities) with major Southern African centres; camp transport will transfer you for a small fee.
■ **Reservations and information:** Okavango Fishing Safaris, PO Box 236, Maun, Botswana. Tel and fax: (09267) 66-0493.

QHAAXWA LODGE

One of the most attractive of the Okavango's camps: a cluster of stylish, twin-bedded, well-appointed reed chalets at the southern extremity of the Panhandle. The chalets look out to the exquisite, papyrus-fringed lagoon that gives the place its unusual name.

Qhaaxwa is one of six lodges recently taken over by the prestigious Orient Express-Mount Nelson joint venture, and facilities are being upgraded. Comfort, cuisine (three table d'hôte meals a day) and service are of an exceptional standard; a notable feature is the charming (and generously stocked) bar raised high above the lagoon's translucent waters.

Guests can fish, boat or walk, and there is excellent birding (slaty egret, Pel's fishing owl, brown firefinch, African skimmer, chirping cisticola, swamp boubou, fish eagle) and sightseeing by mokoro. Fly-in packages are provided by the Gametrackers safari group.

■ **Getting there:** Gametrackers will fly you in.
■ **Reservations and information:** Destination Africa/Gametrackers, PO Box 786432, Sandton 2146, South Africa. Tel: (011) 884-2504; fax: (011) 884-3159.

XARO LODGE

This luxury tented camp is situated on a broad sweep of the Okavango River and, like nearly all the Panhandle's venues but perhaps even more so, caters – and caters in style – for the keen angler. The Meru tents, comfortably fitted out with beds, cupboards and colourful rugs, private bathroom (hot and cold running water; flush toilets); central amenities include a thatched, and very pleasant, complex of lounge, dining room, fully stocked bar and swimming pool.

Though this is essentially a fisherman's lodge, there are plenty of other attractions on offer: game is rather limited, but the area's bird life is superb, seen at its best perhaps on boating trips through the lily-covered waters. Also available are river cruises, light-aircraft flights over the Panhandle and Delta, and excursions (either by road or air) to the Tsodilo Hills.

OPPOSITE: A charmingly embowered corner of the Shakawe camp. The river here is rich in nutrients, which sustain a remarkable number and variety of fish and these, in turn, attract a splendid array of waterbirds.

TOP AND ABOVE: The reed-built Qhaaxwa Lodge, on the edge of a lovely lagoon.

■ **Getting there:** Xaro is accessible only by air; most guests are flown in by Merlin Services.

■ **Reservations and information:** The local booking agents are Merlin Services, Private Bag 13, Maun, Botswana. Tel: (09267) 66-0351; fax: (09267) 66-0571. South African agents include Wilderness Safaris, PO Box 651171, Benmore 2010, South Africa. Tel: (011) 884-1458; fax: (011) 883-6255.

NXAMASERI LODGE

Another angler's and bird-lover's paradise: the waters here are home to nearly 80 different kinds of fish (including 11 types of bream), to the Delta's largest concentration of fish eagle, and to a splendid variety of other avian species – lily-hopping African jacana, kingfisher, darter, heron, skimmer, wattled crane and hundreds more.

The lodge's setting is exceptional: it's on an island in the Nxamaseri Channel some three kilometres from the Okavango River, and can be reached only by boat; the brick and thatch chalets, surrounded by giant ebony trees and designed to blend with the environment, look over a wonderland of lily-covered flood plain, reed and feathery papyrus bed, palm-graced islet and lush riverine woodland.

The camp can accommodate a maximum of just 12 guests; each chalet has its private bathroom; meals are served in the open-air (and fully licensed) Mukwa dining room/bar complex and fish, predictably, features prominently on the menu. The Okavango bream and tigerfish pâté are quite delicious.

Fishing and birding are among the available activities, of course, but there are also wilderness safaris; excursions to see the Bushman

SHINDI CAMP

Set on its own magical island surrounded by the deep waters of the northwestern Delta region, Shindi is known for its fishing and, especially, for the fine birding opportunities it provides, notably on and around the nearby Gadikwe lagoon, home to breeding colonies of various waterbird species. The camp comprises luxury tents; guests enjoy table d'hôte meals and drinks in the central dining area. Game viewing is reasonably rewarding; one can spot crocodile and hippo and the occasional sitatunga antelope; game drives on the island are on the itinerary.

■ **Getting there:** Kerr & Downey will fly you in.
■ **Reservations and information:** Kerr & Downey Safaris, PO Box 40, Maun, Botswana. Tel: (09267) 66-0211/2; fax: (09267) 66-0379.

JEDIBE ISLAND CAMP

Surrounded by the permanent waters of the northwestern Delta some way south of the Panhandle and inaccessible to vehicles, this island camp offers the classic Okavango experience – gentle mokoro excursions across the central flood plains; boat journeys to and along the big rivers, the lagoons and lakes of the north. The camp comprises an eye-catching reed-and-thatch central complex of dining area, bar and boma fringed by spacious, twin-bedded, walk-in Meru safari tents (each has its shower and flush toilet). The tents are scattered beneath a deep shade-giving mantle of palms and handsome indigenous trees.

Wildlife is limited, but interesting: there are hippos and crocodile, of course – the latter are especially prominent in the vicinity, so take good advice before and great care when setting out for a cooling dip – plus red lechwe and the shy sitatunga antelope. Somewhat more rewarding is the bird life: here you can expect to see, among others, African fish eagle, wattled crane, swamp boubou (a species of shrike), whiterumped babbler, slaty egret, copperytailed coucal and Pel's fishing owl (one of which is a familiar visitor to camp: christened Paddington, he was reared by a member of the staff).

TOP: Shindi Camp's rustic dining area.
ABOVE: Relaxing at Jedibe Island.
OPPOSITE: Visitors paddle their way through the Delta's hugely intricate labyrinth of channels.

paintings of the Tsodilo Hills; horseback trails through the western Delta region; light-aircraft flights over the swamplands; mokoro trips and leisurely river cruises; visits to (and champagne brunches on) one or other of the area's lovely, wooded islands. Fishermen have the use of large, stable, flat-bottomed boats powered by quiet engines (some inboard, others outboard).

■ **Getting there:** It is possible to drive to the area but, again, most guests arrive as members of a fly-in package. The airstrip, on one of the larger islands, is a short boat-trip from camp.
■ **Reservations and information:** Merlin Services, Private Bag 13, Maun, Botswana. Tel and fax: (09267) 66-0351/0571. South African agents: Falcon Africa Safaris, PO Box 785222, Sandton 2146. Tel: (011) 886-1981; fax: (011) 886-1778.

A mokoro loaded for the journey.

One of the Delta's larger waterways.

■ **Getting there:** By air from Maun to Jao, and by boat to Jedibe Island (a 10-minute trip). Your safari operator will handle travel arrangements.

■ **Reservations and information:** Jedibe Island is run by Okavango Wilderness Safaris, Private Bag 14, Maun, Botswana. Tel: (09267) 66-0086; fax: (09267) 66-0632. The camp is included in packages offered by other safari operators, among them Wilderness Safaris (based in Johannesburg) and Bonaventure Botswana. See pages 314 and 315 for addresses.

GUMA LAGOON

A lovely little camp of *en suite* chalets and tents – rendered even more appealing by the warmth with which guests are received and looked after – overlooking one of the north-western Delta's largest and most beautiful lagoons, a magnificent place of palm trees, papyrus and reed beds and limpid water.

There's superb tiger and bream fishing in the area, and especially in the Panhandle, a 40-minute boat journey away (fishing gear is provided), though you'll find much else to keep you engrossed – bird-watching (including massed flamingoes if you're lucky), mokoro trails, game viewing (Guma offers island walks), and boating (coxswains are on hand to guide you to the best places; picnics and barbecues are organised en route).

■ **Getting there:** By road, Guma is 315 km from Maun. The only petrol outlet in between (and it's an unreliable source) is the trading store in Etsha 6, so stock up with extra fuel. By air, one of the various charter companies will fly

you in to Guma airstrip. Alternatively, fly to Seronga, where you'll be met and taken on the leisurely boat transfer (fishing/bird-watching on the way) to camp.

■ **Reservations and information:** Merlin Services, Private Bag 13, Maun, Botswana. Tel: (09267) 66-0351; fax: (09267) 66-0571.

WILDERNESS MOKORO TRAILS

This small camp under canvas – it comprises eight twin-bedded Bow and Eureka units – is located on an island in the permanent deep waters of the northwestern Delta: a remote, infinitely peaceful place available only on a block-booking basis (minimum of four guests). As its name suggests, it specialises in exploratory excursions by mokoro, the traditional dug-out canoe of the region, but there is also boating, walking, good fishing (rods and tackle supplied) and even better bird-watching in the area.

Although the camp itself has few claims to sophistication, it's both attractive and comfortable. The tents share two ablution blocks (flush toilets, delightful bucket showers); there is a separate dining area; bar facilities are also available.

■ **Getting there:** Wilderness Safaris will fly you from Maun to Jedibe airstrip, from where a mokoro transports you to camp.

■ **Reservations and information:** Wilderness Safaris, PO Box 651171, Benmore 2010, South Africa. Tel: (011) 884-1458; fax: (011) 883-6255.

THE AFRICAN FISH EAGLE

Perhaps the best known – and certainly the most photographed – of Southern Africa's birds of prey is the fish eagle (*Haliaeetus vocifer*), found in wetlands and near rivers, dams and estuarine lagoons in all the subcontinent's regions except the dry western Cape coastal belt and southern Namibia. The species is especially prolific in Botswana's Okavango Delta and Chobe areas, and in the St Lucia lake system of northern Natal.

This large (240-cm wingspan) raptor, instantly recognisable by its black, white and chestnut plumage, preys mainly on live fish, swooping down at a narrow angle to within a few centimetres of the water's surface and, without a check in its flight, grasping its victim in powerful talons to carry it up to its perch. It is this dramatic sequence, together with the bird's loud 'WHOW-kayow-kwow' scream (heard most often at dawn and in flight, this is, in the minds of many, the quintessential call of Africa), that accounts for its celebrity status and the wide coverage it receives in television documentaries.

Contrary to the image it presents, however, the species is not exclusively predatory. When its preferred food resources are scarce it will cheerfully rob other birds – notably cormorants and herons – of their catches, steal their eggs, kill and eat their nestlings, hunt other waterbirds (up to the size of a flamingo) and, occasionally, take frogs, insects and a variety of land creatures ranging from monitor lizards (leguaans) to dassies (rock rabbits, or hyraxes) and monkeys. Nor is it averse to scavenging when the opportunity presents itself. In normal times, though, fish eagles – those of the permanent wetlands – spend very little of their time actually searching for food (one Kenyan study came up with an average of eight minutes' activity a day!). These are highly sedentary, or resident, birds: they rarely move away from the narrow confines of their clearly defined territories. A pair, indeed, may well remain in the same small patch of watery terrain for its entire lifespan.

In Southern Africa, fish eagles lay their clutch of between one and three (but usually two) plain white eggs during the winter months and, as with other African eagles – though rather less so – sibling aggression often leads to the death of the last-born chick.

BELOW: The eagle lands.

MOREMI WILDLIFE RESERVE AND THE CENTRAL DELTA

The Moremi reserve lies a little more than 100 km to the north of and is accessible by road from Maun, though one really needs a four-wheel-drive to get there – patches of deep sand and fallen trees (pushed over by elephants in their quest for forage) make the going difficult and sometimes hazardous.

The reserve extends across both wetland and dry terrain – a magnificently diverse ecological compound of flood plain, island, lily-covered lagoon, dense reed and papyrus bed, giant fan palm, twisty-rooted strangler fig and magnificent mopane woodland giving way, in the north and east, towards the Chobe park, to riverine acacia.

Some of the islands, like those of the northern Delta, are minuscule, comprising little more than a giant termite mound supporting a fig tree or two, but there are others that are fairly substantial; the largest is Chief's Island, an enormous expanse of grassland and forest flanked by the substantial Santantadibe and Boro rivers and on which the wildlife has been left marvellously undisturbed. Indeed, the whole of the Moremi area is famed for the richness of its animal and bird life. The reserve is not fenced (though there's a veterinary cordon well to the south), and the big game – great herds of buffalo, zebra and elephant (an estimated 70 000 of these) – roam freely between the fringes of the Delta and the Chobe region to the northeast. Kudu, tsessebe, impala, Chobe bushbuck, reedbuck, waterbuck and lechwe are common sights; baboons are everywhere; among the predators are lion and leopard, cheetah, wild dog, and such smaller nocturnal species such as serval and wild cat.

The lagoons – where much of the water is entrancingly mantled by lily-pads and pale blue flowers – and the flood plains are alive with the sound and colourful sights of birds: African and lesser jacana, Egyptian and pygmy goose, knobbilled ducks, saddlebill stork, and around 400 other species. Especially worth visiting are the heronries at Gobega, Xakanaxa and Gadikwe, home to colonies of glossy and sacred ibis, marabou stork,

yellowbilled egret, and many kinds of heron – blackheaded, squacco, greenbacked, rufous, night and purple among them.

There is no permanent public accommodation within the formal boundaries of the Moremi, but four camping sites are available – at the two gates, at Third Bridge and at Xakanaxa, just to the west. Facilities are fairly basic; the camps have showers and waterborne sanitation, but these tend to be overused during peak holiday periods and the systems break down from time to time. Public entrance, vehicle entrance and camping fees here – in common with other Botswana public parks – are comparatively high. In sharp contrast to the paucity of public amenities, an impressive number of private lodges and camps has been established, most of them around the edges of the reserve.

Game viewing

The internal roads – there is a kind of triangular drive traversing the reserve's eastern segment, leading from South Gate westwards to Third Bridge and back eastwards again to North Gate – are sandy and challenging, especially during the wet season. Indeed parts of the Moremi are sometimes inaccessible to motorists in periods of heavy rain.

■ **Getting there:** By road from Maun, take the road northeast towards Chobe for 64 km, turn left and continue for a further 35 km to South Gate. Trips to and around the reserve, by 4x4 and boat, are on offer in Maun.

■ **Information** Department of Wildlife and National Parks, PO Box 131, Gaborone, Botswana. Tel: (09267) 37-1405.

Camp Okavango

A top-of-the-range luxury lodge established by Jessie Neil, a Californian whose perfectionism, good taste and deep love of this wilderness are in plain evidence all around you: in the cordon-bleu cuisine, the elegant silverware, the attentive service, the beautifully appointed East African-style tents and in a myriad other, small and thoughtful, touches. Definitely a place for the discerning safari enthusiast.

The camp, set among the jackalberry and sausage trees of an island in the heart of the Delta's permanent waters, comprises 11 twin-bedded tented units, each with private shower (hot water on tap) and waterborne toilet facilities. The reed-and-thatch central complex houses attractive dining, lounge and bar areas; the bar, in homage to its international clientele, stocks a splendid range of drinks.

Water is the focus of activities; on offer are exploratory trips through the quiet channels and lagoons by mokoro and small fibreglass powerboat, and game walks, led by licensed guides, over neighbouring islands. The birding is superb (400 species have been identified in the vicinity); fishing and photographic expeditions are laid on.

The area is known for its sitatunga antelope, but game viewing is generally pretty limited and, for the total wilderness experience, one should combine one's visit with a few days spent at Okavango's sister Camp Moremi (see below).

■ **Getting there:** Camp Okavango cannot be reached by road. Desert & Delta Safaris will fly you in, to the camp airstrip, from either Maun or Kasane, or transport you by boat from Camp Moremi.

■ **Reservations and information:** Afro Ventures/Desert & Delta Safaris, PO Box 2339, Randburg 2125, South Africa. Tel: (011) 789-1078; fax: (011) 886-2349.

OPPOSITE: The Moremi reserve, a splendid mix of wetland and dry terrain, supports huge numbers of elephant.
LEFT: Game spotting near Xakanaxa.

CAMP MOREMI

Related to and in some ways much like Camp Okavango – both were created by Jessie Neil – Camp Moremi also offers stylish living in the heart of the wilderness. Here, too, there are luxury East African-type *en suite* tents; the cuisine is superb, the service immaculate. One of the camp's special features is its timbered dining, lounge and bar complex, raised high above the waters of the lovely Xakanaxa lagoon.

This is big game country; beautifully maintained safari vehicles take guests on exhilarating exploratory drives; the area's lion and buffalo populations are especially notable; bird life (400 species) outstanding. It's recommended that you divide your safari holiday between the sister camps: Moremi introduces you to the region's wildlife, Camp Okavango to the wonders of its waters. A boat ferries guests from one to the other.

TOP: *The reed and timber 'lofty lodge' at Camp Moremi; guests enjoy fine views of the lagoon.* ABOVE: *Some of the Moremi's stately sable antelope. These animals are usually seen in groups of about 30 individuals, though concentrations of up to 200 have been recorded. The males are fiercely territorial; fights during the rutting season can lead to serious injury, sometimes even death.*

■ **Getting there:** Desert & Delta Safaris will fly you in (to Xakanaxa airstrip) from Maun or Kasane, or transport you by boat from Camp Okavango.

■ **Reservations and information:** Central reservations in South Africa: PO Box 2339, Randburg 2125. Tel: (011) 789-1078; fax: (011) 886-2349.

Tsaro Safari Lodge

Located on the Khwai River just outside the Moremi reserve's northeastern boundary, and a little out of the ordinary: here, instead of the usual reed-and-pole or tented units, there are solid, brick-and-thatch chalets, each with its private bathroom (some are split-level, and have sunken baths). The central amenities also fall outside the orthodox Okavango pattern: they're housed in an elegant, white-walled complex of courtyard, open dining area and lounge/bar, the whole overlooking the flood plain and surrounded by trim lawns and shade-giving trees. The food is excellent; the bar well stocked; the swimming pool beckons.

Activities revolve around the area's magnificent game populations and its spectacular beauty. Early-morning and evening drives are laid on; bird-watching, photographic and boating excursions set out from the Xugana sister-lodge, set beside a large and lovely lagoon some way to the west (see page 197).

■ **Getting there:** Tsaro Lodge is accessible both by road (4x4 vehicles only) and by air. Okavango Explorations will fly you in.
■ **Reservations and information:** The lodge does not cater for the drop-in trade; package bookings through Okavango Explorations, PO Box 69859, Bryanston 2021, South Africa. Tel: (011) 708-1893; fax: (011) 708-1569.

Mombo Camp

A remote camp, situated on Mombo Island (which adjoins the northern tip of Chief's Island) in the northwestern Delta and sister establishment to Jedibe Island Camp (see page 184).

Mombo is popular, and deservedly so: it offers a quite superb all-round wilderness experience – this is a region of both land and water, and it can be explored in privacy: guests and camp staff provide the only human presence for miles around. On offer are morning and afternoon game drives in open land cruisers through the Moremi and Jao areas, and evening drives within the Jao concession. The resident ranger will also take

TOP: Hippo graze on Tsaro's lawns.
ABOVE: Dinner time at Mombo Camp.

you on invigorating, and rewarding, walking safaris. Among the area's wildlife are elephant, buffalo, giraffe, lion, leopard, cheetah, wildebeest, zebra, hyaena (the classic documentary *Sisterhood* was filmed at Mombo), albino lechwe (a local genetic oddity), a variety of other antelope and a fine diversity of bird species.

Accommodation is in seven comfortably spacious twin-bedded Meru tented rooms and one reed chalet, all with *en suite* facilities. Recent improvements include upgraded dining and lounge/bar areas.

■ **Getting there:** Mombo Island has its own 800-m airstrip; the safari operator will fly you in.
■ **Reservations and information:** Agents include Okavango Wilderness Safaris, Private Bag 4, Maun, Botswana. Tel: (09267) 66-0086; fax: (09267) 66-0632. Also its associate, Wilderness Safaris, PO Box 651171, Benmore 2010, South Africa. Tel: (011) 884-1458; fax: (011) 883-6255.

KHWAI RIVER LODGE

This lodge, which overlooks the river's flood plain near the Moremi game reserve's North Gate, is one of the region's oldest and most respected, known over the years for its comfort, its pleasant setting and the excellence of its cuisine. Both these elements have been enhanced since the place was taken over, in 1991, by the Orient Express-Mount Nelson joint venture.

Guests are accommodated in rondavel-type brick-and-thatch chalets (each with *en suite* facilities) that are built beneath a canopy of splendid indigenous trees; resident hippo and, often, visiting elephant and other big game animals can be viewed at leisure from the grounds. Shared amenities include a lounge and dining area, fully stocked bar, filtered swimming pool and shop. Professional rangers conduct you on half- and full-day game drives; the bird-watching (about 350 species have been identified; checklist available) is magnificent.

■ **Getting there:** The lodge is 8 km northeast of the Moremi reserve's North Gate; most guests are flown in by Gametrackers. Those arriving by road should seek specific directions before starting out: the route network over the last stretch is complicated.

■ **Reservations and information:** Destination Africa/Gametrackers, PO Box 786432, Sandton 2146, South Africa. Tel: (011) 884-2504; fax: (011) 884-3159.

house (five metres above the ground; bathroom facilities are some distance away) and an attractively atmospheric, reed-walled complex of bar, dining room (for breakfast and dinner), kitchen and shop. The water runs hot in the showers; the toilets flush; camping gear can be hired.

Oddball's – its full and rather improbable name is Oddball's Palm Island Luxury Lodge – is a casual, undemanding, thoroughly enjoyable base from which to explore this wonderful region, which most guests do by hiring mokoro and guide and disappearing into the watery wilderness for days on end.

Oddball's belongs to Okavango Tours & Safaris, which also runs the much more upmarket Delta Camp just up the river.

■ **Getting there:** Most guests arrive by charter flight from Maun, touching down at nearby Delta Camp and transferring by either road or river. Okavango Tours & Safaris handles its clients' travel arrangements.

■ **Reservations and information:** Okavango Tours & Safaris, PO Box 39, Maun, Botswana. Tel: (09267) 66-0220; fax: (09267) 66-0589. South African contact address: PO Box 52900, Saxonwold 2132. Tel: (011) 788-5549; fax: (011) 788-6575.

OPPOSITE: The attractive Khwai River Lodge.
TOP: Inside one of Delta Camp's huts.
ABOVE: Camp Okuti's boma area.

ODDBALL'S

In some ways well-named – it does tend to attract some eccentrically interesting characters. The camp is set on the southwestern corner of Chief's Island: a self-catering establishment that began life as a base for the budget-conscious rugged individualist determined to see the Delta on his own. But the backpacking trade collapsed in 1989 when Botswana's park entry fees were hiked by a hefty 600 per cent, after which Oddball's was upgraded (though the rates remained modest) and now provides an inexpensive alternative to the standard low-density/high-cost luxury establishment.

Campers comprise most of the clientele; permanent buildings include a rustic tree

CAMP OKUTI

A pleasantly shady camp on the Xakanaxa lagoon within the Moremi reserve, Okuti sets out to provide a 'special African experience', and succeeds admirably in doing so. It's an intimate little place, accommodating just 14 people in its neat, carpeted, spotless, thatched and whitewashed chalets, all of which overlook the waters of the river. Owners Rolf and Helma Schleifer are a charmingly hospitable couple; the all-in tariff includes meals (the food is excellent), drinks, game viewing, bird-watching and boating, and upmarket mobile safaris.

■ **Getting there:** Okuti Safaris will fly you to Xakanaxa airstrip.
■ **Reservations and information:** Okuti Safaris, Private Bag 49, Maun, Botswana. Tel and fax: (09267) 66-0307.

DELTA CAMP

This small, old-established (it was originally – before the Okavango became a tourist mecca – a family getaway) and utterly charming camp offers the ultimate in rustic seclusion: just eight reed, thatch and timber *en suite* huts hidden among the tall trees of the Boro River bank.

Tranquillity is the keyword here: owner Peter Sandenburgh has banished powerboats from the area – as part of a more general campaign against noise pollution in this most pristine of wildernesses – in favour of the graceful, silent and environment-friendly mokoro. Delta's expert 'polers', who are also knowledgeable guides, take you out on extended exploratory trips along the waterways, stopping at the end of the day to pitch tents, cook a surprisingly imaginative campfire meal and share their wisdom with you.

Fishing, bird-watching and walking are also among the attractions. All meals, drinks and excursions are included in the tariff.

ABOVE: The elevated bar at Gunn's Camp.
OPPOSITE ABOVE: Gunn's guests on a relaxing mokoro trail.
OPPOSITE BELOW: The African jacana's long toes enable it to walk on lily pads.

■ **Getting there:** There is no road access; Okavango Tours & Safaris will fly you in from Maun.
■ **Reservations and information:** Okavango Tours & Safaris, PO Box 39, Maun, Botswana. Tel: (09267) 66-0220; fax: (09267) 66-0589. South African contact address: PO Box 52900, Saxonwold 2132. Tel: (011) 788-5549; fax: (011) 788-6575.

GUNN'S CAMP

A small place with a big personality – owners Mike and Lindy Gunn have a lively, very sociable approach to the safari business and your days here will linger in the memory long after your return to the concrete jungle.

There are in fact two venues: the main camp, on Ntswi Island on the western edge of Chief's Island, offers pleasant Meru tents and a central dining area where formal meals are served. Drinks are enjoyed in the well-stocked bar. On the next-door island is a camping site.

Among the options are conducted game-viewing and birding walks and mokoro trails.

■ **Getting there:** The camp is not accessible by road; Mike Gunn will make the travel arrangements (by light aircraft or by boat).
■ **Reservations and information:** Gunn's Camp/Trans Okavango Safaris, Private Bag 33, Maun, Botswana. Tel: (09267) 66-0351; fax: (09267) 66-0571.

SAN-TA-WANI SAFARI LODGE

A cluster of eight African-style brick-and-thatch huts near the Moremi reserve's South Gate, San-ta-Wani is one of the older lodges, its immediate surrounds among the most enchanting: it is set in a garden graced by ancient and beautiful indigenous trees and wild flowers (the grounds are lovingly tended by a blind gardener).

The animals of the area are reputed to be unusually (and inexplicably) tame: one can drive right up to a herd of elephant. Buffalo are especially prolific here; lion, leopard, cheetah and wild dog, sable and roan, eland occasionally seen. Rangers conduct guests on twice-daily and full-day game-viewing drives in open safari vehicles; bird-watching expeditions are also an option; checklists of the local mammals, birds (350 species) and trees are available.

Meals are served (usually) in the reed-enclosed boma, and the cuisine is excellent: San-ta-Wani is one of the lodges recently taken over by the Orient Express-Mount Nelson hospitality group.

■ **Getting there:** San-ta-Wani, close to the Moremi's South Gate, is accessible by road both from Maun and from Kasane in the north. Most guests, however, are flown in by Gametrackers.

■ **Reservations and information:** Destination Africa/Gametrackers, PO Box 786432, Sandton 2146, South Africa. Tel: (011) 884-2504; fax: (011) 884-3159.

XAXABA

Situated on the 'island of tall trees', one of many just to the south of Chief's Island, Xaxaba is an old-established and most attractive camp set in an especially beautiful part of the Delta. To sit in the elevated bar with a long drink in one's hand while the sun sets over the quiet waters is a memorable experience indeed.

Xaxaba is a popular place (book well in advance) that can accommodate up to 24 guests in its comfortable twin-bedded reed chalets (each has its *en suite* facilities); activities on offer include powerboat and mokoro trips, pontoon river-cruises, walking trails (magnificent bird-watching opportunities;

350 species identified; checklist available), fishing and, on request, sightseeing by light aircraft. There are a swimming pool and a small curio shop *in situ*; excellent table d'hôte meals (three a day) are enjoyed in the dining area. The camp is now part of the Orient Express-Mount Nelson joint venture.

■ **Getting there:** Gametrackers will fly you in.
■ **Reservations and information:** Destination Africa/Gametrackers, PO Box 786432, Sandton 2146, South Africa. Tel: (011) 884-2504; fax: 884-3159.

MACHABA CAMP

Situated on the Khwai River near the Moremi reserve's North Gate, Machaba is an outstanding venue for the keen game viewer and photographer (the area, significantly, is a hunting concession).

A great number and variety of animals can be seen; elephant, giraffe, buffalo, various antelope and the big cats are prominent; the bird life is superb. On offer are game drives by both day and night.

Accommodation is in well-appointed, supremely comfortable tents; guests take their meals and drinks either in the reeded restaurant or, more usually, in the open. The campfire dinners are memorable.

■ **Getting there:** Machaba is accessible by both road (via Moremi North Gate) and air. Kerr & Downey Safaris will fly you in.

■ **Reservations and information:** Kerr & Downey Safaris, PO Box 40, Maun, Botswana. Tel: (09267) 66-0211/2; fax: (09267) 66-0379.

XAKANAXA CAMP

The first of the private camps to be established on the entrancing lagoon of that name, and it still has something of the old Africa about it. Its Meru tents, raised on platforms and shaded by tall trees, are unpretentious, comfortable, lit at night by hurricane lamps; guests (maximum 12) take their meals in the informal dining area; a good selection of drinks is available.

The lagoon is home to hippo and crocodile which, together with the presence of the bilharzia snail, discourages swimming, but there is fishing here and superb bird-watching – especially during springtime, when the waters attract great nesting colonies of storks.

■ **Getting there:** Xakanaxa is accessible by both road (via the Moremi reserve's North Gate and Third Bridge) and air.

■ **Reservations and information:** Moremi Safaris, PO Box 2757, Cramerview 2060, South Africa. Tel: (011) 465-3842; fax: (011) 465-3779.

POM POM CAMP

A cosy, very comfortable tented camp on the lower reaches of the Okavango River bordering the new Moremi reserve – that is, in the central Delta region. It's run by Kerr & Downey Safaris; among its attractions are the area's superb bird life, its more limited but interesting mammals, and its fishing. Activities include game walks, game drives and mokoro excursions. Among guest amenities is a restaurant (drinks are included in the tariff).

■ **Getting there:** Kerr & Downey Safaris will fly you in.
■ **Reservations and information:** Kerr & Downey Safaris, PO Box 40, Maun, Botswana. Tel: (09267) 66-0211/2; fax: (09267) 66-0379.

OPPOSITE LEFT: *Xaxaba guests are transported by mokoro, the quietest and least intrusive means of exploring the pristine waterways.*
OPPOSITE RIGHT ABOVE: *A Xakanaxa safari tent.*
OPPOSITE RIGHT BELOW: *Boating near Xakanaxa.*
BELOW: *Hippo and calf in the Moremi wetlands.*

XUGANA LODGE

This splendid, beautifully tree-shaded camp is set beside the Xugana lagoon, one of the Delta's largest and loveliest stretches of open water. The clientele tends to be cosmopolitan and discerning (the Prince of Wales was a guest in 1984); the owners specialise in photographic safaris, but there's much else on offer: game drives, bush walks, cruises across lagoon and through waterway, bird-watching expeditions (superb opportunities), light-aircraft flights over the swamplands and, above all, angling (tiger-fish, bream, catfish). Accommodation is in spaciously comfortable *en suite* chalets raised high above the ground to overlook the lagoon.

■ **Getting there:** Okavango Explorations will fly tourists in.
■ **Reservations and information:** Okavango Explorations, Private Bag 48, Maun, Botswana. Tel and fax: (09267) 66-0528. South African contact address: PO Box 69859, Bryanston 2021. Tel: (011) 708-1569; fax: (011) 708-1893/4.

BOTSWANA'S JUMBO TRAILBLAZERS

One of the most delightfully imaginative ways of seeing something of the Okavango Delta is from your perch on the back of an African elephant.

America's zoo and circus world was home to Abu, Kathy and Bennie until the late 1980s, when biologist and author Randall Moore (he wrote the acclaimed *Back to Africa*, a kind of pachydermal version of Hayley's *Roots*) brought these mature elephants back to their ancestral continent and, patiently and lovingly, retrained them to carry riders through its great sunlit spaces. He then teamed up with Kerr & Downey Safaris of Maun to devise a six-day safari package.

The trail provides an unforgettable experience: you ride high, so your eyes miss very little of what's going on around you; the elephant belong naturally to the environment, which has its very special appeal, and they move with surprising gentleness through it, and, as Moore says, 'you're close to the animals; when they communicate with one another, you are part of their world'.

The trail party (maximum 10 persons) is flown in to Abu's Camp from Maun, and members spend a day getting used to their mounts – and making friends with the seven young elephant that belong to the group – before setting out, with the juveniles in tow, through the wilder- ness of grassland and island-studded flood plain. Tour itineraries are flexible: the trail can be combined with more conventional visits to Kerr Downey Safari's other camps (Shindi, Pom Pom and Machaba: see main text).

The experimental scheme has proved successful, and it could lead to bigger things. Randall Moore's dream is to establish an extensive elephant training centre in Botswana, a

multipurpose endeavour that would, among other things, attract tourists, serve as part of an environmental education programme, produce animals for zoos and for understocked game reserves, help minimise the brutal effects of culling programmes (by taking in the orphans) and perhaps, eventually, show the way towards a viable and far more humane alternative to culling as a means of wildlife population control.

Information and reservations: Kerr & Downey Safaris, PO Box 40, Maun, Botswana. Tel: (09267) 66-0211/2; fax: (09267) 660-6379.

OPPOSITE AND BELOW: On safari. The elephant trails set out from Abu's Camp to explore the wetlands and their islands. Tours are flexible, taking in other camps and different means of transport.
RIGHT: Relaxing in the boma.

THE CHOBE AREA

The Chobe National Park covers some 11 000 km² of northern Botswana, a magnificent, game-rich wilderness of river and flood plain, grassland and flat, rather featureless Kalahari semi-desert interspersed with the occasional sandy depression, natural pan, swampland and with extensive areas of mopane, acacia, teak and kiaat woodland.

For much of the year the pans, most of them, are empty, but the rivers of the north – the Linyanti and the Chobe (they are in fact different sections of the same watercourse, and form the ragged boundary between Botswana and Namibia's Caprivi Strip) – are perennial and life-sustaining, and there are a number of waterholes scattered around the harsh, arid-looking central and southern parts. During the latter half of each year, the river system floods, spilling some of its precious content southwards, very occasionally as far as Savuti Channel to fill the game-rich Savuti marshlands.

So the Chobe park's water resources, although not plentiful, are adequate and, together with the woodlands and the sweet grasses of the plains, they sustain a marvellous array of animal and bird life.

In the dry winter months the herds of buffalo and elephant – there are an estimated 35 000 of the latter, which is the largest concentration to be found within the bounds of any national park in Africa – migrate northwards to congregate around the rivers and their fertile flood plains: an unforgettable sight, especially at the going down of the sun, when this lovely land and its great gatherings of animals are bathed in the reds and golds of a dying day. Other creatures abound in this watery wilderness, among them hippo and crocodile, the Chobe bushbuck (more brightly coloured than its cousins elsewhere), the red lechwe and the fairly rare puku antelope, which is at the southern limit of its range here. White rhino, introduced into the area from Zululand, promised to enrich the wildlife complement at one time but, tragically, poachers have reduced their numbers to the point of local extinction.

Notable, too, is the Savuti Marsh of the west-central region, close to the great Mababe Depression (which was once a great lake). In fact the 'marsh' is a vast, dry grassland plain stretching to far horizons, treeless, apparently devoid of life, but with the rains come the wildebeest, the tsessebe, the giraffe, zebra (some 25 000 of these migrate down from the Linyanti/Chobe area, feeding at Savuti for a few weeks before moving on to the Mababe), buffalo and elephant, and much else. The area is famed for its predators – its lion, leopard and cheetah; hyaena and wild dog.

OPPOSITE: *Game viewing at Chobe's Nogatsaa.*
ABOVE: *Lion are prominent in the Savuti area.*
RIGHT: *4x4s are needed in much of the Chobe.*

The Chobe's bird life, particularly that of the northern wetlands, is quite superb. Around 460 different species have been recorded within the park, among them fish eagle, reed cormorant, saddlebill and marabou stork, knobbilled and whitefaced duck, egret, Egyptian goose, purple heron, sacred ibis, malachite kingfisher, Jameson's firefinch, crested and redbilled francolin, Burchell's coucal, palid harrier, weavers and wagtails, hoopoes, hornbills, shrikes and busy colonies of little carmine bee-eaters.

Exploring the Chobe
The park's administrative headquarters are at Kasane, a small but rapidly growing centre in the far northeast of the region, just to the west of the Kazungula border post. The village boasts three hotels, a bank, bakery, service station, liquor store, small supermarket, a brand new international airport, and a majestic baobab tree whose hollowed-out trunk, at one time in the distant colonial past, served as a prison.

The road from Kasane to Nata, Gaborone, Francistown and points beyond is now fully tarred; there is also trouble-free access from the busy and expanding town of Kasane to two other tourist meccas: Namibia's Caprivi Strip and the Victoria Falls, on the border between Zimbabwe and Zambia.

The 35 km of Chobe River frontage that stretches from Kasane westwards to Ngoma is well developed for tourism; fringing the river are splendid private lodges and hotels; the road network is in generally good condition, negotiable by ordinary saloon car, though the routes can become difficult in wet weather and very sandy in dry.

However, you'll need a four-wheel-drive vehicle to explore the rest of the wilderness: surfaces are sandy and can be treacherous. Most of the park is open throughout the year; the areas around the Savuti Channel and Mababe Depression, though, are open at the motorist's risk during the rainy season (1 December to 31 March).

CHOBE'S PUBLIC CAMP SITES
There are five of these scattered around the park; facilities are, generally, barely adequate; take everything with you that you think you'll need.

SERONDELA is on the Chobe River in the north and comfortably accessible from Kasane: busy, often (in the tourist season) uncomfortably crowded. Showers and toilets are among the few visitor amenities.

LINYANTI is on the Linyanti River bank opposite the Caprivi Strip. A remote site; good game viewing, bird-watching and fishing; basic ablution facilities *in situ*.

SAVUTI is in the west-central area of the park. Splendid game viewing but, again, the camp site tends to be crowded; basic and sometimes unreliable ablution facilities are provided. There are also three private camps in the vicinity (see pages 207 and 208).

TSHINGA is in the east-central region, and a very pleasant site. The general area, cut through by the Ngwezumba River, is graced by mopane woodland and mixed forest, and by a number of pans, and there's fine game viewing – especially just before the rains, when the elephant and buffalo congregate.

NOGATSAA is just to the north of Tshinga. Toilets and showers, borehole, dam and viewing hide *in situ*.

ABOVE: Fishing in the Linyanti; hippo are among the area's impressive wildlife complement.
OPPOSITE: The unusual Chobe Game Lodge.

■ **Getting to the Chobe:** Kasane, as mentioned, is accessible by a good road from the southeast (via Nata), and from Livingstone and Victoria Falls (70 km due east; the Zimbabwe-based United Touring Company operates a daily coach service between the Falls and Kazungula). The road up from Maun, through Savuti, is comfortably negotiable by four-wheel-drive in the dry season. By air: one can fly in to Kasane by private air charter, or take one of the scheduled flights, to either Victoria Falls/Livingstone or Kasane, offered by Air Botswana, Air Zimbabwe, Air Namibia, Zambian Airways and South African Airways. There are airstrips at Linyanti and Savuti.

■ **Reservations and information:** It is not necessary to book your camp site in advance. Entry permits are available (and entry fees payable) at the park gates. Permits and information may also be obtained by writing to the Department of Wildlife and National Parks, PO Box 17, Kasane, Botswana. Tel: (09267) 65-0235.

CHOBE GAME LODGE

This luxurious, five-star lodge/hotel complex is, visually, somewhat at odds with its ruggedly African setting, but the contrast appeals rather than offends: it's been quite beautifully designed, is superbly run, and it enables you to enjoy and explore this most fascinating corner of Africa in style. The clientele speaks volumes about the place: the guest list is cosmopolitan, enlivened here and there by names that are known internationally (Elizabeth Taylor and Richard Burton, for instance, spent their second honeymoon in one of the suites).

Chobe Game Lodge overlooks the Chobe River 12 km west of Kasane and eight kilometres from the park gates. The buildings are Moorish in character, the public rooms spacious, cool, distinguished by high, barrel-vaulted ceilings, graceful archways, Italian-tiled floors. In the reception area is an eye-catching display of African art (including some fine tapestry work); outside are emerald lawns, tropical gardens, lovely indigenous shade trees and an inviting pool.

Accommodation comprises 43 double bedrooms, all with *en suite* bathrooms, and with private balconies that overlook river and flood plain. The rooms are well appointed, furnished with taste, cooled by overhead punkah-fans. More luxurious (and more pricey) are the four suites: each has its private bathroom (two of them have two bathrooms), its secluded garden patio and swimming pool. Among guest amenities are a wildlife reference library, a well-stocked curio shop, a modern conference centre, the stylish Linyanti cocktail bar and lounge, a table d'hôte restaurant (specialities include tigerfish pâté and various, and delicious, venison dishes), and an outdoor barbecue area. Breakfast and lunch are lavish buffet affairs.

On offer is a wide range of activities, though the region's wildlife is the principal attraction. There are conducted game-viewing excursions by open vehicle (one can also embark on self-guided drives), by small boat, and by air – the lodge keeps a Cessna 207 aircraft at Kasane, and lays on flights to, among

other destinations, the Okavango and Moremi in the south, Savuti in the southwest, and north to the Victoria Falls. Much closer to home are the hotel grounds themselves, on and from which you can observe hippo and croc, baboon, a variety of antelope and, often, elephant and buffalo, and a marvellous array of birds.

Then there's the evening cruise on the *Mosi-oa-Tunya*, a two-deck barge that makes its leisurely way past the river banks and their teeming wildlife. Drinks are served on board, the atmosphere is relaxed and sociable, the sunsets quite stunning.

■ **Getting there:** Either by road or air to Kasane, and by road to the lodge (a 10-minute drive). See page 202 for more detailed information on access to and movement around the Chobe region. Safari and tour operators will handle their clients' travel arrangements.

■ **Reservations and information:** Chobe Game Lodge, Reservations and Marketing, PO Box 2602, Halfway House 1685, South Africa. Tel: (011) 315-1695/6/7; fax: (011) 805-2882. Also through Afro Ventures or Desert & Delta Safaris (see page 314 and 315 for contact addresses).

KUBU LODGE

A delightful little cluster of 11 Swiss-type, timber-and-thatch chalets elevated high above the Chobe River near Kazangula, 10 km to the east of Kasane. In the early days the site was used as a labour recruitment centre and the place still has a vaguely colonial feel about it, conferred in part by the handsomely mature flamboyant and jacaranda

The Swiss-style charm of Kubu Lodge.

trees that grace the lovely grounds, in part by the remains of old houses with their gauzed-in verandahs.

The chalets are comfortably appointed; each has its private bathroom, its mosquito nets, overhead fan, coffee machine, hair dryer. Sites have also been established for campers (lovely setting, excellent communal bathroom facilities).

Pride of the lodge is its split-level, wood-and-thatch restaurant and bar complex, the broad balcony of which looks out over the river, offering superb sunset views. The restaurant serves tasty table d'hôte fare; there is also a barbecue area and a swimming pool in the grounds.

Activities include ranger-led game drives through the Chobe park; tiger-fishing excursions; boating (small craft can be hired), and birding. Specialist game drives and more extensive expeditions (to, for instance, the Okavango Delta and the Makgadikgadi areas) are also available through Go Wild Safaris, which can be contacted through the lodge.

■ **Getting there:** By either road or air to Kasane, and then by road to the lodge (a short and easy drive). See page 202 for more information on access to and movement around the Chobe region.

■ **Reservations and information:** Kubu Lodge, PO Box 43, Kasane, Botswana. Tel: (09267) 65-0312; fax: (09267) 65-0412.

CHOBE CHILWERO

Chilwero means (approximately) 'the vista beheld' in the local language – an apt enough epithet because the views from the lodge, set atop a 100-m hill overlooking the Chobe River and the flood plain, are indeed magnificent. The best of them can be enjoyed from the main building, a two-storeyed and beautifully thatched structure that houses the dining room (which is distinguished by its large and lovely kiaat-wood table and cordon-bleu cuisine) and, upstairs, an attractively inviting look-out lounge area. Clustered around are the eight thatched and comfortably appointed A-frame bungalows, all with *en suite* facilities.

Chobe Chilwero, situated between the town of Kasane and the national park's northeastern gate, is a relatively new lodge: it was built in the mid-1980s by Brian and Jan Graham, who also launched the Linyanti and Selinda camps, and who have elevated the running of a safari lodge to an art form. Guests are warmly received and very well looked after; on offer are twice-daily game drives (the guides are unusually knowledgeable and informative) to view the wildlife and scenic splendours of the Chobe National Park, and boat trips on the river (the craft is powerful, but commendably quiet).

■ **Getting there:** Either by road or by air to Kasane; then by road to the lodge (take the route leading to the Chobe National Park, turn left just after Chobe Safari Lodge and continue up the slope for 5 km). See page 202 for more detailed information on access to and movement around the Chobe region.

■ **Reservations and information:** Chobe Chilwero, PO Box 22, Kasane, Botswana. Tel: (09267) 65-0352. Also through Gametrackers (see page 315 for the contact address).

CHOBE SAFARI LODGE

Among the attractions of this old-established, unpretentious and comfortable hotel complex is the *Fish Eagle*, a two-deck barge that takes you on leisurely sunset cruises: there are bar facilities aboard, and it's a most relaxing way of seeing the Chobe River, its animals and splendid bird life. The lodge is also popular among anglers (it's an excellent tiger-fishing venue, especially in spring and early summer).

Accommodation is in comfortable family units and standard *en suite* bedrooms in its main section, and in 22 thatched rondavels (some budget, others more luxurious) strung out along the river bank. There's also a camping site. Among guest amenities are a restaurant, cocktail lounge and bar (the latter is the local pub, patronised by a lively clientele that includes safari guides, game hunters, bush pilots and sundry colourful characters with stories to tell), a curio shop, liquor store and pool. Game drives are available through Go Wild Safaris, which operates from Kasane. The hotel will also organise transfers to the Linyanti and Selinda luxury tented camps in the far west of the Chobe park (see page 207).

TOP: The river-front at Chobe Safari Lodge.
ABOVE: The Chobe River is exclusive home to the rare puku antelope.

■ **Getting there:** Chobe Safari Lodge is situated on the western edge of Kasane village, a short distance from the airport. See page 202 for more detailed information on access to tne region.
■ **Reservations and information:** Chobe Safari Lodge, PO Box 10, Kasane, Botswana. Tel: (09267) 65-0300; fax: (09267) 65-0301.

CRESTA MOWANA SAFARI LODGE

A brand-new luxury hotel set beside the Chobe River near Kasane. Mowana, in the Setswana language, means 'baobab', which refers to the ancient and majestic tree around which the complex has been built.

The two-storey thatched structure, superbly designed to blend with its riverine surrounds, houses the reception area, conference centre, shops, travel offices, à la carte restaurant, cocktail bar and barbecue patio. Extending out in two directions along the river bank are the accommodation wings: the 112 bedrooms have *en suite* facilities, private balconies, and look out to the Chobe. Among the guest amenities are two swimming pools. Activities on offer include game drives, river cruises, facilities for fishing and boating, helicopter flights, game flights, kayaking on the rapids and nature walks, and day trips to the Victoria Falls, 70 km to the west.

BELOW: Linyanti Camp's observation barge.
OPPOSITE ABOVE: Linyanti' sociable bar area.
OPPOSITE BELOW: Allan's Camp receives a visit.

■ **Getting there:** The lodge is 8 km from the Chobe National Park, and easily accessible from Kasane airport (a 10-minute drive). See page 202 for more detailed information on access to the region.

■ **Reservations and information:** Cresta Hotels, Botswana: Private Bag 126, Gaborone. Tel: (09267) 31-2431; fax: (09267) 37-5376. Cresta Hotels, South Africa: PO Box 45, Ferndale 2160. Tel: (011) 787-9500; fax: (011) 787-9757.

LINYANTI CAMP

A most pleasant tented camp set in the far northwest of the Chobe park, in the flood plain of the Linyanti River – an area reminiscent of the wondrous Okavango Delta to the south. Here you'll find the same slow-moving, papyrus-fringed waterways, the magical little palm-fringed islands, the rich profusion of riverine vegetation and of bird life. An exquisite spot. In the surrounding savanna woodland areas are elephant, impala, sable, wild dog, lion and the secretive leopard.

Linyanti's eight tents are large, airy, comfortably appointed (though bathroom facilities are communal), well shaded by a dense canopy of giant knobthorn trees. The

pole-and-thatch dining area (excellent cuisine) and bar look out to the river, and to sit there with a long drink in your hand and the glorious colours of the sunset around you is delight indeed. The camp is now owned by Photo Africa, and is most professionally run.

There's good fishing in the area and, of course, game viewing and birding – which are undertaken either on foot along the forest line in company of a trained guide or, in more leisurely fashion, aboard the camp's gently-floating two-deck river barge.

■ **Getting there:** Linyanti is accessible by road and air, from both Maun and Victoria Falls. Most guests arrive by light-aircraft charter (the airstrip is 10 km from camp). Safari operators handle their clients' travel arrangements.

■ **Reservations and information:** Linyanti Camp, PO Box 22, Kasane, Botswana. Tel: (09267) 65-0383. It features on the itineraries of Gametrackers and Photo Africa Safaris (see pages 315 for addresses).

SELINDA BUSH CAMP

Little sister to Linyanti (see above), Selinda comprises a tiny and most attractive cluster of just four twin-bedded luxury tents (each has its hot-water bucket shower and flush toilet) situated beside the Selinda Spillway close to the Linyanti River – a lovely area of flood plain, lagoon, palm island and riverine forest. Game viewing and birding are excellent: in good seasons the floods attract a marvellous array of waterfowl; and herds of elephant, zebra, wildebeest, buffalo and antelope of various kinds, together with the attendant predators.

On offer are game drives in open four-wheel-drives, and guided walks across the flood plain. Meals are taken and sociable get-togethers enjoyed in the canvas dining area that sits atop a giant termite mound. Selinda is full of character, its ambience that of the authentic Africa.

■ **Getting there:** Selinda is accessible by road and air from both Maun and Victoria Falls. Most guests arrive by light-aircraft charter. Safari operators handle their clients' travel arrangements.

■ **Reservations and information:** Selinda Camp, PO Box 22, Kasane, Botswana. Tel: (09267) 65-0385; fax: (09267) 65-0383. The camp features on Photo Africa Safaris' itinerary (see page 315 for contact addresses).

ALLAN'S CAMP

Situated on the Savuti Channel in the semi-arid, game-rich, west-central region of the Chobe park, Allan's is an attractive little complex of African-style reed-and-thatch A-frame bungalows. The focus of camp life is the spaciously tented area where tasty meals, refreshing drinks and the good company of your hosts and fellow guests are enjoyed.

On offer are conducted birding excursions (around 350 species have been identified in the area; a checklist is available) and game-viewing drives. The viewing – in seasons of good rains – is at its best in the latter part of the year, when great numbers of animals migrate to and congregate around the water-holes just to the south.

Allan's is one of six Gametrackers' venues taken over fairly recently by the Orient Express-Mount Nelson joint venture, and facilities are being upgraded. Gametrackers' clients have exclusive use of the camp. It's recommended you take in Allan's as part of a wider-ranging package.

■ **Getting there:** Gametrackers will fly you in.
■ **Reservations and information:** Destination Africa/Gametrackers, PO Box 786432, Sandton 2146, South Africa. Tel: (011) 884-2504; fax: (011) 884-3159.

SAVUTI SOUTH

Sister to and much like Allan's, which lies just to the east (see above), Savuti South is also a comfortable all-tent camp, one which a variety of animals (including hyaena and the occasional elephant) tends to visit at night – all of which adds spice to your wilderness experience. There's excellent game viewing in this semi-desert, acacia-studded region, particularly when (or if) the Savuti Channel

The rugged surrounds of Savuti South.

floods (although it hasn't done so since 1979); and good birding as well (350 species; checklist available). Guests are conducted on drives; there are some interesting Bushman paintings in the vicinity.

Savuti South is now owned by the presti-gious Orient Express-Mount Nelson group; Gametrackers and their clients have exclusive use of the camp.

■ **Getting there:** Gametrackers will fly you in.
■ **Reservations and information:** Destination Africa/Gametrackers, PO Box 786432, Sandton 2146, South Africa. Tel: (011) 884-2504; fax: (011) 884-3159.

LLOYD'S CAMP

This is a place for the discerning wildlife enthusiast: it specialises in dramatic close-quarter game viewing (from a hide overlook-ing the camp's small waterhole); game drives start at or even before dawn, in order to catch the night prowlers before they rest up for the day; when the sun goes down the camp spotlight illuminates a fascinating parade of nocturnal visitors.

At Lloyd's Camp there are few frills, but owners Lloyd and June Wilmot are dedicated to the wilderness and they offer you a power-ful, and truly memorable, insight into the real Africa.

The camp, set on the bank of the now dry Savuti Channel, comprises comfortable twin-bedded tents with shared amenities (there's hot water on tap). In the evening one relaxes around the campfire in always good and often stimulating company, and the drinks go down a treat.

■ **Getting there:** Lloyd's is accessible by road: it's on the southern bank of the Savuti Channel about 1 km from the public camp site. Most guests, though, fly in (either your hosts or Clive Walker Trails will make the arrangements).
■ **Reservations and information:** Lloyd Wilmot Safaris, PO Box 246, Maun, Botswana. Tel: (09267) 66-0351, or through Clive Walker Trails, PO Box 645, Bedfordview 2008, South Africa. Tel: (011) 453-7646; fax: (011) 453-7649.

THE MONKEYS OF SOUTHERN AFRICA

The chacma baboon (*Papio ursinus*), a species of Old World monkey found (mainly) in hilly country and among the rocky outcrops of the savanna spaces, is among the more commonly seen and most 'visitor friendly' residents of Southern Africa's wilderness areas.

The animal is easily recognised: heavily built (adult males weigh up to 40 kg), it has an elongated, dog-like face, darkish brown hair with lighter underparts, and bare buttocks with patches of thickened skin which, on females, swell and redden according to the phases of the sexual cycle.

Chacmas are remarkably agile, sometimes aggressive and always gregarious creatures, congregating in troops of up to a hundred individuals to forage for the wild fruits, bulbs, roots, leaves and insects that make up the bulk of their diet (though they are omnivorous, able to catch and eat vertebrate animals such as birds, hares, sometimes even small antelope when the opportunity presents itself). They are endowed with good hearing and quite superb eyesight – attributes critical to their survival because, as a ground-dwelling species without powerful natural defences, they are highly vulnerable to leopards and other large predators. When the troop senses danger its members immediaztely cluster together in a 'laager' protected by the dominant males (the belief that baboons post sentries, however, is a myth).

Never feed baboons, however sociable and harmless they may seem. They learn to beg for food, even to raid vehicles, and if thwarted can become hostile (in which case they have to be put down).

The chacma occurs throughout the subcontinent as far north as Angola and Zambia. Its cousin, the large yellow baboon, is found in Zimbabwe; the only two other members of the family Cercopithecidae in Southern Africa

The forest-living samango monkey.

are the little, grey-bodied, black-faced vervet monkey (*Cercopithacus aethiops*), common in all well-treed areas and an endearingly familiar presence in and around lodges and park rest camps; as well as the larger and shyer samango monkey (*C. mitis*), which inhabits the larger, well-watered forests of the eastern Cape, northern Natal, eastern Transvaal and eastern Zimbabwe.

Although the samango is seldom seen it is often heard: the male emits a booming call in troop encounters; its alarm call is a loud, repeated 'nyah' sound.

MAKGADIKGADI AND NXAI PANS

Sprawling across the semi-arid east-central portion of Botswana are two of the largest salt pans in the world – vast, shallow basins that were once, long ago, part of an inland sea the size of, or even bigger than, East Africa's famed Lake Victoria.

These are the Ntwetwe and Sowa pans of the Makgadikgadi complex (there are numerous other, salty depressions in the region, but they're smaller and a lot less distinctive) – vast, featureless, for the most part dust-dry basins, blindingly white in the relentless harshness of the African sun and, like Etosha far to the west in Namibia), deceptively animated by mirages that shimmer and dance in the heat-blasted air.

When the rains come, though, their surfaces are covered by sheets of water just a few centimetres deep, and it is during these times

that the salt desert comes alive. Pelicans, flamingoes, waders and all manner of other waterfowl flock to the water in their tens of thousands: a breathtaking spectacle (one sighting is reputed to have encompassed more than a million birds). Animals, too, are attracted to the pans in their multitudes.

The general region is in fact hugely (though, outside the relatively small proclaimed conservation areas, decreasingly) rich in game animals, which migrate according to the dictates of season and of water and food resources. In dry periods the herds – notably of zebra and wildebeest – tend to congregate in the open country to the west, around the Boteti River, but move off to the east and north when the rains come.

The wildlife is especially prolific in the northern parts, on the broad, palm-studded grasslands between Ntwetwe and Nxai Pan. Here there are springbok and gemsbok, blue wildebeest and plains zebra, red hartebeest and their attendant carnivores – lion, leopard, cheetah, brown and spotted hyaena, jackals and wild dog.

Only a small segment of the Ntwetwe is a proclaimed conservation area: its western extremity forms part of the 4 200-km² Makgadikgadi Pans game reserve. In addition, a 310-km² portion of the Nata Delta to the west – the area at the junction of the sporadically flowing freshwater Nata River and saline Sowa Pan – was recently set aside (on local initiative) as the Nata sanctuary. In times of flood the usually dry and desolate-looking terrain here is transformed into a magical, island-graced waterbird habitat.

Nxai Pan, a separate wilderness area to the north of the Makgadikgadi's Ntwetwe, is somewhat deceptively named. It too was once part of the lakes complex, but today it is grassed over, the flat monotony of the plains relieved by swathes of savanna and mopane woodland and by thickets of acacia. At Nxai the wildlife complement is similar to that of the Makgadikgadi pans but enhanced by the presence of giraffe (groups can number an impressive 50 and more individuals) and, just after the first rains fall, of small numbers of

OPPOSITE: The entrancing carmine bee-eater.
ABOVE: Baines' Baobabs, near Nxai Pan.

elephant from the north. Bird life is prolific: around 250 species have been recorded; Nxai's raptors are particularly notable.

The whole of Nxai Pan, together with a number of subsidiary depressions and a group of large and ancient trees known as Baines' Baobabs (they were painted by the celebrated artist-traveller Thomas Baines in 1862 and have, according to photographs, hardly changed since), lies within the 2 600-km² Nxai Pan National Park.

Exploring the area

The best months to see the Makgadikgadi area are April to July, after which the game moves to the Boteti River. Nxai is at its most inviting between December and April. Some hints for the intending visitor:

❏ A four-wheel-drive vehicle to get around is recommended.

❏ Bring with you everything you think you'll need, and more – food, tents and bedding, vehicle spares, precautionary reserves of drinking water, extra fuel (in metal rather than plastic containers).

❏ The best roads are those that traverse the pans themselves. However, do not stray from them: the salty crust is hard but not unbreakable, and vehicles can sink to their axles and beyond in the soft, mushy sub-surface.

❏ Walking is not permitted: horizons are far, the terrain often featureless and it's only too easy to get lost. Predators are also a hazard.

❏ The Makgadikgadi reserve is served by a network of unsignposted tracks (these are charted on the notice board at the northern entrance). If you're travelling in the area outside the reserve's boundaries, take an experienced guide with you.

❏ Nxai Pan National Park also has its route network. Game scouts are on hand to help you plan your itinerary.

❏ Some of the small Nata sanctuary's roads are suited to two-wheel-drive vehicles. Visitors are encouraged to walk freely, however, and a viewing hide has been erected on the eastern shore of Sowa Pan.

Kubu Island, a place of baobab trees and mysterious stone-walled ruins, rises above the flat wastelands of the Makgadikgadi Pans.

PUBLIC CAMP SITES

There is no permanent accommodation within either the Makgadikgadi reserve or the Nxai park. However, camp sites with rudimentary facilities have been established in both areas.

■ **Getting there:** The Makgadikgadi and Nxai areas can be reached by road from Francistown in the east (via Nata and Gweta) and from Maun in the west. These roads are suitable for ordinary saloon cars, but a 4x4 is recommended (and at times essential) for access to and travel within the proclaimed areas. Scheduled air services link Maun and Francistown with major Southern African centres.
■ **Reservations and information:** It is not necessary to book your camp site in advance. Entry permits are available (and entry and camp site fees payable) at the park/reserve gates. Permits and information may be obtained by writing to the Department of Wildlife and National Parks, PO Box 131, Gaborone, Botswana. Tel: (09267) 37-1405.

NATA LODGE

Conveniently located 10 km south of Nata village, which is on the tarred road linking Francistown with Maun (and the Okavango Delta), Chobe and Victoria Falls, Nata Lodge serves as both a welcome stopover for the long-distance traveller and a comfortable base from which to explore the Makgadik-gadi and, to a lesser extent, the Nxai areas. The lodge is situated just off the northern rim of Sowa Pan.

Accommodation is provided in thatched and well appointed A-frame bungalows (all with *en suite* facilities) in a most pleasant setting of monkeythorn, marula and palm trees. The lodge also has a camp site.

Guest amenities include an à la carte restaurant, takeaways, a bar, a curio shop and a refreshing swimming pool. Four-wheel-drive forays to and across the pans can be arranged; the area offers excellent birding during the rains, when the Nata River floods into Sowa Pan and the Nata sanctuary (see above) plays host to a myriad pelicans and flamingoes. Nata Lodge is a popular venue; book early for holiday periods.

TOP: *Nata Lodge, close to Sowa Pan.*
ABOVE: *Riding at Gweta Safari Lodge, 100 km west of Nata and gateway to Makgadikgadi.*

■ **Getting there:** Nata village is on the tarred road 190 km northwest of Francistown and 403 km east of Maun. The lodge is 10 km to the south: follow the guineafowl-embellished signs.
■ **Reservations and information:** Nata Lodge, Private Bag 10, Francistown, Botswana. Tel and fax: (09267) 61-1210.

THE TULI AREA

To the east of the great, sandy wastelands of the Kalahari, in the well-watered, comparatively lush, wedge-shaped region between the Limpopo and Shashe rivers and fringing Botswana's border with the Transvaal province of South Africa, is what is known as the Tuli Block. The countryside is ruggedly beautiful, graced by starkly shaped granite hills and outcrops, open plains, mopane woodlands and, in the riverine parts, by acacia, sycamore fig, winterthorn and nyalaberry, or mashatu, trees. The region is fairly heavily populated, but the majority of people live in the urban centres, leaving the land, still rich in game, to sprawling farms and ranches and to the occasional private reserve.

There is easy road access to the Tuli area from the Transvaal and Bulawayo in Zimbabwe (via Francistown). Many visitors, however, arrive on fly-in safaris.

MASHATU GAME RESERVE

Pride of the region is Mashatu, the largest privately owned game reserve in Southern Africa, and home to the world's largest privately conserved elephant population. The latter are known as the 'relic herds of Shashe', remnants of the once-great pachyderm populations of the Limpopo Valley. The animals, mercilessly slaughtered for their ivory, became locally extinct and remained so for about 60 years until, in the later 1940s, a few refugee groups began filtering back to the sanctuary of the Tuli enclave. Today Mashatu supports about 700 elephant.

The reserve occupies some 30 000 hectares at the tip of Botswana's eastern, wedge-like enclave, a magnificent wilderness of grassland, rocky ridge and narrow flood plain that sustains a great deal of wildlife besides the elephant. Here you'll find giraffe and zebra, eland, impala, steenbok and, in the more densely vegetated parts, lion, leopard, spotted hyaena, an occasional cheetah, kudu, bushbuck, waterbuck, the stately eland, warthog, baboon and a host of smaller,

mainly nocturnal, creatures. Some 375 bird species have been identified in the area.

Guests see all this in style: radio-linked four-wheel-drive vehicles set out at dawn and again at dusk; the Tswana rangers and trackers are superb guides, profoundly wise in the ways of the wild and more than willing to share their knowledge with you. For the closer, more intimate bush experience there are conducted walks that introduce you to the secrets of tracking, and stalking, and to the intricacies of a finely balanced ecosystem.

Mashatu falls into the luxury bracket; its clientele is cosmopolitan; guests are very well looked after, even spoiled. There are two choices of accommodation.

MASHATU'S CAMPS

MAIN CAMP, also known as Majale Lodge, comprises comfortably furnished and very well appointed chalets and rondavels, each with 'his' and 'hers' shower-rooms and toilets and a private verandah with a fine bushveld view. Guests (the camp can accommodate a maximum of 30) enjoy drinks around the filtered swimming pool and in The Gin Trap bar, which is strategically raised to overlook the large and well-patronised waterhole. Dinner (venison specialities; excellent wine list) is usually served in a boma enclosed by reeds and lala palms and which has a viewing window. Also looking out to the waterhole is a thatched, open-sided verandah used for buffet-style breakfasts and lunches.

MASHATU TENT CAMP, also known as Thakadu Camp and situated in the remoteness of the game reserve's northern section,

accommodates 14 people in its twin-bedded, attractively fitted-out canvas units. The tents are insect-proof; each has an *en suite* shower and toilet. Dinner is enjoyed in the firelit boma (again, venison features prominently); breakfast and lunch on the open-sided thatch-covered deck; drinks around the plunge-pool.

■ **Getting there:** By road from the Transvaal, take the N1 to Pietersburg, turn left onto the R521 (signpost: Dendron) and follow the 210-km route northwest to the border post at Pont Drift. Mashatu staff will collect you on the South African side and accompany you through immigration. Most guests, however, fly in. Owners Rattray Reserves offer direct flights between Johannesburg and Tuli airfield in chartered, pressurised King Air aircraft. Immigration clearance facilities are available at the airstrip by prior arrangement. Air Botswana provides regular flights (in a 16-seat Dornier) from Gaborone, Maun and Victoria Falls to Mashatu and Francistown, with connections to Johannesburg. Special charter flights can also be arranged from Gaborone, Maun and Kasane.

■ **Reservations and information:** Rattray Reserves, PO Box 2575, Randburg 2125, South Africa. Tel: (011) 789-2677; fax: (011) 886-4382.

TULI SAFARI LODGE

This splendid lodge, located on a 7 500-hectare private game reserve close to the border at Pont Drift, was fairly recently and extensively upgraded to luxury standards. Accommodation comprises seven twin-bedded and six family rooms in attractively furnished and decorated thatched chalets with private bathrooms.

The central complex has been quite beautifully designed: it houses a dining room (glassed in, but contrived on the indoor/outdoor principle; guests enjoy three lavish meals a day), a bar (built around a tree), patio and filtered pool, the whole embraced by landscaped and lovingly tended gardens of lush plantings, lawns and some of the oldest, tallest and most handsome nyalaberry (mashatu) trees you're likely to see anywhere. From the patio you look out to a waterfall

OPPOSITE: The pool area at Mashatu's Main Camp.
ABOVE: Walking trails in the Mashatu reserve.
RIGHT: Part of Mashatu's tented camp.

that is enchantingly floodlit at night, and which attracts a steady parade of animals (klipspringer, bushbuck, the occasional leopard and a host of smaller nocturnal species). All in all, a venue for the most relaxed and comfortable of bush holidays, and for away-from-it-all business conferences (the conference centre is modern and well equipped).

Among the reserve's wildlife complement are elephant, lion, leopard, hyaena, eland and a wide variety of plains game; included in the daily tariff are two conducted game drives in open four-wheel-drives (wrap up warmly in winter: it can be bitterly cold on the back of the vehicle) and a bush walk. Three viewing hides have been established in the reserve, each sited by a waterhole. Guests can arrange to spend the night in one of them. There's also good birding in the area: among the impressive raptor population are fish, snake and black eagles.

■ **Getting there:** By road from Johannesburg/Pretoria, take the N1 to Pietersburg, turn left onto the R521 (signpost: Dendron) and follow the

210-km route northwest to the border post at Pont Drift. Leave your car on the South African side of the border (the access road can be rough, and floods may be an inhibition during the wet season). Lodge staff will meet you and accompany you through customs and immigration. Most guests, however, fly in from either Johannesburg's Lanseria airport (charter flights) or from Gaborone (twice-weekly scheduled flights). Tuli Safari Lodge has its own international airfield (with customs and immigration facilities *in situ*).

■ **Reservations and information:** Tuli Safari Lodge, PO Box 945, Gaborone, Botswana; or PO Box 41478, Craighall 2024, South Africa. Tel: (011) 788-1748/9; fax: (011) 788-6804. Bookings can also be made through Bushbabies (see page 313 for the contact address).

THE KALAHARI RESERVES

Around two thirds of Botswana is covered by the red sands and sparsely grassed plains of the Kalahari – commonly termed a desert but in reality a wilderness, one that sustains its own, distinctive and in some instances unique animal and plant life.

And its hardy human presence as well. The great, forbidding spaces are home to some of the last of the traditional Bushman communities, small groups of semi-nomadic hunter-gatherers who have managed to resist the pressures exerted and the temptations offered by encroaching Western culture. They are simple, gentle people who own only what they can carry, and who are in total harmony with their environment.

The true desert people – and there are very, very few of them left – still live much as their ancestors did, moving across the parched plains in small clans, each with its defined territory, in search of sustenance. The women customarily gather edible roots and berries, wild cucumbers and tsamma melons, which are a source of both food and water; the men hunt with sinew-strung wooden bow and arrows, which they keep in a skin or bark quiver (though clubs and spears are also used as occasion demands). The arrowheads – once made from chips of stone but now fashioned out of nails and pieces of wire fencing – are tipped with poison extracted from particular insects, spiders or plants. The toxins are slow-acting, and the hunters may have to follow the stricken animal for days, and over long distances, before they can close in. When the kill is finally made, the whole group joins in the feast, singing and dancing in trance-like ritual around the fire.

Game meat, however, is something of a bonus for these people: the hunt has social and spiritual significance, and an antelope carcass provides welcome culinary variation, but for the most part the Bushman's diet comprises, as mentioned, the plants of the desert, supplemented by the smaller mammals, rodents, tortoises, birds and their eggs,

TOP: A young lion drinks at one of the Kalahari region's rare waterholes.
ABOVE: A bush camp in Deception Valley, on the edge of the Central Kalahari reserve.

snakes, lizards, locusts, termites and insects. In the Kalahari, where drought is a permanent condition and surface moisture virtually nonexistent, water is a precious commodity indeed. In especially dry areas the Bushmen use ostrich-egg shells for storage, burying them deep below the sandy surface. These they are able to locate again with uncanny accuracy, perhaps months later, even though the terrain is seemingly featureless and no signs of the cache are visible.

Large parts of the Kalahari wastelands – some 75 000 km² in all – have been set aside as protected areas. None has been extensively developed for tourism; roads, where they exist, are challenging; facilities are few, far between and rudimentary.

CENTRAL KALAHARI GAME RESERVE

Almost 60 000 km² in extent and occupying, as its name suggests, much of the central Kalahari region (it's the second largest conservation area in the world), the reserve is home to scattered groups of Bushmen and haven to large numbers of game animals, among them gemsbok and springbok, blue wildebeest, eland, red hartebeest, and to such predators as lion, leopard, cheetah, hyaena and wild dog. This is an exceptionally dry region – rainfall is rare, and there are no rivers or permanent waterholes – but wildlife is superbly adapted to the conditions: moisture is obtained from such unlikely sources as the dew-covered nighttime plants, the deep roots of the succulents, the moisture-laden tsamma melon and wild cucumber.

There are no visitor facilities, though water is available from the game scouts' camp.

■ **Information:** Department of Wildlife and National Parks, PO Box 131, Gaborone, Botswana. Tel: (09267) 37-1405.

KHUTSE GAME RESERVE

The Khutse forms a 2 600-km² appendage to the Central Kalahari game reserve (see above), and is much more accessible to visitors than its vast northern neighbour. The terrain comprises broad, sandy, scantily grassed plains, fossile dunes, dry river beds, scatters of acacia and other drought-resistant trees and, its most distinctive feature, many seasonal Kalahari pans, most of them sandy but some shrub- and grass-covered. These depressions were once part of an extensive but now long-dry river system. The reserve, despite the lack of surface water, sustains flourishing populations of migratory antelope, together with lion, cheetah, hyaena, black-backed jackal and bat-eared fox.

Visitors can choose between four demarcated camping sites. Bring everything you need with you: there are no facilities whatsoever, though water is available from the game scouts' camp.

■ **Getting there:** The reserve is accessible from Gaborone via Molepolele and Letlhakeng; the road beyond Letlhakeng is suitable only for four-wheel-drive vehicles. Okavango Moving Safaris offer weekend excursions to the Khutse from Gaborone. Tel: (09267) 31-2228.
■ **Reservations and information:** It is not necessary to book your camp site in advance. Entry permits are available (and entry and camp site fees payable) at the entrance gate. For information, contact the Department of Wildlife and National Parks, PO Box 131, Gaborone, Botswana. Tel: (09267) 37-1405.

GEMSBOK NATIONAL PARK

The ancient bed of the Nossob River delineates part of the border between Botswana and South Africa and also the technical boundary between the two gemsbok parks. In ecological terms, however, the latter form a single entity, though the larger portion – Botswana's 11 000-km² Gemsbok National Park – has not yet been developed for tourism. The terrain is typical of the Kalahari's drier regions; among the more pronounced physical features are deep fossil river beds and high red-sand dunes. For a more detailed description of the wider area and its tourism facilities, see page 162.

■ **Getting there:** Access from the Botswana side is via Tsabong. One can also enter via Twee Rivieren in South Africa's Kalahari Gemsbok National Park, and via Mata Mata in the Namibian section of the Kalahari.
■ **Information:** Department of Wildlife and National Parks, PO Box 131, Gaborone, Botswana. Tel: (09267) 37-1405.

ZIMBABWE

Zimbabwe, known as Rhodesia in the years of white rebellion that came to an end with formal independence in 1980, is a large and landlocked country that occupies 390 000 km² of south-central Africa, its sunlit spaces bordering (in clockwise order from the west) on Botswana, Zambia, Mozambique and South Africa.

This is a potentially rich land, fertile in its soils, generous (usually) in its rains, home to something over 10 million people, economically advanced by African standards. And a most inviting one as well – Zimbabwe is endowed with a magnificent wildlife heritage, and blessed by scenic splendour.

Geophysically, the land falls into a number of distinct regions. A high and scenically stunning mountain rampart runs down the country's eastern border from the rugged Nyanga range through the more rounded, tree-mantled, misty hills of the Vumba, to the stark majesty of the Chimanimani in the south. Below the uplands are wide, enchanting and immensely fertile valleys. By contrast, the western and southwestern regions are lower lying, flattish, semi-arid, covered by the sandy soils and hardy dryland vegetation of the Kalahari fringes.

The country's southern frontier is formed by the Limpopo River, its northern by the

OPPOSITE: The Zambezi River, Africa's fourth largest watercourse, thunders over the Victoria Falls.

mighty Zambezi, Africa's fourth largest and arguably its most pristine watercourse. Between the two river systems is the Highveld watershed, a broad ridge rising 1 500 m above sea level and extending southwest to northeast across the width of the country. The Highveld encompasses Zimbabwe's capital – the neat, modern, jacaranda-garlanded little city of Harare – and covers about a quarter of the country; the plateau terrain sloping away on either side of the central ridge a further two-fifths. Bulawayo, the second city, lies some 500 km southwest of Harare.

Beneath the slopes in the southeast is the Lowveld plain, a land of heat and dust, of mopane and ancient baobab tree, leached soils and sparse grasses – but also of irrigated and remarkably productive farmlands, and of countryside rich in game.

Zimbabwe's finest wildlife areas, though, are on the other side of the watershed, along a relatively narrow arc that runs almost continuously from the superb Hwange National Park in the west up to the Zambezi at the Victoria Falls, the country's premier tourist attraction, and then northeast to Lake Kariba and beyond, along the Middle Zambezi valley and its high escarpment to the Mozambique border. It is within this belt of water and wilderness that the great game parks, together with their attendant safari lodges and bush camps, are concentrated.

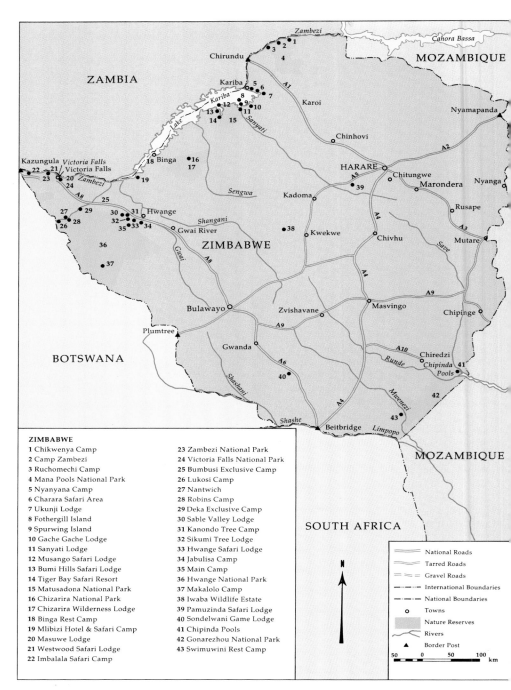

ZAMBIA

ZAMBEZI

Cahora Bassa

MOZAMBIQUE

Chirundu

Kariba

Kariba

Lake

Chinvu

Kadoma

Kwekwe

Mutare

Masvingo

Chipinge

Bulawayo

Zvishavane

Plumtree

Gwanda

Chiredzi

BOTSWANA

Beitbridge

SOUTH AFRICA

MOZAMBIQUE

ZIMBABWE

1 Chikwenya Camp	23 Zambezi National Park
2 Camp Zambezi	24 Victoria Falls National Park
3 Ruchomechi Camp	25 Bumbusi Exclusive Camp
4 Mana Pools National Park	26 Lukosi Camp
5 Nyanyana Camp	27 Nantwich
6 Charara Safari Area	28 Robins Camp
7 Ukunji Lodge	29 Deka Exclusive Camp
8 Fothergill Island	30 Sable Valley Lodge
9 Spurwing Island	31 Kanondo Tree Camp
10 Gache Gache Lodge	32 Sikumi Tree Lodge
11 Sanyati Lodge	33 Hwange Safari Lodge
12 Musango Safari Lodge	34 Jabulisa Camp
13 Bumi Hills Safari Lodge	35 Main Camp
14 Tiger Bay Safari Resort	36 Hwange National Park
15 Matusadona National Park	37 Makalolo Camp
16 Chizarira National Park	38 Iwaba Wildlife Estate
17 Chizarira Wilderness Lodge	39 Pamuzinda Safari Lodge
18 Binga Rest Camp	40 Sondelwani Game Lodge
19 Mlibizi Hotel & Safari Camp	41 Chipinda Pools
20 Masuwe Lodge	42 Gonarezhou National Park
21 Westwood Safari Lodge	43 Swimuwini Rest Camp
22 Imbalala Safari Camp	

	National Roads
	Tarred Roads
	Gravel Roads
	International Boundaries
	National Boundaries
○	Towns
	Nature Reserves
	Rivers
▲	Border Post

N

50   0   50   100
km

THE HWANGE AREA

Hwange National Park, in the far northwest of Zimbabwe, ranks among the princes of Africa's great game reserves: it covers nearly 15 000 km^2 of heat-blistered Kalahari sand country – mainly grassland plains with scattered bush and trees – and it sustains a greater variety and density of wildlife than any other conservation area in the world. Until recently it was known as the Wankie area, but the name has reverted to its authentic origins: Hwange Rosumbani was a 19th-century Rosvi subchief whose misfortune it was to occupy land selected by Mzilikazi, the great Ndebele warrior-king, as a royal hunting ground. Some 90 years later – in 1928, after a slow half-century recovery from the great rinderpest epidemic – his domain was proclaimed a game reserve, and in 1950 it became a national park.

The northern sector of the Hwange is characterised by rocky outcrops, extensive teak forests and mopane woodlands, but for the rest the terrain is fairly flat and open – which of course is ideal for game viewing. It is the northern section, however, that has been most extensively developed for tourism (this is where the public rest camps and most of the private camps and lodges have been established), while the central and southern areas – most of the park – remain a pristine wilderness in which the animals are left virtually undisturbed.

Hwange has no perennial streams, but there is plenty of water in the pump-supplied waterholes and in the many natural pans that fill up after the start of the summer rains. These sources nurture great numbers of elephant, giraffe, zebra, buffalo, sable, roan and other antelope (16 species of buck altogether, including a small number of gemsbok that have made their home in the southwestern corner), and an impressive 25 different kinds of predator, including lion, leopard, cheetah, spotted hyaena and wild dog. The park is especially renowned for its elephant: during the rains (November to February)

The turkey-sized ground hornbill.

many migrate across the border into northern Botswana, but in the dry season Hwange is home to more than 20 000 of these gentle but destructive giants – which at times is rather too many for the countryside to sustain. Rhino, of both the white and black varieties, were reintroduced into the park a few years ago but the populations have been savagely depleted by poachers.

Around 400 bird species have been identified in the park, among them a splendid variety of raptors. Many of Hwange's trees, too, are worth more than a passing glance. Here you'll find the African ebony and the wonderboom, the giant red mahogany *Khya nyasica* (one specimen, at Mount Selinda far to the east, is fully 60 m high), and its smaller and most attractive creeper-covered Natal cousin (*Trichilia emetica*); the bloodwood or mukwa tree, much favoured by the makers of solid furniture, and the renowned Zimbabwe teak (*Baikiaea plurijuga*), known locally as the mgusi.

HWANGE'S CAMPS

There are three major and four smaller, more exclusive, public rest camps (they're available on a block-booking basis) within the park, all located in the northern region. The larger venues each have a grocery store that stocks basic provisions, a limited number of caravan and camping sites (with waterborne ablutions and toilet facilities) and a fuel outlet; the nearest vehicle repair garage is in the town of Hwange.

MAIN CAMP offers self-catering, one- and two-bedroomed cottages, chalets and lodges. The fully equipped cottages incorporate a bathroom and verandah; cooking facilities are communal; electric hotplates are provided; and there's a thatched, open-sided dining area in which there are fridges. The camp restaurant (see below) is nearby. The chalets have barbecue-type wood fires and a communal kitchen area, but are not provided with cutlery and crockery. The lodges are fully equipped, and have electric hotplates. Main Camp's amenities include a fully licensed bar and restaurant.

SINAMATELLA CAMP, with much the same choice of accommodation as Main Camp (cottages, chalets, lodges), is sited on a 55-m-high, boulder-strewn plateau from which there are fine views of the surrounding countryside and, especially, of the game-rich Sinamatella valley below. Here, too, there's a restaurant and bar.

BUMBUSI EXCLUSIVE CAMP, located 24 km northwest of Sinamatella, offers four two-bed A-frame huts and a two-bed cottage (which has a central lounge area that can accommodate two extra guests). The cooking and ablution arrangements are communal. The access road to Bumbusi is rugged, and can be negotiated only by four-wheel-drive during the rains, although an ordinary saloon car will get you there during the dry season.

LUKOSI CAMP Much the same as Bumbusi, and also in the Sinamatella area, Lukosi accommodates groups of up to 12 guests from November through to April.

Game-viewing in the Hwange area.

ROBINS CAMP The third and least sophisticated of the major public venues, Robins is open throughout the year, although the area's game-viewing roads are closed off between November and April. The camp has chalets only, with outdoor cooking facilities (bring your own cutlery and crockery) and communal ablutions. The electricity (generated *in situ*) is switched off at 10 pm.

NANTWICH, 11 km from Robins Camp, is a small camp of two-bedroomed, fully self-contained cottages.

DEKA EXCLUSIVE CAMP, situated 25 km west of Robins, comprises just two two-bedroomed (six-person) family units, each with its own bathroom and toilet, and a communal dining room, sitting room and fully equipped kitchen. The access road is suitable only for four-wheel-drive vehicles, and is sometimes closed off entirely during the rainy season.

Game viewing

The various rest camps are linked by about 500 km of dirt roads along which there are fine picnic spots and viewing sites, most of which overlook waterholes. Some of the routes are shut off during the rainy season. The main picnic sites are enclosed, well shaded, served by small ablution and toilet blocks, and staffed by an attendant who will provide boiling water for your tea. Generally speaking you'll probably find it more rewarding to spend several patient hours beside one waterhole rather than drive through the great spaces hoping for sightings en route.

At Main Camp you can observe the animals by moonlight – an unforgettable experience. Escorted walks are conducted from the three major rest camps, and wilderness trails set out from two (Sinamatella and Robins) between April and October.

A game-viewing expedition with a charming difference is the five-day steam-train safari that begins and ends in Bulawayo, taking in both the Hwange park (two days) and the Victoria Falls area. Accommodation is in vintage coaches with luxurious compartments (though one can choose to spend some of the nights at a hotel or lodge); the steam locomotives are among the largest ever built; the food is excellent; the champagne breakfasts special.

■ **Getting there:** By road: access to all the camps is from the main Bulawayo-Victoria Falls highway. For Main Camp the turn-off is at the 264,5-km mark, the access road a further 25 km; a second turn-off is at the 280-km mark. For Sinamatella, Bumbusi and Lukosi a tar road turning to gravel branches off the main route just south of Hwange town; the 45-km access road runs through Mbala Lodge and the Deka safari area to Sinamatella. Robins, Nantwich and Deka Exclusive are reached by the turn-off 48 km south of Victoria Falls; continue for 70 km on gravel. Robins can also be reached through the park from Main and Sinamatella, but check road conditions before setting out. By air: there are scheduled Air Zimbabwe flights to the national park aerodrome near Main Camp; transport to camp is arranged through the United Touring Company. Main Camp also has an unlicensed airstrip for private/charter aircraft. By rail: the Zambezi Special steam safari from Bulawayo takes in the Hwange park and the regular Bulawayo-Victoria Falls passenger trains stops at Dete; transport from the station, and tours within the park, can be arranged through United Touring Company.

■ **Reservations and information:** The Central Booking Office, Department of National Parks and Wildlife Management, PO Box 8151, Causeway, Harare, Zimbabwe. Tel: (09263-4) 70-6077.

■ **Zambezi Special steam safari:** Rail Safaris, PO Box 4070, Harare, Zimbabwe. Tel: (09263-4) 73-6056; or (09263-9) 7-5575.

OPPOSITE: The delightfully informal Robins Camp.
TOP: Cottages at Hwange's Main Camp.
ABOVE: Sinamatella's dining area. The camp is sited atop a rocky plateau.

SIKUMI TREE LODGE

An enchanting cluster of tree houses (supported by stilts and built into immense mangwe trees) set in an extensive private wildlife estate on the northeastern fringes of the Hwange National Park. There are eight twin-bedded and two double-storeyed family units, all beautifully constructed, at varying heights to suit guests' preferences, from thatch and Zimbabwe teak; each is carpeted and has its own *en suite* facilities (shower, basin, flush toilet). The central complex, also attractively designed in safari style (local woods are

Sable Valley Lodge

Sable Valley, set within its own forestry reserve bordering the Hwange park, is an exceptionally attractive safari lodge, designed and built with the surrounds very much in mind: pink slate, Gwayi River stone and the rich tropical hardwoods of the region have been used extensively in the construction of the buildings; roofs are quite beautifully thatched in traditional Ndebele style. The lodge played host to Queen Elizabeth and the Duke of Edinburgh on their visit to Zimbabwe in 1990; accommodation and amenities are top of the range. The luxury lodges – there are three double-bedded and eight twin-bedded units, each with its bathroom, floor carpeting and solar-powered electric lighting – are sited among indigenous shade trees to give guests an unusual degree of privacy.

Features of the spacious central complex are its soaring hexagonal roof (a theme carried through to the individual living units) and its magnificent bar and dining area, which incorporates an observation platform looking down onto the well-patronised waterhole. The menu is table d'hôte; the cuisine excellent. Amenities include a swimming pool.

extensively used) encompasses a dining area and bar; the grounds are graced by shade-dappled lawns and a swimming pool.

Game viewing

Guests are conducted on day and night game drives, both into the national park and around the private concession area. Bush walks are also an option at times (these depend on the availability of a professional ranger). Wildlife around the lodge is prolific; there are excellent opportunities for bird-watching and for photography.

■ **Getting there:** By road: the lodge is 7 km from the main Bulawayo-Victoria Falls highway; turn off at the 264,5-km mark and left, after 6 km, at the Sikumi sign. Most guests, however, fly in: Sikumi is a 30-minute drive from the Hwange park's air-field; a Touch the Wild representative will meet and transfer you.

■ **Reservations and information:** Touch the Wild, Private Bag 5779, Dete, Zimbabwe. Tel: (09263-18) 273. Private Bag 6, PO Hillside, Bulawayo, Zimbabwe. Tel: (09263-9) 7-4589; fax: (09263-9) 4-4696.

Game viewing

One can spend rewarding hours at the lodge's own waterhole; the general area is renowned for its sable herds (the largest in Africa) and its elephant; lion, leopard and wild dog are among the carnivores seen in the immediate vicinity; the bird life is superb; the splendours of the national park are within easy reach. Sable Valley guides take you out on day drives and night excursions; strategically sited observation hides offer splendid opportunities for photography.

■ **Getting there:** Sable Valley is not accessible by private vehicle. By air: guests are met at the Hwange's airport or at Hwange Safari Lodge and transferred by a representative of Touch the Wild.

■ **Reservations and information:** Touch the Wild, Private Bag 5779, Dete, Zimbabwe. Tel: (09263-18) 273. Private Bag 6, PO Hillside, Bulawayo, Zimbabwe. Tel: (09263-9) 7-4589; fax: (09263-9) 4-4696.

OPPOSITE: The spotted sandgrouse often gather in their thousands to drink.
ABOVE: Close encounters in the Hwange park.

HWANGE SAFARI LODGE

This is a three-star luxury hotel that offers all the comforts of big-city sophistication, but has been built and is run with the lover of the wilderness in mind. Located just outside the Hwange National Park, close to its Main Camp, the lodge is particularly noted for its magnificent viewing platform – part of the bar complex – that overlooks the waterhole and, beyond, a spectacular landscape of pristine bush and teak forest.

Hwange Safari Lodge can accommodate around 190 guests in its comfortable, airconditioned, *en suite* rooms (double and family) and suites. À la carte and table d'hôte fare are enjoyed in the restaurant; the service is superb; the lunchtime barbecues, laid on in the most tranquil of outdoor settings, are special. Among the lodge's amenities are tennis courts, a swimming pool, an aviary and a small museum.

Game viewing

The lodge's waterhole – which can be seen from the patio as well as the observation platform – provides an endless source of interest; bunker hides here and elsewhere promise even closer wildlife encounters. On offer are game drives in open vehicles, bush walks, sunset trails, and one- and two-night safari excursions into the wilderness (on which one sleeps out in tree houses).

■ **Getting there:** By road: access is from the main Bulawayo-Victoria Falls highway. Turn off either at the 264,5-km or the 280-km mark and follow the signs. By air: Hwange Safari Lodge is 4 km from the Hwange park's airport, to which there are scheduled flights; visitors are transferred by coach.
■ **Reservations and information:** Hwange Safari Lodge, Private Bag DT5792, Dete, Zimbabwe. Tel: (09263-18) 331/2/3/4/5/6; fax: (09263-18) 337. Zimbabwe Sun Hotels central reservations, PO Box 8221, Causeway, Harare, Zimbabwe. Tel: (09263-4) 73-6644; fax: (09263-4) 73-4739. Garth Thompson Safari Consultants in Harare, Tel: (09263-4) 79-5202; fax: (09263-4) 79-5287.

KANONDO TREE CAMP

A small, new, exclusive venue, designed along the lines of, but perhaps less elaborately than, Sikumi Tree Lodge (see page 225), Kanondo comprises six tree houses set on the fringes of Kanondo Pan, one of the Hwange park's busiest watering points. The renowned 'presidential herd' of elephant (they are protected by a special presidential decree) is resident in the vicinity.

Each tree house has basic *en suite* facilities (bathroom and showers are in a separate building at ground level) and enjoys a splendid view of the waterhole. Electricity throughout the camp is provided by solar panels. The central boma area, where companionable meals are served and enjoyed around the campfire, also encloses an observation platform.

ABOVE: Lunchtime at Ivory Lodge.
OPPOSITE: A duet of little bee-eaters.

Game viewing

The sunken hide, just three metres from the water's edge, provides exceptional opportunities for close-up viewing and photography. On offer are game drives and bush walks.

■ **Getting there:** Kanondo is located within the same private estate as Sable Valley (see page 226). The camp is not accessible by private vehicle; leave your car at either the airport or at Hwange Safari Lodge; a representative of Touch the Wild will meet and transfer guests arriving by both road and air.

■ **Reservations and information:** Touch the Wild, Private Bag 5779, Dete, Zimbabwe. Tel: (09263-18) 273. Private Bag 6, PO Hillside, Bulawayo, Zimbabwe; Tel: (09263-9) 7-4589; fax: (09263-9) 4-4696.

IVORY LODGE

This rustically elegant venue provides an atmospheric setting for the classic African experience: guests are accommodated in twin-bedded teak-and-thatch tree houses set in a rugged wilderness estate on the northern fringes of the Hwange park. The rooms – there are 10 units in all – are furnished in attractively ethnic style, sited for privacy and linked together by winding bush paths; each has its private bathroom, and a verandah that overlooks the attractive 'red waterhole'. Two are close to the ground (for those who don't fancy climbing stairs), the others at tree-top level. The central structure, built of local woods and thatch, houses the bar and dining areas (the lodge prides itself on its excellent home-style cuisine), the boma and a splendid observation platform. Among other amenities is a swimming pool.

Game viewing

Professional guides conduct guests on drives through the Hwange park, and on bush walks. The lodge's own waterhole attracts a wide variety of wildlife.

■ **Getting there:** Ivory Lodge, 6 km from Hwange airport, is not accessible by private vehicle; leave your car at the airport; a representative of the lodge will meet and transfer (by land rover) guests arriving by either road or air.

■ **Reservations and information:** Ivory Lodge, PO Box 55, Dete, Zimbabwe. Tel: (09263-18) 3402. PO Box 9111, Hillside, Bulawayo, Zimbabwe. Tel: (09263-9) 6-5499. Among agents associated with the lodge are Wild Africa Safaris, PO Box 1737, Harare, Zimbabwe. Tel: (09263-4) 73-8329; fax: (09263-4) 73-7956. Garth Thompson Safari Consultants, PO Box 5826, Harare, Zimbabwe. Tel: (09263-4) 79-5202; fax: (09263-4) 79-5287.

JABULISA CAMP

The name, in SiNdebele, means 'place of happiness' – an apt enough epithet for this enchanting venue located on a 30 000-hectare private estate close to the Hwange National Park. Focal point of the camp is a converted 70-year-old farmhouse whose ceil-ing, at one end, has been raised to accommodate a most attractive dining and observation area; below is an open-plan arrangement of spacious lounge (from which drinks are served), main dining room and, outside, landscaped spaces for lazing around in pleasantly shady surrounds. Scattered around the central complex are the five twin and two double cabins, each charmingly furnished and decorated in African style (earthy ethnic prints and ornaments are much in evidence), each with an *en suite* bathroom. The bath, cleverly positioned, affords the reclining occupant a fine view over the vleis of the Gwayi River valley – luxury indeed.

Game viewing

Safari drives through the Hwange park, and around the estate, are conducted in open land cruisers.

■ **Getting there:** By road: access is from the main Bulawayo-Victoria Falls highway; turn off at the Gwayi River Hotel, and left immediately onto gravel (just behind the hotel); follow the Jabulisa signs. By air: the camp is 45 minutes' drive from the Hwange park airfield, along the road leading southwest through the Gwayi River valley; a Jabulisa representative will meet and transfer you.

■ **Reservations and information:** Jabulisa Camp, PO Dete, Zimbabwe. Tel: (09263-18) 2306; fax: c/o (09263-18) 375.

NEMBA SAFARI CAMP AND WILDERNESS TRAILS

Nemba is an exclusive little family-run tented camp located in the Linquasha area of the Hwange National Park – one of only two safari outfits operating within this game-rich wilderness. Accommodation is in three comfortable huts and four large, insect-proof tents under thatch, all with shower and toilet. There is also a rather more luxurious executive (or honeymoon) suite.

Game viewing

Nemba tailor-makes its excursions to suit individual preferences; options include game drives, bush walks and night excursions conducted by professional guides, and visits to hides strategically sited beside several of the pans. The emphasis, however, is on the walking safari, both from Nemba camp within the Hwange park and farther to the east, in the Mzola wilderness. Nemba Safaris runs three-day trails (maximum six persons) through the fertile, game-rich and scenically beautiful flood plains of the Shangani and other rivers; participants experience the unusual pleasure of walking unburdened through the veld while their equipment and luggage is transported ahead by ox-wagon. Overnight accommodation is in Tonga-style thatched huts built on stilts (there are bush showers and flush toilets); camp beds, sleeping bags, mosquito nets and so forth are provided.

■ **Getting there:** Nemba Camp is about three hours' drive from the Hwange park's airport; the route cuts through the park, and there is game to be seen, and a picnic lunch enjoyed, *en route*. For the wilderness trails, guides meet clients at and transfer them from the Hwange park airport. Alternatively, drive to the first camp site (seek directions from Nemba Safaris, see below) or leave your vehicle at Hwange Safari Lodge or another prearranged collection point.

■ **Reservations and information:** Nemba Camp: PO Box 4, Gwayi, Zimbabwe. Tel: (09263-9) 7-8775; fax: (09263-18) 375. Mzola wilderness trails: Chris van Wyk, Nemba Safaris, PO Box 4, Gwayi, Zimbabwe.

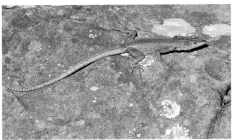

CHOKAMELLA CAMP

A fairly new tented camp located in a prime game-viewing area on the very edge of the Hwange National Park (entry from Chokamella is via the Inyantue gate). The tents – nine twin-fly units and a special 'honeymoon suite', all with *en suite* facilities, hot and cold running water and electric lighting – are set on platforms overlooking a natural pan that attracts great numbers of animals in the dry season. Among the guest amenities is a swimming pool.

Game viewing

Chokamella specialises in photographic safaris, offering day-time game drives and night excursions, in open land rovers, through the national park. Guided bush walks are also on the itinerary.

■ **Getting there:** By road: access is from the main Bulawayo-Victoria Falls highway and Hwange airport; however, you'll need a 4x4 to negotiate the last, mainly gravel, stretch. By air: Chokamella is an hour's drive from the Hwange

park airport; guests arriving by both road and air are met and transferred to camp by land rover.

■ **Reservations and information:** Landela Safaris, PO Box 66293, Kopje, Harare, Zimbabwe. Tel: (09263-4) 70-2634. Among agents are Wild Africa Safaris, PO Box 1437, Harare. Tel: (09263-4) 73-8329; fax: (09263-4) 73-7956.

MAKALOLO CAMP

This luxurious tented camp is situated in the vast and pristine parklands of the Hwange park's southern region – a wilderness area that comes as close to the 'real' Africa, the one that Mzilikazi hunted in, Selous explored and Hemingway wrote about, as you'll find anywhere.

Makalolo, set in a countryside of white sands, palm trees and giant termite mounds, overlooks the Samavundhla pan, a dry-season magnet for a splendid number and variety of wild animals. Especially notable are the area's elephant and buffalo, giraffe and sable, lion and white rhino, and its bird life.

The camp can accommodate 18 guests at a time in its spacious twin-bedded, insect-proof

OPPOSITE ABOVE: One of Jabulisa's chalets.
OPPOSITE BELOW: A colourful flat lizard.
ABOVE: Big Tom's waterhole, Hwange.

tents; each has its shower, basin and flush toilet; solar power heats the water and provides the lighting. Meals are enjoyed in the boma; the food is good, the bar fully stocked; your hosts are friendly and well versed in the ways of the wild.

Game viewing

There are open-vehicle game drives by both day and night, through terrain populated by a splendid diversity of animals and birds and to the teeming plains of Ngamo. Makalolo is also known for its walking safaris.

■ **Getting there:** Makalolo is between two and three hours' drive, through the park, from the airport. Touch the Wild will meet and transfer you.
■ **Reservations and information:** Touch the Wild, Private Bag 5779, Dete, Zimbabwe. Tel: (09263-18) 273. Private Bag 6, PO Hillside, Bulawayo, Zimbabwe. Tel: (09263-9) 7-4589; fax: (09263-9) 4-4696.

THE VICTORIA FALLS: A SCENE 'GAZED UPON BY ANGELS'

The Kololo people of the Zambezi's upper reaches call them *Mosi-oa-Tunya*, the Ndebele *aManzi Thungayo*, both of which describe the great clouds of spray, or 'smoke', that rise far above the thunderous waters. Most of the world, though, know them as the Victoria Falls, named in honour of England's long-reigning queen by the missionary-explorer David Livingstone, reputedly the first white person to see them. Livingstone reached the Falls by dugout canoe, catching his first glimpse of the awe-inspiring spectacle on 17 November 1855. 'Scenes so lovely,' he later observed, 'must have been gazed upon by angels in their flight.' The next day he planted commemorative seeds of apricot, peach and coffee, and carved his name on a nearby tree – the only time in his life, he recalled, that he had 'indulged in this weakness'.

Livingstone's uncharacteristic display of enthusiasm is understandable enough. The Victoria Falls, the most striking feature along the entire 3 540-km length of the Zambezi River, are almost twice as deep and wide as their Niagara cousins; during the peak April period the waters, flowing at a prodigious 545 million litres a minute (which is equivalent to four times Johannesburg's yearly consumption), plunge over the 1 700-m rim in a series of grand cataracts that create the great cloud. On a clear day the rising spray can be seen 80 km away; and at night, during the full-moon phase, an eerily eye-catching lunar rainbow arcs across the gorge. To get to one of the best viewing points you walk through the rainforest, an enchanted and enchanting place of moist, tangled undergrowth and trees whose leaves glisten and drip in the fine mist.

The Falls are at their most dramatic in the months following the rainy season – between February and May. During the period of lowest flow, from September to November, most of the water finds its way through and over the Devil's Cataract, leaving three of the other falls virtually dry. Even at this time, though, their bare faces have their special grandeur.

On the opposite side is Zambia, the border between the two countries running down the middle of the river.

BELOW: The Falls in full flood.
OPPOSITE: The view from Devil's Cataract.

THE VICTORIA FALLS AREA

ABOVE: The thick-tailed galago, one of the larger of several small tree-living primates found in the forests. They are nocturnal, insect-eating creatures.

OPPOSITE: Shangaan traditional dancers give lively performances at the Victoria Falls.

The Victoria Falls – the *Mosi-oa-Tunya* ('smoke that thunders') of the region's Kololo people – are among the most spectacular of the world's great natural wonders. They are certainly Zimbabwe's premier tourist draw-card, although until about three decades ago surprisingly little effort was made to attract visitors to their splendours.

The Falls, in the far northwestern corner of the country, straddle the Zambezi River, a mighty watercourse – Africa's fourth largest (and least spoilt) – that rises in the Lunda uplands far to the north, running south and then east to form the Zimbabwe-Zambia border before entering Mozambique to discharge into the Indian Ocean, 3 540 km from its source. Downstream from the Falls is the great man-made lake of Kariba; upstream is the small town of Kazungula and the eastern tip of Namibia's Caprivi region (see page 153), meeting point of four countries. Here the river is at its widest, its banks fringed by dense green forest, its immense flow sluggish, giving no hint of the sudden and tumultuous violence with which it descends into the 108-m deep gorge.

The railway bridge across the river just below the Falls was completed in 1905 – for that time, a quite magnificent feat of civil engineering and a standing monument to the driving ambition of Cecil John Rhodes, the financial magnate, politician and empire-builder whose vision encompassed no less than a map of Africa painted an Imperial red. The bridge, which formed part of his grand Cape-to-Cairo road, would have been a lot easier and cheaper to build upstream from the cataracts, but he insisted on the more scenic route.

Inevitably a township grew up close to the crossing, though prior to the 1960s it comprised little more than a splendid Edwardian-colonial hotel, a trading store, a few curio outlets and a scatter of storage and rest huts. Today, by contrast, Victoria Falls has a permanent population of well over 10 000, half

a dozen luxury hotels, casinos, restaurants, a sophisticated shopping centre, banks, service stations and an international airport. Visitors spend their days viewing the drama and beauty of the tumbling waters, exploring the river (the more intrepid on foot, by canoe and by raft, the less so by sunset cruise and the 20-minute 'Flight of Angels' light-aircraft trip), lazing by the pool and playing golf (wildlife is a feature of the lovely fairways); their evenings dining, wining, gambling and being entertained.

Special drawcards in and around the town are the crocodile ranch, which contains about 2 000 of these giant reptiles; the multi-cultural craft village, a marvellously evocative exposition of traditional lifestyles, architecture, handwork, ornamentation, custom, music and drama; and two national parks.

The latter do not rank among the country's foremost game sanctuaries, but they nevertheless have their wildlife interest, and one of them is a scenic and botanical gem.

VICTORIA FALLS NATIONAL PARK

This 2 350-hectare area fringing the Falls and extending over a narrow strip along the river's southern bank has been set aside to preserve both the aspect and the famed rainforest, a magical place rich in birds and butterflies, animals and, especially, in plants. Here, nurtured by the mists and the humus of the soil, are dense profusions of ferns and orchids, vines and lianas, creepers and climbers of all kinds tangled among tall fig and ebony, palm and sausage trees.

A path leads through the forest to the edge of the gorge, and steps cut into the cliff take you down to an observation platform. The awesome cataracts, the forest, the spray, the rainbows fashioned by the diffused sunlight, the soft colours of dawn and of the golden evenings create images that remain long in the memory. There are several other routes and many fine viewpoints, among them the bridge itself, though you'll have to complete customs formalities before entering the Zambian section.

■ **Getting there:** The park is adjacent to the town of Victoria Falls.

■ **Information:** Department of National Parks and Wildlife Management, PO Box 8151, Causeway, Harare, Zimbabwe. Tel: (09263-4) 70-6077. The Secretary, Victoria Falls Publicity Association, PO Box 97, Victoria Falls, Zimbabwe.

ZAMBEZI NATIONAL PARK

This 56 000-hectare sanctuary, which flanks the river above the Victoria Falls and extends southwards for about 25 km, is home to elephant and buffalo, giraffe, white rhino, zebra, splendid herds of sable, eland, kudu, Sharpe's grysbok, reedbuck, impala, waterbuck, lion, leopard and cheetah, and an impressive array of birds.

THE ZAMBEZI PARK'S CAMPS

Permanent accommodation, available in the park's riverbank camp, comprises self-catering, fully equipped, two-bedroomed (six-person) lodges. The camp has neither shop nor restaurant, but Victoria Falls township is

just six kilometres downstream, and the road is tarred. Other options are:

❏ Three exclusive 10-person (block bookings only) fishing camps, each set in enchanting surrounds. Sansimba (30 km upstream) and Mpala Jena (17 km) are officially open only in the dry season; Kandahar is available throughout the year. Facilities are basic: simple sleeping shelter; cement tables, benches and barbecue units; cold showers; flush toilets.

❏ Four 'minimum development' camp sites (barbecue stands and bush toilets only), all sited on the riverbank in wild and quite beautiful surrounds.

❏ The Chamabonda platform, an observation point 25 km along the southern game-viewing route (30 km from Victoria Falls), available for overnight camping. Here there's a cold-water shower and flush toilet.

ABOVE: Rafting below the Falls – a virtually risk-free sport, even though there's white water on some stretches.
OPPOSITE: Sightseeing by riverboat.

Game viewing

Some of the wildlife mentioned above, together with hippo and crocodile, can be spotted on the scenically fascinating drive that leads along the 46-km river frontage. *En route* there are more than 20 demarcated, shady and most attractive riverbank sites where you can stop for a picnic, or to fish in the big, slow waters (bream and tigerfish are the main catches; a licence is not required).

The 25-km Chamabonda game drive cuts through the southern section of the park and is, usually, the more rewarding route in terms of the larger game species.

■ **Getting there:** The park is adjacent to the town of Victoria Falls.

■ **Reservations and information:** Bookings for accommodation should be made through the National Parks Central Booking Office, Department of National Parks and Wildlife Management, PO Box 8151, Causeway, Harare, Zimbabwe. Tel: (09263-4) 70-6077. The Bulawayo Booking Agency, PO Box 2283, Bulawayo, Zimbabwe. Tel: (09263-9) 6-3646. Information is also available from the Victoria Falls Publicity Association, PO Box 97, Victoria Falls, Zimbabwe; Tel: (09263-13) 4202.

MASUWE LODGE

The lodge, which takes its name from the Masuwe River, a tributary of the Zambezi, is situated in a 300-hectare concession on the eastern edge of the Zambezi National Park just 7 km from Victoria Falls township.

Accommodation is in 10 roomy, walk-in safari tents (one of them serves as a 'honeymoon suite') on platforms raised on stilts – which provides guests with fine views of the river reaches and surrounding countryside. The tents, each erected under a shade-giving thatched structure, are pleasantly furnished, unusually well appointed; features include a private balcony, wall-to-wall reed matting, ethnic décor; cupboard, dressing table, and *en suite* facilities (shower, basin, flush toilet).

The most attractive central dining and lounge complex, built of thatch and stone, opens onto a balcony and bar area which looks out to the pleasant swimming pool and the river beyond.

Game viewing

The Masuwe River flows for up to nine months of the year, but even in the dry late-winter season there are permanent pools along its reaches, watering points that attract a variety of wildlife from the national park. Game drives are laid on, both through the park and around the lodge's concession. Bush walks are by prior arrangement. The lodge will organise trips to the Victoria Falls, its crocodile ranch, the craft village and other points of interest.

■ **Getting there:** Masuwe Lodge is 7 km south of Victoria Falls; your hosts can arrange transport from the town centre. By air: guests will be met at and transferred from Victoria Falls airport by a lodge representative.

■ **Reservations and information:** Landela Safari Adventures, PO Box 66293, Kopje, Harare, Zimbabwe. Tel: (09263-4) 70-2634 or 73-2091; fax: (09263-4) 70-2546.

WESTWOOD SAFARI LODGE

This exclusive little camp (it can accommodate a maximum of six guests) nestles beneath the towering trees of the Zambezi River bank about an hour's drive upstream from the Victoria Falls. The three attractive double lodges, each with its private bathroom, are within a few metres of the water's edge, and the views across the broad reaches and their palm-fringed islands are quite splendid. Focal point of the place is its thatched dining and relaxation area.

Game viewing and exploring

Professional guides conduct guests on game drives and night excursions through the Zambezi National Park; the Hwange is within easy travelling distance, as are the impressive number of wildlife and scenic delights of the beautiful Caprivi region of Namibia just to the west (visitors must have visas to enter this area). Other options include escorted bush walks, river cruises in a small launch, enjoyable sundowner cruises, and tours of the Victoria Falls area.

ABOVE: The old-style Victoria Falls Hotel.
OPPOSITE: A'Zambezi River Lodge.

■ **Getting there:** Westwood is a 30-minute drive from Victoria Falls; you'll need a 4x4. Most guests fly in, and are met at and transferred from either the airport or the Victoria Falls Hotel by a representative of the lodge.
■ **Reservations and information:** Westwood Safari Lodge, PO Box 132, Victoria Falls, Zimbabwe. Tel: (09263-13) 4614. Garth Thompson Safari Consultants, PO Box 5826, Harare, Zimbabwe. Tel: (09263-4) 79-5202; fax: (09263-4) 79-5287.

IMBALALA SAFARI CAMP

One of the most inviting of venues, Imbalala is, like Westwood (see above), situated on the Zambezi close to Kazungula and the Caprivi wetlands. It's a beautiful spot, landscaped into the dense riverine forest overlooking the flood plain; the river and its changing moods are a constant delight to the eye. Vistas encompassing the broad waters can be enjoyed wherever one happens to be: in the pool bar, in the dining area, lunching beneath the handsome shade trees, relaxing in one's private chalet. This last – there are eight *en suite* units in all – is an attractive thatched-roofed structure, its thatch extending from ground to high apex.

Game viewing

This is especially rewarding in the dry season, when one can often see elephant swimming across to the islands, buffalo wallowing at the water's edge, the occasional sitatunga

antelope and much else. Walks and drives along the flood plain bring into view a wonderfully varied bird life. For close-up wildlife encounters there are cruises by small boat and leisurely, drifting journeys by pontoon.

Imbalala is also for the fisherman (bream and, especially, tigerfish: your catch is cooked for you in and served from the camp's kitchen). Fishing equipment is available on site, but some types of lure are in short supply and keen anglers are advised to bring their own tackle (notify the management beforehand that you want to fish).

■ **Getting there:** The camp will arrange transfer from either its permanent office in the town of Victoria Falls or Victoria Falls airport.
■ **Reservations and information:** Imbalala Safari Camp, PO Box 110, Victoria Falls, Zimbabwe. Tel: (09263-13) 4219.

VICTORIA FALLS HOTELS

Visitors who intend taking in the wilderness scene as part of a broader itinerary and who prefer sophisticated hotel accommodation to the rather more rugged charms of a safari camp have an attractive choice of venues.

MAKASA SUN CASINO HOTEL

Modern, smart, luxurious, with plenty laid on in the way of diversion and recreation. The hotel has a four-star rating, nearly 100 rooms and suites, a magnificent pool area (with poolside bar and barbecue; the garden surrounds are quite lovely) and a rooftop cocktail area from which you can see the billowing spray-cloud thrown up by the falls.
Food, drink and amenities: Excellent à la carte fare is served in the Baccarat restaurant; there's live entertainment in the evenings and, of course, games of chance in the casino: blackjack, roulette, punto banco, and the ubiquitous fruit machines.
Reservations and information: PO Box 90, Victoria Falls, Zimbabwe. Tel: (09263-13) 4275; fax: (09263-13) 4782. Zimbabwe Sun Hotels central reservations: PO Box 8221, Causeway, Harare, Zimbabwe. Tel: (09263-4) 73-6644; fax: (09263-4) 73-4739.

VICTORIA FALLS HOTEL

The grand old lady of the Falls area: it opened its hospitable doors in 1905, the year the Zambezi bridge (see page 234) was inaugurated. And the place hasn't changed all that much since: high ceilings, long, wide hallways and shade-dappled verandahs are among its many attractively Edwardian features, legacies of a more leisurely, more graceful era. The main verandah is a popular meeting place. The 140 or so rooms and suites, though, have all the modern comforts and conveniences (the hotel is a four-star establishment).

Food, drink and amenities: Meals (à la carte and lavish buffet; nightly dancing) are served either in the elegantly decorated dining room or on the terrace, from which there's a splendid view of the old iron railway bridge. Evening events include a barbecue and a magnificent display of traditional African dancing on the hotel's sweeping lawns. Among guest amenities are a sparkling swimming pool, floodlit tennis courts, a hairdressing salon, as well as banking and touring/sightseeing services.

Reservations and information: Victoria Falls Hotel, PO Box 10, Victoria Falls, Zimbabwe. Tel: (09263-13) 4751/4761; fax: (09263-13) 4586. Zimbabwe Sun Hotels central reservations: PO Box 8221, Causeway, Harare. Tel: (09263-4) 73-6644; fax: (09263-4) 73-4739.

ELEPHANT HILLS HOTEL

Gutted some years ago, during the bush war, and now quite beautifully reconstructed in cool, vaguely Mediterranean style (though the décor has strong ethnic African overtones), the stylish 260-room, 13-suite, five-star hotel offers just about everything the leisure-bent holidaymaker could need or want. Its water complex (incorporating a swimming pool) is the country's largest; the atrium – the renowned rainforest in microcosm (birds and small mammals included) – can be seen and enjoyed from the accommodation block; among the sporting facilities are the 18-hole golf course, originally designed by Gary Player.

Food, drink and amenities: Meals are enjoyed in the Samukele, Kasibi and Terrace restaurants and in the pool area; there are four cocktail bars; food and service are top of the range; live entertainment and a casino bring sparkle to the evenings.

Reservations and information: PO Box 300, Victoria Falls, Zimbabwe. Tel: (09263-13) 4793; fax: (09263-13) 4655. Zimbabwe Sun Hotels central reservations: PO Box 8221, Causeway, Harare, Zimbabwe. Tel: (09263-4) 73-6644; fax: (09263-4) 73-4739.

A'ZAMBEZI RIVER LODGE

Sited on the Zambezi just upstream from the falls, this three-star, rustically attractive hotel is a member of the respected Rainbow Group. Architecture and décor draw their inspiration from traditional Africa; thatch and panga-panga timber are much in evidence, blending beautifully with the natural surrounds (the hotel is said to be the largest thatched complex in Africa). The 83 airconditioned rooms and suites are laid out in a curving sweep to overlook the river.

Food, drink and amenities: Guests relax in the central pool area, where barbecue lunches and drinks are served to the accompaniment of a marimba (African string-instrument) band; meals are also enjoyed in the Makorekore grill room (à la carte) and in the Batonka table d'hôte restaurant. The Huntsman is a companionable cocktail bar.

Reservations and information: The Rainbow Group, PO Box 5418, Harare, Zimbabwe. Tel: (09263-4) 72-8303 or 77-0585.

RAINBOW HOTEL
An exceptionally handsome establishment, Moorish in concept, designed along flowing, decoratively arabesque lines – a place of white walls and cool courtyards. The rooms (there are 48 units, four of them suites) are airconditioned and have private bathrooms.
Food, drink and amenities: Among other attractions are the pool patio, the unusual 'swim-in' bar and the daily barbecue lunches. And, of course, the Victoria Falls, whose rainbow can be viewed over a drink in the hotel's roof bar. Cordon bleu à la carte and table d'hôte meals are served in the restaurants.
Reservations and information: The Rainbow Group, PO Box 5418, Harare, Zimbabwe. Tel: (09263-4) 72-8303 or 77-0585.

ILALA LODGE
The smallest and newest of the hotels, and one of the most stylish. Situated just one kilometre from the falls, Ilala – the name is taken from the area's lala palms – has just 16 twin rooms; each has a private bathroom, and French windows that open out onto lawn and the natural bush of the private estate. In an unusual departure from standard architectural practice, the accommodation section is positioned below the public rooms, among which are the à la carte restaurant and pool bar.
Reservations and information: Garth Thompson Safari Consultants, PO Box 5826, Harare, Zimbabwe. Tel: (09263-4) 79-5202; fax: (09263-4) 79-5287. Zambezi Wilderness Safaris, PO Box 18, Victoria Falls, Zimbabwe. Tel: (09263-13) 4737; fax: (09263-13) 4417.

KARIBA AND ZAMBEZI UPSTREAM

At the narrow Kariba gorge, some 450 km downstream from the Victoria Falls, the Zambezi has been dammed to create what was, until recently, the largest man-made lake in the world. The massive project was launched in the 1950s, was formally inaugurated by Queen Elizabeth the Queen Mother on 17 May 1960, and has radically changed the character of the countryside.

The lake is 280 km long, 40 km at its widest, 5 180 km² in extent and, when full, contains 160 billion cubic metres of water. To skirt its perimeter involves a 4 000-km trek. The dam wall comprises a 126-m-high, 21-m-thick concrete arch that runs 600 m from one bank of the river to the other. The six sluice gates are capable of discharging 9 400 cumecs of flood water; the power plant, its giant turbines and its alternators are housed in a massive chamber carved out of solid rock.

So much for the statistics: they say much about the dimensions and scope of the reservoir and hydroelectric scheme, but tell you nothing of the wild beauty of the place, of its inlets and islands, of the resorts and marinas that make Kariba one of Africa's most appealing leisure areas. Nor do they hint of the romance, the mystery and the drama of its beginnings – of the displacement, by the relentlessly rising waters, of some 50 000 Tonga tribesmen and the anger of Nyaminyami, the great river god; of the unprecedented floods that killed 17 workers (altogether, more than 70 people died during the four-year construction period) and which threatened to destroy the dam; and most notably of the myriad animals that were trapped on the shrinking patches of dry land by the nascent lake. Most of the game – about 5 000 head in all – was rescued by Rupert Fothergill and his rangers during the massive, and heroic, relocation scheme known as Operation Noah.

Above the dam wall is Kariba township, originally created to house the project's skilled workers (many of them Italians) and

■ **Getting there:** Bumi Hills, 50 km across the lake from Kariba township, is accessible by boat (transfers are arranged by the lodge) and by air (the airstrip can take craft up to DC3s). A twin-engined UAC Private Islander flies guests to and from Kariba. Another option is to drive in from Kariba; petrol is available *in situ*.

■ **Reservations and information:** Bumi Hills Safari Lodge, PO Box 41, Kariba, Zimbabwe. Tel (09263-61) 2353; fax: (09263-61) 2354. Zimbabwe Sun Hotels central reservations: PO Box 8221, Causeway, Harare, Zimbabwe. Tel: (09263-4) 73-6644; fax: (09263-4) 79-4739.

SANYATI LODGE

An unpretentious camp, situated on Kariba's lakeshore just 300 m from the rugged faces of the gorge, Sanyati is known for the personal attention extended to its guests, for its excellent cuisine, for the tranquillity of the setting, and for the splendid wildlife of the immediate area.

The camp is small: a scatter of rustic thatch-and-stone cottages and chalets sited well apart from each other to confer an unusual degree of privacy; all are comfortably appointed, each has its own bathroom and its view of the lake.

The central dining and relaxation patio looks out across Kariba's eastern basin; the food is of cordon bleu standard; dinner by gaslight (there's no generator to break the silence; power is supplied by solar panels), with moonglow illuminating the still waters, is a magical occasion indeed. On especially bright nights you can enjoy the meal at candlelit tables set aboard a pontoon out on the lake. Among the lodge's amenities is a swimming pool.

Game viewing and fishing

On offer are conducted exploratory expeditions along the Matusadona shoreline by boat, land rover and on foot; guests can expect to see elephant, buffalo, hippo, a variety of antelope species, perhaps lion, and a goodly number of the area's 200-odd different kinds of bird. The lodge's pontoon

OPPOSITE: Bumi Hills Safari Lodge from the air.
TOP: Saddlebilled storks feed among the aquatic plants of the water's edge.
ABOVE: The pool area at Bumi Hills.

doubles as a comfortable, shady observation platform, and as a fishing spot. More dedicated anglers can hire boats and tackle; helpers are on hand to clean your catch and generally look after you on trips onto the lake and along its shoreline. The area is especially well endowed with tigerfish.

■ **Getting there:** The lodge will arrange a boat transfer from Kariba.

■ **Reservations and information:** Sanyati Lodge, PO Box 4047, Harare, Zimbabwe. Tel: (09263-4) 70-3000.

SPURWING ISLAND

The attractively grass- and tree-covered island, set close to the shore in a bay flanked by the high Matusadona hills and the rugged Sanyati gorge, was once described by Thor Heyerdahl (of *Kon-tiki* fame) as 'a truly perfect place for all animal lovers'. And indeed the passing parade of game – buffalo grazing, hippos wallowing, elephants sporting in the shallows – is wonderful to behold. So, too, are the birds: around 150 species are resident in the immediate vicinity, among them fish eagle, Narina trogon and the rare African finfoot. The camp's social hub is its central semi-open complex of dining area and two-storeyed, gazebo-type, very companionable pub, all of which overlook the waters of the lake. Accommodation is of three kinds: rustic but beautifully maintained chalets (two of which are in the semi-luxury class) with bathrooms *en suite*; cabins with showers and toilets; and tents under thatch, which have shared ablution facilities.

Game viewing

Much can be seen on and from the island itself. Farther afield, there are conducted game drives and bush walks; boat, pontoon and canoe forays onto the lake and around its many creeks and backwaters (perhaps the most appealing way of seeing the wildlife; the evening excursions are memorable) and, of course, fishing trips.

More enthusiastic and fitter game-lovers are offered a three-day backpacking expedition into the Matusadona mountains – a trail through rugged countryside famed for both its wildlife and its scenic splendours.

■ **Getting there:** Guests either fly or drive in to Kariba, from where they are transferred to the island by speedboat. Alternatively one can take a charter flight to nearby Fothergill Island (see next page) and transfer by boat.

■ **Reservations and information:** Spurwing Island, PO Box 101, Kariba, Zimbabwe. Tel: (09263-61) 2466/2275/2290; fax: (09263-61) 2301.

TIGER BAY SAFARI RESORT

The resort is situated on the Ume River south of Bumi Hills and on the boundary of the Matusadona park, an attractive, family-style venue of 12 thatched, fan-cooled double chalets with private bathrooms. The units are beautifully sited: each has lovely views of mountain and water, and when the lake is at its normal level (recent years have been plagued by drought), guests can bring their boats right up close to the chalet door.

Tiger Bay is a relaxed place, popular for its friendly atmosphere and the casual lifestyle visitors are encouraged to follow. The main lodge offers full catering facilities (table d'hôte menu), a pleasantly convivial bar (the U-Me Rendezvous) and a swimming pool. Drinks are also enjoyed outside during the glorious sundown hour; barbecue dinners are served around the campfire.

Game viewing and exploring

The lodge lays on late-afternoon game-viewing cruises, game drives and bush walks. This is a renowned tigerfishing area; boats are available for hire.

■ **Getting there:** By boat: Kariba is a 90-minute voyage away. By air: the resort will transfer you from Kariba in its own aircraft; transfers connect with scheduled flights from/to Victoria Falls, Hwange National Park and Harare.
■ **Reservations and information:** Tiger Bay Safari Resort, PO Box 102, Kariba, Zimbabwe. Tel: (09263-61) 2569. Conquest Tours, PO Box 714, Harare, Zimbabwe. Tel: (09263-4) 79-4351.

MUSANGO SAFARI CAMP

This fairly new venue, established and run by professional guides Tim Atkinson and Steve Edwards, is sited on a small island close to the lakeshore between Bumi Hills and Tashinga. Accommodation is in comfortably spacious safari tents under thatch, each with twin beds (reading lights are solar-powered), a private outdoor sitting area and an *en suite* shower and flush toilet.

Meals and drinks are served in the most pleasant open-air dining room.

TOP: *Tiger Bay's inviting pool area.*
ABOVE: *The often-seen wattled plover.*
OPPOSITE: *A Bumi Hills safari boat.*

Game viewing and exploring

Professional guides escort guests on drives and walks through the Matusadona National Park, and on occasional night excursions around the island. There are also game-viewing cruises along the lake shoreline, and afternoon canoe trips. Fishing is seasonal.

■ **Getting there:** Visitors are met at Kariba airport and flown by light aircraft to the Bumi Hills airstrip, where they are collected and driven to the water's edge. A motor launch takes them on the final 15-minute journey to camp.
■ **Reservations and information:** Musango Safari Camp, PO Box UA306, Union Avenue, Harare, Zimbabwe. Tel: (09263-4) 79-6821/2 or 70-7713/4; fax: (09263-4) 79-6822.

KARIBA'S FLOATING CAMPS

Intriguing alternatives to the land-based lodge are small craft specially built and appointed for the visitor who wants the best of both water and wilderness.

Typical is *Zambezi Spectacular*, a six-person floating safari camp of three boats, each fitted with twin beds, moored inshore in a secluded area of the lake. The comfortably furnished cabins have small adjoining dressing rooms, hot- and cold-water showers, chemical toilets, and game-viewing verandah-decks. Within easy rowing or paddling distance is the 'mother ship', where guests get together of an evening to relax over sociable sundowners and to dine (the food is well above the ordinary). The shoreline teems with game animals and birds; the setting is marvellously serene: there are no generators, no motors, no sounds but those of untouched Africa.

Game viewing and exploring

A surprising variety of wildlife can be observed from the cabin windows and the deck, and from the mother ship. In addition, though, there are boat and canoe trips along the lakeshore and guided game walks and longer trails into the hinterland.

■ **Getting there:** Access is by boat or air; your hosts will organise the transfers.
■ **Reservations and information:** Zambezi Spectacular: Private Bag 2015, Kariba, Zimbabwe. Tel: (09263-61) 2526. Livingstone Safaris, PO Box 7245, Harare, Zimbabwe. Tel: (09263-4) 70-2005. Among the other floating safari camps are Water Wilderness, associated with Bumi Hills Safari Lodge (see page 244), PO Box 41, Kariba, Zimbabwe. Tel: (09263-61) 2353. Also *Nyakasanga* and *Nyakasikana* houseboats: Lake Wilderness Safaris, PO Box 113, Kariba, Zimbabwe. Tel: (09263-61) 2645. All these are based in the Matusadona area.

CHARARA SAFARI AREA

This magnificently rugged wilderness hugs the eastern shores of the lake (Kariba township and the dam are at its northwestern corner; Bumi Hills and the Matusadona National Park lie along the lakeshore to the west): a 1 700-km^2 expanse of miombo and mopane woodland countryside that sustains a splendid number and variety of game animals – elephant, buffalo, kudu, waterbuck, lion and leopard among them.

NYANYANA CAMP There is no permanent accommodation within the safari area. However, 20 camping and 15 caravan sites are available near the Nyanyana River estuary, just 100 m from the lake shore.

Amenities include fireplaces (firewood is available) and water standpipes, baths, showers, basins and flush toilets. There's also a slipway for those visitors with boats, although it cannot be used when water levels are low (as they often have been in recent years). The nearest food and petrol outlets are at Kariba, 28 km away.

Game viewing

Much of the wildlife can be seen close to Nyanyana; beware the elephant and lion that tend to loiter on the access road (elephant sometimes wander into the camp itself). Visitors can explore the area on foot, but only if accompanied by a qualified guide (who can be hired *in situ*, for a small fee). The Wildlife Society of Zimbabwe has developed picnic sites and an observation platform.

■ **Getting there:** By road from Harare: along the Great North Road via Karoi; turn off towards Kariba at Makuti and again, at the 56-km mark, for Nyanyana. By boat: craft can be hired at Kariba.
■ **Reservations and information:** Camp site bookings through The Central Booking Office, Department of National Parks and Wildlife Management, PO Box 8151, Causeway, Harare, Zimbabwe. Tel: (09263-4) 70-6077. Bulawayo Booking Agency, PO Box 2283, Bulawayo, Zimbabwe. Tel: (09263-9) 6-3646. Information can also be obtained from Charara Safari Area, Private Bag 2002, Kariba, Zimbabwe. Tel: (09263-61) 557 (warden's office) or 2337 (camp).

GACHE GACHE LODGE

A new camp (it was opened in 1993, and is pronounced 'gatchee gatchee') of comfortable thatch and brick units, all with *en suite* facilities, designed to overlook lake and river and the wild countryside of the Charara area.

Game viewing and exploring

Among activities on offer or planned are riverine and lakeshore game-viewing expeditions, bird-spotting by canoe and power-boat; drives in open vehicles; bush walks conducted by a professional guide; and fishing trips.

■ **Getting there:** A minibus transports guests from Kariba to the Kariba Breezes Hotel, from which they are transferred by power-boat (a 40-minute journey). Alternatively, a private air charter will get you there, from Kariba airport, in about 7 minutes.

■ **Reservations and information:** Landela Safaris, PO Box 66293, Kopje, Harare, Zimbabwe. Tel: (09263-4) 70-2634. Wild Africa Safaris, PO Box 1737, Harare, Zimbabwe. Tel: (09263-4) 73-8329; fax: (09263-4) 73-7956.

CHIZARIRA NATIONAL PARK

The park extends across 192 000 hectares of spectacular hill terrain – part of the Zambezi escarpment – to the southeast of Lake Kariba's upper reaches and, although home to an abundance of animals and birds, it does not play host to too many visitors: the area is remote, accessible only by four-wheel-drive, and one needs permission to enter. The nearest food and petrol outlets are at Binga, 90 km from the park. Visitors should report to the warden's office on arrival.

Once you are in, though, you're rewarded by splendid landscapes of msasa-covered mountainside and deep ravine, river and stream and natural spring, and by a wildlife complement that includes elephant and buffalo (about 1 000 of each are resident in the park), sable, roan, tsessebe, lion, leopard and some crocodile.

Among Chizarira's numerous birds are the crowned eagle, the bat hawk, Livingstone's fly-catcher and the elusive Taita falcon.

CHIZARIRA'S CAMPS

The park has no permanent accommodation. There are, however, six exclusive camping sites (available on a block-booking basis; maximum 12 persons), three with ablution facilities. Kasiswi bush camp, along the upper reaches of the Lusilukulu River, and Busi bush camp, on the Busi River, have raised sleeping and dining shelters; the other three camp sites are undeveloped.

Game viewing

There are no game-viewing roads, but one may explore the park on foot provided one is accompanied by a qualified guide. The Department of National Parks and Wildlife Management run backpacking wilderness trails, conducted by an armed ranger, during the dry season. The trails last for up to 10 days. Also on offer are escorted day trails.

■ **Getting there:** Access is complicated. By road from Harare, go via Karoi; from Bulawayo, via Kamativi towards Victoria Falls. In both cases continue on the Binga road to the signposted turn-off.

TOP: Shade trees grace Mlibizi's grounds.
ABOVE: Bushbuck are common in the Kariba area.

■ **Reservations and information:** Reservations for both the camp sites and the wilderness trails should be made through The Central Booking Office, Department of National Parks and Wildlife Management, PO Box 8151, Causeway, Harare, Zimbabwe. Tel: (09263-4) 70-6077. Bulawayo Booking Agency, PO Box 2283, Bulawayo, Zimbabwe. Tel: (09263-9) 6-3646.

CHIZARIRA WILDERNESS LODGE

One of the Kariba region's most secluded camps, located on the remote northern boundary of the Chizarira National Park some 85 km from Binga. This is the edge of the high Zambezi escarpment, and there are fine views across the valley to the lake shore 30 km away.

The small, attractive complex comprises eight two-bedded stone-and-thatch lodges (all with private bathrooms) set in the shade of handsome mountain acacia trees. Guests get together in the central dining, leisure and bar area, and around the rather lovely swimming pool that has been built among, and which blends into, the rocky outcrops and boulders of the hillside.

Game viewing

The countryside here is splendidly wild, wholly unspoilt; among its animals are elephant, buffalo, plains game and, until recently, one of Zimbabwe's largest population of black rhino. The game generally is not all that prolific or visible; the last-named species is a prime target of poachers throughout the subcontinent, and the numbers have dwindled alarmingly (indeed, only the country's private reserves now provide safe sanctuary for the species), but the landscapes are magnificent.

The lodge is run by a charming husband-and-wife team; the former, a professional guide, takes guests out on foot safaris through the national park, and on longer backpacking trails around the wider region. Daily game drives are also on offer.

■ **Getting there:** Access to the lodge is by air, from either Harare or Victoria Falls, to the Chizarira National Park's all-weather airfield, a 30-minute drive from camp.
■ **Reservations and information:** Zambezi Wilderness Safaris, PO Box 18, Victoria Falls, Zimbabwe. Tel: (09263-13) 4637; fax: (09263-13) 4417. Sun Link International, PO Box HG529, Highlands, Harare, Zimbabwe. Tel: (09263-4) 70-4085 or 72-9025; fax: (09263-4) 72-8744.

MLIBIZI HOTEL AND SAFARI CAMP

Situated at the confluence of the Zambezi and Mlibizi rivers at the southwestern end of the lake (and actually closer to Victoria Falls than to Kariba), Mlibiz is a largish collection of thatched buildings set in 10 hectares of lawns and shade trees. The fan-cooled, four-person, serviced bungalows, built of stone and thatch, have private bathrooms and their own patches of garden. Rather special are the two self-catering, double-storeyed chalets designed for families and fishing parties of from 12 to 20 people.

The entire lodge complex is set high on a ridge, and there are delightful views of the grounds and, beyond, the lake. Amenities include a cocktail bar, playground, craft shop, swimming pool and tennis courts.

Game viewing

On offer are morning and evening game drives and longer (one- to three-day) game-viewing and photographic expeditions organised in association with Chizarira Wilderness Lodge (see previous page) and Ilala Lodge (see page 240), from which transfers are

Sundown in the hills above Lake Kariba.

arranged. One can also make one's way by small boat or canoe up Devil's gorge, and take a pontoon/ raft houseboat ride (the vessel has bar and cooking facilities, shower, toilet) past the Batonka villages of the Mlibizi River bank; a speciality is the breakfast cruise. There's good fishing in the area.

■ **Getting there:** By road: Mlibizi is a four-hour drive (370 km) from Bulawayo; the route is tarred all the way. Take the Victoria Falls highway past Gwayi River Lodge, and then the Kamativi road; turn right onto the Binga road after about 40 km and continue for about another 45 km; turn left at the Mbilizi signpost and continue for 10 km. By water: the Kariba ferry calls in at Mlibizi (a 22-hour voyage; excellent scenic and wildlife viewing en route). Guests may also of course make the journey in their own or hired boats. By air: transfers are arranged from Victoria Falls and Hwange airports. For charter flights, there's a 1 200-m dirt airstrip 5 km from Mlibizi; transport to the hotel is laid on.

■ **Reservations and information:** Mlibizi Hotel and Safari Camp, PO Box 6294, Harare, Zimbabwe. Tel: (09263-4) 6-7537/8; fax: (09263-4) 6-3019.

KARIBA'S HOTELS

The handful of hotels that fringe the lake offer comfortable and in some instances luxurious accommodation, splendid vistas, plenty of sporting and recreational facilities, boat hire, sightseeing packages and, most of them, game-viewing opportunities.

LAKE VIEW INN

A spacious, airy, most pleasant two-star family hotel tucked away on the Matusadona hillside looking down to the lake. The views, as the name suggests, are magnificent at any time of the day but especially so as the sun sets over the still waters.

Food, drink and amenities: The most inviting vantage point is probably the patio restaurant. There's also a cocktail bar, the Kariwa à la carte and table d'hôte restaurant (live band Tuesday to Saturday) and an attractive pool area. On offer are game drives, fishing excursions, watersports, and nightly transport to and from the Caribbea Bay casino.

Getting there: Lake View Inn is 17 km from Kariba airport; access is by road or water.

Reservations and information: Zimbabwe Sun

Lake View's pleasant pool area.

Hotels central reservations: PO Box 8221, Causeway, Harare, Zimbabwe. Tel: (09263-4) 73-6644; fax: (09263-4) 73-4739.

CUTTY SARK HOTEL

Another charming family hotel in the Matusadona area, but in this instance right on the lake shore. Accommodation is in thatchroofed 'lodges', all with private bathrooms.

Food, drink and amenities: The restaurant offers both à la carte and table d'hôte fare and on most evenings one dines, and dances, to the sound of a live band. The hotel runs a bar-service cruise boat that puts out twice a day – a relaxing way to explore the watery wilderness and view the game. Other amenities include a pool, tennis court, and fishing boats that can be hired complete with crew, cold box for the catch and a packed lunch.

Getting there: Access is by boat or road from Kariba (coach transfers are laid on).

Reservations and information: PO Box 1490, Harare, Zimbabwe. Tel: (09263-4) 70-5081; fax: (09263-4) 70-7599.

LIVING ON THE WATER

There are around 50 houseboats and cruisers available for charter on the lake, well-equipped and spacious craft that vary in design from the comfortable but functional to the luxurious, and in size from 12 m to 30 m, to accommodate anything from four to 12 passengers. The larger boats have a captain who is intimately familiar with the lake, its islands, inlets and secrets places, and its many moods, and a small crew of helpers who look after the food and drink, the fishing and game-viewing arrangements.

In the middle range of craft and typical of the breed is the *MV Tropicana*, a sturdy, 17-m, two-storeyed monohull cruiser (optimum speed seven knots) with three cabins: a master one with *en suite* shower and toilet, and two smaller double units that share bathroom facilities. Apart from its berths, each cabin has a dressing table, mirror and wardrobe. Mattresses and bed linen are available if you want to sleep on deck (a pleasant way to pass the warm and starlit nights). Indeed, much of one's time is spent on the upper-storey sun deck, which is equipped with a collapsible shade canopy and sun beds, and on the equally inviting afterdeck, where there's a dining table and bar. Some of the bigger vessels incorporate surprisingly spacious lounges, or saloons, complete with television and hi-fi. Life aboard is relaxed and undemanding, the routines flexible. One's days are occupied with sunbathing, sociable lunches, afternoon siestas, evening parties; with water-skiing, fishing, exploring, game- and bird-spotting.

Different owners and tour operators offer different kinds of houseboat holiday. Some emphasise luxury living, others fishing, or watersports, or the wilderness experience – a package may, for instance, encompass trips to the Matusadona and Mana Pools parks, a visit to the Victoria Falls, a canoe safari, a bush trail or white-water rafting down the Zambezi.

In a rather different category is the Cresta hospitality group's *Zambezi* paddle steamer, an ultra-luxurious 'floating hotel' of 20 cabins, four staterooms, dining saloon, cocktail bar, ballroom and casino.

Tied up in a secluded corner of the lake.

ABOVE: *Elephant in the Mana Pools area.*
OPPOSITE ABOVE: *A waterbuck in the shallows.*
OPPOSITE BELOW: *An Egyptian goose.*

CARIBBEA BAY RESORT AND CASINO

An imaginatively conceived Sardinian-style lakeshore maze of twin rooms, suites, 'casitas', courtyards and arched walkways set in beautifully maintained grounds.

Food, drink and amenities: The place – technically classed as a resort – offers both comfort and diversion: there are three cocktail bars, Pedro's à la carte restaurant, a self-service diner, two swimming pools (each has its bar), a supermarket and, of course, the gaming rooms. Entertainment is laid on in the evenings, and there's a lot available in the way of watersports: the resort complex overlooks beach and private marina.

Getting there: Access from Kariba is by boat or road (transfers are by coach).

Reservations and information: Caribbea Bay is a member of the Zimbabwe Sun group; local address: PO Box 120, Kariba, Zimbabwe. Tel: (09263-61) 2454/5. Zimbabwe Sun Hotels central reservations: PO Box 8221, Causeway, Harare, Zimbabwe. Tel: (09263-4) 73-6644; fax: (09263-4) 73-4739.

THE ZAMBEZI VALLEY

Downstream of Lake Kariba the Zambezi River thunders through a short, narrowish gorge before widening and emerging into one of Africa's last great wilderness areas.

This is what is known as the middle Zambezi valley, a splendidly rugged stretch of river, flood plain and alluvial terrace, acacia, mopane and mahogany woodland, jesse bush and high flanking escarpment that runs from Kariba to the Mozambique border. Its riverine reaches, together with great tracts of land on the southern side, are given over almost entirely to wildlife and the preservation of its habitats. The magnificent Mana Pools National Park covers 2 200 km² of the region; much of the remainder has been set aside as proclaimed safari areas – huge, virtually untouched wilderness expanses that are used for controlled hunting but otherwise left alone. Among the latter are the Chewore (3 390 km² in extent), the Dande (523 km²), the Urungu (2 870 km²), the Sapi (1 180 km²) and the Doma (764 km²). The safari areas, together with the Mana Pools park, are a declared World Heritage Site. The Zambezi valley is not the healthiest of places, nor, in

KARIBA BREEZES HOTEL

This popular venue is on the waterfront, next to a tiny harbour (where boats and fishing tackle can be hired). Accommodation is in 30 or so airconditioned double rooms and one suite, all with bathrooms.

Food, drink and amenities: Both à la carte and table d'hôte fare are served in the restaurant. Among amenities are two swimming pools.

Getting there: Access from Kariba is by water and by road.

Reservations and information: PO Box 3, Kariba, Zimbabwe. Tel: (09263-61) 2433/4/5 or Harare (09263-4) 79-0173.

tourist terms, the most comfortably accommodating. The terrain is rugged, the routes through it rough, sometimes – in the rainy season – impassable. The malarial mosquito, the tsetse fly and the bilharzia snail are all too common residents of the lower lying areas. But for all that, the valley has a very special place in the discerning visitor's itinerary.

MANA POOLS NATIONAL PARK

This is the Zambezi valley in all its wild splendour. Fronting 70 km of the river's reaches, the park's most prominent features are the flood plains – or, more accurately, the fertile riverine terraces that have been formed over the millennia as the Zambezi's sluggish waters flowed northwards, depositing rich alluvial soils and creating seasonal pools and channels. The moisture and the lush vegetation – the sweet grasses, the acacia and mopane – attract great numbers of game animals. Beyond, to the south, rise the tree-mantled hills of the escarpment.

The middle Zambezi valley is haven to around 12 000 elephant, the largest concentration in the world after the Hwange herds. Other large mammals abound, among them about 16 000 buffalo, huge numbers of plains zebra, antelope of many kinds, lion, leopard, cheetah, hyaena and packs of wild dog. Mana Pools also sustains one of the country's two groups of nyala (the other is at Gonarezhou; see page 265). There are some black rhino, too. Until a few years ago – until the poachers moved in in force – the park was home to Zimbabwe's premier population of the species, but tragically few are left today.

In the dry season the game comes down from the high country to the south for the life-giving waters of the river and for the lush grazing of its terraces, and to be there just before the onset of the summer rains, in October and November, is to witness a unique and spectacularly memorable part of the wilderness cycle. There are so many elephant that, after a while, one tends to regard them as commonplace. Buffalo can be seen in herds of 2 000 and more; hippo and baboon are everywhere; the antelope roam in

TOP: *Camping out at Mana Pools.*
ABOVE: *Buffalo thrive in the Zambezi area.*
OPPOSITE: *Bird-spotters in the Mana Pools park.*

their multitudes – and the predators congregate for the easy pickings. Avian life is as fascinating if not quite so dramatic. The park plays host to a variety of both woodland and water species – eagles and vultures, Goliath herons, Egyptian and spurwing geese, storks, cormorants and a myriad smaller birds.

A pristine paradise indeed – but one that is under threat. There has been talk of damming the river farther downstream, thus permanently inundating the terraces. The poachers continue to operate with deadly persistence despite the most strenuous countermeasures. There is the possibility that oil, in commercially exploitable quantities, could be found in the area. And schemes to eradicate the tsetse fly will, if undertaken, open up the region to cattle – perhaps the quickest and surest way to destroy the natural environment. But, for the time being, this marvellous part of Africa remains a wild kingdom without parallel.

MANA POOLS' CAMPS

Permanent accommodation in Mana Pools is available in two pleasant riverside lodges, Musangu and Muchichiri. Each eight-bed unit is self-contained, furnished, equipped (bedding, gas stove and gas fridge/freezer, cutlery, crockery) and serviced.

Mana Pools' main camp is Nyamepi, a 29-site caravan and camping ground downstream from the two lodges. Here there are communal ablution blocks housing baths, showers, washbasins (hot and cold running water) and toilets. Firewood is supplied in limited quantities; visitors are advised to bring their own gas stoves.

In addition, there are four remote camp sites, available on an exclusive (block booking) basis, each restricted to two vehicles and 12 persons; and the Vundu camp, which comprises two sleeping huts, a living hut, kitchen and small ablution facility.

Mana Pools is open to campers only in the dry season (May to October), although the dates may change from time to time depending on weather conditions. The lodges, however, are available throughout the year.

The number of vehicles allowed within the park at any one time is restricted to 50, so day visitors should enquire about access before setting out.

Game viewing

The park has a road network. The dry season, and especially the October-November period, is the best time to visit; the most rewarding viewing hours are early in the morning and mid- to late afternoon, when many of the larger mammals emerge onto the river terraces from their hillside cover.

Mana Pools is the only Zimbabwean game park containing such species as elephant, buffalo and the larger carnivores in which visitors are allowed to walk unaccompanied. You do so, though, at your own risk: this is very wild country, and one should always remember that pretty well any animal can be dangerous if startled, irritated, or cut off from its line of retreat.

Boating and fishing are also permitted; boats can be hired locally, and provide game viewers with a splendid alternative to the drive and the bush walk.

■ **Getting there:** By road from Harare: access is via the main highway that leads north to Chirundu and Zambia. Drive 16 km beyond Makuti (269 km from Harare) to Marongora, where bookings are confirmed and entry permits obtained. Continue north for 6 km, turn right onto gravel and follow the road for 30 km to the Nyakasikana gate. The Nyamepi camp office is 42 km farther on. The main highway to the turn-off is tarred; the route from the turn-off to Nyamepi is negotiable by ordinary saloon cars but conditions can be rough. The last fuel outlet is at Makuti; petrol and oil are not obtainable within the park. From Kariba, travel via Makuti, which is 80 km from Kariba township.

■ **Reservations and information:** The Central Booking Office, Department of National Parks and Wildlife Management, PO Box 8151, Causeway, Harare, Zimbabwe. Tel: (09263-4) 70-6077.

CHIKWENYA CAMP

Associated with Fothergill Island and the first private photographic safari camp to be established in the Zambezi valley (it made its appearance in 1982), Chikwenya has become a highly respected leader within the conservation world. It's also a popular venue, favoured by bush-lovers for its isolation and for the beauty of the surrounding wilderness.

The camp is at the confluence of the Zambezi and Sapi rivers, just outside the north-eastern corner of the Mana Pools National Park, in a remote and marvellously unspoilt area of riverine forest and game-rich flood plain. Guests are accommodated in eight thatched, Batonka-style, semi-open chalets, sited along the riverbank to allow unrestricted views of the waters and a welcome degree of privacy. Each has its private facilities (hot and cold showers, flush toilet). Nearby, beneath an enormous canopy of lovely mahogany shade trees, is the dining area, where the tables are of rough-hewn timber, the pottery hand-crafted, and where one relaxes in the company of hosts who are steeped in the lore, and dedicated to the preservation, of the wilderness.

The camp is open only during the dry season – from early April to mid-November.

TOP: *Chikwenya trailists examine a termite mound.*
ABOVE: *Setting out on a game drive.*
OPPOSITE: *River viewing near Chikwenya.*

Game viewing and exploring

Specially adapted boats and open vehicles take guests out on trips that are, usually, very rewarding. Chikwenya's speciality, however, is the escorted bush walk. Chikwenya is the start and finish point of the five-day Natureways combined foot and canoe trails.

■ **Getting there:** By charter flight from Harare, and regular air transfers to the camp from Kariba.
■ **Reservations and information:** Chikwenya Camp, PO Box 292, Kariba, Zimbabwe. Tel: (09263-61) 2525. Foot and canoe trails: Natureways Wilderness Trails, PO Box 5826, Harare, Zimbabwe. Tel: (09263-4) 79-5202/5287 or 70-4501; fax: (09263-4) 79-4501.

CAMP ZAMBEZI

This small (12-guest) private tented camp is set among handsome Natal mahogany trees a few metres from the banks of the Zambezi in the heart of the Mana Pools park. Across the river, on the Zambian side, the escarpment rises up in all its rugged magnificence; the flood plain is both scenically lovely and rich in wildlife – elephant and buffalo are especially common, and the great concentrations of plains game support an impressive array of predators.

Accommodation is in comfortable two-bed tents equipped with mosquito nets and washbasins; bathroom facilities consist of bucket showers and short-drop toilets. The tariff includes three good meals a day.

Camp Zambezi functions from Mondays to Fridays between July and October – the months in which the game is at its most prolific and visible.

Game viewing

There are game drives in open vehicles for the keen photographer; canoe trails on the water of the Zambezi for the bird-watcher and fisherman. Guests are also conducted on bush walks – highly informative and sometimes exciting forays on which one can (usually) observe game at close quarters, and learn something of the ecosystem and its myriad elements.

■ **Getting there:** By road: a minibus collects guests from Harare's Monomotapa Hotel early in the morning; a land cruiser takes over at Makuti for the journey into the valley, and the party arrives in time for lunch. By air: the Mana Pools airstrip is 12 km from camp; Camp Zambezi will arrange air charter and transfer.

■ **Reservations and information:** Camp Zambezi, PO Box 5826, Harare, Zimbabwe. Tel: (09263-4) 79-5202; fax: (09263-4) 79-5287.

RUCKOMECHI CAMP

An exceptionally attractive riverside venue, set in a majestic stand of mahogany and acacia trees on the western boundary of the Mana Pools park. The area's different habitats – river and flood plain, jesse bush, mountain and ancient forest – are home to a remarkable variety of animals and birds.

Ruckomechi, open during the dry season (April to November), caters for a maximum of 20 guests in its 10 wood-and-thatch chalets, each of which has *en suite* facilities (shower, washbasin, toilet). Electricity is laid on, but only between six and eleven at night; paraffin lamps and candles do duty at other times. The camp's thatched bar, dining and lounge area – the latter a companionable deck arrangement where guests relax at the glorious sunset hour – overlook the river. An occasional game of cricket is played on the island sandbanks; third man and long on watch out for crocodiles.

Game viewing and exploring

Ruckomechi has four experienced resident guides; on offer are morning and afternoon conducted drives and night excursions; bush

The sylvan charm of Ruckomechi.

walks led by a professional (and armed) hunter/guide, and sunset canoe trips.

More ambitious is the three-night Mana canoe trail, between Ruckomechi and the Mana Pools park's eastern boundary – a route that takes you through one of Zimbabwe's most richly populated wildlife areas. Trailists are backed by a four-wheel-drive and a support crew that establishes the night camps (tents and dining tables are set up at the river's edge; the cuisine is surprisingly sophisticated; the setting, and the company, delightful). Ruckomechi's guides also know a great deal about the river's fish; guests have the use of the camp's boat and tackle; the local tigerfish record stands at 10 kg.

■ **Getting there:** Access is by road and water from Kariba. Guests are collected – from either airport or hotel – at 9.45 am and driven to Chirundu (a two-hour trip), and then taken by boat on the one-hour second leg to arrive in time for lunch.
■ **Reservations and information:** Shearwater Adventures, PO Box 3961, Harare, Zimbabwe. Tel: (09263-4) 73-5712; fax: (09263-4) 73-5716.

THE LOWVELD AND CENTRAL REGIONS

Zimbabwe's great central spaces, sliced through by the Highveld, flanked by high and lovely mountains in the east and by the Kalahari semi-desert in the west, are not known for the richness of their wildlife: in large part they are well populated, intensively farmed and ranched.

Several sanctuaries have been proclaimed, among them the Mushandike, in the south-central region, and the scenically grand Matobo Hills National Park near Bulawayo, but none of the areas can really be classed as classic big-game country. More immediately attractive to the game viewer, perhaps, are some of the larger private properties that sustain impressive numbers of game animals and which offer lodge facilities.

In the far southeast, however, the scene is very different. This is the Lowveld, a sun-scorched, once fever-ridden plain which remains bone dry for much of its extent, but whose rivers have been harnessed to feed hugely productive irrigation schemes, and the lush-looking land yields bountiful crops of sugarcane, citrus and winter wheat. Beyond these, to the south, lies one of Southern Africa's bigger, wilder and more exciting game conservation areas.

GONAREZHOU NATIONAL PARK

The name means 'place of many elephants', and this is indeed elephant country. Gonarezhou, 5 000 km² in extent, sprawls over the hot, low-lying, ruggedly remote, flattish mopane and baobab country of the southeastern border area fringing Mozambique and close to South Africa's famed Kruger National Park. Many of the larger animals move freely over the frontiers; the Kruger's elephant and eland, in particular, migrate seasonally.

The wildlife, which can perhaps be seen at its best in the Chipinda Pools section, is prolific, encompassing among others buffalo, giraffe, zebra, hippo and crocodile, the rare Lichtenstein's hartebeest, the shy suni and

The solitary large-spotted genet.

many other antelope – including the beautiful nyala, at one time scarce but now well established and regularly seen, especially along the riverine belt. Among the predators are lion and leopard.

And, of course, there are the elephant – about 6 000 of them. Though these giants are gentle enough in most other parts of Southern Africa, those of the Gonarezhou tend to be unusually temperamental and should be treated with the utmost respect. The official pamphlet warns that 'they bear a grudge against man due to persecution and harassment over the years ...'. The Gonarezhou's major river is the Save; also prominent is the Runde, which is flanked by dramatic red-sandstone cliffs and which, curiously enough, is home to two marine species (swordfish and tarpan) as well as to bream, tigerfish and the 'living fossil' lungfish.

The park is potentially one of Southern Africa's finest game conservation areas, but it has its problems: the vegetation has suffered from bush-burning (part of the tsetse fly control programme), and from damage caused by

ABOVE: Cresta Sandstone's Kwali camp.
OPPOSITE: Bushman art on the Lone Star ranch.

the over-large elephant population; the waters of the two rivers are being siphoned off for irrigation; savage droughts – together with the bands of poachers, many of whom cross over from strife-torn Mozambique – have been decimating the herds.

Still, Gonarezhou remains a magnificent wilderness and, once the difficulties have been overcome, may well rival mighty Hwange in its splendour. At the time of writing (1993), the park was temporarily closed to the public.

GONAREZHOU'S CAMPS

The park is divided into two quite separate sections: Chipinda Pools in the north (which encompasses the Runde and Save subsections) and Mabalauta in the south. The nearest supplies of fuel and provisions are at Chiredzi, some 60 km north of Chipinda Pools and principal centre of the Lowveld's irrigated farming region. In normal times (that is, when the park is open to the public), accommodation comprises:

CHIPINDA POOLS and **CHINGULI**, in the Chipinda Pools section, are two developed six-person camps. Both have open dining rondavels and ablution blocks; caravans can be accommodated at the former; several undeveloped sites, offering only the most basic of amenities, are also available. In addition, four delightful picnic sites/hides have been opened in the area for those who want to camp out in a true wilderness area.

SWIMUWINI REST CAMP (the name means 'the place of the baobabs'), in the Mabalauta section, is a pleasant place overlooking the Mwenezi River. It has three five-bedded thatched chalets with enclosed verandahs and two three-bedded chalets with open verandahs. All the units are furnished and equipped (beds, linen, gas fridge/freezer, basic cooking utensils, solar lighting); the bathrooms and toilets are communal. Wildlife is very much in evidence at Swimuwini; elephant, buffalo and lion sometimes move around near and even through the grounds, and nyala drink at the fishpond. The Mabalauta area also offers five camping/ caravan sites.

Game viewing and exploring

Gonarezhou's two sections have their own road networks; the land between remains an entirely untouched wilderness. Much of the Chipinda Pools area is suitable only for four-wheel-drive vehicles. In normal times the camps are open throughout the year but travel within the park is restricted during the rains (seek advice before embarking on a drive). Attractive picnic sites have been established. Take note that the rivers are infested with bilharzia.

Among particular points of interest within the Gonarezhou are the Runde River's spectacular Tjolotjo cliffs, cut through by gullies that animals follow to get to the water; the Tambohanta Pan, which in the rainy season covers the full eight kilometres between the Save and Runde rivers near the Mozambique border; the Chivilila rapids, a series of 10-m falls through the Runde's gorge just south of Chipinda Pools; the Samahena gorge; and the Mwatomba Pools. The Manjinji Pan, 25 km from the park office (and outside the boundary) is the focal point of a splendid bird community.

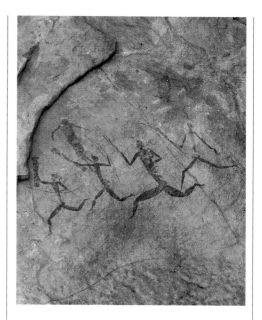

■ **Getting there:** By road from Harare and Bulawayo: via Ngundu Halt, turning left for Chiredzi and Chipinda Pools, and via Rutenga, turning off for Boli and Mabalauta. From South Africa, travel via Beitbridge and either Rutenga or Ngundu Halt.

■ **Reservations and information:** The Central Booking Office, Department of National Parks and Wildlife Management, PO Box 8151, Causeway, Harare, Zimbabwe. Tel: (09263-4) 70-6077.

CRESTA SANDSTONE LODGES

The respected Cresta hospitality group operates two Lowveld lodges, both outside but with easy access to the Gonarezhou National Park – and to the splendid game populations (elephant, black rhino, buffalo, lion, leopard and a host of antelope) of the 30 000-hectare Lone Star ranch.

KWALI CAMP, near the wall of the life-sustaining Malilangwe dam, offers attractively rustic, ethnic-style, wood-and-thatch *en suite* bungalows that blend beautifully with the rugged outcrops and handsome trees of their surrounds. The camp, a charmingly tranquil place billed as 'an affordable retreat for the

ABOVE: A corner of Pamuzinda's dining area.
OPPOSITE: Elephant at Pamuzinda Lodge.

family', can accommodate 22 guests. Excellent meals are served in the riverside dining and barbecue area. Game viewing is conducted in open vehicles and by boat.

INDUNA SAFARI LODGE has a more unusual character: weathered rock, thorn trees, thatch, window nets and the open sky have been incorporated into the design of the chalets – most imaginative, and very effective. Nearby is a lake; all around are the rocks of an ancient natural amphitheatre. Gourmet meals are enjoyed in the open. Induna does not cater for children.

On offer are game drives, nature walks, fishing excursions, and trips to the massive Tjolotjo sandstone cliffs that fringe the Runde River. Fine examples of Bushman art can be seen in the area.

■ **Getting there:** The lodges are accessible by road from Chiredzi and by private aircraft; Buffalo Range airport, which is served by scheduled Air Zimbabwe flights, is within easy driving distance.
■ **Reservations and information:** Cresta Hotels and Safaris, PO Box 2833, Harare, Zimbabwe. Tel: (09263-4) 70-7411; fax: (09263-4) 79-4655. Johannesburg contact number: (011) 787-9757.

SONDELANI GAME LODGE

One of Zimbabwe's most sophisticated lodges, Sondelani is set among the baobabs, pod mahoganies and acacia trees of an extensive (25 000-hectare) western Lowveld wilderness, an area that is home to elephant, buffalo and rhino, to large populations of plains game (including gemsbok), and to leopard, cheetah and other carnivores.

Accommodation is in attractive, individually styled *en suite* chalets built of thatch, wood and local stone. Meals are rather special: beautifully prepared and served in either the outdoor boma or the enclosed dining room, they invariably feature imaginative local specialities and, of course, venison. Amenities include a fully stocked bar and a most pleasant swimming pool area.

Game viewing

Professional ranger-guides take guests out on game drives, on spotlit night excursions, on bush- and river-walks and on backpacking trails (overnight accommodation is in the lodge's tent camp). One can also ride through the game-rich countryside on horseback. Other activities on offer include fishing in the river, bird-watching, and visits to Bushman art sites.

■ **Getting there:** Sondelani is 135 km from the southern border town of Beitbridge, just off the main road to Bulawayo and Victoria Falls. Access is by road, and by air. The lodge has its own airstrip; alternatively, fly to Bulawayo, from where Sondelani will arrange transfer to camp.
■ **Reservations and information:** Sondelani Game Lodge, PO Box 1472, Bulawayo, Zimbabwe. Tel: (09263-9) 6-8739 or 6-0430; fax: (09263-9) 6-4977. Johannesburg contact number: (011) 880-6458.

IWABA WILDLIFE ESTATE

Primarily a big-game hunting enterprise, Iwaba also conducts photographic safaris on, and welcomes non-hunters to, the estate, a 100-km^2 property on the Munyati River in central Zimbabwe. Accommodation is in thatched *en suite* rondavels; meals are taken in the thatched central dining area.

Game viewing

Guests are conducted on game-viewing excursions by qualified guides. The estate is haven to a number of endangered species, among them rhino, cheetah, pangolin and python; other wildlife on view includes wildebeest, zebra, sable, kudu, eland, water-buck and the occasional leopard. But, wrote one guest after his visit, 'the stars of Iwaba are the rhino – both species, the black brought in from the Zambezi valley and the white from Natal way back in 1974. We all enjoyed watching the giraffe, which are new animals there, and searching for the small herd of young elephant.' Incidentally, he added that 'the evening meal around the campfire was really something to remember – first-class food and wine (Zim wine is OK!).'

Iwaba Safaris, your hosts, also have hunting access to a huge (2 000-km²) area extending northwards from the village of Gokwe to the Zambezi escarpment.

■ **Getting there:** Iwaba Wildlife Estate lies east of the midlands town of Kwekwe, from which there is easy road access. Clients arriving at Harare by air will be met and transferred to camp by car (a journey of between four and five hours).
■ **Reservations and information:** Iwaba Safaris, PO Box 5, Kwekwe, Zimbabwe. Tel: (09263-55) 2477.

PAMUZINDA SAFARI LODGE

This luxurious bush venue is situated on a private estate just off the main Harare-Bul-awayo road and just an hour's drive from the Zimbabwean capital. The extensive property is home to a variety of game animals, though the thrust of the conservation effort is the protection and propagation of a small number of endangered species.

Set among attractive shade trees beside the quiet Seruwi River, Pamuzinda caters for a maximum of 26 guests in its 11 quite beauti-fully appointed double lodges and one two-bedroomed 'royal suite' secluded on its own island. The latter has two *en suite* bathrooms and its own swimming pool. The central complex, an open-air arrangement of dining and bar areas, looks out over the main pool and the pan. Cuisine is cordon bleu; the ser-vice meticulous.

On offer are early morning and evening conducted game walks and drives.

■ **Getting there:** By road from Harare, take the Bula-wayo highway to a point just beyond Selous; turn left at the Pamuzinda sign and continue for 6 km.
■ **Reservations and information:** Pamuzinda Safari Lodge, Cresta Hotels and Safaris, PO Box 2833, Harare, Zimbabwe. Tel: (09263-4) 70-7411; fax: (09263-4) 79-4655.

ZAMBIA

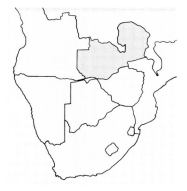

This kidney-shaped, landlocked country extends over 750 000 km² of the Central African plateau – a huge country, as large as France, Austria, Switzerland and Hungary put together. It shares its northern border with Zaire and Tanzania, its eastern with Malawi, its southeastern with Mozambique, its western with Botswana and its southern – formed by the wide and wonderful Zambezi River – with Zimbabwe.

The country lies within the tropics, but because of its fairly high general elevation it enjoys a remarkably kindly climate. There are three distinct seasons: a hot, dry early summer between August and October; a warm and wet high summer from November through to March or April, when heavy tropical downpours cool the afternoon and early evening air; and the winter months that extend from April to July, a bone-dry period of clear, sunfilled skies during the days and cold nights diamond-bright with stars.

Generally speaking, there is little of the dramatic about the Zambian countryside: much of it is remarkably flat, the terrain broken only occasionally by widely dispersed hills and modest ranges. For the most part the ground is covered by a savanna of small trees and tall perennial grasses, though there are splendid teak forests in the southwestern

OPPOSITE: The Zambezi at last light. The Zambian side of the river remains a pristine wilderness.

region, and the lakes area of the far north is a delight to the eye. Zambia's scenic pride, however, are its two great watercourses and their valleys: the Zambezi and the Luangwa. Along the former are the Victoria Falls, arguably the most spectacular of the world's natural wonders, and the Kariba Gorge, its colossal dam and the 5 200-km² lake.

The Luangwa, which runs down the country's eastern flank, and which forms part of Africa's Great Rift Valley, is a wide swathe of river and flood plain, ox-bow lagoon, forest, woodland and grassland that sustains a marvellous variety of wildlife.

Altogether, 19 national parks have been created to conserve the country's impressive natural heritage. Not all of them have been developed for tourism, and only four major areas are featured in the following pages. More will undoubtedly merit inclusion in the years to come: the Zambian economy, and its tourist industry, tended to stagnate during the two decades following independence in 1963, but with the change of administration in the early 1990s there was a fresh commitment to free enterprise and to the exploitation of the country's full potential, and a new spirit is abroad in the land. The region will become, more and more, a prime destination for those who are attracted to the wide and sunlit spaces of Africa, to their far horizons and their wild animals.

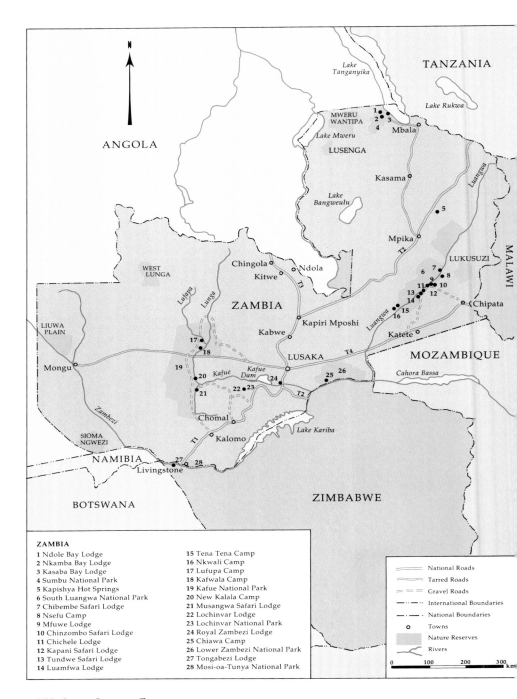

ZAMBIA

1 Ndole Bay Lodge
2 Nkamba Bay Lodge
3 Kasaba Bay Lodge
4 Sumbu National Park
5 Kapishya Hot Springs
6 South Luangwa National Park
7 Chibembe Safari Lodge
8 Nsefu Camp
9 Mfuwe Lodge
10 Chinzombo Safari Lodge
11 Chichele Lodge
12 Kapani Safari Lodge
13 Tundwe Safari Lodge
14 Luamfwa Lodge

15 Tena Tena Camp
16 Nkwali Camp
17 Lufupa Camp
18 Kafwala Camp
19 Kafue National Park
20 New Kalala Camp
21 Musangwa Safari Lodge
22 Lochinvar Lodge
23 Lochinvar National Park
24 Royal Zambezi Lodge
25 Chiawa Camp
26 Lower Zambezi National Park
27 Tongabezi Lodge
28 Mosi-oa-Tunya National Park

National Roads
Tarred Roads
Gravel Roads
International Boundaries
National Boundaries
○ Towns
Nature Reserves
Rivers

0   100   200   300
km

THE KAFUE REGION

The long and lovely Kafue River, Zambia's most valuable watercourse (among other things it feeds the industrialised Copper Belt area) rises in the northwest, near the country's border with Zaire, and flows southwards for 300 km before abruptly swinging east to meander through the Kafue Flats, or wetlands. It then plunges through the magnificent Kafue Gorge to reach its junction with the Zambezi 96 km west of Kariba.

Some 400 km of the river's middle reaches are flanked by the Kafue National Park, Zambia's largest conservation area. There are two other, much smaller parks on the Flats – the Blue Lagoon (closed to the public for the time being) and the Lochinvar.

KAFUE NATIONAL PARK

The park extends over 22 500 km² (an area about the size of Wales) to the west of the Kafue River, a countryside that is enormously varied both in its landscapes and its wildlife complement. Much of the region is covered by dryish miombo woodland and by broad, grassy expanses known as 'dambos' which sustain great numbers of buffalo and zebra, wildebeest, sable and hartebeest. Less common are the patches of mopane country, found mainly in the south, and the tall stands of teak and candelabra trees.

Then there is the river itself, its clear, blue-green waters fringed by a narrow belt of lush forest, a riverine wonderland that is home to water pear and coconut ivory, to bushbuck, puku, monitor, hippo and crocodile and to a superb array of birds – giant kingfisher, African darter and finfoot, purplecrested loerie, stork, crane and fish eagle (this last is one of Zambia's national emblems). At Kafwala the river opens out into channels to race past emerald-green islets, and then reforms, continuing south to fill the splendid, 370-km² Lake Itezhi-tezhi.

Most inviting of the park's wildlife areas, though, is the great Busanga flatland of the north, a region of grassland and flood plain dotted with 'islands' of vast termite mounds that support fig and phoenix palm and other handsome trees. The river terraces and the marshlands beyond sustain herds of graceful,

A chacma baboon surveys his domain from the heights of a giant termite mound.

The Zambezi escarpment's rare taita falcon.

water-loving red lechwe, an antelope species that, during the earlier decades of the century, was hunted and poached to the edge of extinction (by the 1940s fewer than a hundred individuals remained) but which has made a remarkable recovery and now roams the wetlands in great multitudes. Here, too, you'll find the elusive, swamp-living sitatunga, the reedbuck and the bushbuck. In the drier parts of the Busanga, and in the flood plain when the waters recede after the rains, are impressive numbers of game animals and their attendant predators, notably lion, leopard and cheetah.

Game viewing in the Kafue
The national park has a fairly extensive network of roads, which are in tolerable condition during the dry season. Most visitors, however, arrive as clients of one or other of the safari companies, who conduct drives in open land cruisers and, some of them, lay on trips and longer expeditions by boat.

Accommodation The Kafue National Park offers a variety of accommodation; there are about a dozen camps, all of them privately run, ranging from the budget self-catering to the exclusive lodge. Visitor facilities here, as in the country's other game areas, are subject to rapid change: some long-established places have been closed down, others are being upgraded, new ones are being built or planned. The following is a select list.

■ **Getting to the Kafue:** By road from Lusaka: take the main route westwards via Mumbwa, Kaoma and the turn-off to Lake Itezhi-tezhi, a four- to five-hour (330-km) drive. The road is potholed in places but otherwise in reasonable condition. One can also drive north from Livingstone, on the Zambezi River at the Victoria Falls: follow the main road towards Lusaka, turning left at Kalomo for the park's Dumdumwense gate. This route is difficult in the wet season. By air: private operators and charter firms fly in to the park's Ngoma and other airstrips.

NEW KALALA CAMP
This is a small (eight-person), fully catered venue of comfortably furnished (local woods are used extensively), insect-proofed, airconditioned rondavels overlooking the waters of Lake Itezhi-tezhi. Warm natural springs rise in the vicinity; available are escorted day game-viewing drives, night excursions, boat trips on lake and river, and island walks. The area's bird life is enchanting; among the 400-plus species to be seen are fish eagle, Pel's fishing owl, black stork and the rare taita falcon. The camp is open throughout the year.

■ **Getting there:** See above for general directions to the national park. Travel arrangements for most New Kalala guests are handled by the safari operator.
■ **Reservations and information:** Eagle Travel, PO Box 35530, Lusaka, Zambia. Tel: (09260-1) 22-6857; or African Outposts, PO Box 4148, Randburg 2125, South Africa. Tel: (011) 884-6847/8.

MUSUNGWA SAFARI LODGE
The camp is in the same area as New Kalala, but is set high above the southern shore of Lake Itezhi-tezhi and is altogether a much more ambitious establishment. Here there are 23 pleasantly appointed twin- and four-bedded chalets, simply but comfortably furnished, each with its *en suite* facilities and private verandah. The Sable suite is more special: it boasts two bedrooms and a lounge with its own bar.

Guests get together to relax in the central complex of bar and restaurant, which has been designed and decorated in attractively ethnic style. The former is well stocked, the latter offers a surprisingly varied menu; vegetables and fruit come from the lodge's own garden, fish (the bream is delicious) is fresh from the lake. Convivial outdoor barbecues are enjoyed on fine summer nights and in the dry season; traditional Ila dancers provide the 'cabaret'.

Musungwa, which is open throughout the year, is unusually well endowed with visitor amenities: it has a library, curio shop and conference centre, a swimming pool and sauna, squash and tennis courts, as well as facilities for boating, fishing, windsurfing and waterskiing.

There's plenty laid on, too, for the game viewer and those who want to explore the wider region. Among the options are two- to three-hour morning, afternoon and evening landrover drives along the lake route and into the national park; all-day safaris (lunch is taken at the lodge's Nanzhilia bush camp), and bush walks. There are also river cruises, fishing expeditions (rods and tackle are available) and boating tours of the lake's islands. For a more intimate wilderness experience guests can arrange to spend a night at Nanzhilia (the area is noted for its buffalo, zebra, roan, sable and the smaller antelope, and for lion, cheetah and wild dog) or on Chongo Island.

Then there are the cruises on the *Sea Truck*, a 24-seat riverboat that sets out along the Kafue from the lodge, stopping here and there at local points of interest (the villages of the Ila people, the hot springs and so forth) and lake trips on the renowned *Zambezi Queen*. The latter, which has an upper deck for game viewing, was built in the 1950s as a luxury vessel for the Zambezi River run (among her more distinguished passengers was Queen Elizabeth the Queen Mother), but has since been completely refitted and now plies the quieter waters of Itezhi-tezhi.

■ **Getting there:** Musungwa is 1 km from the Kafue National Park's Musa gate, which is the main entrance to the southern sector. For general route directions to the park, see page 274; travel

Musungwa's spacious pool area.

arrangements for most Musungwa guests are handled by the safari operator.

■ **Reservations and information:** Musungwa Safaris, PO Box 31808, Lusaka, Zambia; Tel: (09260-1) 27-3493/4233; or T G Travel (Tours Division), PO Box 20104, Kitwe, Zambia. Tel: (09260-2) 21-5188.

BUSANGA TRAILS CAMPS

This private safari company operates three lodges in the game-rich northern sector of the Kafue National Park, a region well watered by the Kafue, Lufupa and Lunga rivers and their tributaries and which is dominated by the Busanga plain (see page 273). Accommodation is in rustic but comfortable thatched chalets. There aren't too many sophisticated luxuries – they would be out of place in this marvellously untouched wilderness – though the Lufupa venue has a swimming pool.

Busanga Trails offer safaris that take in, among other things, the Victoria Falls as well as the three camps, which comprise:

LUFUPA, the most centrally situated and headquarters of the park's northern region. It's an attractive place, popular (especially among fishermen) for its setting on a high bank overlooking the broad waters at the confluence of the Kafue and Lufupa. Anglers can expect excellent catches of pike, bream and silver barbel; game viewers are treated to nocturnal drives, a speciality of the camp. The pans and lagoons around Lufupa are a bird-watcher's joy.

KAFWALA, set among the palms and handsome indigenous trees of the Kafue River bank, looks out on the Kafwala rapids. The area is home to a multitude of elephant and buffalo, to all the larger antelope, and to lion and cheetah (sightings of the latter are unusually commonplace).

SHUMBA, sited among giant fig trees, is on the Busanga plain proper and ranks as probably the most strategically placed of all three for game viewing. The plain is one of the wildlife wonders of Southern Africa; a specially designed, high, shady platform provides a superb vantage point.

■ **Getting there:** For general directions to the Kafue park, page 274. Busanga Trails will handle its clients' travel arrangements.

■ **Reservations and information:** Busanga Trails, PO Box 30984, Lusaka, Zambia. Tel: (09260-1) 22-1197/2075/3628; fax: (09260-1) 22-2198/1157.

LOCHINVAR NATIONAL PARK

Located on the Kafue Flats some 100 km to the east of the Kafue National Park, the small Lochinvar wetland wilderness is famed for its population of the Kafue lechwe antelope and for its magnificent bird life. More than 70 000 Kafue lechwe – a subspecies of the better known red lechwe and found only in this particular area – inhabit the lush flood plain. They are lovely animals, easily recognised by their smooth chestnut coats, black-marked legs, long and narrow toes and their prominent, lyrate horns. In the dry season herds of wildebeest and zebra move into the park.

The World Wildlife Fund has acknowledged Lochinvar's status as an outstanding bird sanctuary: it supports over 400 species, many of which can be seen throughout the year. Notable among them are spurwinged geese, whitefaced and fulvous tree-ducks, and grey and purple goliath herons.

ABOVE: Lake Kariba's Siavonga resort area.
ABOVE RIGHT: Butterfly of the family Acraeidae.

LOCHINVAR LODGE Run by the National Hotels Development Corporation, the lodge has recently been refurbished and extended, and is now a full-catering, 60-bed venue centred around a converted but still charming old farmhouse.

■ **Getting there:** It is 234 km from Lusaka and 48 km from Monze (the turn-off from the Lusaka-Livingstone road; the final stretch is all-weather gravel). Admission by permit, obtainable at the gate or from the Wildlife Department at Chilanga, though the most convenient way of getting to and seeing the park is on a National Hotels holiday package.
■ **Reservations and information:** National Hotels Development Corporation, PO Box 33200, Lusaka, Zambia. Tel: (09260-1) 24-1023 or 24-9144/8; fax: (09260-1) 24-8352.

THE ZAMBEZI REGION

The Zambian side of the great river, in marked contrast to what the Zimbabweans have done along the southern bank, has not been extensively developed for tourism. The Victoria Falls area and the town of Livingstone boast a couple of lodges and some good hotels, but there's little in the way of visitor amenities farther downstream, along the shores of Lake Kariba and in the spectacular middle Zambezi valley beyond. Just two national parks have been created along the entire length of the watercourse: a small one around the Falls and a larger, barely accessible area at the valley's eastern extremity.

MOSI-OA-TUNYA NATIONAL PARK AND LIVINGSTONE

The 66-km^2 park has been established to preserve the Falls, the riverine reaches above them and the gorges below. These wonders of nature, described in some detail in the previous chapter, are Zambia's prime tourist attraction; best vantage point is the Knife Edge footbridge, which spans a narrow, rocky ridge between the high bank and a downstream island (the spray here is drenching, and you'll need a raincoat and umbrella).

Livingstone, 10 km away, is an attractive little town that offers all the modern comforts and services. Of special interest to visitors are the main museum (prehistory, natural history, cultural exhibits, and memorabilia relating to the missionary-explorer David Livingstone); the field museum (archaeology); the steam railway museum (on display, among

other fascinating relics, is an 1892 Class 7 loco), and the Maramba cultural village. This last is a 'living museum' of traditional Zambian art, crafts, lifestyles, music and movement; especially popular are the reed-garbed Makishi dancers.

Just outside town is the zoological park, in which there are various mammal species (the smaller and rarer ones are in enclosures) and aviaries of indigenous birds.

Accommodation Visitors to the Falls area are able to choose from a number of hotels, all of which offer solid comfort and at least one of which is ranked as a luxury establishment. Among them are:

THE NEW FAIRMOUNT HOTEL A three-star, 170-guest venue. The *en suite* rooms are air-conditioned and pleasantly furnished and decorated; amenities include a casino, a swimming pool and a conference room (maximum 60 delegates).
Reservations and information: PO Box 60096, Livingstone, Zambia. Tel: (09260-3) 32-0726.
THE ZAMBEZI MOTEL Two-star rating; 50-bed capacity; airconditioned rooms; conference facilities for 30.
Reservations and information: PO Box 60700, Livingstone, Zambia. Tel: (09260-3) 32-1511.
RAINBOW LODGE An attractive, 76-guest, resort hotel comprising luxury rooms and self-contained, traditional-style chalets; amenities include an airconditioned restaurant and swimming pool.
Reservations and information: PO Box 60090, Livingstone, Zambia. Tel: (09260-3) 32-1806/8.
MOSI-OA-TUNYA INTERCONTINENTAL HOTEL A sophisticated (five-star) venue located within the zoological park. Accommodation comprises 100 double rooms and six suites, all with private bathrooms. The hotel is being extended. There are two excellent restaurants, where special 'theme nights' are staged: Indian, Italian, German, Chinese, 'Safari BBQ', 'Western' and so on.

Among activities on offer are game-viewing drives, river cruises, helicopter excursions over the Falls, visits to and picnics/cocktails at the various museums. Amenities include

OPPOSITE: The Zambezi Gorge at Victoria Falls. The cataracts are at their most dramatic in the months following the rainy season.
ABOVE: Chalets at Rainbow Lodge.

a pleasant swimming pool and a conference centre (150 delegates).
Reservations and information: PO Box 60151, Livingstone, Zambia. Tel: (09260-3) 32-1121 or 32-1129. Bookings may also be made through Intercontinental Hotels worldwide.

Game viewing in Mosi-oa-Tunya
The 12-km drive along the riverbank from Songwe Gorge offers splendid scenery and a number of pleasant picnic spots. Also on offer are cruises upstream on the luxurious Makumbi riverboat, from which the Zambezi's prolific wildlife – the hippo and crocodile, elephant and various other animals that are drawn to the banks and the islands – can be observed in comfort. The riverine bird life is superb.

■ **Getting there:** Livingstone is accessible by road from Lusaka; from Zimbabwe via the Victoria Falls bridge, and from Botswana via Kasane. By air: Zambia Airways operates scheduled flights to Livingstone; other major Southern African and overseas airlines operate into Lusaka (see Advisory, page 312).
■ **Information:** The Zambian National Tourist Board; The National Hotels Development Corporation (see Advisory, page 313).

TONGABEZI LODGE

This stylish camp, situated 25 km upstream from the Victoria Falls, accommodates its guests in eight stone-and-thatch two-bed chalets (double beds, double baths) and five tents under thatch, which also have *en suite* facilities (reed-enclosed open-air shower and a 'loo-with-a-view'). All the units are imaginatively designed and attractively appointed; special among the chalets are the Tree House, the Bird House and the Honeymoon House. This last, set atop a cliff overlooking the Zambezi and its palm-fringed islands, has a four-poster bed, a sunken bath and a private garden. The vistas, particularly at sunrise and sunset, are spectacular.

Companionable meals are enjoyed around the single, large dining table; the food is excellent, as is the service (staff outnumber guests two to one). Amenities include a charming pool area and its artificial waterfall, and a rather bumpy 'house rules' croquet lawn. A grassed tennis court is planned.

Tongabezi's small sister-camp, Sindabezi, nestles on an island downstream and can be reached only by boat. Here there are four two-bed *en suite* chalets and a thatched dining area, the whole overlooking a flood plain that plays host to a variety of game animals and to some lovely birds.

There's also a six-person fly camp (set up afresh for each new group of visitors) on Livingstone Island, literally a stone's throw from the Victoria Falls.

Game viewing and exploring

Tongabezi's special drawcards are the one-, two- and three-day guided canoe expeditions along the upper reaches of the river. En route one stops at some of the many game- and bird-rich islands; nights are spent in a fly-camp. Incidentally, the canoes are stable touring craft and one doesn't need to be an experienced paddler to take to the waters.

For the less energetic, there is a motorised banana-boat, which provides a leisurely and most attractive means of getting to know the river, its many moods and its wildlife. The lodge also lays on trips to Livingstone, the Falls and the Mosi-oa-Tunya park.

- **Getting there:** Tongabezi is 25 minutes by road from Livingstone airport, 75 minutes from Victoria Falls airport across the river in Zimbabwe, and just over two hours' drive from Kasane in Botswana. The lodge will arrange transfers.
- **Reservations and information:** Tongabezi Lodge, Private Bag 31, Livingstone, Zambia. Tel: (09260-3) 32-3235/96; fax: (09260-3) 32-3224.

THE MIDDLE AND LOWER ZAMBEZI

The Zambian portion of Lake Kariba is a fairly popular recreational destination, especially among residents of and visitors to Lusaka, which lies 150 km to the north.

They come for the fishing, the boating and watersports, or simply to relax at one or other of the casually attractive resort venues, among which are Manchinchi Bay Lodge, Lake Kariba Inn and Zambezi Lodge, all of them in the town of Siavonga, close to the dam wall. The area, though, has comparatively little to offer in the way of safari facilities and game viewing: there are no parks or reserves on or close to the lakeshore.

OPPOSITE: One of the few wilderness lodges on the Zambian side of the river is Tongabezi, a delightful camp of stone, timber and thatch chalets and luxury tents under thatch.
ABOVE LEFT AND TOP: Among Tongabezi's chalets are the Honeymoon House, set in its private garden high above the Zambezi, and Bird House.
ABOVE: Tongabezi's secluded pool area; the entire river frontage has been lawned.

However, downstream from Kariba, along the stretch opposite Zimbabwe's splendid Mana Pools wilderness (see page 260), is the Lower Zambezi National Park, a lovely region of wooded hills, riverine forests and valleys dense with acacia and mopane. Poaching has reduced the game populations, but one can still see plenty of elephant and buffalo, antelope, hippo and crocodile, the occasional lion and leopard, and a fine array of birds. And the scenery, particularly on the imposing Zambezi escarpment, is magnificent.

At the time of writing, two private concerns were active in the area, each of which offered outstanding safari amenities.

ROYAL ZAMBEZI LODGE

This most attractive camp – it gets its regal prefix from its association with the Royal Chieftainess Chiyaba – is situated near the confluence of the Zambezi and Chongwe rivers, the latter serving as gateway to the Lower Zambezi National Park.

The setting is really lovely: above there's a spreading canopy of tall evergreen trees; in front are the waters of the larger river, a full kilometre wide at this point; just downstream are reed-lined islands that sustain a wondrous bird life and also play host to elephant, buffalo, hippo and various other animals.

Guests – a maximum of just 12 – are accommodated in spacious, pleasantly furnished tented chalets (cooling thatch over canvas), each with its *en suite* bathroom. The units are well ventilated and mosquito proof; the showers run hot and cold water, and the toilets flush. At one end of the camp is the open-sided dining and terrace area and the unusual Kigelia bar, built around and anchored to a quite enormous sausage tree

(*Kigelia africana*). The views across the majestic river, from both bar and terrace, are a joy, most especially as the sun sets over the waters.

The Lower Zambezi park is a half-hour journey from camp; after crossing the Chongwe, you emerge onto wide, sandy plains that teem with wildlife. The plains are girded by the Zambezi, its inlets and lagoons and fringing forest.

Game drives penetrate 20 km into this pristine wilderness; up to 30 mammal species (including lion and other large predators) and 350 different kinds of bird can be seen

OPPOSITE ABOVE: Boating on a twilit Lake Kariba. There are three attractive lakeshore resort venues, from which craft of various kinds can be hired.
OPPOSITE BELOW: One of the lake's kapenta boats.
ABOVE: A more adventurous canoe safari.

during a single excursion. The party breaks off during the afternoon drive – just before the light fades – for a welcome riverbank sundowner before continuing with the aid of a powerful spotlight.

For the rest, there are enjoyable launch and canoe safaris – led by trained guides – on which guests explore (and photograph) the river's banks, channels and islands.

Boats and tackle are also available for a day's tiger-fishing (the best months for this are August and September).

■ **Getting there:** Access is by boat (from Kariba or Chirundu); by road (from Lusaka; a 4x4 is needed for the last stretch) and by air. Much depends on the time of year; check directions with the lodge when making your bookings.

■ **Reservations and information:** Ms Jackie Gibbs, Marketing Director, Royal Zambezi Lodge, PO Box 31455, Lusaka, Zambia. Tel: (09260-1) 22-3952 or 22-3504; fax: (09260-1) 22-3504.

CHIAWA RIVER CAMP

Chiawa is set on the riverbank within the Lower Zambezi park, and is a pleasant little camp that pays homage to the pristine character of the area: it is dismantled at the end of each tourist season (November) to allow the environment to recover, and erected afresh after the rains.

The amenities, in these circumstances, are surprisingly sophisticated: the tents are spacious, comfortable, insect-proof; the showers run hot water; the toilets flush; solar power provides electricity throughout, and there's even a facility for re-charging video-camera batteries. The camp provides a full catering and bar service.

On offer are game walks and game drives (including a pleasant sundowner excursion followed by a night drive), fishing expeditions and boating trips on the Zambezi River. The early morning river-side outing to watch the sun rise over the water is an experience to be savoured.

There are no giraffe in the area, but almost every other major species can be seen: elephant, buffalo, a variety of antelope, zebra, warthog, hippo, crocodile, good leopard, serval, civet and, if you're lucky, one of Africa's largest prides of lion (36 individuals at the time of writing). The bird life – especially raptor and waterfowl – is prolific.

■ **Getting there:** Access is by road from Lusaka to Chirundu (either direct or via Kariba) and then by launch. By air: to Kariba, by road to Chirundu, by launch to Chiawa. G & G Safaris will make the travel arrangements. Guests flying into Lusaka spend a night at Lilayi Lodge (south of the city) before continuing on to Chiawa.
■ **Reservations and information:** G & G Safaris, PO Box 30972, Lusaka, Zambia. Tel: (09260-1) 26-1588; fax: (09260-1) 26-2683. In Johannesburg: contact Pathfinder Travel. Tel: (011) 442-8007; fax: 011) 442-8015.

RIDING THE WHITE WATERS

Visitors of the more adventurous kind are able to explore almost the entire Zambian stretch of the mighty Zambezi by canoe and raft – on one of the white-water expeditions mounted by Sobek, an American outfit that, since its inception in 1973, has pioneered more than 200 rivers in 60 countries. The name, incidentally, is taken from the ancient Egyptian crocodile god – an act of propitiation that seems to have worked, since Sobek's safety record remains unblemished.

The safaris operate through the gorges downstream from the Victoria Falls, and in the Lower Zambezi valley below Kariba. On offer are one-, three- and five-day expeditions; exhilarating rapids and challenging turbulence feature prominently, of course, but there's also more leisurely flat-water canoeing, game viewing (in Mana Pools on the Zimbabwean side as well as in the Lower Zambezi National Park) and bird-watching. Participants stay overnight in camps that are competently staffed (cook and assistant) and comfortably appointed.

Shearwater Adventures are Sobek's counterparts on the Zimbabwean side of the Zambezi. This large and superbly organised outfit offers seven different canoe safaris between Kariba and the Mozambique border, including the famed Ruchomechi canoe trail (see page 264), rafting in the Victoria Falls gorges, and walking and horse trails. For information on itineraries and options, contact Sobek and Shearwaters direct; see pages 315 and 316 for addresses.

BELOW: Riding the rapids below the Falls.
BOTTOM: Rafters assemble in the Batoka Gorge.

THE LUANGWA VALLEY

The Luangwa River, one of the Zambezi's biggest tributaries, rises in the Zambia-Malawi border area to flow 770 km south-westwards through the fertile grasslands of the country's eastern region. In seasons of good rains it will break its banks to inundate the surrounding countryside and sometimes, after the floods, change its course to leave behind a scatter of ox-bow lakelets – a cycle that creates a splendid diversity of landscape and habitat.

The valley, part of Africa's Great Rift Valley system, lies a full 800 m below the plateau on either side, and in summer the air can be suf-focatingly hot. The countryside, though, is spectacular in its rugged beauty, the vegeta-tion thick and, near the Luangwa and its many feeder watercourses, lushly green the year round. Here you'll find the giant mahogany and leadwood, coconut ivory palm and rain tree and huge baobabs, the 'upside down trees' of African lore.

Flanking the river's western banks are two national parks: the magnificent South Luang-wa and, separated from it by the 30-km Mun-yamadzi corridor, the smaller and less well known North Luangwa, a 4 700-km² expanse of miombo woodland that supports a fine variety of wildlife. To the east, on the rocky uplands beyond the flood plain, is the 2 720-km² Lukusuzi National Park. Neither the North Luangwa nor the Lukusuzi have been developed to any significant degree for tourism: there is no permanent accommoda-tion (though a couple of private ventures operate in the former), access is difficult, and there are no internal roads.

SOUTH LUANGWA NATIONAL PARK

Despite the depredations of poachers, the park – an impressive 9 050 km² in extent – is sanctuary for one of the world's largest and most varied concentrations of game animals: the black rhino population has been reduced to the point of local extinction, and the

TOP: *Kudu and friend. Only the males of these large antelope have horns.*
ABOVE: *The regal African fish eagle.*

elephant herds are depleted, but the latter are still plentiful and great numbers of buffalo, giraffe and zebra, impala and kudu roam the plains; waterbuck, reedbuck and hippo haunt the riverine stretches.

Among the less common antelope are the roan, the eland, Lichtenstein's hartebeest, the puku and the golden-coated oribi. The park

TOP LEFT AND CENTRE: Out on a limb – gregarious vervet monkeys are a familiar sight in the Luangwa Valley; trees afford them refuge from most predators, though the nocturnal leopard is almost equally at home in the high branches.
LEFT: A spotted hyaena mother and her pups, born in a hole in the ground. These massive-jawed animals are hunters as well as scavengers.
ABOVE: Baobabs and handsome vegetable ivory palms in the South Luangwa park.

also sustains the endemic Thornicroft's giraffe and small herds of Cookson's wildebeest, a subspecies which is also unique to the region (one individual was found to have a record 82,5-cm horn spread). Carnivores are represented by, among others, lion, leopard, spotted hyaena, wild dog and a number of smaller, nocturnal predators.

The South Luangwa is a bird-watcher's delight. Around 400 different species have been identified; notable are the raptors, and such waterbirds as the saddlebilled stork, egret, spurwing goose, goliath heron and sacred ibis (see also page 297).

Most foreign visitors savour the splendours of the South Luangwa as clients of the National Hotels Development Corporation or of one of the half-dozen or so private operators whose lodges and bush camps and, especially, walking safaris provide a striking insight into this superb wilderness. Among the various venues are the following.

KAPANI SAFARI LODGE

This exclusive, medium-sized camp, set beside the waters of one of the Luangwa River's quiet ox-bow lagoons, is owned and run by the renowned Norman Carr, who is to Zambia what George Adamson was to East Africa and Rupert Fothergill to Zimbabwe. Norman has known and loved the region for the past half-century, and he and his meticulously trained guides provide a memorable bush experience.

The lodge comprises four tiled-roofed stone chalets and eight twin-bedded rooms that have been designed with the heat of the Zambian day in mind – they have high ceilings, gauzed windows, overhead fans. Each incorporates *en suite* bathroom facilities and has its private verandah (with bar fridge). Guests get together in the thatched central complex of open-air bar, dining and sitting area; the passing parade of animals can be observed from its raised viewing platform; among the amenities is a secluded pool.

Longer-staying visitors – those who like to walk and want a closer encounter with the

wilderness – can spend time at one of Kapani's two bush camps. Both are sited beneath handsome evergreen trees on the banks of a sand river; each accommodates six people and operates during the dry months (from June to October).

Kapani's game-viewing itinerary is flexible: small parties set out twice a day in open vehicles; there are spotlit night drives, and marvellously instructive walking safaris. The guides are masters of bush lore, immensely knowledgeable about the animals, birds and plants of the region; back at camp, in the

OPPOSITE ABOVE: Relaxing at Kapani's Nsolo camp.
OPPOSITE BELOW: Nsolo bush camp interior.
TOP: Mfuwe Lodge's attractive surrounds.
ABOVE: A hippo in the Mfuwe area.

evenings, Norman gives informal, and spell-binding, chats on the Luangwa Valley, its problems and its potential. Bird-watching is at its best during the 'green season' (November to April), when the rich diversity of the resident species is enhanced by migrants from the north. If you're booked in to Kapani for three or more days, the lodge will arrange leisurely picnic drives and visits to a local village, and to the local crocodile farm.

■ **Getting there:** Kapani is 670 km from Lusaka, 270 km from Lilongwe in Malawi, and a 40-minute drive from Mfuwe airport, which is served by scheduled flights and from which the lodge will arrange transfer. For general directions to the South Luangwa park, see page 297.

■ **Reservations and information:** Norman Carr Safaris, PO Box 100, Mfuwe, Zambia. Tel and fax: (09260-62) 4-5015.

MFUWE LODGE

This National Hotels venue has an exquisite setting (some say the best in the Luangwa Valley) beneath the ebony and *Codilla africana* trees that flank one of the river's many permanent lagoons. The waters here are home to a profusion of hippo and croco-dile (they sunbathe in their dozens in full view of the guest rooms), and are often visit-ed by herds of elephant.

Mfuwe is a popular lodge, geared perhaps to more of a mass market than some of the smaller private camps. Its 12 comfortably fur-nished twin-roomed chalets (each sleeps four people) have *en suite* facilities; guest ameni-ties include a pleasant restaurant (local as well as standard international dishes feature on the menu), well-stocked bar, swimming pool, curio shop, video viewing, and provi-sion for conferences.

On offer throughout the year are morning, afternoon and nocturnal drives and, between June and November, guided walking safaris. The area's bird life is superb; much of it can be observed from the lodge's neat lawns.

■ **Getting there:** For general directions to the South Luangwa park, see page 297. The lodge will arrange transfers from Mfuwe airport.
■ **Reservations and information:** PO Box 69, Mfuwe, Zambia. Tel: (09260-62) 4-5018 or 4-5062. National Hotels offer all-inclusive packages; for details, contact the corporation at PO Box 33200, Lusaka. Tel: (09260-1) 24-1023 or 24-9144/8; fax: (09260-1) 24-8352. Bookings also through and information from Eagle Travel, PO Box 33530, Lusaka. Tel: (09260-1) 22-9060, or though any travel agent.

CHINZOMBO SAFARI LODGE

A year or so ago the prestigious *Illustrated London News* gave the Luangwa Valley 'top marks for game viewing', and added that 'Chinzombo is highly praised ... thatched cottages, excellent food'.

The assessment is well founded: the lodge is indeed an inviting venue – it is set among huge, shade-giving mahogany, ebony and winterthorn trees; its nine twin-bedded

en suite thatched chalets and central dining and bar area overlook the wide sandbanks of the Luangwa River; hippo are everywhere; in the dry season a great many animals come down to drink from the waters. Elephant and giraffe often wander into camp.

Chinzombo is very professionally run; cuisine and service are of an unusually high standard, and the management is very serious about the environment and its preservation. The lodge helps fund the Save the Rhino Trust, founded in 1980 to assist the government in its efforts to stop commercial poaching (of elephant as well as rhino). The Trust keeps about a hundred men in the field; patrols are concentrated in the Luangwa Valley.

The lodge encourages the patronage of special-interest groups (ornithologists, botanists, keen photographers). For these and for the non-specialised guest there are morning walks or drives in open vehicles, a choice of late-afternoon and night excursions, sundowner get-togethers beside the quiet and lovely river. Supplementary attractions include all-day outings into the remoter parts

■ **Getting there:** For general directions to the South Luangwa National Park, see page 297. The lodge will arrange transfer from Mfuwe airport or the local Kanumbe airstrip.
■ **Reservations and information:** Chinzombo Safari Lodge, PO Box 85, Mfuwe, Zambia. Tel: (09260-62) 4-5053; fax: (09260-62) 4-5076. Zambian agents: T.G. Travel, PO Box 20104, Kitwe. Tel: (09260-2) 21-5188; and Andrews Travel & Safaris, PO Box 31993, Lusaka. Tel: (09260-1) 21-3147.

CHICHELE LODGE

Also owned by the National Hotels group, Chichele is similar in some ways to Mfuwe Lodge (see page 289), but the setting is quite different – the camp is perched atop a hill overlooking the Luangwa flood plain and the Muchinga escarpment beyond. The views, especially from the spacious lounge area, are splendid. Accommodation is in 18 comfort-ably appointed rooms (12 twin-bedded, five single, one family); guests take their meals in the airconditioned restaurant, their drinks in the well-stocked cocktail bar, their daytime leisure around the swimming pool.

On offer are the standard game drives and walks; other excursions include visits to a tra-ditional African village nearby and to the crocodile farm.

■ **Getting there:** For general directions to the South Luangwa park, see page 297. Chichele Lodge will arrange transfer from the airport.
■ **Reservations and information:** Reservations and information: This is a National Hotels venue; for contact details, see Mfuwe Lodge, page 289.

ABOVE: Chinzombo, on the Luangwa River bank.
ABOVE RIGHT: Some of Chinzombo's thatched chalets.

of the park; old-fashioned portered walking safaris that recall an earlier and perhaps more romantic era; visits to local villages for an insight into traditional lifestyles.

The lodge's Kuyenda bush camp caters for families and small parties (up to six people) who like to walk and to commune with nature in seclusion. Accommodation is in reed-and-grass huts with *en suite* facilities. The camp is open from 1 June to 31 October.

LUAMFWA LODGE

Set beside an entrancing lagoon in the far southern segment of the park and a two-minute walk from the Luangwa River bank (here a favoured haunt of the busy little carmine bee-eater), Luamfwa caters, rather stylishly, for a maximum of 16 guests in its attractive wood-and-thatch, *en suite* chalets. Meals are invariably served around the campfire; French and other Continental dishes feature on the menu.

This is a superb game area. Leopard are surprisingly visible; elephant, lion and much else can be seen around the lagoon. On offer are walking safaris, and game drives.

■ **Getting there:** For general directions to the South Luangwa park, see page 297. The lodge will transfer its guests from the Mfuwe airport (game viewing en route). Charter and private aircraft use the lodge's airstrip.

■ **Reservations and information:** Transcat, PO Box 32540, Lusaka, Zambia. Tel: (09260-1) 26-1683, or 26-1732; fax: (09260-1) 26-2438.

TENA TENA AND NKWALI

These two camps are owned and run by Robin Pope, protégé of the celebrated Norman Carr (see Kapani Safari Lodge, page 288) and a moving spirit within the Central African conservation brotherhood. Robin is known for, among other things, his superbly conceived and executed walking trails – mobile safaris – both within the Luangwa Valley and in the remote, seasonally flooded western region of the country.

Tena Tena is one of only two tented safari camps within the South Luangwa National Park, an attractive collection of six Manyara-style safari tents (they're under thatch) set beneath shade-giving mahogany trees on the banks of the Luangwa River. The comfortable units have *en suite* facilities; guests congregate of an evening in the roomy bar and dining area – an open-sided 'citenje' – overlooking the broad waters. Tena Tena is open only during the dry months – from 1 June to 31 October.

Nkwali Camp, a little more informal, comprises six safari chalets (with shared bathroom facilities) located in the 'all-weather' Mfuwe area 30 km south of Tena Tena. The camp, which lies just outside the national park, also looks onto the Luangwa River. The dining room is built around a giant Natal mahogany, the bar around an ebony tree; the company is convivial, the service friendly, highly personalised.

Both camps offer bush walks, morning and night drives (often led by Robin) and all-day picnic outings. The itineraries are flexible; mealtimes fit in with guests' game-viewing preferences. Excursions from Tena Tena take in the game-rich lagoons, pans and sandbanks of the river; close to camp is a waterhole and its attractive hide. The Nkwali area is beautifully wooded.

■ **Getting there:** For general directions to the South Luangwa park, see page 297. Robin Pope Safaris will organise transfers to the camps.
■ **Reservations and information:** Robin Pope Safaris, PO Box 320154, Lusaka, Zambia. Tel: (09260-62) 4-5017; fax: (09260-62) 4-5076.

OPPOSITE ABOVE: Robin Pope's Tena Tena camp comprises spacious tents under thatch.
OPPOSITE BELOW: Tena Tena bush trailists break for coffee and sandwiches.
TOP: The central area at Tena Tena.
ABOVE: Sobek Adventures' Tundwe camp.

TUNDWE SAFARI LODGE

This is a fairly new camp, sited well away from the other venues, and the game animals of the area are still a bit skittish, wary of the human presence, but things are settling down very nicely.

The location is quite superb: Tundwe nestles beneath enormous shade trees on the Luangwa River bank; less than a kilometre away there's a permanent lagoon that beckons the game-viewer and picnicker.

Tundwe's accommodation comprises reed-and-thatch units with *en suite* facilities. Meals are enjoyed in the pleasant central area. On offer are day and night game drives, and when conditions are favourable guests are poled down the river in a banana-boat – a

memorable experience. Tundwe's speciality, however, is the walking safari, for which it operates two trail camps (they're accessible only on foot and by boat).

■ **Getting there:** For general directions to the South Luangwa park, see page 297. Sobek Adventures will arrange transfer from the airport.
■ **Reservations and information:** Sobek Adventures, PO Box 30263, Lusaka, Zambia. Tel: (09260-1) 22-4248; fax: (09260-1) 22-4265.

CHIBEMBE SAFARI LODGE

This is the most northerly of the South Luangwa's private camps, though it is situated on the river's east bank and thus falls just outside the park proper.

Chibembe, operated by Wilderness Trails, specialises in the longer walking safari, but there's much to recommend the lodge itself and its immediate area. Large by Zambian standards, the timbered chalets (each has its *en suite* facilities and private verandah) accommodate 40 guests in single, double and family units. The camp has a pleasant

ABOVE: On a Chibembe wilderness trail.
OPPOSITE ABOVE: Game-viewing at Chibembe camp.
OPPOSITE BELOW: Chibembe's central area.

setting, well-shaded by loftily spreading Natal mahogany and winterthorn trees; guests relax in the central dining and bar area; until recently their frequent companions were two orphaned animals – Moto the elephant and Ebba the zebra, who were rescued by Chibembe staff (Moto after a panic-stricken and near-suicidal attempt to cross the crocodile-infested river).

A recent addition to (or rather, remote extension of) Chibembe is the six-person Mupamadzi river-camp, sited among enormous *Adina microcephala* trees on the banks of the Mupamadzi River some two to three hours' drive north of the mother lodge in a hitherto undeveloped area of quite remarkable beauty. Nearby are the game-rich Chifungwe and Lunda plains. The main lodge and its river-camp are open only during the dry season (1 July to 31 October).

Game viewing around Chibembe

The itinerary takes in a morning and an afternoon drive and a rather special 'sundowner' excursion that gives guests a last look at the diurnal animals, and which concludes with a pleasant drink or two at a river-side stopover.

The drive then continues by spotlight and ends back at camp in time for dinner. Also available are day trips by five-seater light aircraft to the Bangweulu swamps, a region that sustains a wealth of water-related birds and an animal life that is quite different to that of the Luangwa Valley (it includes, among many others, the sitatunga antelope and black lechwe).

Chibembe is well-known for the 'Walk on the Wild Side' safaris that begin and end at the lodge. Trailists overnight at two of the three bush camps, where a cook, waiter and bedroom attendant are in permanent residence. Drinks are available; the showers have hot water.

Wilderness Trails also operate in the wilds of the North Luangwa National Park, an area that was until recently barred to all but a few researchers and government rangers. Here, too, there's a comfortable bush camp, sited on an attractive stretch of the Mwaleshi River. The park is renowned for its wildlife, and in particular for its lions; game viewing is conducted principally on foot; parties are restricted to six persons.

■ **Getting there:** For general directions to the South Luangwa park, see page 297. The safari operator will arrange transfer from either Mfuwe airport (a two-hour drive; game viewing en route) or the Lukuzye airstrip (a 10-minute drive).

■ **Reservations and information:** Wilderness Trails, PO Box 30970, Lusaka, Zambia; Tel: (09260-1) 21-5946. Main agents: T.G. Travel (Tours Division), PO Box 20104, Kitwe. Tel: (09260-2) 21-5188; and Adventure Centre, PO Box 35058, Lusaka. Tel: (09260-1) 22-0112/ 3/4/5; fax: (09260-1) 22-0116. South Africa: African Outposts, PO Box 4148, Randburg 2125. Tel: (011) 884-6847/8; fax: (011) 883-9684; and Hartley Safaris, PO Box 69859, Bryanston 2021. Tel: (011) 708-1893/5; fax: (011) 708-1569.

NSEFU CAMP

Sister venue to Chibembe and the oldest of Zambia's tourist camps (it retains much of its charmingly old-fashioned character), Nsefu is located on a broad sweep of the Luangwa River, its six twin-bedded *en suite* thatched rondavels enjoying fine views of water and wilderness. This is a small, friendly place whose guests enjoy an unusual degree of personal attention; meals are sociable affairs; there's a full bar service.

Nsefu's flexible game-viewing timetable includes open-vehicle day and night drives

ABOVE: The small, informal and in some ways delightfully old-fashioned Nsefu camp, set on the Luangwa River bank.
OPPOSITE ABOVE: Nsefu game drive.
OPPOSITE BELOW: Sundowner time.

and short walks through the bush. There are hides and a waterhole (visible from the bar) close by; the wider area offers magnificent game viewing (elephant, buffalo, the endemic Thornicroft's giraffe and Cookson's wildebeest, kudu, eland, puku, zebra, waterbuck, lion, leopard, hyaena) and bird-watching (Pel's fishing owl, saddlebilled stork and carmine bee-eater).

■ **Getting there:** For general directions to the South Luangwa park see page 297. The safari operator will arrange transfer from Mfuwe airport (1,5 hours' drive) or the Lukuzye airstrip (50 minutes' drive).
■ **Reservations and information:** For contact addresses, see Chibembe, page 295.

KAPISHYA HOT SPRINGS

Located some 100 km northwest of the North Luangwa National Park, on the famed Shiwa Ngandu ('Lake of Royal Crocodiles') private estate, Kapishya serves as a kind of base camp for extensive forays into the Luangwa Valley, to the Bangweulu flood plains and to the Victoria Falls. The camp is on the banks of the Manshya River about half-an-hour's drive from the elegant 40-room colonial mansion built by the pioneering Gore-Brown family in the 1920s (tours are part of the visitor's itinerary) and comprises pleasant, ethnic-style 'pole-and-dagga' chalets. Each has its *en suite* facilities and private verandah.

Among local attractions are the warm, palm-fringed and relaxing mineral springs; the eye-catching Chusa Falls; and Nachipala Hill, where the explorer David Livingstone stopped to get his bearings in 1867. Activities on offer include river-rafting trips and bird-watching walks.

During the dry season Shiwa Safaris operates eight-person excursions into the North Luangwa park, where guests explore the game-rich terrain on foot.

Nights are spent in the Buffalo camp's comfortably spacious tents (each tent has its own bathroom facilities); the North Luangwa, a region of shady mopane woodland, thicket, grassland, riverine forest and lagoon, is magnificent walking country.

As mentioned earlier, these safaris are part of more wide-ranging expeditions that take in the Bangweulu wetlands as well as the Victoria Falls.

■ **Getting there:** By road from Lusaka: Kapishya is some 100 km north of Mpika; turn left off the Great North Road and continue for 32 km through the Shiwa Ngandu estate.

■ **Reservations and information:** Shiwa Safaris, Private Bag E395, Lusaka, Zambia. Tel and fax: (09260-1) 61-1171.

Game viewing in the South Luangwa

Safari operators and the staff of the private camps conduct their guests on exploratory drives and bush walks. Independent visitors are able to embark on self-guided drives along the shortish circular route within the Mfuwe area of the park. An ordinary car will get you around this, but you'll need a 4x4 to explore the rest of the South Luangwa. Unaccompanied walking is not permitted.

■ **Getting to the South Luangwa:** It's about 600 km from Lusaka and 250 km from Lilongwe in Malawi. By road from Lusaka: take the route east to Chipata and then the road northwest to Mfuwe. An ordinary car will get you there. Safari operators will meet clients at and transfer them (by road or by air) from Lusaka. By air: Zambia Airways operate four flights a week into Mfuwe airport, from which the lodges (or safari companies) will arrange transfer. Charter and private aircraft: use either Mfuwe airport or the South Luangwa's private airstrips.

THE NORTHERN LAKES REGION

A small segment of Zambia's far northern border is washed by the waters of Lake Tanganyika, Africa's second largest and the world's second deepest lake (after Russia's Baykal). Indeed its size – 700 km long and 70 km at its widest point – and its depth could qualify it as an inland sea, though there are no tides and the waves are more in the nature of gentle swells.

The lake's shores are scenically lovely, fringed by strangler fig and candelabra tree, boulder strewn in parts (some of the rocks are of the balancing kind, and feature strikingly in local lore and legend), graced by attractive beaches in others. The literature claims that there's good, safe bathing here, but crocodiles and hippos lurk in and around the shallows.

More attractive is the fishing, especially along the lake's shelves, with which the local coxswains are intimately familiar. Boats are available for hire, and fishermen come from afar to troll for the fighting goliath tigerfish, which can weigh up to 30 kg; the Nile perch (50 kg) and the rare, much sought after golden perch; the giant 'vundu' catfish (60 kg); the delicious lake salmon and yellow-belly, or 'nhupe'.

The lake also sustains kapenta, a sardine-like fish relished by Zambians and caught in great quantities, together with a variety of less commercial species, including colourful ciclids, some of which are exported for the tropical fish trade.

To the east are two other lakes: Mweru, which straddles the border with Zaire, and Mweru Wantipa. Between the two is the Mweru Wantipa National Park; a little way to the south is the Lusenga Plain National Park. Neither park has been developed for tourism; access is difficult, the area is densely populated, and the game has suffered grievously from the predations of poachers.

The northeastern region's third wildlife area, though, is a lot more hospitable and attractive to visitors.

SUMBU NATIONAL PARK

The park extends across some 2 000 km² of open grassland and miombo woodland stretching south from the shores of Lake Tanganyika. Here, too, the poachers have been active but there are still elephant to be seen, together with buffalo, zebra, roan, sable and eland, Lichtenstein's hartebeest, puku, waterbuck and duiker. The bird life – both Southern and East African species are represented – is superb, especially along the lakeshore. Flamingoes are among the more spectacular migrants; other notables include storks,

ABOVE: The attractive bar area at Kasaba Bay. Beach barbecues are a feature of camp life; swimming and golf are among the amenities. OPPOSITE BELOW: The ubiquitous scrub hare.

herons and wild ducks, skimmers, whiskered terns and spoonbills.

Two of the area's more prominent points of interest are the magnificent Kalombo Falls, on the Kalambo River to the east (they fall sheer for 220 metres) and the Kasaba Bay crocodile farm, home to around 70 breeding females and thousands of their hatchlings.

SUMBU'S LODGES

Three beach resorts have been established on the lake's shore, pleasantly unpretentious, well-maintained, modestly comfortable and usually uncrowded places that offer fishing, boating, relaxation in quiet and attractive surrounds – and a modicum of game viewing.

KASABA BAY LODGE is situated a hundred or so metres from the beach and, because elephant and other animals regularly beat a path through the area to get to water, visitors are escorted on the short walk over the lawn by a game guard. Accommodation is in 14 double chalets, each with a spacious bedroom and *en suite* bathroom. Meals are served either in the main dining room (fresh fish invariably features), on the beach (barbecues), or in the thatched bar area, which is sited beneath a giant winterthorn tree. Diners are sometimes joined by Tusker, an unusually friendly and inquisitive elephant. Lodge amenities include a large swimming pool, and there's a golf course nearby.

NKAMBA BAY LODGE, 24 km along the lakeshore to the west, has been built on the hillside, its grounds overlooking the beach.

LEFT: *Ndole Bay Lodge – a splendid venue for the fisherman and water sportsman.*
ABOVE: *The swallow-tailed bee-eater.*

Game viewing in the Sumbu

The road network is restricted, the routes rugged, and one really needs a 4x4 to get around. Guards are available to take you out, either in a vehicle or on foot. The game is not all that prolific but the landscapes – grassland, riverine forest, patches of marsh, hills and steep valleys – are a photographer's delight. Even more rewarding, perhaps, are the excursions by launch: the animals tend to concentrate along the water's edge, especially in the dry months; the crocodiles are the biggest you're likely to see anywhere; the birds are beautiful and the sunsets glorious.

■ **Getting there:** By road from Lusaka: through Mpika and Mporokoso, but the road is long and lonely, there aren't too many amenities en route, and the last stretch, on dirt, can be rough. By air: most visitors take the Zambian Airways ATR 42 turboprop flight from Lusaka (via Ndola, on the Copper Belt) to Kasaba Bay. Best way to get from Kasaba Bay to the other two lodges is by boat. Circuit Safaris and other tour operators will handle their clients' travel arrangements.

■ **Reservations and information:** Lodge bookings may be made through Circuit Safaris, PO Box 22890, Kitwe. Tel: (09260-2) 21-5826 or 21-6873; fax: (09260-2) 21-6715. Other safari and tour firms operate into the area. Information also from the Zambian National Tourist Board, PO Box 30017, Lusaka. Tel: (09260-1) 22-9807.

NDOLE BAY LODGE, just outside the park's boundary, is the newest of the three and, unlike the others, the waters here are free of hippo and crocodile so one can bathe, snorkle and waterski from the lovely, golden-brown beach. Again, amenities are similar to those of Kasaba Bay. There is accommodation for 60 guests in the double chalets – more than enough to cope with demand, even in peak season. At the time of writing Ndole Bay, indeed all three lodges, had a low occupancy rate, partly because the area is difficult and expensive to get to.

VISITOR'S ADVISORY

SOUTH AFRICA

In brief
Currency The South African Rand (R), divided in 100 cents. *Telephone and fax international calls* International code + 27 + area code + subscriber's number. Internal calls: area code + subscriber's number; all numbers within this chapter are prefixed by the relevant area code. *Local time* Universal Central Time plus two hours. *Principal centres* Pretoria (administrative capital); Cape Town (legislative capital); Bloemfontein (judicial capital); Durban; Pietermaritzburg; Port Elizabeth; Kimberley; East London. *Official languages* English and Afrikaans (subject to political debate).

Climate
Northern Natal and Zululand This is mainly but not exclusively a summer rainfall region. It falls within the transitional zone between the tropics and subtropics; there is considerable winter precipitation. The weather is kind to holidaymakers throughout the year, though summers can be very hot and, especially on or near the coast, uncomfortably humid. Winter days are mild, the nights cool.

Eastern Transvaal Lowveld A summer-rainfall region, with a subtropical climate, though it has tropical characteristics in the northern areas. Summers (Nov-Feb) are very hot, often humid; thunderstorms usually occur in the late afternoons and last, at most, for little more than an hour; the thunder and lightning can be of Olympian proportions, the downpours torrential. Winter days are cloudless, the air warm and invigorating; nights are cool and sometimes downright cold. The high escarpment region to the west is of course cooler in summer and a lot colder in winter.

Northern and Western Bushveld Much the same as the Lowveld, though these areas have a lower summer rainfall, and the winters tend to be colder. The region enjoys an average nine hours of sunshine a day throughout the year.

Travel
Entry documents Most visitors need visas as well as valid passports to gain entry into the country. Travellers from the United Kingdom and Eire, and from the neighbouring states of Lesotho, Botswana and Swaziland, are exempt from visa requirements if their visit does not exceed 14 days. Multiple-entry visas may be issued if your tour involves visits to and re-entry into South Africa from neighbouring countries.

Customs Visitors are allowed to bring in, free of duty, moderate quantities of alcohol, cigarettes, perfume and personal gifts; further items, up to a stipulated maximum value (this is subject to change: the amount was a modest R1 000 at the time of writing), may be brought in at a flat rate of 20 per cent.

Health requirements Visitors coming from or passing through a yellow-fever zone should have a valid International Certificate of Vaccination. The zone extends over much of tropical Africa and South America (including Brazil). Airline passengers in transit through the zone, though, are exempt from the requirement providing they do not leave the transit airport. Note that cholera and smallpox vaccination certificates are no longer required. There are no Aids screening procedures in force.

Special precautions Visitors to Northern Natal and Zululand, and to the Transvaal Lowveld, are urged to begin a course of anti-malaria tablets before starting out. The bilharzia snail (see page 11) is also prevalent in the lower lying parts of the two regions. Beware crocodiles and hippos generally, but especially in the St Lucia shallows. Sharks, and a variety of toxic marine life (fire- fish, scorpionfish and stonefish) are hazards off the northern Natal coast.

Travel by air After years of partial isolation, South Africa is now well served by international flights. South African Airways, the national carrier, operates over a network that spans most of the globe; a score and more other international airlines offer services to and from the country. The main ports of entry into the country are

Jan Smuts international airport, which serves both Johannesburg and Pretoria; Durban's Louis Botha airport and Cape Town's DF Malan airport. The latter two also have international status. Jan Smuts is by far the biggest and busiest entry point. Domestic air services are provided by South African Airways and a dozen or so smaller, private airlines. Specifically:

Northern Natal and Zululand Among scheduled carriers serving the region are Comair (Johannesburg/Richards Bay/Mkuze); Link Airways (Johannesburg and Durban to Phinda), and Mac Air (Johannesburg to Richards Bay and Vryheid).

Eastern Transvaal Lowveld The regional airports are at Skukuza (Kruger), Phalaborwa, Nelspruit, Tzaneen and Thohoyandou (Venda). Among the services at the time of going to press were Comair, from Johannesburg to Phalaborwa and Skukuza; the airline is also a tour operator, offering 'Costcutter Safari' conducted excursions to and around the Kruger Park, and accommodation in the secluded Comair camp and Skukuza; Link Airways (Johannesburg and Durban to Nelspruit); Theron Airways (from Lanseria, near Johannesburg, to Thohoyandou); Metavia (Johannesburg/Nelspruit), and Letaba Airways (Johannesburg/Phalaborwa and Tzaneen).

Small private airlines and charter firms also use airport facilities at Hoedspruit for the central Kruger region, and the new airport at Malelane, on the park's southern boundary. Most of the private reserves and lodges have their own landing strips; that at MalaMala (Rattray Reserves) has international status. These are used by charter firms – many of them operating out of Lanseria and Grand Central airports in the Johannesburg/Pretoria area, and from Durban – as well as by private aircraft.

Northern and Western Bushveld There are regular flights between Jan Smuts international airport and Sun City; contact your travel agent for details. Charter facilities are also available.

Travel by road. Travellers intending to bring their own vehicles into the Common Customs Area that embraces South Africa, Namibia, Botswana, Lesotho and Swaziland must obtain the necessary documents – a triptyque or carnet authorising temporary importation – from an internationally recognised motoring organisation (the Automobile Association for instance) in their country of origin.

A foreign driver's licence is valid in South Africa provided it carries the photograph and signature of the holder or, failing this, is accompanied by a certificate of authority (in English) issued by an embassy or other competent authority. Alternatively, obtain an International Driving Permit before your departure – the application procedure is straightforward; the licence is valid for 36 months. Licences should always be carried when driving in South Africa.

South Africa has an extensive and excellent road network comprising 200 000 km of national and provincial highways, 85 000 km of which are fully tarred. Surfaces are generally in good condition, though the going can be rough in some of the remoter and more hilly rural areas. Among the regional routes are:

Northern Natal and Zululand The main highway north from Durban is the N2, which ends near the Swaziland border north of Mkuze. There are several routes from Johannesburg/Pretoria; recommended is that via Ermelo and Piet Retief.

Eastern Transvaal Lowveld From Johannesburg to Nelspruit and the southern Kruger, take the R22 and then the N4 near Witbank; from Pretoria: take the N4 direct. An alternative route to the central and northern Kruger areas: take the N1 national highway (the Great North Road), turn right on to the R71 at Pietersburg for the Tzaneen area and Phalaborwa.

Northern and Western Bushveld General access to the northern areas is via the N1 from Johannesburg/Pretoria, branching off at one or other of the main towns (Warmbaths, Nylstroom, Potgietersrus, etc); see main text for specific directions. Access to the Pilanesburg and Sun City is via Rustenburg, 116 km to the northwest of Johannesburg (take the R24) and 105 km to the west of Pretoria (take one of several routes linking up with the R27).

Minibus and car hire: Rental facilities are available in all major centres and in some of the smaller ones close to the main game areas: at Richards Bay for the northern Natal reserves; at Skukuza, Phalaborwa, Nelspruit and Lydenburg for the Kruger National Park; at Rustenburg and Sun City for the Pilanesberg.

Useful Contacts

■ Automobile Association, Head Office, AA House, 66 Korte Street, Braamfontein 2001. Tel: (011) 403-5700. The AA maintains offices in all the major centres (consult the relevant telephone directories for details) and within the Kruger National Park (PO Box 13, Skukuza 1350. Tel: (01311) 6-5606).

■ Bophuthatswana Directorate of Tourism, Garona Government Offices, Private Bag X2008, Mafikeng, Bophuthatswana. Tel: (01401) 29-2000.

■ KwaZulu Department of Natural Resources, 367 Loop Street, Pietermaritzburg 3201. Tel: (0331) 94-6698; or Private Bag X23, Ulundi 3838. Tel: (0358) 907-5061.

■ Natal Parks Board, PO Box 1750, Pietermaritzburg 3200. Tel: (0331) 47-1981.

■ National Parks Board, Head Office, PO Box 787, Pretoria 0001. Tel: (012) 343-1991; Cape Town: PO Box 7400, Roggebaai 8012. Tel: (021) 419-5365; Southern Cape: PO Box 774, George 6530. Tel: (0441) 74-6924/5.

■ Professional Hunters' Association of SA, PO Box 781175, Sandton 2146. Tel: (011) 706-7724.

■ Satour (South African Tourism Board), Head Office, Private Bag X164, Pretoria 0001. Tel: (012) 47-1131/348-9521; Natal: Suite 520, 5th Floor, Southern Life Centre, 320 West Street; PO Box 2516, Durban 4000. Tel: (0331) 304-7144; fax: (0331) 305-3877; Eastern Transvaal: Ground Floor, Joshua Doore Centre, Cnr Louis Trichardt and Paul Kruger Streets, PO Box 679, Nelspruit 1200. Tel: (01311) 5-2934. Satour also maintains offices in Johannesburg (city and Jan Smuts international airport), Pietersburg, Bloemfontein, Kimberley, Cape Town, Port Elizabeth, East London, and George.

Satour's representation outside South Africa is expanding; among its offices at the time of writing were those in the United Kingdom (London), the United States (New York and Los Angeles), France (Paris), Germany (Frankfurt), Israel (Tel Aviv), Italy (Milan), Japan (Tokyo), Netherlands (Amsterdam), Switzerland (Zurich), Taiwan (Taipeh), and Zimbabwe (Harare).

■ South African Hiking Way Board, Private Bag X447, Pretoria 0001. Tel: (012) 299-9111.

■ St Lucia Publicity Association, PO Box 80, St Lucia 3936. Tel: (03592), ask for 217.

■ Wildlife Society, The Education Officer, PO Box 44344, Linden 2104. Tel: (011) 782-5461.

■ Zululand Publicity Association, PO Box 1265, Richards Bay 3900. Tel: (0351) 4-2243.

SWAZILAND

In brief

Currency The lilangeni (E; plural emilangeni), divided into 100 cents. The South African Rand currency (notes only) is also legal tender; the two currency units are on a par. *International telephone and fax* From South Africa: 09268 + subscriber's number; from other countries: international code + 268 + subscriber's number. *Local time* Universal Central Time plus two hours. *Principal centres* Mbabane (administrative capital); Lobamba (royal and legislative capital); Manzini. *Official languages* SiSwati and English.

Climate

Much the same as that of the eastern Transvaal Lowveld (see page 302). Summer (November-March) is the rainy season; the winter months are dry. Precipitation is heaviest – between a healthy 1 000 and even healthier 2 000 mm a year – on the higher country to the west; the lowveld of the eastern parts records between 500 and 900 mm. Temperatures are also influenced by altitude: the higher parts are temperate and seldom uncomfortably hot, winter days are sunny and warm, winter nights chilly and often cold. Summer temperatures on the lowveld, on the other hand, can reach 40 °C and more.

Travel

Entry documents All visitors require valid passports for entry into Swaziland. However, many foreign nationals, including South Africans, and citizens of the United Kingdom, most Commonwealth countries (exceptions at the time of writing were Mauritius, Bangladesh, India and Sri Lanka), the United States and a number of European countries are exempt from visa requirements. Citizens of France, Germany, Austria and Switzerland can obtain visas free of charge at the point of entry.

Customs Swaziland is a member of the Southern African Customs Union; visitors from or entering through South Africa are not liable for customs duties on goods originating in South Africa, Botswana, Lesotho and Namibia. Other goods may require an import permit.

Health requirements Visitors coming from or who have travelled through a yellow-fever zone need an International Certificate of Vaccination.

Special precautions Visitors are urged to take a course of anti-malaria tablets prior to arrival. Other health risks are rabies (outbreaks are sporadic and infrequent) and, in Swaziland's dams and slower-moving rivers, the bilharzia snail (see page 11).

Travel by air Swaziland's national airport is at Matsapha, eight kilometres from Manzini. Manzini is 42 km from Mbabane. Royal Swazi National Airways operates regular flights to and from Johannesburg, Durban and various Southern and East African countries. The national airlines of Lesotho, Zimbabwe, Zambia and other African states offer regular services to Swaziland, as do one or two South African private airlines, including Comair.

Travel by road Swaziland is connected with major centres in Southern Africa through South Africa's well-maintained road network. There is also a tarred road through southern Mozambique to Maputo (at the time of writing – 1993 – this was a hazardous route for travellers).

Visitors are served by 12 border posts, some of which close earlier than others. The Oshoek-Ngwenya, Mahamba and Golela-Lavumisa posts stay open until 22h00. The Oshoek-Ngwenya post, on the most direct route from Johannesburg, is the busiest. Motorists take the N4 highway via Middelburg and Carolina; Oshoek is 17 km from Mbabane. Road distances, in kilometres, from Southern African centres to Mbabane are: Johannesburg (Transvaal) 371; Durban (Natal) 635; Richards Bay (Natal) 343; Skukuza (Kruger National Park) 208; Maputo (Mozambique) 235; Maseru (Lesotho) 736; Gaborone (Botswana) 718. Roads within Swaziland are generally adequate, but tarred stretches can become pot-holed, and gravelled ones muddy, during heavy rains. Beware animals on country roads.

Driving licences issued in most countries are valid in Swaziland for up to six months provided they are printed in English or accompanied by a certified translation. International driving permits are, of course, also recognised. Motorists are advised to carry their driver's licences at all times. The general speed limit in Swaziland is 80 km/h, reducing to 60 km/h in urban and designated areas. Petrol-filling stations are open throughout the week during daylight hours; petrol is available 24 hours a day in the tourism-developed Ezulwini Valley; a number of garages also offer a round-the-clock repair service; there are AA-appointed tow-in facilities at Mbabane, Manzini, Pigg's Peak and Nhlangano.

Car hire: Rental services are available at Matsapha airport (Hertz agent. Tel: (09268) 8-4393) and Manzini (Avis agent. Tel: (09268) 5-2734).

Photography Visitors may not take photographs of the Royal Palace; the Royal Family; Parliament buildings; or of police and military installations, vehicles and uniformed personnel; post offices and bank buildings. It is courteous to ask permission of the headman should you wish to photograph village scenes and people.

Useful Contacts

■ Swaziland Government Tourist Office, PO Box 451, Mbabane, Swaziland. Tel: (09268) 4-2531.
■ Tourism representation in South Africa: SARTOC, PO Box 600, Parklands 2121. Tel: (011) 788-0742; fax: (011) 788-1200.

NAMIBIA AND THE KALAHARI

In brief

Currency The South African Rand (R), divided into 100 cents; Namibia is planning to introduce its own currency. *Telephone and fax* Namibia is still served by the South African telecommunications system. International calls: international code + 27 + area code + subscriber's number; all numbers within this chapter are prefixed by the relevant area code. *Local time* Universal Central Time plus two hours. *Principal centres* Windhoek (capital), Luderitz, Walvis Bay (within a South African enclave; future ownership and administration are the subject of negotiation), Swakopmund, Keetmanshoop, Oranjemund (a closed mining town), Tsumeb, Omaruru, Outjo, Oshakati, Otjiwarongo, Grootfontein, Karibib, Gobabis. *Languages* English is the official language; Afrikaans and, in the main centres, German are widely spoken. Principal indigenous languages are Kwanyama (Ovambo), Kwangali (Kavango) and Herero.

Climate

Namibia's climate falls into the 'continental-tropical' category, though there is in fact very little of the lushness that one associates with the latter word (except perhaps in the far northeast). This is indeed a hot country, but for the most part dry. The rains, such as they are, fall during the summer months, the 'small' ones in October/November, the 'big' ones from January through to April. Mean annual precipitation is around the 250-mm mark, though the arid lower Orange and Namib regions receive less than 100 mm a year and frequently a lot less. The central highlands enjoy an average of 350 mm, the far northern areas up to 600 mm a year.

The country as a whole averages a little over 300 days of sunshine a year. Temperatures vary according to region: the coastal belt, its climate influenced by the cool Benguela current, is often fogbound and chilly (mean 16 °C); in the interior, summer days are hot to very hot; winter days are generally sunny and mild, the nights often very cold and sometimes bitter.

Travel

Entry documents All visitors require valid passports for entry into Namibia. However, many foreign nationals are exempt from visa requirements, among them visitors from South Africa, Britain and most Commonwealth countries, Eire, Switzerland, Germany, Austria, Italy, France, the Scandinavian countries, the United States, the Commonwealth of Independent States (CIS) and Japan.

Customs Namibia is a member of the Southern African Customs Union; visitors from or entering via South Africa are not liable for customs duties. Overseas visitors arriving direct are allowed to bring in moderate quantities of alcohol, tobacco and perfume duty-free.

Entry is permitted for a maximum of 60 days, though extensions are easily arranged.

Health requirements Health certificates are not normally required.

Special precautions Visitors to Etosha and the Caprivi are advised to take a course of anti-malaria tablets prior to arrival. Most of Namibia's wilderness areas are vast and remote: if you're travelling by car, check routes and conditions with the authorities, and stock up with spares – and with water. Do not stray from the established routes. Beware crocodile, and hippo, and the bilharzia snail (see page 11), in the northeastern areas.

Travel by air Scheduled international flights connect Windhoek's Eros airport with, among other countries, South Africa (Johannesburg/Pretoria and Cape Town), Germany (Frankfurt), Botswana (Gaborone and Maun), Zimbabwe (Harare and Victoria Falls), and Zambia (Lusaka). *Internal services:* Air Namibia operates Boeing 737 and Beechcraft 1900 turboprop flights from Windhoek to Tsumeb, Rundu and Katima Mulilo in the northern regions; Oshakati in Ovambo; Swakopmund, Luderitz and Alexander Bay on the coast, and Keetmanshoop in the southern interior. The Katima Mulilo flights continue to Johannesburg, the Alexander Bay ones to Cape Town. Air Namibia and Namibia Commercial Aviation (see Useful Contacts, page 307) offer charter services.

Travel by road Namibia has a 42 000-km road network. The main highways radiating from Windhoek to the major centres are tarred; tarred roads lead to the southern (South African) and northern (Angolan) borders, and for most of the way to the Botswana border. Secondary roads are maintained to all-weather standards; those in the interior are gravelled; some of the coastal stretches are of 'salt' (gypsum soaked with brine and compacted).

Foreign nationals should be in possession of an International Driver's Certificate. Motorists are advised to carry their driver's licences with them at all times. Speed limits are 120 km/h on tar; 100 km/h on gravel; 60 km/h in the urban areas. Drive carefully on gravel (the loose surface can cause you to skid, and dust is a problem), and on salt (treacherous when wet). Beware kudu and other animals that stray onto highways – especially at night, when they tend to be dazzled, and immobilised, by the headlights. Four-wheel-drive vehicles are needed to negotiate

the desert tracks and those in some of the northern areas. If you intend digressing from the beaten path, leave word of your intended destination and route; carry basic spares, extra fuel and oil, a first-aid kit, and plenty of food and water. Most petrol stations are open 24 hours a day. Fuel supplies, however, tend to be erratic in the remoter areas. The Automobile Association has an office in Windhoek (see Useful Contacts below), and there are AA-appointed agents in the major centres.
Car hire: Rental services are available at Windhoek (airport and city) and in bigger urban centres.

Useful Contacts

■ Air Namibia, PO Box 731, Windhoek 9000, Namibia. Tel: (061) 3-8220; fax: (061) 30-6460.
■ Automobile Association, PO Box 61, Windhoek 9000, Namibia. Tel: (061) 22-4201.
■ Caprivi Wildlife & Tourism Association, PO Box 67, Katima Mulilo 9000, Namibia. Tel: (067352) 322; fax: (067352) 446.
■ Ministry of Home Affairs, Private Bag 13200, Windhoek 9000, Namibia. Tel: (061) 398-9111; fax: (061) 22-3817.
■ Ministry of Wildlife, Conservation and Tourism, Private Bag 13267, Windhoek 9000, Namibia. Tel: (061) 3-6975/6 (reservations) and (061) 3-3875 (information); fax: (061) 22-4900.
■ Namibia Commercial Aviation, PO Box 30320, Windhoek 9000, Namibia. Tel: (061) 22-3562; fax: (061) 3-4583.
■ Namibia Professional Hunting Association, PO Box 11291, Windhoek 9000, Namibia. Tel: (061) 3-4455; fax: (061) 22-2567.
■ Windhoek Publicity Association, PO Box 1868, Windhoek 9000, Namibia. Tel: (061) 22-8160.

BOTSWANA

In brief

Currency The pula (P), which is the Setswana word for 'rain', divided into 100 thebe. *International telephone and fax* From South Africa: 09267 + subscriber's number; from other countries: international code + 267 + subscriber's number. *Local time* Universal Central Time plus two hours. *Principal centres* Gaborone (capital), Francistown, Maun, Kasane. *Official language* English.

Climate

Botswana is a summer-rainfall region. The wet season begins (usually) in late October or early November to peak in December and January, and to end in March. Average precipitation over the whole country is around the 475-mm mark, but there are sharp regional variations: the northern areas receive up to 700 mm a year, the dry Kalahari spaces of the south a low 225 mm.

Summers are hot, daytime temperatures sometimes rising to 40 °C and more, though the nights are generally much cooler (around 25 °C). Winter days are sunny, cool to warm, the nights chilly and sometimes downright cold. Best months to visit are April through to October, both from a weather point of view (the days are filled with sunshine, and temperatures rarely reach uncomfortable levels) and, generally, for game viewing. This is the dry season and the wildlife, congregating around what surface water there is, is at its most visible.

Travel

Entry documents All visitors require valid passports for entry into Botswana. However, many foreign nationals are exempt from visa requirements, among them visitors from South Africa, Britain, all Commonwealth countries, Austria, Belgium, Eire, Finland, France, Germany, Greece, Iceland, Italy, Liechtenstein, Luxembourg, Netherlands, Norway, Pakistan, Samoa (Western), Sweden, Switzerland, Uruguay and the USA.

Entry is permitted for a maximum of 90 days, though extensions are easily arranged. Contact the Chief Immigration Officer, PO Box 942, Gaborone, Botswana. Visitors wishing to break their stay for a short trip to a neighbouring country – for example, through Kasane to the Victoria Falls in Zimbabwe – are advised to make prior arrangements with the immigration authorities for re-entry.

Customs Botswana is a member of the Southern African Customs Union; arriving visitors from or through South Africa are not liable for customs duties. Overseas visitors arriving direct are allowed to bring in moderate quantities of alcohol, tobacco and perfume duty-free.

Health requirements Health certificates are not normally required. However, you may be asked to produce a yellow-fever vaccination certificate if you are from or have travelled through a yellow-fever zone.

Special precautions Malaria is a potential hazard, especially during the wet summer months (October to March), and visitors are advised to take a course of tablets prior to arrival.

Many of Botswana's wilderness areas are vast, remote and difficult to get to. If you're travelling by car, check routes and conditions beforehand with the authorities, and stock up with spares – and with water. Do not stray from the established routes. Beware crocs and hippos, and the bilharzia snail (see page 11), in the Okavango Delta and northern Chobe areas.

Travel by air Principal point of entry is Gaborone's Sir Seretse Khama international airport (15 km from the city centre); there are regional airports at Francistown, Kasane (recently upgraded), Maun, Tuli and Selibe Phikwe, all of which are served by Air Botswana (whose fleet includes the British Aerospace BAe142, the world's quietest jetliner); by some of the smaller airlines and by the air charter firms. Scheduled carriers servicing Gaborone include British Airways and UTA direct from Europe; South African Airways, Air Malawi, Kenya Airlines, Zambia Airways, Air Tanzania and Lesotho Airways. Flight enquiries Tel: (09267) 31-4517.

Travel by road Motorists have a choice of 12 entry points into Botswana from South Africa; one from Namibia; three from Zimbabwe; and one from Zambia (the Kazungula ferry). In addition, there are several other points without border posts on the Botswana side, and visitors arriving through these are required to report to the nearest police station. Border posts are open only during the day, the precise times varying according to the post. Many close at 16h00.

Foreign driver's licences are valid in Botswana for six months provided they are printed in English or are accompanied by a certified translation. Alternatively, obtain an International Driving Permit before departure.

Botswana is a large and sparsely populated country, and its road network is still under development. At present there are about 3 000 km of permanently surfaced roads, and it is possible to drive on tar from Johannesburg through Gaborone to both Francistown in the central-eastern region and Maun in the northwest, and then on to Shakwe. However, many other routes are of a much lower standard, their surfaces varying from well-maintained gravel to loose sand. Conditions also vary with the seasons. Four-wheel-drive vehicles are needed to negotiate the desert tracks in the central and southern areas and many of the routes within and around the Okavango Delta and the Chobe park.

The general speed limit is 120 km/h; in urban areas it is 60 km/h; parks and reserves impose their own limits, which are clearly signposted.

If you intend digressing from the beaten path, leave word behind of your intended destination and route, and carry a good stock of spares, extra fuel and plenty of water. Petrol outlets in Gaborone, Francistown, Mahalapye and Maun are open 24 hours a day; outlets in other centres tend to close around six in the evening, though their owners/attendants will invariably open up if you really need help. Third-party insurance is a requirement; cover obtained in South Africa, Lesotho and Swaziland is valid in Botswana; for the rest, third-party insurance can be purchased at the border post.

Vehicle hire: Rental services (including Avis and Hertz Holiday Car) are available in the major centres, at Sir Seretse Khama international airport and at the smaller regional airports.

Useful Contacts

■ Air Botswana, PO Box 92, Gaborone, Botswana. Tel: (09267) 35-1921; fax: (09267) 37-4802. Flight enquiries: (09267) 31-4517. South African office (Jan Smuts airport): Tel: (011) 975-3614.

■ Botswana Bird Club, National Museum, PO Box 71, Gaborone, Botswana. Tel: (09267) 35-1500.

■ Chobe Wildlife Trust, PO Box 32, Kasane, Botswana. Tel: (09267) 25-0340.

■ Hotel & Tourism Association, PO Box 968, Gaborone, Botswana. Tel: (09267) 35-7144.

■ Department of Tourism, Private Bag 004, Gaborone, Botswana. Tel: (09267) 35-3024.

■ Department of Wildlife and National Parks, PO Box 131, Gaborone, Botswana. Tel: (09267) 37-1405. PO Box 17, Kasane, Botswana. Tel: (09267) 65-0235. PO Box 11, Maun, Botswana. Tel: (09267) 66-0368.

■ Kalahari Conservation Society, PO Box 859, Gaborone, Botswana. Tel: (09267) 31-4259.

■ Okavango Wildlife Society (South African office), PO Box 52362, Saxonwold 2131, South Africa. Tel: (011) 880-3833.

■ Tourism Development Unit, Private Bag 0047, Gaborone, Botswana. Tel: (09267) 35-3024; fax: (09267) 37-1539.

ZIMBABWE

In brief

Currency The Zimbabwean dollar (Z$), divided into 100 cents. *International telephone and fax* From South Africa: 09263 + area code + subscriber's number; from other countries: international code + 263 + area code + subscriber's number. *Local time* Universal Central Time plus two hours. *Principal centres* Harare (capital), Bulawayo, Mutare, Gweru, Masvingo, Kwekwe, Kadoma, Chinoyi, Marondera, Victoria Falls and Kariba. *Official language* English.

Climate

Zimbabwe as a whole enjoys a marvellously temperate climate: although the country lies within the tropics, its inland position and elevation on Southern Africa's high interior plateau moderate humidity and temperature, which remain within comfortable ranges (in most regions), even in high summer and the so-called 'suicide' months of October and November. However, summer days can be ferociously hot (40 °C plus) in the lower-lying parts – the southern and southeastern (Lowveld) and western fringes, and along the Zambezi Valley and escarpment in the north – which, between them, encompass the major wildlife areas. Overall, daytime temperatures range between 20 and 27 °C in summer.

This is a summer-rainfall region; in normal years great storm clouds begin darkening the afternoon sky from about mid-October; the rains proper – brief but noisily torrential downpours – begin about a month later and continue into February. Rainfall increases as you travel from west to east; Beitbridge, the country's southern border town, gets about 400 mm a year; Chipinge, in the eastern highlands, receives a generous 1 100 mm. Winter days are bone-dry, sunny and warm (average 14 to 19 °C); the nights and early mornings chilly and often, in the higher regions, very cold (sub-zero nighttime temperatures are common on the Highveld in June and July).

Travel

Entry documents All visitors require valid passports and visas for entry into Zimbabwe. However, nationals of many countries, including those of the Commonwealth, South Africa, the United States, Japan and most European states, may obtain visas at the ports of entry on presentation of their passports, return or onward tickets and proof of financial independence during their visit.

Customs Visitors are allowed to bring in, free of duty, moderate quantities of alcohol (maximum 5 litres, of which 2 litres may be spirits), tobacco (200 cigarettes), perfumes (1 pint) and personal gifts (up to Z$150 worth).

Currency and payment Foreign currency declaration forms (cash and traveller's cheques) must be completed on entry, stamped, and retained during the visit for presentation when exchanging the currency. In terms of the government's foreign exchange requirements hotels and other operators are able to retain 7,5 per cent of all such currency earned. Non-resident visitors must therefore pay for air fares and settle hotel and safari accounts in full in foreign currency. Dispensation from this requirement is granted to certain establishments; seek advice from the hotel, operator, travel agent or from a bank.

Health requirements Visitors arriving from or who will be passing through yellow-fever zones must be able to produce a vaccination certificate.

Special precautions Malaria is a potential hazard, especially in the lower-lying areas, and especially in summer. Visitors are advised to take a course of prophylactic tablets prior to arrival. The bilharzia snail (see page 11) is prevalent throughout the country. Do not bathe in the rivers or small dams, or on the shores of the larger stretches of water (Lake Kariba, for example). Beware croc and hippo in the riverine areas and the Kariba Lake area (even mid-lake); do not embark on unaccompanied walks in game areas, even where this is permitted (in the Mana Pools park, for instance).

Travel by air Principal port of entry is Harare's international airport. The national carrier is Air Zimbabwe, which operates scheduled flights between Harare and major Southern African, continental and overseas destinations. The airline also operates scheduled flights between Bulawayo and Johannesburg.

The country is served by South African Airways (SAA) and some 15 other international airlines. SAA operates direct flights to both Harare and Victoria Falls. Air Zimbabwe's domestic network covers the country's main centres and tourist venues (among them Bulawayo, Kariba, Victoria Falls, Hwange National Park, Gweru in the midlands region, Masvingo in the south-central region, and Buffalo Range in the Lowveld).

Private charter companies offer unscheduled services between the major airports and airfields, and to many of the remoter airstrips. Largest of these independent carriers is United Air Charter, a subsidiary of United Touring Company (UTC).

Travel by road Zimbabwe has an excellent route network comprising some 5 000 km of first-class highways and 43 000 km of well-maintained secondary roads linking the major centres and tourist destinations. However, the routes through many of the game areas can be rough, especially during the rainy season; some can be negotiated only by four-wheel-drive.

There are 10 entry points from neighbouring countries. The principal route from South Africa is the Great North Road (the N1) leading from Johannesburg and Pretoria, which crosses the Limpopo River via the Beit Bridge (the border town is Beitbridge). Other entry points are: from Botswana, at Plumtree and Mpandamatenga; from Namibia, at Kazungula; from Zambia, at Victoria Falls, Kariba and Chirundu; from Mozambique, at Mutare, Mount Selinda and Nyamapanda. Opening times vary; some posts are closed over weekends.

Excellent road maps are available from the Automobile Association of Zimbabwe (see Useful Contacts, page 311), and ordinance maps from the Department of the Surveyor General.

Petrol outlets in the major and many of the minor centres are open 24 hours a day; outlets in the more remote areas tend to close at around six in the evening, though their owners/attendants will invariably unlock the pump if you're in difficulty. In Zimbabwe, one drives on the left; the general speed limit is 100 km/h; national parks impose their own restrictions, which are clearly signposted.

Driver's licences issued in certain African countries (among them South Africa, Namibia, Botswana, Malawi and Swaziland) are valid in Zimbabwe. Other foreign licences are valid for 90 days provided they are printed in English or are accompanied by a certified translation and photograph. Alternatively, visiting motorists should obtain an International Driving Permit prior to arrival. Those who arrive in their own vehicles also require a triptyque or carnet authorising temporary importation, together with a vehicle-registration certificate and an International Certificate of Insurance.

Car rental: The major international rental firms maintain offices in the larger centres and in the tourist areas; Avis and Hertz (run by UTC) are represented at Harare international airport; Europcar will meet flights. Smaller local firms also offer vehicles for hire.

Coach services of luxury standard operate between Johannesburg, Bulawayo and Harare, and between Bulawayo and Victoria Falls. The major Zimbabwean destinations are also linked by regular (and inexpensive) coach services. Tour operators provide coach and minibus transport for their clients.

Travel by rail Zimbabwe maintains a 3 400-km rail network. Domestic passenger services connect the main commercial and some of the tourist centres. Passenger services also link the country's rail network with those of South Africa (entry point Beitbridge), Botswana (Plumtree), Zambia (Victoria Falls) and Mozambique (Mutare and Sango). South Africa's Spoornet operates excellent (once-weekly) Johannesburg-Harare and Johannesburg-Bulawayo services. Most of the country's locomotives are diesel- or electricity-driven, but working steam trains still ply some of the routes. The luxurious rail safari that takes passengers past the Hwange National Park to the Victoria Falls is renowned among steam enthusiasts (see page 85).

Useful Contacts

■ Automobile Association of Zimbabwe, Ground Floor, Fanum House, Samora Machel Avenue; PO Box 585, Harare, Zimbabwe. Tel: (09263-4) 70-7021.

■ Bulawayo Booking Agency, 104A Fife St; PO Box 2283, Bulawayo, Zimbabwe. Tel: (09263-9) 6-3646.

■ Department of National Parks and Wildlife Management, PO Box 8151, Causeway, Harare, Zimbabwe. Tel: (09263-4) 70-6077.

■ Kariba Publicity Association, PO Box 86, Kariba, Zimbabwe. Tel; (09263-61) 2328.

■ Victoria Falls Publicity Association, PO Box 97, Victoria Falls, Zimbabwe. Tel: (09263-13) 4202.

■ Zimbabwe Association of Tour & Safari Operators, PO Box A483, Avondale, Harare, Zimbabwe.

■ Zimbabwe Professional Hunters and Guides Association, PO Box UA191, Union Avenue, Harare, Zimbabwe. Tel: (09263-4) 73-0771.

■ Zimbabwe Tourism Development Corporation, PO Box 8052, Harare, Zimbabwe. Tel: (09263-4) 70-6511.

■ Zimbabwe Tourism offices abroad: South Africa: Town Mall, Upper Carlton Centre, Commissioner St, Johannesburg 2001. Tel: (011) 21-1541. United Kingdom: The Strand, London WC2R 0514. Tel: (0944-71) 836-7755. USA: 35 East Wacker Drive, Chicago, Illinois 6061. Tel: (091312) 322-2601.

ZAMBIA

In brief

Currency The kwacha (ZMK), divided into 100 ngwee (n). *International telephone and fax* From South Africa 09260 + area code; from other countries: international code + 267 + area code. *Local time* Universal Central Time plus two hours. *Principal centres* Lusaka (capital), Kitwe, Ndola, Livingstone. *Official language* English.

Climate

The country is located between eight and 18 degrees south of the equator, but because of its elevation – it lies on the high Central African plateau – the climate is generally temperate. Nevertheless, summer days can be very hot, the highest temperatures usually recorded in October, just before the onset of the annual rains. The heat is especially intense along the middle and lower Zambezi valley and in the Luangwa Valley. The summer rains – invariably in the form of brief but torrential afternoon and early-evening downpours – occur between November and March or April. Annual precipitation varies between 700 mm and 1 600 mm. Best months to visit are April to October.

Travel

Entry documents All visitors require valid passports for entry into Zambia. However, nationals of Commonwealth countries, Eire and citizens of states with which Zambia has entered into visa abolition agreements (these include the Scandinavian countries, Finland, Pakistan and Romania) do not require visas. For the rest, visa procedures were recently streamlined and tourist documents may be obtained on arrival at the port of entry; South African citizens require four passport-size photographs for visa purposes.

Customs Visitors are permitted to bring in, free of duty, moderate amounts of alcohol (2,5 litres), tobacco (400 cigarettes or 0,5 kg of pipe tobacco or cigars), perfume, personal gifts and personal effects 'considered reasonable by the Controller of Customs'. Visitors are advised to arrange for a representative of a local travel agency or tour operator to be present at the airport to help complete the customs and immigration formalities.

Currency and payment All foreign currency (cash and traveller's cheques) must be declared at customs. The duplicate of the declaration form should be retained for presentation when exchanging foreign for local currency. Keep the form and all receipts in a safe place: they are required by customs on departure.

Health requirements Visitors who are from or who will be passing through a yellow-fever zone or a region in which cholera is prevalent need to produce the appropriate inoculation certificates.

Special precautions Malaria is a hazard, especially in the northern areas (those bordering on Zaire and Lake Tanganyika), where mosquitoes tend to be resistant to chloroquine. Travellers are urged to take a course of anti-malaria tablets prior to arrival; make sure your pharmacist knows which specific areas you intend visiting.

The bilharzia snail (see page 11) is prevalent throughout the country; do not bathe in dams or along stretches of slow-moving water. Aids is rife in Zambia; take the standard and well-publicised precautions. Beware croc and hippo in the riverine areas. Be prepared throughout your stay in Zambia to pay for 'extras' that may be added to your account. Accommodation, for example, attracts a 15 per cent sales tax and a service charge of around 10 per cent.

Travel by air Principal point of entry is Lusaka international airport, 24 km from the city centre. The airport has banking and telecommunications facilities, car-hire services, an information centre and a restaurant. Tour operators offer transfer facilities between airport and city.

An airport tax is payable on departure. The amount varies from time to time; consult your travel agent or tour operator, or the Zambian mission in your country.

The national carrier is Zambia Airways, which operates scheduled flights to and from Europe – five per week at the time of writing, three of them non-stop between Lusaka and London – and one to India via the Seychelles. The country is also served by British Airways and UTA. Among other airlines operating into Lusaka are South African Airways (SAA), Kenya Airways, Air Tanzania, Royal Swazi Air, Angola Airlines, Air Malawi, Air Botswana, Mozambique Airlines, Air Zaire, Air Zimbabwe and Air Namibia. There are frequent connections to major Southern and East African centres, among them Nairobi (Kenya), Harare, (Zimbabwe), Gaborone (Botswana), Dar-es-Salaam (Tanzania) and Mauritius. SAA operates flights from Johannesburg to Lusaka on Wednesdays, Saturdays and Sundays.

Zambia Airways' domestic network links Lusaka with Livingstone and other major tourist destinations; there are direct flights into the major national parks. Private charter companies offer one-off services between all the major and some of the minor airports and airfields.

Travel by road Zambia is a big country; distances are huge; many stretches of road are in poor condition and facilities en route – fuel outlets, breakdown and repair services, accommodation and so forth – tend to be few, far between and unreliable. Generally speaking, visitors to the game areas would do better to place themselves in the hands of a reputable safari or tour operator rather than set out independently.

However, for those intent on going it alone, the two main entry points from the south are through Zimbabwe's Chirundu and Victoria Falls border posts. The former is on the direct route between Harare and Lusaka; the latter on that linking Bulawayo with Livingstone and Lusaka. One may also cross at Kariba.

Travellers from East Africa enter via the Tunduma post; from Zaire through either Kasumbalesa or Mokambo; from Botswana and Namibia's Caprivi region through Kazungula; and from Malawi through Lundazi or Mwami (the most convenient route to the Luangwa valley). There are 11 other, less important entry points. Opening times vary; that at Kariba functions from 06h00 to 18h00.

Visitors arriving in their own cars should be in possession of a triptyque or carnet, issued by a recognised motoring association, though under certain circumstances it is possible to obtain a temporary import permit at the entry point. For information on this and related matters, contact the Controller of Customs and Excise, PO Box 60500, Livingstone, Zambia.

Visiting motorists must take out third-party insurance cover at the port of entry, and must be in possession of a valid International Driver's Permit (licences of other countries are not acceptable in Zambia). Be prepared for police road-blocks on the open road (they are after contraband, and will check your customs clearance documents, and insurance cover; a polite smile rather than irritation is the recommended response).

Bus services: The United Bus Company of Zambia and other private firms run domestic services; schedules tend to be unreliable and, all in all, as one official publication puts it, this means of transport is suitable only 'for the visitor who wants to experience adventurous Zambian travel'.

Travel by other means An inexpensive TAZARA rail service connects Dar-es-Salaam in Tanzania with Zambia's Kapiri Mposhi railhead. Tourists with time to spare can also take the lake steamer from Kigama in Tanzania: it calls at several moorings on its way to Mpulungu in northern Zambia.

Useful Contacts

▪ National Hotels Development Corporation, PO Box 33200, Lusaka, Zambia. Tel: (09260-1) 24-1023 or 24-9144/8; fax: (09260-1) 24-8352.

▪ National Parks and Wildlife Service, Post Bag 1, Chilanga, Zambia. Tel: (09260-1) 27-8366.

▪ Professional Hunters' Association of Zambia, PO Box 32104, Lusaka. Tel: (09260-1) 21-9815.

▪ Tour Operators' Association of Zambia, PO Box 30263, Lusaka, Zambia: Tel: (09260-1); fax: (09260-1) 22-4265.

▪ Zambia Airways, PO Box 30272, Lusaka, Zambia. Tel: (09260) 22-9162; fax: (09260-1) 27-1422. Johannesburg: Second Floor, Nedbank Mall, Commissioner St. Tel: (011) 331-2240/49; Durban: Suite 1422, 320 West Street. Tel: (031) 31-8605.

▪ Zambia National Tourist Board, Century House, Lusaka Square, PO Box 30017, Lusaka, Zambia. Tel: (09260-1) 22-9807/90; fax: (09260-1) 22-5174. Johannesburg: 1st Floor, Finance House, Ernest Oppenheimer Drive, Bruma; PO Box 591232, Kengray 2100. Tel: (011) 622-9206/7,

SAFARI OPERATORS

The following is an extensive but by no means exhaustive list of safari and tour companies operating from and into Southern Africa's wilderness regions. They are grouped together under the various countries, but this does not imply that their services are necessarily confined within those national boundaries. Big game is the principal focus, though many operators offer special-interest safaris, their itineraries devised specifically for the photographer, the bird-watcher, the fisherman, the hiker, the river-rafter and so on. Packages and prices vary, and the options can be bewildering. A safari consultant will have the relevant information; so too will a good travel agent. Alternatively, write direct asking for catalogues and brochures.

SOUTH AFRICA

Action Adventure Tours, PO Box 784327, Sandton 2146. Tel: (011) 887-7870.

African Outposts, PO Box 4148, Randburg 2125. Tel: (011) 884-6847/8.

Afro Ventures, PO Box 2339, Randburg 2125. Tel: (011) 789-1078 or (011) 886-1524; fax: (011) 886-2349. Also in Kasane, Botswana; Windhoek, Namibia, and Victoria Falls, Zimbabwe.

Bonaventure Tour Operators, PO Box 84540, Greenside, Johannesburg, 2034. Tel: (011) 646-6120; toll-free 0800-111007; fax: (011) 886-3125. Also in Maun, Botswana.

Bushbabies, PO Box 721, River Club 2149, South Africa. Tel: (011) 706-2692; fax: (011) 463-2534.

Bushdrifters, PO Box 785743, Sandton 2146. Tel: (011) 659-1551; fax: (011) 659-1122. Also in Maun, Botswana.

Bushveld Breakaways, PO Box 1089, Edenvale 1610. Tel: (011) 609-6158; fax: (011) 452-4550; and PO Box 926, White River 1240. Tel: (01311) 5-1998; fax: (01311) 5-0383.

Call of Africa Safaris, Bonnyrigg Road, Constantia, Cape 7800. Tel: (021) 794-2284.

Clive Walker Trails, PO Box 645, Bedfordview 2008. Tel: (011) 453-7645/6/7; fax; (011) 453-7649.

Comair: PO Box 7015, Bonaero Park 1622. Tel: (011) 973-2911; fax: (011) 973-3913.

Desert & Delta Safaris, PO Box 2339, Randburg 2125. Tel: (011) 789-1078; fax: (011) 886-2349. Also in Maun, Botswana.

Destination Africa, PO Box 78823, Sandton 2146. Tel: (011) 803-4132.

Drifters Adventours, PO Box 48434, Roosevelt Park 2129. Tel: (011) 888-1160; fax; (011) 888-1021.

Falcon Africa Safaris, PO Box 785222, Sandton 2146. Tel: (011) 886-1981; fax: (011)886-1778.

Gametrackers/Safariplan, PO Box 4245, Randburg 2125. Tel: (011) 886-1810; fax: (011) 886-1815. Also in Maun, Botswana.

Holiday Tours, PO Box 4942, Randburg 2125. Tel: (011) 787-0512; fax: (011) 886-4460.

Kariba Houseboat Safaris, PO Box 1765, Honey-dew, Johannesburg 2040. Tel: (011) 788-0740.

Karibu Safaris, PO Box 35196, Northway, Durban 4065. Tel: (031) 83-9774; fax: (031) 83-1957. Also in Maun, Botswana.

Okavango Explorations, PO Box 69859, Bryanston 2021. Tel: (011) 708-1893; fax: (011) 708-1569. Also in Maun, Botswana.

Okavango Tours & Safaris, PO Box 52900, Saxonwold 2132. Tel: (011) 788-5549/0260; fax: (011) 788-6575. Also in Maun and Gaborone, Botswana.

Okavango Wilderness Safaris, PO Box 651171, Benmore 2010. Tel: (011) 884-1458/9; fax: (011) 883-6255. Also in Maun, Botswana.

Overland Safaris, PO Box 81192, Parkhurst 2120. Tel: (011) 442-8007; fax: 442-8015.

Papadi Tours, PO Box 3684, Honeydew 2040. Tel: (011) 679-3525; fax: (011) 455-5369.

Penduka Safaris, PO Box 55413, Northlands 2116. Tel & fax: (011) 883-4303.

Safari SA, PO Box 4942, Randburg 2125. Tel: (011) 787-0512; fax: (011) 886-4460.

Safariplan: see Gametrackers/Safariplan.

Springbok Atlas Safaris, PO Box 819, Cape Town 8000. Tel: (021) 448-6545; fax: (021) 47-3835.

Thompsons International Tour Operators, PO Box 41032, Craighall 2024. Tel: (011) 788-0810; fax: (011) 788-2664.

Tsaro Safaris, PO Box 651171, Benmore 2010. Tel: (011) 884-1458; fax: (011) 883-6255.

Ubizane Safaris, PO Box 102, Hluhluwe 3960. Tel: (03562) ask for 3602; fax: (03562) ask for 193.

Wild Africa Safaris, PO Box 68132, Bryanston 2021. Tel: (011) 792-2353; fax: (011) 792-2833.

Wilderness Safaris, PO Box 651171, Benmore 2010. Tel: (011) 884-1458; fax: (011) 883-6255.

Wildlife Safaris, PO Box 3134, Randburg 2125. Tel: (011) 886-4065; fax: (011) 886-1275.

Zululand Safaris, PO Box 79, Hluhluwe 3960. Tel and fax: (03562) 144.

SWAZILAND

Umhlanga Tours, PO Box 2197, Mbabane. Tel: (09268) 4-5222 or 6-1431.

NAMIBIA

Africa Adventure Safaris, PO Box 20274, Windhoek. Tel: (061) 3-4720.

African Extrvaganza, PO Box 22028, Windhoek. Tel: (061) 6-3086.

Afro Ventures, PO Box 11176, Klein Windhoek. Tel: (061) 3-6276.

Bushland Safaris, PO Box 11880, Windhoek. Tel: (061) 3-3977/3-2507; fax: (061) 22-5003.

Charly's Desert Tours, PO Box 1400, Swakopmund. Tel: (0641) 4341.

Desert Adventure Safaris, PO Box 1428, Swakopmund. Tel: (0641) 4459/4072; fax: (0641) 4664.

Encounter Namibia, PO Box 9924, Windhoek. Tel: (061) 22-8474.

Etosha Fly-in Safaris, PO Namutoni via Tsumeb. Tel: (0671) 11.

Kaokohimba Safaris, PO Box 30828, Windhoek. Tel: (061) 22-6779; fax (061) 22-3540.

Namib Adventure Safaris, PO Box 6348, Windhoek. Tel: (061) 4-2388; fax: (061) 3-7175.

Namib Wilderness Safaris and The Namib Travel Shop, PO Box 6850, Windhoek. Tel: (061) 22-5178 or 22-6174; fax: (061) 3-3332.

Oryx Tours of Namibia, PO Box 2058, Windhoek. Tel: (061) 22-4252/3; fax: (061) 3-5604.

Sobek Expeditions (SWA Safaris), PO Box 20373, Windhoek. Tel: (061) 3-7567; fax: (061) 22-5387.

Southern Cross Safaris, PO Box 20373, Windhoek. Tel: (061) 3-7567.

BOTSWANA

Africa Calls, Private Bag 83, Maun. Tel and fax: (09267) 66-0614.

Africa-in Tours & Safaris, PO Box 614, Francistown. Tel: (09267) 21-3208; fax: (09267) 21-4552.

Afro Ventures, Private Bag 13, Maun. Tel: (09267) 66-0351; fax: (09267) 66-0571; and PO Box 323, Kasane. Tel: (09267) 65-0456; fax: 65-0119.

Bird Safaris, PO Box 15, Maun. Tel and fax: (09267) 66-0614.

Bonaventure Botswana, PO Box 201, Maun. Tel: (09267) 66-0503; fax: (09267) 66-0502.

Bushdrifters and Capricorn Safaris, Private Bag 35, Maun. Tel: (09267) 66-0351; fax: (09267) 66-0571.

Capricorn Safaris, Private Bag 21, Maun. Tel: (09267) 66-0265; fax: (09267) 66-0571.

Chanouga Safaris, Private Bag 44, Maun. Tel: (09267) 66-0647; fax (09267) 66-0571.

Desert & Delta Safaris, Private Bag 10, Maun. Tel:(09267) 66-0564/85; fax:(09267) 66-0569.

Gametrackers/Safariplan, PO Box 100, Maun. Tel: (09267) 66-0302; fax: (09267) 66-0571.

Go Wild Safaris, PO Box 56, Kasane. Tel: (09267) 25-0237/25-0336; fax: (09267) 25-0223.

Karibu Safari, Private Bag 39, Maun. Tel: (09267) 66-0493.

Kerr & Downey Safaris, PO Box 40, Maun. Tel: (09267) 66-0211/2/3; fax: (09267) 66-0379. Also in London, UK. Tel: (0944-71) 629-2044; fax: (0944-71) 49-1977.

Koro Safaris, Private Bag 22, Maun. Tel: (09267) 66-0307.

Kudu Travel, PO Box 1241, Gaborone. Tel: (09267) 37-2224; fax: (09267) 37-4224.

Linyanti Explorations, PO Box 22, Kasane. Tel and fax: (09267) 25-0352.

Map Safaris, Private Bag 44, Maun. Tel: (09267) 66-0647; fax: (09267) 26-0571

Merlin Services, Private Bag 13, Maun. Tel: (09267) 66-0351; fax: (09267) 66-0571.

Okavango Explorations, Private Bag 48, Maun. Tel and fax: (09267) 66-0528.

Okavango Tours & Safaris, PO Box 39, Maun. Tel: (09267) 66-0220/339; fax: (09267) 66-0589.

Okavango Wilderness Safaris, Private Bag 14, Maun. Tel: (09267) 66-0086; fax: (09267) 66-0632.

Okuti Safaris, Private Bag 49, Maun. Tel and fax: (09267) 66-0307.

Pan Africa Travel, PO Box 1443, Gaborone. Tel: (09267) 35-2321; fax: (09267) 37-4290.

Penstone Safaris, PO Box 330, Maun. Tel and fax: (09267) 66-0520.

Photo Africa Safaris, PO Box 11, Kasane. Tel: (09267) 65-0385; fax: (09267) 65-0383.

Phuti Travel, PO Box 40534, Gaborone. Tel and fax: (09267) 31-4166.

Safari & Bush Services, PO Box 1051, Gaborone. Tel: (09267) 35-2729.

Travel Wild, PO Box 236, Maun. Tel and fax: (09267) 66-0493.

Trans Okavango Safaris, Private Bag 33, Maun. Tel: (09267) 66-0351; fax: (09267) 66-0571.

Tsaro Safaris, Private Bag 26, Maun. Tel and fax: (09267) 66-0528.

Wildlife Safaris, PO Box 236, Maun. Tel and fax: (09267) 66-0493.

Wilmot Safaris, PO Box 246, Maun. Tel: (09267) 66-0351; fax: (09267) 66-0571.

ZIMBABWE

Abercrombie & Kent Safaris, PO Box 2997, Harare. Tel: (09263-4) 72-1340; fax: (09263-4) 72-9617.

Africa Dawn Safaris, PO Box HG632, Highlands, Harare. Tel: (09263-4) 70-7138; fax: (09263-4) 73-5615.

African Adventures, PO Box A88, Avondale, Harare. Tel: (09263-4) 70-8727.

Afro Ventures, PO Box 125, Victoria Falls. Tel: (09263-13) 4648; fax: (09263-13) 4341.

Conquest Tours, PO Box 714, Harare. Tel: (09263-4) 79-4351.

Garth Thompson Safari Consultants, PO Box 5826, Harare. Tel: (09263-4) 79-5202; fax: (09263-4) 79-5287.

Landela Safaris, PO Box 66293, Kopje, Harare. Tel: (09263-4) 70-2634.

Livingstone Safaris, PO Box 7245, Harare. Tel: (09263-4) 70-2005; fax: (09263-4) 70-2006.

Manica Touring Services, PO Box 429, Harare. Tel: (09263-4) 73-6091; fax: (09263-4) 70-5590.

M'Pole Executive Tours & Travel, PO Box 6966, Harare. Tel: (09263-4) 73-7071; fax: (09263-4) 72-8647.

Peter Garvin Safaris, PO Box UA93, Union Avenue, Harare. Tel: (09263-4) 70-2781; fax: (09263-4) 70-1049.

Safari Interlink, PO Box 5920, Harare. Tel: (09263-4) 72-0527; 70-0911/2.

Safari Par Excellence, PO Box 5920, Harare. Tel: (09263-4) 72-0527; fax: (09263-4) 72-2872.

Safari Promotions, PO Box BW96, Borrowdale, Harare. Tel: (09263-4) 72-9025; fax: (09263-4) 72-8744.

Shearwater Adventures, PO Box 3961, Harare. Tel: (09263-4) 73-5712; fax: (09263-4) 73-5716.

Sun Link International, PO Box HG529, Highlands, Harare. Tel: (09263-4) 70-4085/ 72-9025; fax; (09263-4) 72-8744.

Sunset Tours (Sunsafaris), PO Box 5405, Harare. Tel: (09263-4) 79-5386.

Sunshine Tours, PO Box 447, Bulawayo. Tel: (09263-9) 6-7791/7-7540.

Touch the Wild, PO Box 735, Harare. Tel: (09263-4) 4-5400/4-8347; also Private Bag 6, PO Hillside, Bulawayo. Tel: (09263-9) 7-4589; fax: (09263-9) 4-4696; and Private Bag 5779, Dete. Tel: (09263-18) 273.

United Touring Company/Safaritrails (Zimbabwe; Botswana), 4 Park St/Cnr Jason Moyo Ave, Harare. Tel: (09263-4) 79-3701; fax: (09263-4) 79-2794. Also in Bulawayo, Tel: (09263-9) 6-1402; Hwange, Tel: (09263-18) 393; Kariba, Tel: (09263-61) 2662; and Victoria Falls, Tel: (09263-13) 4267/8.

Wild Africa Safaris, PO Box 1737, Harare.
Tel: (09263-4) 73-8329; fax: (09263-4) 73-7956.
Zambezi Wilderness Safaris, PO Box 18,
Victoria Falls. Tel: (09263-13) 4737;
fax: (09263-13) 4417.
Zimtours, PO Box 8052, Causeway, Harare.
Tel: (09263-4) 70-6511; fax: (09263-4) 79-3669.

ZAMBIA
Africa Bound, PO Box 60036, Livingstone.
Tel: (09260-3) 32-1606.
Andrews Travel & Safaris, PO Box 31993,
Lusaka. Tel: (09260-1) 21-3147.
Big Five Travel and Tours, PO Box 60926,
Livingstone. Tel: (09260-3) 32-1432.
Busanga Trails, PO Box 30984, Lusaka. Tel:
(09260-1) 22-1197/2075; fax: (09260-1) 22-2198.
Circuit Safaris, PO Box 22890, Kitwe. Tel:
(09260-2) 21-5826; fax: (09260-2)21-6715.

Eagle Travel, PO Box 35530, Lusaka.
Tel: (09260-1) 22-6857.
G & G Safaris, PO Box 30972, Lusaka.
Tel: (09260-1) 26-1588; fax: (09260-1) 26-2683.
Robin Pope Safaris, PO Box 320154,
Lusaka. Tel: (09260-62) 4-5017;
fax: (09260-62) 4-5076.
Shiwa Safaris, Private Bag E395, Lusaka.
Tel and fax: (09260-1) 61-1171.
Sobek Adventures, PO Box 30263, Lusaka.
Tel: (09260-1) 22-4248; fax: (09260-1) 22-4265.
PO Box 60957, Livingstone. Tel: (09260-3)
32-1432. Also in Windhoek, Namibia.
TG Travel (Tours Division), PO Box 20104,
Kitwe. Tel: (02960-2) 21-5188.
Transcat, PO Box 32540, Lusaka. Tel: (09260-1)
26-1683; fax: (09260-1) 26-2438.
Wilderness Trails, PO Box 30970, Lusaka.
Tel: (09260-1) 21-5946.

PHOTOGRAPHIC CREDITS

ABPL = Anthony Bannister Photo Library **AI** = African Images **BNPB** = Bophuthatswana National Parks Board **NPB** = Natal Parks Board **PA** = Photo Access **SIL** = Struik Image Library
African Outposts: p 72. **S Adey:** Front cover, top right; p 16 (NPB); 21 left & right (NPB); 27; 29 top & bottom; 38 above (NPB) & below; 49 right (NPB), centre left & bottom left (NPB); 50 above (NPB). **A Bannister:** p 61 (ABPL); 66 (ABPL); 83; 99 below; 106 (ABPL); 149 (ABPL); 173 (ABPL); 187 (ABPL). **D Balfour:** p 32 (ABPL); 140 (ABPL); 175 below, 176; 177 above; 178 above; 181 below; 184 below; 188; 190 below; 197 (ABPL); 201 left; 210; 211; 212; 229. **C Bell:** Front cover, centre left; p 41 below; p 264 (AI) **Big Game Parks:** p 122 below; 123 below; 127; 128 above & below. **R Boycott:** p 124 left. **R Bush:** p 99 above (ABPL). **D Butchart:** p 12 (AI); 44 below (AI); 45 below (AI); 73 (AI). **D Carew:** p 230 above (ABPL). **P Comley:** p 214. **Conservation Corporation:** p 34; 35 above; 88. **M Coppinger:** Front cover, centre right. **G Cubitt:** p 62; 71; 91; 118; 124 right; 135 above & below; 139 above & below; 143 below; 145; 146 left & right; 152; 156; 158; 159 above & below; 160 above; 161; 180; 192; 196 left; 207 below; 208; 218; 221; 223; 224; 225 above & below; 227; 228; 230 below; 231; 233; 234; 235; 237; 241; 243; 244; 245 above & below; 246; 247; 248; 249; 250 above; 251; 253; 262 above & below; 263; 265; 266; 267; 268; 269; 270; 271; 277; 278; 284. **R de la Harpe:** Back cover, left (NPB) & spine (NPB); p 15 above & below (NPB); 17 above left, below left (NPB) & right (NPB); 18 above (NPB), left, right (NPB); 22; 24 (NPB); 25 (NPB); 26 above left (NPB), below left (NPB) & right; 28 (ABPL); 29 centre (NPB); 30 above (NPB) & below; 31 centre (NPB) & bottom (NPB); 36 left (NPB); 37 (NPB); 39 above (NPB) & below; 42 above; 46 above (NPB); 49 top; 50 below (NPB); 51 above (NPB); 52 (NPB); 64 above left & below left; 70 below left; 101; 132; 143 above; 168 left & right; 209; 226. **N Dennis:** p 36 right (ABPL); 45 above (ABPL); 195 below (ABPL). **GPL du Plessis:** p 41 above (PA). **R du Toit:** p 58 (ABPL). **H & J Eriksen:** p 126. **P Funston:** p 57 (ABPL); 75 (ABPL); 258 (ABPL); 260 below (ABPL). **C Haagner:** p 59 (ABPL); 67 centre (ABPL); 144 (ABPL); 150 (ABPL); 151 (ABPL); 164/165 (ABPL); 181 above (ABPL); 202 (ABPL); 226 (ABPL). **L Hay:** p 69 above (ABPL). **L Hes:** p 46 below; 47; 54/55; 60 (PA); 78 left; 80; 81 left; 122 above; 124 above; 125; 163; 216 above (PA). **L Hoffmann:** p 43; 121 above & below; 160 below (all SIL). **P Lawson:** p 216 below (PA). **N Mann:** p 74 above right (ABPL) & below right (ABPL); 112 (ABPL). **R Matthews:** p 107 (BNPB); 108 (BNPB). **S Meyer:** p 178 below; 179; 190 above; 191 above; 193 below; 194; 195 above; 200; 201 right; 203; 204; 205 above & below; 207 above; 213 above & below; 215 above & below. **RC Nunnington:** p 63 right (ABPL); 64 right (ABPL); 79 (ABPL). **W & S Olivier:** p 137 above. **J Paisley:** 185 (PA); 186 right (PA). **M Patzer:** p 259 below; 276; 279; 281 left, above right & below right; 282 above; 285 above & below; 286-291; 292 above & below; 294; 295 above & below; 296; 297; 298 below. **B Peterson:** p 23 (AI); 44 above (AI); 169 (AI). **P Pickford:** p 20; 175 above; 242; 250 below; 259 above. **H Potgieter:** p 35 below; 114, 115 left & right; 116; 117 above & below. **A Ramsay:** p 102 below (PA). **Rovos Rail:** p 85 above & below. **Safari Plan:** p 82. **J Ryder:** p 301 (ABPL). **L Stanton:** p 70 above left (ABPL); 74 left (ABPL); 78 right (ABPL). **Sun International:** p 129 above; 130. **D Steele:** p 31 top; 63 top left and below left; 65; 67 bottom; 68; 76 above; 77; 86 (PA); 102 above (PA); 166; 167 above & below; 184 above; 189; 191 below; 196 above left (all PA). **P Steyn:** p 236 (PA); 240 (PA); 261; 274. **M Tennant:** p 40 (AI). **G Thomson:** p 154 (ABPL). **M van Aardt:** p 53 below; 136; 137 below; 142; 147; 148; 170; 254 above. **H von Hörsten:** Front cover, bottom left (ABPL); p 69 below (ABPL). **P Wagner:** p 129 below; 131 above & below; 177 below; 186 left; 193 above; 206; 243; 255; 257; 280; 282 below; 283; 284; 299; 300 (all PA). **C Weiss:** p 141 above & below; 162. **B & L Worsley:** p 252 (PA); 260 above (PA).

INDEX